THE DEATH AND LIFE OF GERMANY

THE DEATH
AND
LIFE OF
GERMANY

AN ACCOUNT OF
THE AMERICAN OCCUPATION

Eugene Davidson

UNIVERSITY OF MISSOURI PRESS   COLUMBIA AND LONDON

Copyright © 1959 by Eugene Davidson
First published by Alfred A. Knopf, Inc. in 1959.
First University of Missouri Press paperback edition, 1999.
University of Missouri Press, Columbia, Missouri 65201
Printed and bound in the United States of America
All rights reserved

5   4   3   2   1   03   02   01   00   99

Library of Congress Cataloging-in-Publication Data

Davidson, Eugene, 1902–
    The death and life of Germany : an account of the American
occupation / Eugene Davidson.
        p.   cm.
    Originally published : New York : A.A. Knopf, 1959.
    Includes bibliographical references and index.
    ISBN 0-8262-1249-2 (alk. paper)
    1. Germany—History—1945–1955.   2. Reconstruction (1939–1951)—
Germany.   3. Germany (West)—History.   I. Title.
DD257.D33   1999
943.087—dc21   99-15520
                                                                 CIP

♾™ This paper meets the requirements of the
American National Standard for Permanence of Paper
for Printed Library Materials, Z39.48, 1984.

Cover designer: Kristie Lee
Typesetter: Bookcomp, Inc.
Printer and binder: Edwards Brothers, Inc.
Typefaces: Electra

In memory of
Suzette Morton Davidson
1911–1996

PUBLISHER'S NOTE

T HE PAGES that follow were written a generation and more ago, but they are as luminous now as they were then. Time has not in any way dimmed their significance. Indeed, at the very end of the present book when the author assumes the present tense, describing what for him had happened only yesterday, he is as prescient as he possibly could be; this is a book that has endured.

The new printing offers opportunity to look back over what has happened in our now almost finished century, and observe the many, many errors of policy, large and small. But it is necessary to admit that despite error, the broad outlines of U.S. policy for Germany in the crucial decade of 1945–1955 have stood the test. As the author says, citing Konrad Adenauer, "Never in history has a conqueror done so much for the nation she had conquered." In a moment when grave mistakes were easy to make, policy turned out quite well.

ACKNOWLEDGMENTS

Many people have helped in the making of this book. Wallace Notestein, seconded by Harry Rudin, urged me to write it, to go out into the countryside in Germany to discover as much as I could from plain people of what they had seen and experienced. I have tried to follow his knowledgeable advice and over a period of years have talked with a large number of Germans, mainly in the West but also in and from the East zone, to ask what happened to them during the period of the occupation. Among them have been farmers and workers, politicians, businessmen, and newspapermen in the various parts of the Bundesrepublik.

A special debt is owed to Gisela Hensel Fairley, who well before the fall of the Third Reich understood the German predicament and, from the end of the war, worked long hours at the task of re-establishing the lines of communication from "the other" anti-Nazi Germany to the West. Ernst Lemmers, Hubertus zu Loewenstein, Reinhold Maier, Willy Brandt, Franz Böhm, Walter Schreiber, and the late Robert Tillmanns have greatly aided my knowledge of the political and social changes, as have, among the scholars, writers, and experts in various fields, Heinz Proebst, Ernst Mueller-Meiningen, Jr., Martin Horn, Wilhelm von Cornides, Viktor von der Lippe, Rudolf Pechel, General Adolf Heusinger, Lieutenant Colonel von Freytag-Loringhoven, Klaus Harpprecht, Edwin Redslob, Konrad von Ilberg, Kurt Hesse, Karl Jaspers, Giselher Wirsing, and Rainer Hildebrand. The officials of the Bank Deutscher

Länder, members of the staff of the Foreign Office, of the library of the Bundestag, of the Ministry for All-German Questions, of the Institut für Zeitgeschichte, and of the Nuremberg archives have been unfailingly co-operative. Among other competent observers of Germany I am obligated to Robert and Louis Lochner, Irving Brown, Melvin Lasky, Frank Howley, M. W. and Dennis Fodor, Richard C. Hottelet, Brewster Morris, Jack Tuthill, Laughlin Campbell, Sir Vaughan Berry, Leo Crespi, and George Henry. James B. Conant was most helpful while he was high commissioner and later ambassador; General Lucius Clay and John McCloy have readily answered questions about their respective terms of office as military governor and high commissioner. My indebtedness is also great to Major General Reber and to the staffs of the historical division at Karlsruhe, the public-information section at Heidelberg, the Kansas City Document Center, and to the library of the American Embassy at Mehlem for many courtesies and efficient assistance.

The chapter on Nuremberg, in somewhat different form, was presented at a symposium at the University of Kansas in the summer of 1957 and had the benefit of the criticism of the members of the group under the benign chairmanship of George Anderson. Parts of the manuscript have been read by Samuel Bemis and Pieter Geyl; all of it has been read by David Dallin and Robert Ferrell, and has greatly profited from their sagacious comments. Colonel Truman Smith, who with Colonel I. L. Hunt and others wrote an official history of the American occupation of the Rhineland after World War I, has kindly made available a manuscript copy of their book [1] and has also put me in touch with American and German military and other authorities. Finally, it is a pleasure to thank my bursary student, David Sumner, and, above all, my devoted friends and

---

[1] *American Military Government of Occupied Germany, 1918–1920.* Report of the Officer in Charge of Civil Affairs, Third Army and American Forces in Germany. Mimeographed.

ACKNOWLEDGMENTS

colleagues at the Yale University Press for their tireless editorial assistance. Without the critical aid of Roberta Yerkes, David and Elinor Horne, and Gertrude Hopkins, the book would have taken far more time to get ready for the press and would have many more defects in its presentation. I should also like to express my appreciation of the perceptive criticisms made by Henry Robbins of the editorial staff of Alfred A. Knopf, Inc.

New Haven
November 21, 1958

CONTENTS

THE DEATH AND LIFE OF GERMANY

I

THE FACE OF THE ENEMY

During the critical days of World War II, when the decisions were being made which would shape the fate of Germany and of the world for the years of peace to come, there was no authoritative or acknowledged voice to speak on behalf of a future Germany. All the instruments of power inside and outside her borders seemed brought together for her destruction, and in the last months of the war no foreign enemy was more single-mindedly concentrated on this end than Adolf Hitler himself. Not a foot of territory, he had ordered, was to be given up along the vast Russian front. If the ground was too frozen to dig trenches, then the guns could be used to plow furrows in the earth and give protection to the fighting troops; and in the West as well, including Germany itself, everything that could produce or be used in commerce—wharves, power stations, factories, mines—was to be blown up before the advancing Allies. They were to find nothing but the scorched earth of the Leader's vengeance against the enemy and against the German people who had failed him and lost their right to any kind of future. The enemy—above all, the Russian—had proved himself stronger; and as Hitler saw his empire shatter and planned his own destruction it was an easy matter to send boys of fourteen and even twelve and ten, in flapping uniforms made for their fathers, into the front lines; to order the execution of commanders who, to save the lives of soldiers and civilians, failed to fight to the last man and bullet; and to destroy anything of value not only to the enemy but even to the Germans. Women and girls were sent to take over antiaircraft defense; prisoners in concentration camps were ordered killed; and the enemy's bombing of German men, women, and children in the gaping cities went on month after month, day and night.

The men who on July 20, 1944, tried to win control of the country from the Nazis—the alliance of soldiers and civilians who hoped to replace Hitler and his men and in some fashion preserve a Germany for the future—were almost all killed; there were more than five thousand death sentences. One of the defendants who, turning to his judge at his trial in Berlin, said: "If I am hanged, Mr. President, you, not I, will be afraid," [1] seemed to be talking vainly not only against the power of the Nazis in his own country but to the equally deaf ears of the enemies of his enemies. For the Allied leaders, when they heard the news, were unimpressed. "The highest personalities in the German Reich are murdering one another," Churchill said.[2] The American high command, civilian and military, attached no more weight to the uprising. Hitler's merciless total war seemed to have resulted now in making the final identification between himself and the German people which he had so long preached. In these last months of his power he and the Allies both spoke of the plots as having been inspired by a small band of Junkers and generals.

The Germans were seen by Allied leaders as in need of more of the bitter and deadly lessons they were getting. Although both Churchill and Roosevelt declared that they had no thought of exterminating or enslaving the German people, Roosevelt said that unconditional surrender applied to them too, not only to the armed forces. And the plans being prepared by Washington for the occupation were designed to bring home to the German people that they had lost the war, to smash at the outset any legend of treason or partial defeat. The Germans—all

[1] Joseph Wirmer, quoted in Annedore Leber: *Das Gewissen steht auf,* p. 124.
[2] Quoted in *The New York Times,* Aug. 3, 1944.

Germans—were to be punished for having backed the war and the criminal Nazi regime that had started it, and for keeping them going so long.

At Yalta, Roosevelt, Stalin, and Churchill agreed that German labor was to be used to help repair the enormous damage the German armies had caused in the Allied nations. There were to be reparations in goods and in dismantled factories; the subsequent directives to the American troops ordered that there be no reconstruction except for the benefit of the allied armies of occupation, and food was not to be given to the civilian population except in cases where the famine would affect the Allied forces. From 1942 to 1945 there were a variety of plans for splitting Germany into from two to seven separate states. In 1942 Stalin and Churchill were both in agreement that Prussia, the chief symbol and source of German militarism, was to be separated from the rest of Germany, and a number of states made of the rest. Churchill, like many of the other Allied leaders, was anti-Prussian, seeing in Prussia's tradition and in the German General Staff one of the evils of the twentieth century. At Yalta he told Stalin that he would deal harshly with the northern Germans but mildly with the southern ones, to which Stalin answered that they all seemed to him to fight like devils. Churchill, however, distinguished to a degree between the kinds of Germans who were fighting; at least twice during the war he paid tribute to the valor of the enemy: to Rommel and his North African corps and to the German soldiers at Cassino, where, he quoted General Alexander as saying, probably no other troops in the world could have stood up against the punishment they were taking. And when Stalin at Teheran said he would like to kill fifty thousand German officers and technicians, Churchill said he would rather sacrifice his own life. It was the German, especially the Prussian, military machine he wanted to see dismantled; he said he made no war against races. In 1941, before the United States entered the war, he had differentiated between the slogans of war and the political realities; he ex-

5

plained: "The phrases 'Nazi tyranny' and 'Prussian militarism' are used by us as targets rather than as any implacable general condemnation of the German peoples. We agree with the Russian Government in hoping to split the Germans and to isolate the criminal Nazi régime." [3]

Roosevelt, on the other hand, while he too disliked the Prussians, was strongly anti-German, and so were the chief advisers who surrounded him and in whom he placed his confidence. At Teheran he agreed with Stalin that there were no important differences between the German states: Bavaria did not have the officer class that Prussia had; that was all. According to Mrs. Roosevelt, he had approved the Morgenthau plan for making a pasture of Germany, not only at the Quebec conference in September 1944, when he persuaded Churchill to accept it, but even later after he had publicly repudiated it. Basically, she says—and other evidence bears her out—he preferred the Morgenthau plan to the views of Hull and Stimson. In 1943, before Secretary of State Hull went to Moscow, Roosevelt spoke of the need for splitting up Germany and moving out the dangerous elements of the population from East Prussia, which would go to Poland, and he voiced his opposition to any plan for a soft peace. At Yalta, after he had seen the destruction the Germans had brought to the Crimea, he said he was in a more bloodthirsty mood than before. He thought the Army handbook, of which Mr. Morgenthau and his advisers in the Treasury complained, "pretty bad," so bad that he called a news conference to criticize it.[4] The handbook foresaw a food ration of two thousand calories or less for the Germans, along with some heavy and some light industry; but it failed to promise punishment and retribution. The men around the President—Sumner Welles, Hopkins, Hull—were mostly of the same opinion as Roosevelt. Stimson said that Hull's plan for Germany was

[3] Winston Churchill: *The Second World War*, III, 200, 523, 628, 853; V, 509.
[4] *The New York Times*, Sept. 24, 1944.

scarcely less punitive than Morgenthau's; Stimson himself wanted Germany disarmed and her industries controlled.[5]

Roosevelt, like many English, Americans, and French of his generation, had taken an early dislike to the Germans, to their "provinciality" and their "arrogance." He had spent time in their country as a child, and subsequent events had borne out his impressions. Unlike Churchill or Stalin, he would have little to do with the idea of any "other Germany"—he had no interest before the war in seeing a member of the opposition to Hitler who came to the United States, nor did he in the course of the war distinguish between Germans. It was the German people, he said in 1944, who needed to know they had engaged in a lawless conspiracy against the decencies of modern civilization. He too denounced the Prussian military clique and the gangs of militarists—Sumner Welles at the same time was speaking of the perennial poison of the German General Staff. Always anxious to avoid the mistakes of World War I, Roosevelt wanted no armistice, no reparations in money, which had caused so much recrimination and had failed so disastrously after the First World War. Nor would the whole of Germany escape an occupation this time as it had after that war, although he believed that the Germans would characteristically throw up the sponge when their borders were crossed in order to escape the consequences of their lost and criminal war.[6] The young German prisoners the Americans had captured, Roosevelt thought, were worse than the old, and the peril of Nazism remained in their fanaticism. It would be enough for the Germans to eat soup after the Allied victory, soup three times a day served by Army soup kitchens. "If I had my way," he was reported as saying, "I would keep Germany on a breadline for the next 25 years."[7] To avoid the mistakes of the past, he urged uncondi-

[5] Henry L. Stimson and McGeorge Bundy: *On Active Service in Peace and War*, p. 570.

[6] *The New York Times*, Aug. 18, 1944.

[7] Stimson and Bundy: *On Active Service . . .* , p. 573. Fred Smith: "The Rise and Fall of the Morgenthau Plan," *UN World*, March 1947.

tional surrender instead of the fourteen points of Wilson. He also would have no repetition of Clemenceau's error of wanting to divide Germany by force; instead he favored, as did Hull, encouraging the separatist movements that already existed.[8]

Among the advisers around Roosevelt, Stimson and Forrestal took a more moderate view of the character of the Germans and the treatment to be given them than did Hull, Morgenthau, Welles, or Hopkins. Stimson had learned from his father to mistrust the Prussians and admire the French. For him war was the basic crime, and Imperial Germany had resembled the Nazi state in its warlike postures. This time, he believed, a defenseless Germany would be the best protection against a revival of militarism; but he opposed what he regarded as the extreme proposals of both Hull and Morgenthau and what he called clumsy economic vengeance. The plans for keeping Germany near the margin of hunger he thought a great mistake. At the time it was written he believed JCS 1067, the Army directive that governed the conduct of the American troops in Germany and forbade fraternization or giving food to the Germans, to be a "fairly good paper," although some two years later, in 1947, he had come to think it "a painfully negative document." Stimson's opposition to Hull's and Morgenthau's harsh economic policies toward Germany was reinforced by his concern for a wider area. He wrote: "He[Hull] and Morgenthau wished to wreck completely the immense Ruhr-Saar area of Germany and turn it into second-rate agricultural land regardless of all that area meant not only to Germany but to the welfare of the entire European continent. Hopkins went with them so far as to wish to prevent the manufacture of steel in the area, a prohibition which would pretty well sabotage everything else." [9]

But Roosevelt's Cabinet committee was unanimous in recommending the demilitarization of Germany, punishment of war criminals, controls over communications and education. "It was

[8] James F. Byrnes: *Speaking Frankly*, pp. 181–84.
[9] Stimson and Bundy: *On Active Service . . .*, p. 570

only on the issue of the destruction of German industry that Stimson was violently opposed to his colleagues." [1] Forrestal too said that the American people would not support the mass murder or enslavement of the German people or its industrial devastation. Hull wanted the power of large industry and land-owners eliminated, the standard of living of the German population to be held no higher than subsistence levels, and Germany's self-sufficiency and her economic position of power in Europe destroyed, his main objective being the establishment of a system of collective security. During the first years of the war he was not anxious for the dismemberment of Germany, but thought rather she should be kept under military control for some twenty-five or fifty years. In 1944, although violently opposing the Morgenthau plan, he came to favor the separation of the Ruhr and Saar from Germany. He wanted a common occupation and control of the country, decentralization of the political structure; and his views, he reports, were enthusiastically accepted by the Russians.

Stimson wanted Germany punished. But he wrote of the Morgenthau plan: "The question is not whether we want the Germans to suffer for their sins. Many of us would like to see them suffer the tortures they have inflicted on others. The only question is whether over the years a group of seventy million educated, efficient, and imaginative people can be kept within bounds on such a low level of subsistence as the Treasury proposals contemplate. . . . It would be just such a crime as the Germans themselves hoped to perpetrate upon their victims—it would be a crime against civilization itself." [2]

Roosevelt's convictions about the future plans of German militarists were shared by many, including Under Secretary of State Sumner Welles, who thought the German General Staff knew it was defeated but would play for time and differences "between the United Nations." Welles believed that the Gen-

[1] Ibid.
[2] Ibid., p. 578.

9

eral Staff was only half visible, that the other half of its mechanism was secret and would remain so; it had made detailed plans for a later renewal of its attempt to dominate the world— and the Anglo-Saxon powers were its only permanent antagonists. He opposed a centralized Germany, which he thought would start another war of revenge; and, like Roosevelt, he favored a partition of Germany into a number of states, with Poland to get East Prussia. He thought the first stratagem of the postwar German military command would be to stimulate the growth of communism in its "world revolutionary form," which he distinguished from its Stalinist form, and that a long occupation would be needed. German policy for fifty years had been directed to world conquest; for two hundred years the German people had been a destructive force in the family of nations; and the same sinister alliances of big industrialists and the General Staff had been behind the Weimar Republic, in temporary concealment, that had been behind the Nazis. He believed that there should be no hurry to develop German self-government, but he did not favor the extreme economic devastation that Morgenthau and his advisers in the Treasury Department were advocating. Men who were close to the President believed he favored Welles over Hull. It was sometimes said that Welles was running, in effect, a second state department; and toward the end of the war there was even a third one when the Treasury Department took part in negotiating political settlements and Henry Morgenthau went to Quebec to present his plan for the treatment of Germany at a conference in which the State Department was not represented.[3]

Morgenthau's was the most radical of the blueprints for the destruction of German military, economic, and political power. Although the acceptance of the Morgenthau plan in September 1944 was short-lived and the plan was promptly and violently attacked by all the other members of the Roosevelt Cabinet, it was never completely disentangled from the procedures of

[3] Robert. E. Sherwood: *Roosevelt and Hopkins*, I, 135.

the occupation until 1947. Roosevelt and Churchill withdrew their approval of the plan within a few days of initialing it, yet some of its articles became part of JCS 1067 and of the Potsdam agreement. Morgenthau and his principal adviser, Harry Dexter White, to whom the plan owed many if not all of its features, believed with Welles that the Germans and the Nazis were identical and that the Germans were already preparing for the next war. Somewhere in Germany, Mr. Morgenthau wrote in 1945 in *Germany Is Our Problem* (in which the plan was printed for the first time), a fanatical young corporal was plotting as Hitler had in 1918. The mobilization of World War III was already beginning—it was a proved and demonstrated fact, he wrote, that there were plans for financing the Nazis after their defeat, that factories were to have their research bureaus hidden in cities or villages, with liaison agents in touch with the party.[4] So there could be no halfway measures in uprooting the sources of power and infection as there had been after World War I. Germany was to be dismembered; large estates were to be broken up; German heavy industry was to be eliminated. There were to be no diesel engines manufactured, no steel rails, no tractors; not even perfume was to be produced, for the factories manufacturing it could be converted to make poison gas; there was to be no machinery for the manufacture of light metals, since that could be turned to the making of light planes. Factories to be left the Germans were those for making toasters, hair-curlers, and other such light objects of consumption.

Originally Mr. Morgenthau would have stripped the Ruhr of industry and closed the mines; later he wanted the area interna-

[4] This was to be often repeated. On July 11, 1945, the *Stars and Stripes* wrote that the Germans had already set in motion plans for a third attempt to enslave the world. An article in the same paper on September 28 reported the first of the secret postwar meetings of SS leaders. They were to lie low for the present and prepare to capitalize on the trouble to be expected between the Allies. Others wrote in 1945 that the officer corps had secret arms caches on the estates of the German Junkers (Michael Sayres and Albert E. Kahn: *The Plot against the Peace*).

tionalized but no German allowed in it. There was to be no trade between the Ruhr and a divided Germany; the miners and factory hands were to go back to the farms and shops of a deindustrialized Reich; the cartels were to be broken up and a careful watch maintained. I. G. Farben, he believed, was at the end of the war concealing its important documents in beer halls, caves, salt mines, and monasteries. Farben and other organizations that had permitted Germany to export manufactures and to buy food instead of growing it would now be destroyed, and Europe would feed itself instead of feeding Germany. There would be mass unemployment, and this would help the Allies to use German labor battalions to repair the war damage. The Germans were not to be allowed to have laboratories or centers of research, though without them, Mr. Morgenthau thought, German scientists would surreptitiously use their homes or barns for such purposes.

The Nazis had succeeded in so alienating the sympathies of the civilized world that such views as these got a hearing they could scarcely have received otherwise. A reviewer of *Germany Is Our Problem* in *The New York Times Book Review* wrote that no book since *Mein Kampf* had offered the American people information so important to their survival; reading it, he believed, would help prevent World War III. Another reviewer called the author a hardheaded, logical realist—not completely persuasive on every point, but so cogent and reasonable on many that it would be well for the world if copies reached President Truman and Secretary of State Byrnes and General Eisenhower, then the key people among the Americans making decisions on what to do with the Germans.[5]

Although the Morgenthau plan was withdrawn because of the storm of criticism both inside and outside the administration, the Secretary of the Treasury announced to his colleagues in the Cabinet that the President wanted him to have an im-

[5] *The New York Times*, Oct. 7, 1945. Orville Prescott in ibid., Oct. 5, 1945.

portant voice in all decisions on Germany, and the State Department memoranda and briefings of Roosevelt before his journey to Yalta bear traces of the conflict, which did not result in a complete victory for the opponents of the plan. In the directive of September 22, 1944,[6] which became the basis for JCS 1067, Germany was to be kept to a minimum standard of living; it was to be treated as a defeated enemy nation, and fraternization was to be strongly discouraged. All General Staff officers were to be arrested; no steps were to be taken for German economic rehabilitation; relief was to be given to the civilian population only to the extent necessary to prevent disease and such disorder as might interfere with military operations. The State Department in later memoranda repeated that the occupation should be "severe," although it continued to oppose sweeping deindustrialization and looked forward to a minimum German economy and the eventual assimilation of the German people into world society. These later memoranda spoke of a rock-bottom standard of living for the German people and repeated that Germans should provide labor for the rehabilitation of devastated parts of Europe. The primary Allied objective, the State Department believed, was to prevent Germany from again disturbing the peace of the world.

JCS 1067 went further than this. Like the Morgenthau plan, it said that the Germans could not escape responsibility for what they had brought upon themselves, and Germany was to be occupied not for the purpose of liberation but as a defeated enemy nation. The directive forbade research activities, cartels, military pensions, fraternization. Measures were to be taken to make sure that former Nazis were not used in military government, regardless of administrative necessity; there were to be "no German parades, military or political, civilian or sports"; the political administration was to be decentralized, and re-

---

[6] This was drafted by the State and War departments and approved by the Treasury representatives after long debate (Paul Y. Hammond: "The Origins of JCS 1067").

gional and local autonomy encouraged. No merchant ships were to be built, no oil or rubber was to be manufactured, there were to be no aircraft. A paragraph read:

> You will estimate requirements of supplies necessary to prevent starvation or widespread disease or such civil unrest as would endanger the occupying forces. Such estimates will be based upon a program whereby the Germans are made responsible for providing for themselves, out of their own work and resources. You will take all practicable economic and police measures to assure that German resources are fully utilized and consumption held to the minimum in order that imports may be strictly limited and that surpluses may be made available for the occupying forces and displaced persons and United Nations prisoners of war, and for reparation. You will take no action that would tend to support basic living standards in Germany on a higher level than that existing in any one of the neighboring United Nations and you will take appropriate measures to insure that basic living standards of the German people are not higher than those existing in any one of the neighboring United Nations when such measures will contribute to raising the standards of any such nation.[7]

JCS 1067 was to some degree a victory of the men in the Treasury Department who persistently held out against the plans of the State Department, the Army, and the British for a treatment of Germany that would be stern but would look to her eventual recovery. Morgenthau's assistant, Harry Dexter White, thought the British plan envisaged too much political freedom for Germany; after the Morgenthau plan had been rejected by the men who initialed it, he and his colleagues were ever on the alert to restore as many features of it as they could.

To get a hearing, memoranda to the President had to take into account his conviction that it was necessary to deal harshly

[7] *Germany, 1947–1949*, pp. 21–33.

with the Germans. No one, Roosevelt declared in response to the attacks on the Morgenthau plan, wants to make Germany a wholly agricultural nation again or desires the eradication of German industrial capacity in the Ruhr and Saar; but he continued after the rejection of the Morgenthau plan to urge the Secretary of the Treasury to publish his book. In an introduction to it Roosevelt wrote what were perhaps his minimum requirements for the treatment of the Germans: "The German people are not going to be enslaved because the United Nations does not traffic in human slavery. But it will be necessary for them to earn their way back into the fellowship of peace-loving and law-abiding nations. And, in their climb up that steep road, we shall certainly see to it that they are not encumbered by having to carry guns. They will be delivered of that burden—we hope forever."

Stalin's view of Germany was in contrast to that of both Churchill and Roosevelt. From the start of the war he distinguished between the Nazis and the German people, seeking to drive between the government and the governed a wedge that would one day be used to overturn the Nazis. The Russian foreign commissar, Viacheslav M. Molotov, in a radio broadcast in 1941 immediately after the German attack, said: "This war was not forced on us by the German people, workers, peasants, intelligentsia, whose sufferings we know so well, but by a clique of bloody fascist rulers. . . ." [8] Stalin repeatedly proclaimed that the Russian war was a holy war of liberation against the fascist bandits and was not directed against the peaceful German people. In his order of the day of February 23, 1942, he said:

> It is sometimes rumored in the foreign press that the Red Army has the aim of exterminating the German people and destroying the German state. That is of course a stupid lie and an absurd calumny on the Red Army. The Red Army does not have and cannot have such idiotic aims. The Red

[8] Wolfgang Leonhard: *Die Revolution entlässt ihre Kinder*, p. 108.

Army sets itself the goal of driving the occupier out of our country and of freeing Soviet soil from the fascist German invasion. It is very likely that the war for the liberation of Soviet soil will lead to the driving out or destruction of the Hitler clique. We should welcome such a result. But it would be laughable to equate the Hitler clique with the German people, the German state. The lessons of history teach us that the Hitlers come and go but the German people, the German state remain.[9]

In July 1943 in Moscow the Free Germany Committee, made up of captured German generals, officers, and men, was founded, and in September the Union of German Officers. The aim of both was the overthrow of the Nazi tyranny that was leading Germany to disaster. Hitler's irresponsible and criminal acts had freed them, the manifesto of the Committee said, of their soldiers' oaths. As patriotic Germans they called on the Army and the people to get rid of him and to establish a strong, united Germany with weapons in its hands.

For Stalin and the Russians, propaganda was a vital part of the successful conduct of the war, and German broadcasters representing the Free Germany Committee moved with the front-line Russian troops urging surrender on the German soldiers, not as treason but as an act on behalf of their country and its future. The same tactics were used in the broadcasts and pamphlets aimed at the civilian population: "Attention—this is the broadcast of the Free Germany Committee. We speak in the name of the German people. We call for the rescue of the Reich." Stalin did not demand unconditional surrender of the German people—only, he said, of the Hitlerite armies. (At Yalta it was Churchill who wanted to change the word "Hitlerite" to "Nazi" to make the application broader.) Stalin in February 1943 said the Red Army was created not for the conquest of foreign countries but to defend the frontiers of the

---

[9] Boris Meissner: *Russland, die Westmächte und Deutschland*, p. 13.

Soviet land and drive the German invaders from the borders of the country. Propaganda of the Free Germany Committee in the summer of 1943 urged the German troops to retreat to their borders, keeping their arms.

The implications of those words were alarming to Britain and the United States, especially as they were accompanied by Russian accusations that the Allies were seeking a separate peace; there were rumors that Stalin himself might be negotiating with the Germans. With Stalin's speech before him, President Roosevelt inquired of Ambassador William H. Standley in Moscow whether he thought Stalin was in fact considering an agreement with Germany. There is some substantial evidence that Stalin in those months after Stalingrad was ready to negotiate— either as a means of putting pressure on the West or as a move toward a separate peace. Delay in opening the second front had been the cause of increasingly angry explosions on the part of the Russian leadership and Communist sympathizers in England and the United States. In addition, there had been no American and British approval of Stalin's repeated territorial demands on Poland and the Baltic countries. So the rumors went: Stalin was turning, as he had before, to the possibility of dealing with Hitler. The negotiations that the Kremlin initiated failed to develop, according to Peter Kleist, through whom Russian agents three times attempted to get in touch with Hitler, because of the Führer's intractability. Kleist says that in 1943 the Russians offered Germany the borders of 1914, but Hitler would not deal with them. There is, however, evidence that Hitler was anxious in that period to come to an agreement with Russia. But what he proposed was preposterous: a secret armistice. A report of the "Fuehrer Conferences on Matters Dealing with the German Navy" for July 17 and 18, 1943, quotes Hitler as saying: "We can hope to win this war only if we stop expending our forces in the East. . . . Russia is getting considerable supplies via the Far East. Therefore the question arises whether a threat by Japan that she will enter the war against Russia will help to make the latter accept the German offer of an unannounced armistice on the Eastern front, to be kept secret from the Anglo-Saxons. Russia would continue to accept Lend Lease materials. This political goal is worth *every* sacrifice." [1]

Whatever weight one wishes to give to the evidence for Stalin's readiness to make a separate peace, there is no doubt that he always recognized the existence of a number of Germanies within the Nazi state. They were made up of Germans who were useful to him at a particular moment in history—the Junkers and generals of the Free Germany movement in 1943, the Communist Germans of the 1930's (some of whom he delivered to Hitler in 1939), the so-called democratic Germany of the future which would include even SS men. All these were welcomed or slain impartially with only one judgment upon them—their usefulness to Stalin's plan for a conquest far wider than the occupation of East Germany. Churchill could talk of his own sympathy for the toiling masses; Stalin was unimpressed by the familiar words or by any distinction other than the one he made between the men who collaborated and those who did not. Stalin's demands changed as the military and political situations changed. In 1941 he told Eden he wanted Germany divided; at Teheran he inclined toward Roosevelt's plan of five German states; at Yalta he wanted the plans for German dismemberment to be included in the communiqué issued at the end of the conference, but a few months later the Russians dropped the idea, although the American administration still favored it. As victory came closer, the tone of the propaganda from Moscow hardened. In 1945 forty captured German generals urged the army to surrender, saying the Germans would

[1] There is additional support for the theory that in this period the Russians and Germans were in some sort of diplomatic touch. See H. von Einsiedel: *I Joined the Russians*; Leonhard: *Die Revolution entlässt ihre Kinder*; Peter Kleist: *Zwischen Hitler und Stalin, 1939–1943*; "Fuehrer Conferences on Matters Dealing with the German Navy."

have to be punished but could earn their way back to a respectable place in the community of nations.

"The Hitlers come and go but the German people, the German state remain." Placards bearing these words appeared all over Berlin when the Russians entered the ruined city. Like the propaganda posters that appeared in the other countries the Soviet dominated—great colored murals showing processions of well-fed, happy, bronzed workers—the placards were in dazzling contrast to the thin, gray-faced citizenry walking past them. The words were fair, but they bore little relationship to the harsh realities of life in the plundered city.

The words of Churchill and Roosevelt, on the other hand, were meant to teach a moral lesson; they were addressed to all Germans, making no distinction between the party fanatics and those who had fought against them or who might be used against them. Their technical advisers were of another mind. The Advisory Committee set up in 1941–2 recommended, as did the State Department, strict controls but no dismemberment of Germany. At the time of the Moscow conference in 1943 both the American and the British experts accompanying Hull and Eden opposed the strong measures being discussed by the foreign ministers (as Molotov reported, the Russian experts did too), and in 1944 the United States Army psychological-warfare division wanted to distinguish the Nazi party and the high command from the German people.

Nor were all the men who were making the decisions of one mind or always of the same mind. General Eisenhower, who believed the war to be more of a holy war than any in history, thought the United States was bound to feed Germany and wanted the Ruhr restored instead of dismantled. Roosevelt said he desired no starvation and enough production so that Germany would not be a burden on the rest of the world, although he was to say at Yalta that he did not want to help keep the Germans from starving. But it was in fact the hard policy that won out in the American directives—the Germans were not often fed from the Army soup kitchens that Roosevelt had favored. They were kept at arm's length as a hostile, conquered people who were biding their time for revenge.

These differences between the Russian views of the occupation and the American were apparent too in the technical preparations. The American military-government officers who, beginning in 1942, were trained in Charlottesville, Virginia, in Michigan, and elsewhere, including a final period of training in England, were mainly civilians either detached from other branches of the Army or commissioned directly from civil life; they were given rapid courses in German and history and military law and were marched and drilled in conditioning exercises which, since most were middle-aged men, were patently needed. In addition, units of enlisted men were given instruction at various universities—so-called area studies of the people and language. From the beginning it had been clear that military government in the early stages would be under the control of the Army rather than the State Department; and, while there were many committees, international, departmental, and technical, dealing with the problems of the occupation, the training of the military-government personnel was the job of the Army.[2]

The Russian system was of another kind; the party and the Army together ran the occupation. The personnel that was to reorganize the German political and social system consisted almost entirely of German Communists who had fled to Russia during the Nazi period, and all of them had been trained not for months but for years for the job they would have to do. All of them spoke fluent German. They knew precisely what their political assignments were and the reasons for them; there were

[2] Late in 1941 the Advisory Committee on Postwar Policy was appointed by the President; in addition there were technical committees; combined committees; the Working Security Committee, made up of representatives of the State, War, and Navy departments; and the Foreign Economic Administration, which was to co-ordinate War, Treasury, and OSS activities in Germany after the surrender.

few wasted motions as the first of them came in with the Soviet troops to organize the defeated Germans, their industries, their unions, their police, their newspapers, their political parties, their farms. By the time the Americans got to Berlin, the Russians had been in the city for nine weeks; a single Communist-controlled union, four political parties, a police force, and a municipal government were already established; and 80 per cent of the factories that had survived the war had been dismantled.

On the Russian side there was remarkably little hate of the Germans despite the ferocious fight they had been waging, the scorched earth where there had been Russian cities and towns, the atrocities committed against the Russian civilian population and prisoners of war. It is true that Stalin at Yalta said the Germans were savages, people who delighted in destroying the work and civilization of others; on other occasions he had called for the extermination of the invader, and he had wanted German workers' homes bombed as well as the factories. But these remarks were asides—they had little place in the public pronouncements, the propaganda, or the indoctrination given the troops. There was no counterpart to the American instructions telling the GI's they were not to be moved by the hunger of the yellow-haired German child or the attractive German girl because under these outward signs—so the warnings went—there lurked the Nazi.

The behavior of the troops, however, bore only a vague relation to the directives. Photographs of the Americans entering Rötgen showed them giving candy and food to German children. The reaction in the United States to these pictures was so violent that recurrences were strictly forbidden; but they never stopped. The Russians had no such orders—and they regarded the Germans with no more or less suspicion than they did any other outpost of the capitalist world, which in all its forms, whether German or Allied, threatened the revolution until it could be converted by force or propaganda. Before them fled thousands of terrified Germans trying to make their way to the West. The Russian soldiers plundered and raped in the East German towns and villages as they had in the other countries they invaded or liberated. Their demands for watches and women—"*Uhri, Uhri, Frau komm*"—were insatiable (the raping usually followed after troops had got hold of alcohol); this wildness, combined with the threat of arrests and deportations, sent panicky masses of the German civilian population and of German soldiers to try somehow to get to the West. The last defenses of the German high command were organized to permit their troops, as far as possible, to surrender to the British or Americans.

Stalin and the Russian leaders had no anti-German sentiments of the kind that forced the revision of the American Army handbook for the occupation of Germany. Stalin observed to Churchill and Roosevelt that the Germans were too subservient and too law-abiding; he told how in 1907 he had gone to what was to be a workers' meeting in Leipzig. The meeting had failed to take place because there was no one to punch the railroad tickets of the two hundred German workers so they could feel free to leave the platform of the station. Once he even expressed his sympathy for the German soldiers who were being killed like pigs, he said, because Hitler had ordered them not to retreat. Stalin's demand for four million Germans to be used as forced laborers to repair the destruction by their armies, his demand for reparations, even for the killing of the fifty thousand officers, were no more than he required of any other country under Soviet control, including his own. Purges, forced labor, the state taking what it needed without regard to the population—there was nothing new in this, certainly nothing specifically anti-German.

II

THE FACES OF THE FRIENDS

ALL THE full-dress conferences ended in public texts and affirmations of agreement among the Russians, British, and Americans as to how the Germans were to be dealt with. The difficulties and differences appeared in other events, but they were always there below the surface during the whole course of the war, becoming more evident as victory came nearer. They appeared when Churchill asked Stalin if he wanted only small defenseless powers in East Europe and Stalin retorted by asking Churchill if he foresaw a Danubian confederation in the same area. They were to be seen in the relations with the two Polish governments, the two Yugoslav factions, in Greece, and when Stalin told Churchill his threats against Russia would have reverse results. The occasions multiplied as victory came nearer. But in the large formulations about the future of Germany there was substantial agreement. All three nations— Britain, Russia, and the United States—wanted to weaken Germany's military power and potential. In the darkest days of the invasion when the Germans were at the gates of Moscow, Stalin had Russian postwar boundaries in mind. He told Anthony Eden in December 1941—the same month the Union of Polish Patriots, which would soon be contesting the authority of the London Poles, was established under Russian auspices—that he wanted the recognition of Russian frontiers as they were after the pact with Hitler. While the Americans, owing to the opposition of Stimson and perhaps with unhappy memories of the

23

secret treaties of World War I, were unwilling at this point to talk about the details of borders, there was never to be any serious objection to the loss of German territory in the East, especially of East Prussia, or to Stalin's desire for having friendly governments on the Russian frontiers. Some territorial changes for the benefit of Poland and the Soviet Union, the occupation of Germany (either, as the British first suggested, by the victorious powers acting together, or by the three powers in separate zones), war trials, reparations, forced labor, reform of the German economy, the destruction of Nazism and militarism, the need for re-education—on these broad principles there was never any fundamental disagreement.

The Allies met on common ground in the decisions to decentralize the German political structure and to break up large corporations, the German banking system, and large estates—essential elements in providing the economic backing and officer cadres of Prussianism. But from the very beginning of the German attack on Russia, Stalin seems never to have doubted that Germany, the Hitler state, was but the foremost of his enemies, and that when the war was over the Germans would be replaced by a hostile Anglo-Saxon capitalist world across whatever boundaries were drawn; so the farther west these boundaries were, the better. Such forebodings were naturally more evident outside the convivial banquets of Teheran and Yalta, although they appeared during the meetings there too.

The first necessity, of course, was the defeat of the invader, and to this end the same antifascist front that Stalin had tried to create in the 1930's became a powerful reality. But if victory over Hitler came first, it would be merely a stage in the other, long-range conflict. There were many reassurances for Stalin's allies. In November 1941 he said Russia had no goal of invading foreign soil or bringing foreign countries under a Russian yoke; he dissolved the Comintern in 1943; he readily accepted the American blueprints for postwar cooperation. Hull describes Molotov as radiant when he read the American plan that Hull gave to him informally in Moscow. It was a plan for the control of Germany and—above all, in the mind of the American administration—for the postwar collaboration of the peace-loving nations. In the genial atmosphere of Teheran, Roosevelt welcomed Stalin as a new member of the family, and again at Yalta he compared the meeting to a family gathering.

Despite these general agreements, there remained many signs of Stalin's abiding suspicions of his allies. In the days of gravest danger to the Soviet state, when the decision of Stalingrad was still in the balance, he refused to let American-manned planes fly to the Caucasus to aid the Russian armies. Churchill early remarked on the unsatisfactory state of British consultations with the Russian ally on military matters. As the Germans were advancing in the Caucasus and the Baku oil fields, Churchill wrote to General Ismay on November 5, 1941: "The Russians tell us nothing, and view with great suspicion any inquiries we make on this subject." [1] When Field Marshal Sir A. P. Wavell went to Tiflis at this time, he found no one in authority to talk to, although he spoke Russian well. The crew of a British plane that flew to Archangel soon after the German attack on Russia was quartered in a houseboat and not permitted on shore. General John R. Deane was told by the American Chief of Staff, General Marshall, that he should not try to find out anything about Russia since such inquiries would irritate the Soviet government. And Churchill reports that when in 1942 Molotov visited England, he kept guns under his pillow, his doors were locked, and he brought with him his own police and cleaning-women.

The lack of a second front was a continuing cause of friction. With millions of Germans heavily engaged on the Eastern front, occupying thousands of square miles of Russian territory, Stalin could ask the British and Americans what they were waiting for. The bulk of the German armies and Hitler's best troops were in the East. Stalin was convinced that the West could, if it would,

[1] Winston Churchill: *The Second World War*, III, 525–6.

open up a diversionary front in Europe, and Roosevelt had told Molotov in May 1942 that there would be a second front that year. When it did not appear, Stalin's view of *Realpolitik* was confirmed; it was the same strategy he was to follow, if on a far smaller scale, when the Poles in Warsaw rose against the Germans and the Russian armies stopped just outside of Warsaw while the Germans crushed the resistance inside the city. Certain that the West wanted Russia to do the fighting and then enter the continent of Europe triumphant and fresh when Russia was exhausted, he demanded to know from every emissary who came to Moscow the reasons for the delay. He taunted Churchill with being afraid of the Germans. At the same time the Communist parties and others, filled with admiration for the wartime qualities of the Russians, staged rallies in Britain and America to call for the second front, which the Russians and many non-Communists as well were sure was being deliberately postponed. There were always signs of Russian doubts of the West. Americans were refused permission to inspect Soviet air bases. The Allies continually urged the Russians to let their planes attack the German troops on the Eastern front, but shuttle bombing with Allied planes using Russian bases was never permitted on any large scale, although for a short time there was an American air base in the Ukraine. The plans were made and approved at conferences, but somehow the practical arrangements came to be sidetracked or the directives misunderstood. Allied military observers were kept from the Russian front; weather stations were promised but never provided.[2]

Lend-lease was regarded by the Russians as a most useful increment to their arsenals; it had to be provided in vast convoys

[2] In 1939 Stalin had been more anxious to please Hitler, who wished him ill, than he would be in later years to co-operate with his admiring friends of the West. The Russians in 1939 and 1940 offered the Germans repair bases near Murmansk and actively aided their use by German ships. "Fuehrer Conferences on Matters Dealing with the German Navy," Report of the Commander-in-Chief to the Führer, Oct. 10, 16, Dec. 30, 1939; Jan. 26, June 4, 1940, all in Vol. II, 1940.

that were heavily attacked by the Germans. Any delay in shipments was protested by the Soviets as intentional.[3] American
lend-lease planes were welcome, but American crews were not
permitted to fly them in—the Russians sent their own fliers to
Alaska to pilot the planes to Siberia. A request to land dis-
abled planes on Russian fields at the time of the bombing raid
of the Ploesti oil fields was answered a week after the raid took
place. When the Russians asked for two million pairs of shoes
and the Americans said they could not supply that number of
new ones but would have to send repaired ones, the Russians
refused to take them. A complete tire plant was shipped to
Russia, but no American engineer could go with it. A radio station was sent, but the freight planes bringing it had to stop at
Teheran, where it was transshipped. British medical personnel at
Vaenga and elsewhere were subjected to severe restrictions.
Medals could not be presented by the American ambassador,
Admiral Standley, but had to be turned over for presentation
by Mr. Molotov. When Russian troops were inadvertently
strafed by American planes on one of the relatively few occasions when they were allowed to attack German targets on the
Russian front, Molotov said it could not have been an error, although similar mistakes were made on all fronts during the war,
as innumerable infantrymen have testified.

Nor were Russian suspicions wholly unjustified in the light of
their far-reaching plans for the countries they were liberating
and for those the West would liberate. Churchill in October
1942 wrote in a memorandum to Anthony Eden of "the meas-
ureless disaster" if Russian barbarism overlaid the culture and independence of the ancient states of Europe. To build a dike
against it, he thought of a Council of Europe, a United States
of Europe, and an international police force. But as the war
progressed, it became clear to him that only the United States
could balance Russian power. Even then there would be no se-

---

[3] Ambassador Standley reported that the Russian newspapers never mentioned American relief shipments being sent to the Soviet Union.

curity for Europe unless Russia could be persuaded to be co-operative and to accept reasonable compensation in territory and goods for her losses.

The attempts of the Allies, therefore, to deal with Russia's preponderant power and her evident forebodings were unceasing. Churchill's method—tried later in the war, in 1944—was the time-honored one of parceling out spheres of influence, sharing power in areas important to both sides, and satisfying reasonable demands for territory and friendly governments on Russia's borders. But Soviet Russia represented for many of the men of the New Deal another pariah government of the Left. Its leaders were the survivors of an upheaval that, like the American and French revolutions, had had its enemies in the rich and powerful of an old reactionary order and would always have them there. These enemies were also the enemies of the New Deal; they were the same ones who hated Roosevelt and his economic reforms. So men such as Hopkins became suspicious, not of Stalin's plans for extending Russian influence, but of Churchill's imperialism, although Hopkins's admiration of the British Prime Minister had been well-nigh boundless when the British alone were fighting the Germans. These men said it was impossible to organize the postwar world without the Russians being brought in as equal partners with the United States. Forrestal reports that no criticism of the Russians could be tolerated in these circles. "I find," he wrote in September 1944, "that whenever any American suggests that we act in accordance with the needs of our own security he is apt to be called a god-damned fascist or imperialist, while if Uncle Joe suggests that he needs the Baltic Provinces, half of Poland, all of Bessarabia and access to the Mediterranean, all hands agree that he is a fine, frank, candid, and generally delightful fellow who is very easy to deal with because he is so explicit in what he wants." [4] These "liberals," as they were called, believed that the Russians had good cause to be suspicious, that the Munich Pact,

[4] Walter Millis, ed., with E. S. Duffield: *Forrestal Diaries*, p. 14.

the invasion of Russia by Allied armies in 1918, and English and American imperialism were not far from what Stalin said of them.

Under the influence of the fervors and passions of the war and to enable themselves to believe in the good intentions of the Russian ally, many serious observers came to believe in a new interpretation of historical facts that they had not observed before. Walter Lippmann, for example, wrote that, wide apart as the two systems of government had been both in the times of the Tsar and under the Communists, there had been an underlying admiration and understanding: the United States and Russia had wanted each other to be strong, each had supported the other in critical times. Books, articles, and editorials were written to show how alike the Russians and Americans were—a sentiment echoed by many, including people of such different political philosophies as Henry Wallace, General Eisenhower, and Joseph E. Davies, the former American ambassador to Russia and an indefatigable defender of Russian activities. The Soviet attack on Finland and the pact with Hitler were represented as devices for gaining time before fighting the Nazi enemy. Roosevelt, before the Russians had been attacked by Hitler, said the Russian dictatorship was as brutal as any in history— but all this changed after the German invasion. The hatred of the Nazis was powerful enough to divert any anti-Russian sentiments; and in the course of the war, with victories and defeats on a scale never seen before, for many people it was the Russians, not the British or even Americans, who were the heroic figures. For many of the New Dealers, too, big business was not unlike the Marxists' view of it; its international cartels, its anticommunism, and its lack of any sense of social responsibility would need vigilant policing after the war. Hopkins mentioned how certain industrial quarters in the United States would want to build up German industry again.

Many who were implacably opposed to Roosevelt's domestic policies shared his generous feelings for Russia. Hull believed

Russia fundamentally changed during the war and reminded himself and Roosevelt of the traditional friendship between the two countries. In general, he thought, Russia had been peaceably inclined, and Roosevelt said he agreed entirely.[5] Stimson said the Russians were "in their own strange way . . . magnificent allies," and on "the central political issues of the war, the alliance with Britain and Russia," he was "a wholehearted supporter of the President." [6] Stettinius said cautiously that there were many in the United States who viewed Russia as a threat and many in Russia who suspected Western democracy, but that there was no need to fear Russia. Wendell Willkie urged the second front and, taking the same view as Hopkins, told Stalin that the Americans wanted a second front but the British did not. Davies thought that what they were practicing in Russia was close to real Christianity, and Roosevelt too was ready to think that religion had more influence on the Russians than appeared on the surface when he referred to the possibly beneficent effect of Stalin's early theological training. "They all seem really to want to do what is good for their society," he told Frances Perkins, "instead of wanting to do for themselves. We take care of ourselves and think about the welfare of society afterward." [7] Like many others—including Sumner Welles, who believed that the Russians had abandoned any notion of world revolution, at least temporarily [8]—Roosevelt thought that there was a new kind of communism. Writing to Frank Knox on the question of permitting members of the Communist party to be radio-operators on American ships, he remarked: "The Soviet people in Moscow are said to have little liking for the American Communist Party and their methods—especially because it seems true that the communist party of twenty years ago has

[5] Cordell Hull: *The Memoirs of Cordell Hull*, p. 297.
[6] Henry L. Stimson and McGeorge Bundy: *On Active Service in Peace and War*, pp. 527, 528.
[7] Frances Perkins: *The Roosevelt I Knew*, p. 87.
[8] Sumner Welles: *The Time for Decision*, p. 406.

practically ceased to exist in Russia." [9] At Teheran he refused to lunch alone with Churchill so that Stalin would have no cause for suspicion that the two Western statesmen were combining against him, and he stayed near Stalin's villa for reasons of security. Stalin had suggested that he would be safer there, an anxiety that apparently did not extend to Churchill, who had quarters some distance away. Roosevelt, sure of his own good intentions and confident of his personal powers, wrote to Churchill in 1942: "I think I can personally handle Stalin better than either your Foreign Office or my State Department. Stalin hates the guts of all your top people. He thinks he likes me better, and I hope he will continue to do so." [1]

The profound desire to think well of Stalin, to explain away any seeming intransigence, was widespread among people of many nationalities, American, British, French, Czech, and German. It was proof against any disagreeable interpretation of the march of events. It was often said when he was unyielding, or failed to carry out an agreement, that he could not because the Politburo had prevented it. Even Churchill wondered how far his power went, and in a letter to Eden written in 1944 still referred to him in a hopeful moment as "that great and good man." [2] Some thought that Molotov's failure to keep Stalin informed accounted for his otherwise incomprehensible behavior.

At the Moscow conference in 1943, Hull, along with a rejoicing American press, believed that one of the great victories over an evil past had been won: Stalin had agreed to join a system of collective security after the war. The conference was widely spoken of as the crowning achievement of Hull's career. The Secretary of State himself said: "There will no longer be need for spheres of influence, for alliances, for balance of power or for any other of the special arrangements through which, in

[9] Eastland Committee, p. 44 (Jan. 3, 1955).
[1] Churchill: *The Second World War*, IV, 201.
[2] Ibid., VI, 712.

the unhappy past, the nations strove to safeguard their security or to promote their interests." [3]

There was no denying Stalin's charm for his American visitors. He could be affable, a good listener, sensible, and humorous—the travelers saw in him the man they had come to see. Hopkins called him a football coach's "dream of a tackle," about five feet six inches (he was actually five feet two), quiet, courteous, and easy to deal with.

"He is a man," said Mr. Roosevelt on Christmas Eve of 1943, "who combines a tremendous, relentless determination with a stalwart good humor. I believe he is truly representative of the heart and soul of Russia; and I believe that we are going to get along very well with him and the Russian people—very well indeed." [4] At his first meeting with Stalin at Teheran he left his translator behind, to emphasize his complete trust in his host.

The desire to please Stalin and get along with him was proof even against the hitherto strongly supported Stimson doctrine, according to which the United States (and presumably other nations) would not recognize territory acquired by aggression. The British were prepared early in 1942 to recognize Russian claims to strategic borders, but the Americans, as we have seen, wished to delay any discussions of actual boundaries. [5] Stalin continued to press for recognition of the Russian claims, which were strongly resisted by the Poles, both in London and Washington; and by the time of the Teheran conference in December 1943, Roosevelt joined Churchill in agreeing to the Curzon line for the west Russian boundaries; the Baltic states, he thought, would probably vote to become part of the Russian

[3] Quoted in *The New York Times*, Nov. 19, 1943.

[4] Robert E. Sherwood: *Roosevelt and Hopkins*, II, 804.

[5] Churchill told Roosevelt that if Russia's claims were not recognized, there was no guarantee she would not make a separate peace; and in March he wrote: "The increasing gravity of the war has led me to feel that the principles of the Atlantic Charter ought not to be construed so as to deny Russia the frontiers she occupied when Germany attacked her" (Churchill: *The Second World War*, IV, 327). See also Hull: *Memoirs*, pp. 1171–2; Boris Meissner: *"Stalin und die Oder Neisse Linie,"* Ost Europa, Vol. I (1951), No. 1, p. 343.

security system, and the Russians, he said, should trouble them-selves to get this done. At Teheran, Roosevelt wanted Germany divided into five parts, a position that Stalin seemed to regard favorably, although Stalin was sure Churchill did not. Churchill had talked of a Danubian federation, and Stalin asked ironically whether he envisaged Hungary and Rumania as part of it—a federation being favored by the London Polish government too, but vigorously opposed by the Russians, who had very different plans for the Balkans and Poland. Stalin played out little comedies of that kind; while Roosevelt was talking of the division of Germany, he said: "See," pointing to Churchill, "he isn't listening."

Churchill was in an awkward position. If he could not persuade the London Poles to agree to the Curzon line—which was, after all, a boundary that a British foreign secretary had once laid out—there would be no London Poles in the later Warsaw government. On the other hand, the London Poles felt that they had not fought the war to lose Polish territory, and some of them at least had wildly ambitious plans for a Polish-dominated Eastern Europe which could only come about through the exhaustion of both Russia and Germany. Churchill was willing to see Poland recompensed for loss of the eastern provinces by acquisition of purely German territory up to the Oder-Neisse boundary, and no objections were raised to the Soviet demand for the German city of Königsberg as a warm-water port. Roosevelt expressed his belief that if the legitimate demands of Russia were met she would be more co-operative, and a warm-water port he regarded as one of them. Churchill's own plan at Teheran was for the detaching of Prussia and the inclusion of a South Germany in some sort of federation. Stalin had no intention of permitting non-Communist alignments in this area and merely pointed out that Germany would soon dominate such a federation.

Harry Hopkins took with him to the first Quebec conference in 1943 "a very high-level United States military strategic estimate" that the Russian position in postwar Europe would be dominant and that there would be no power in Europe to oppose her tremendous military forces. England might not be able to balance her power in the Mediterranean unless supported. The report concluded that every effort should be made to gain Russia's friendship.

By the time of Teheran, Churchill no longer held high cards. The battle of Stalingrad had been won early in 1943 and the Russian armies were sweeping toward the German borders. The English had little to offer them. A man of the nineteenth century, Churchill thought in terms of federations when such devices no longer could play a role in the power relations of Europe. Roosevelt let him carry the brunt of the discussion with Stalin at Teheran on the Polish question, intent only on winning Stalin to co-operation in the postwar world, convinced that almost no sacrifice was too great for this goal. Hopkins said that the more the State Department warned against the power and purposes of the Russians in postwar Europe, the more obstinate the President became in his Russian policy. Hull, deeply devoted to the cause of international co-operation, had written Roosevelt in a memorandum of February 1942: "There is no doubt that the Soviet government has tremendous ambitions with regard to Europe and that at some time or other the United States and Great Britain will be forced to state that they cannot agree, at least in advance, to all its demands. It would seem that it is preferable to take a firm attitude now. . . ." [6] No firm stands were taken, for these, it was felt, would be resented and would reinforce Russian suspicions of the West.

Roosevelt was convinced that Russian ambitions could be curbed and domesticated by bringing Stalin into the family circle, and he was convinced that he could do it. At Teheran he had his first opportunity to talk face to face with Stalin, something he had long wanted to do. Avoiding active participation in any discussion of prickly subjects such as the Polish bound-

[6] Hull: *Memoirs*, p. 1169.

aries, he worked deliberately on the human side of Stalin, joking about Churchill's fat cigars and his John Bullishness; when he left he was sure that he and Stalin had become friends: "We got on beautifully. We cracked the ice if there ever was any ice; and since then there has been no ice." [7]

Stalin meanwhile had broken relations with the London Polish government late in April 1943, when the London Poles wanted the International Red Cross to investigate the German charges that the Russians had killed some fifteen thousand Polish officers, many of whose bodies had been found in a mass grave at Katyn. It was at this point that the Communist Union of Free Polish Patriots was called to active duty by the Soviets to replace the London Polish regime, which up to then had been recognized by the three powers. This was the cause of the first major crisis among the Big Three. Roosevelt sought to avoid it, again by personal appeals. He assured the Polish Prime Minister, Mikolajczyk, that the Russians were not imperialists, and he explained to Stalin that with the election coming in 1944 he must reckon with some six or seven million Polish votes in the United States, whereupon Stalin said that he understood this but that some propaganda work should be done among them. In fact it was Churchill's imperialism rather than Stalin's that Roosevelt came to admonish. "You have 400 years of acquisitive instinct in your blood," he told Churchill at Yalta. "A new period has opened in the world's history and you will have to adjust yourself to it." [8] Churchill's fiery refusal to give up any portion of the British empire, despite the hopes of many Americans for a free India and Hong Kong's return to China, was a continuing if minor source of friction between the two men. Roosevelt was willing to take a more lenient view of international morality than Hull when, in Moscow in 1944, Churchill and Stalin worked out a division of spheres in the Balkans. Under this arrangement the rough division of influence was to be

[7] *The New York Times*, Aug. 24, 1944.
[8] Edward R. Stettinius: *Roosevelt and the Russians*, p. 237.

in Rumania 90 per cent Russian and 10 per cent British; in Hungary 70 per cent Russian and 30 per cent British; in Greece 90 per cent British and 10 per cent Russian; and in Yugoslavia 50–50. Although such practices were gravely offensive to Hull, the President agreed to allow a three-month trial of the formula. This was a return in one sense to the malign past, but it also held the possibility of future collaboration, a concession both to the British and to the Russians in an area where America had neither strong emotions nor interests.

Roosevelt and many of his advisers came to think not only that Churchill, much as they had loved him, was imperialistic but also that his mind was too concerned with the balance of forces which would exist after the war. They were suspicious of his pressure for a campaign in the Balkans; as the war progressed, they took more the Russian view of what was needful than the British. They had two major aims. The first was to win the war; in Mr. Roosevelt's trope, Doctor Win-the-War was the new physician now, having replaced the New Deal diagnostician who had been needed in the days of the depression. Second only to that was the need to gain the friendship and confidence of the Russians, for without it, they told one another, there would be no peace. The question was how to win it. There was no disagreement on the first goal or how to attain it. On the second there came to be sharp differences as the danger of a German victory receded, as officials in direct touch with the Russians reported on their difficulties, and as Churchill, the Polish government-in-exile, and the anti-Tito Yugoslavs attempted to combat the Communist drive for the control of Eastern Europe. In the State Department too the technical reports were widely different from the views and purposes of the administration, and some of them clearly pointed out the Russian danger. But the higher councils of the New Deal were peculiarly open to Soviet influences. Much has been written and reported on the widespread Communist infiltration of American government agencies, and there is no doubt of its influence, although its importance in the German question may well be exaggerated.

At Yalta, of course, Alger Hiss was one of the American delegation. Roosevelt's telephone number was 1, Hiss's was 4. He was but one among many high government officials who were in later years to be accused and some of them convicted of having acted against the interests of the United States on behalf of the Soviet Union. Hiss's influence at Yalta, however, seems to have been confined almost exclusively to United Nations affairs. Harry Dexter White, the chief author of the Morgenthau plan, was only one of several men in the Treasury Department who were later accused of being Communist agents; there were others in important positions in the government who were to meet the same charges in years to come—many of them connected with the occupation of Germany. The head of the denazification branch of American military government in 1945, George Shaw Wheeler, took refuge in 1947 in Czechoslovakia.[9] Gerhart Eisler, the chief of the broadcasting station of the OWI which was sending propaganda to Germany, later took refuge in the East zone.[1] White was in charge of all foreign affairs as they affected the Treasury Department; he was Morgenthau's alternate on the Economic Defense Board, and in charge of American economic policy for Germany. It was through him that a set of American-made plates of the occupation marks was delivered to the Russians, and it was he who told Lord Cherwell, who accompanied Churchill to Quebec in 1944, that if the British signed the Morgenthau plan they could have the loan they were seeking. The Morgenthau plan itself bears a strong resemblance to the proposal of the Soviet economist Eugene Varga, published in Russia in 1943 under the title *War and the*

[9] Eastland Committee, pp. 9, 10.
[1] On May 30, Leahy reports (*I Was There*), the State Department told him that two of its employees and an officer in Naval Intelligence were giving confidential information to persons outside the government. The OWI broadcasts to Poland were indistinguishable, according to Stanislaw Mikolajczyk (*The Rape of Poland*), from those emanating from Moscow.

Working Class, which foresaw use of German labor, dismantling of industrial plants and equipment for reparations, breaking up of estates into small farms, and denial of all economic aid to Germany, including food, clothing, and means for the repair of the devastation. In addition, the Varga plan included the confiscation of all German property held abroad.

But the dismemberment of Germany was no longer a Russian goal at the end of hostilities; the United States discovered then that only we and the French continued to favor it. Dismemberment was but one of a number of possibilities for Germany, as the Russians saw the matter. In 1943 Moscow had another plan based on the National Committee for Free Germany. The patriotic manifestoes of the committee, the publication in Moscow of its newspaper *Free Germany,* emblazoned with the black, white, and red colors of Imperial Germany, were part of a design for a possible future armed Germany in alliance with Russia. Thus while, as one observer has said, "those fellows were having a lot of fun cutting up Germany down there in the Treasury Department," the American arm of the Communist forces was merely doing its best to follow the Varga rather than the Free Germany line of Moscow. The activities of the American Communists had no influence whatever on the ultimate decisions as to which course the Russians would follow.[2] Their influence as far as American decisions were concerned was undoubtedly important in minor matters, and, had the situation developed in Europe as it did in the Far East, it might have had as far-reaching consequences.

[2] The opposite Russian attitudes toward the dismemberment of Germany may be attributed to alternate political possibilities. A unified Germany or a large section of it dominated by Russia—as might have resulted if the Free Germany Committee had been successful in causing a revolt—would have been far more useful to Stalin than the creation of five separate German states. On the other hand, a divided Germany with Russian influence even in one part of it might have been brought into the Russian orbit through its inherent weakness. The division of the zones at Yalta was in effect a division of Germany; and after that decision, the Russians could use the slogan of unification to win Germans to the Communist cause.

Hull thought White "a very high class fellow"; [3] and the Treasury Department asked for a special passport from the State Department for Irving Kaplan, one of the men who was later to be identified as a Communist agent and who was Economic Adviser on Liberated Areas. General Eisenhower's financial adviser, supplied by the Treasury Department, was Bernard Bernstein.[4] He was to be later identified as a strong supporter of pro-Communist causes. During the war and until 1946 he had the rank of lieutenant colonel, and afterward he was put in charge of decartelization in Germany. He was also to defend Russia's methods of carrying out the Potsdam agreement. "Only the Russians," the *Daily Worker* of February 21, 1946, reported him as saying, "have shown that they mean to exterminate fascism and nazism, and have already taken decisive steps in that direction." It is unlikely that these men or others like them had any long-range or decisive effect on what was actually done or that they did more than add a chorus of voices to the prevailing anti-German sentiment. They could influence policy up to a point where they met a barrier of equally stubborn opinion, as in the case of the Stimson-Hull resistance to the Morgenthau plan. Their great strength lay in the weakness of the opposition, the lack of a viable policy with regard to Europe, including Germany, among the high officials of the administration. What the Communists did in the government or could do, aside from passing along classified information and helping their friends get important posts, was to promote the general feeling of benevolence toward the Russians and help inflame the passion for a hard peace on which the administration had already decided. Just as the Carnegie Endowment was later able to hire Alger Hiss as its president, the administration, with its declared all-encompassing postwar goal of an organized world peace, could fit anyone into its purposes who talked convincingly

[3] Jenner Committee (1954), p. 12.
[4] Ibid., July 1953; Nov. 12, 17, 23, 1953; Dec. 2, 3, 10, 1953.

of collective security and, with this in view, of the need to get along with the Russians.

Yalta confirmed the decisions that were made at Teheran. The Poles were to lose territory in the east and gain it in the west, although the precise western boundaries were left for the peace conference; some eight or nine million Germans— Churchill said six—would have to be moved from those areas, but by this time the Russian armies had driven deep into German territory and Stalin could report that there would be no great problem. Most of the Germans, he said, had run away. The American State Department's briefing of Mr. Roosevelt, while it did not favor the mass exodus of so many people into a shrunken Germany, said the point was not worth making a stand on, and this was Roosevelt's position.

For Churchill, by the time of the Yalta conference, there was no longer any doubt of the lengthening shadow of the Russian danger; the only question was what could be done about it. Already in May 1944 he had written to Anthony Eden asking: "Are we going to acquiesce in the Communization of the Balkans and perhaps of Italy? I am of the opinion on the whole that we ought to come to a definite conclusion about it, and that if our conclusion is that we resist the Communist infusion and invasion, we should put it to them pretty plainly at the best moment that military events permit." [5] The British, Churchill reports, were given inferior quarters at Yalta, but these were not so poor as their bargaining position. Roosevelt told him that American troops would remain in Europe no longer than two or three years; and while the United States made it plain that it would take a leading part in the postwar organization of peace, Churchill above all needed troops at hand. This was one of the reasons he urged a zone for France.

A few months before the Yalta conference, a shocking episode had taken place which should have left little doubt of the shape of the future. As the Russian armies rolled toward Warsaw, the

[5] Churchill: *The Second World War*, V, 708.

Moscow radio called for the rising of the Polish resistance forces in the city. The battle for Warsaw had long been prepared for; there were organized formations with hidden arms, and as the Russians came within a few miles of the city these formations sallied into the streets on the given signal and attacked the Germans. The Russian Army, however, stopped, and for sixty days the forty thousand Poles fought until fifteen thousand were dead and the rest, including their commanding general, Bor-Komorowski, captured. The London Poles and the British government were in despair. Churchill begged the Russians for permission at least to drop arms and supplies to General Bor and his men. Stalin regarded Warsaw, like Katyn, as an opportunity to get rid of supporters of the London Poles, to show their helplessness, to prepare for the new friendly power of a Communist-dominated Poland. Churchill saw it as a catastrophe: here were men being slaughtered fighting for the principles for which England had gone to war.

On August 16, 1944, Churchill records, Andrei Vyshinsky in Moscow asked the United States ambassador to call and, "explaining that he wished to avoid the possibility of misunderstanding, read out the following astonishing statement":

> The Soviet Government cannot of course object to English or American aircraft dropping arms in the region of Warsaw, since this is an American and British affair. But they decidedly object to American or British aircraft, after dropping arms in the region of Warsaw, landing on Soviet territory, since the Soviet Government do not wish to associate themselves either directly or indirectly with the adventure in Warsaw.[6]

That remained the Russian position despite Churchill's entreaties, backed somewhat halfheartedly by Roosevelt, who telegraphed:

[6] Ibid., VI, 133.

Stalin's reply to our joint proposal for assisting the Warsaw Poles is far from encouraging.

The supply by us of the Warsaw Poles is, I am informed, impossible unless we are permitted to land and take off from Soviet airfields. Their use for the relief of Warsaw is at present prohibited by the Russian authorities.

I do not see what further steps we can take at the present time that promise results.[7]

As Stalin remained adamant, Churchill begged Roosevelt to join him in sending a final message to attempt to persuade Stalin; but the President on August 26 refused, saying:

I do not consider it would prove advantageous to the long-range general war prospect for me to join with you in the proposed message to Stalin, but I have no objection to your sending such a message if you consider it advisable to do so.[8]

By the time of the Yalta conference the Lublin Polish government which had been formed from the Union of Polish Patriots had announced its intention of trying the men responsible for the uprising. "This causes us," said Churchill, "great anxiety and distress"; and he entreated Stalin "with patience and kindness to consider our position"[9]—something that Stalin was never ready to do.

Stalin agreed at Yalta to permit free Polish elections—all that Churchill and Roosevelt could salvage from their support of the London Poles. Churchill asked Stalin if Mikolajczyk's party would be authorized, and Stalin said benignly that as an anti-fascist party of course it would be. But it was clear at Yalta that the cause of the London Poles was hopeless despite the fact that, as Churchill pointed out, England had gone to war on behalf of the territorial integrity of Poland; and Roosevelt, pur-

[7] Ibid., p. 139.
[8] Ibid., p. 140.
[9] *Foreign Relations . . . Malta and Yalta*, p. 852.

suing the same tactics as at Teheran, asked that Stalin as a sign of generosity let Poland keep Lvov. He assured Stalin that he wanted a Polish government friendly to Russia, to which Stalin replied: "To all three."

Stalin got all he demanded: the new eastern Polish boundaries; recognition of the Lublin government, which would absorb the London Poles and become the Provisional Government of National Unity after the elections; and, in effect, extension of the Russian sphere to the Oder. His permission for the antifascist parties to participate in the new government became meaningless with the Polish Communist cadres organizing the voting and with the country under Russian occupation. There were forty-five toasts at Yusupov Palace in the course of the dining, and the outward expressions of boundless good will and mutual congratulations were many, but any doubt in the minds of Churchill and some American observers as to what the future portended could not have lasted long. Allied representatives never had the promised voice in the reorganization of the Polish government. Sixteen Poles from the Warsaw Underground, who were invited to Moscow to represent the non-Communist political parties, simply disappeared. When news of them came, it was through Stalin, who announced that they had been arrested and would be tried for their crimes. No concessions changed the course of the Russian plans. Churchill had recognized the pro-Communist Tito government in Yugoslavia over the bitter protests of the Yugoslav government-in-exile. In the United States the Royal Yugoslav government was presented with a number of planes on the graduation of a group of Yugoslav air cadets; the gift was immediately denounced by Tito. There was no recurrence of it—Roosevelt joined the British in accepting the Communist regime in Yugoslavia.

Yalta, in fact, confirmed the end of any idea of freely chosen governments in Poland and Yugoslavia; it confirmed the decision to occupy Germany and divide it into zones, the payment of reparations in kind, the use of German forced labor, and the likelihood of the dismemberment of Germany, which Stalin wanted inserted in the final communiqué. He also reluctantly approved the inclusion of a French zone in the occupation, providing it came out of the British and American portions; but he was contemptuous of the French, saying that the Yugoslavs had fought better and had provided more troops against the Germans.

On the larger issues Roosevelt, still in pursuit of postwar collaboration, agreed to the Russian demand for three additional Assembly votes in the United Nations; and there was another charade on the question of the voting and the rights of the small powers. Stalin and Molotov said they were confident they could get the agreement of the Ukraine and White Russia to join the UN while the Yalta conference was in session. Stalin had no great opinion of the rights of small nations if that meant judging the conduct of the big ones—he had had some experience of that when Russia was expelled from the League of Nations. He said it was absurd to pretend that a nation like Albania should have the right to judge the actions of the Soviet Union. But Churchill clung to his British notions of the international proprieties, pointing out that even with the right to vote in the Assembly there would be a veto power in the Council, and thus, while the small nations would be heard, the Soviet would have the right to say "no" after they had spoken. Would England, asked Stalin, be ready to hear the Chinese on the subject of Hong Kong or the Egyptians on the Suez? "Certainly," said Churchill, and added that, as in Hyde Park, all shades of opinion could be heard. Stalin said he thought that if the Chinese brought up the subject they would want more than a hearing; they would want action. On the question of the democracy of the Lublin Poles, Stalin assured his colleagues that the number of Poles supporting them was at least as large as the number of French who supported De Gaulle, and that these Poles were as democratic as the French. Stalin also said the rate of literacy in Poland was pretty high and asked Churchill how it compared with Egypt's.

But now both Churchill and Roosevelt were critical of the London Poles too—how else could they urge them to accept boundaries the Poles didn't want and become a part of the government that was denouncing them as agents of the Nazis? Roosevelt said the Poles were quarrelsome and had been a source of trouble in Europe for five hundred years. He did not attach much importance, he declared, to the question of a legal Polish government: there had not been one anyway. Churchill admitted that he had great difficulties with the London Poles, who were deaf to advice and lived in an unreal world. He told Stalin that after the Russian agony, Soviet claims to the east Polish boundaries were based not on might but on right—a curious transmutation of power into spiritual values.

Yalta, like all the other conferences, left the participants in varying states of euphoria. The press of the United States hailed it. *The New York Times* said it surpassed "most of the hopes placed on this fateful meeting"—it showed "the way to a . . . secure peace, and to a brighter world. . . . The alliance of the Big Three stands firm. . . . This conference marks a milestone on the road to victory and peace." [1] Senator Claude Pepper called it the greatest step toward peace in history. Hopkins asked Roosevelt during one of the sessions not to demand more of the Russians since they had already conceded so much more to the United States and Britain than they to her. Edward R. Stettinius, Roosevelt's new Secretary of State, reported a most successful meeting. Russia, he said, gave every evidence of desire to co-operate along all lines with the United States. Roosevelt told Congress: "I am convinced this agreement on Poland is the most hopeful possible . . . for a free, independent, prosperous Poland." There would be, he said, a more stable political Europe than ever. Roosevelt's close friend and adviser Judge Samuel Rosenman reports that the President was certain Yalta had paved the way for the kind of world he had been dreaming about. He understood Stalin and Stalin him.

Russia's joining the war against Japan was assured, and the

[1] *The New York Times*, Feb. 14, 1945.

arrangement included a trusteeship for Korea. Would there be any foreign troops in Korea? asked Stalin. Roosevelt said there would not—and these arrangements too were made in a conspiratorial atmosphere of good fellowship without the presence of Churchill. He would "kill us," [2] said Stalin, "if he was not included in the arrangement"; but Roosevelt was mainly intent on bringing Stalin into camp, and these little games were a calculated part of his campaign. Roosevelt told Stalin that he was affectionately known as Uncle Joe to Churchill and himself; and when Stalin became irate at what he took to be an indignity, Byrnes saved the day by pointing out that Uncle was a term of affection in the United States—witness the symbol of Uncle Sam.

The agreement reached at Yalta began to disintegrate immediately. Averell Harriman, the American ambassador, reported from Moscow that the Russians were overrunning entire populations, making no distinction between friends or foes of the United Nations. He noted that the Russian papers were calling Iran fascist and asserting that there was no legal basis for American troops being there. A *Putsch* in Rumania some two weeks after Yalta put a Communist government in power. The Provisional Polish Government of National Unity never functioned except as the inheritor of the Lublin Poles. No Allied missions were allowed to see to the care of liberated Allied prisoners behind the Russian lines.

One month after Yalta, Winston Churchill wrote: "If we did not get things right the world would soon see that Mr. Roosevelt and I had underwritten a fraudulent prospectus when we put our signatures to the Crimea settlement." [3] In April he reported an aching heart amid the triumph, and by May, he was to reveal some years later, he wanted the German troops to keep their weapons—so far had the Russians come and so one-sided was their power.

[2] *Foreign Relations . . . Malta and Yalta*, p. 770.
[3] Churchill: *The Second World War*, VI, 422.

III
LANDSCAPE OF THE MOON—
WITH FIGURES

Hopkins told his biographer that after the Yalta conference "we really believed in our hearts that this was the dawn of the new day we had all been praying for and talking about for so many years. We were absolutely certain that we had won the first great victory of the peace—and by 'we' I mean *all* of us, the whole civilized human race. The Russians had proved that they could be reasonable and far seeing and there wasn't any doubt in the minds of the President or any of us that we could live with them and get along with them peacefully for as far into the future as any of us could imagine." [1]

One of the things that had helped to convince Hopkins and others of the essential reasonableness of the Russians had been the matter of the voting. The Russians had originally asked for sixteen votes in the United Nations Assembly and had come down to three. Not only that, but when Roosevelt pointed out that public opinion in his country might be aroused by awarding three votes for Russia to one for the United States, and asked Stalin whether he would not be willing to support more American representation in case of need, Stalin said he would. This concession caused considerable elation among the Americans at Yalta, and when matters began to go badly, as they did immediately, there were various comforting explanations. Stettinius attributed the deterioration not to the decisions made at

[1] Robert E. Sherwood: *Roosevelt and Hopkins*, II, 870.

Yalta but to the fact that Russia was not living up to them.

Stalin's swift suspicion of the West was nowhere more evident in the post-Yalta months than in the exchange he had with Churchill and Roosevelt over the surrender of a German army in Italy. The surrender had been accepted by the Western Allies, and a Russian participant belatedly included. There was a mighty explosion from Stalin. Roosevelt and Churchill explained at length, but in vain, that this was a tactical surrender which any commander in the field was entitled to accept. Stalin spoke darkly of bad faith, seeing without difficulty both what the Germans were trying to do and what he expected the Allies would be doing. The German Army commanders at the end were mainly trying to hold a line against the Russians to save not territory or supplies but people from falling into Soviet hands. But subsequent German offers to surrender an army, whether tactical or strategic, were cleared with Moscow.

Thousands of Germans escaped to the West as a result of this last defense—so many, in fact, that General Eisenhower had to threaten to seal off his lines. And there was no immediate difference, at least, for those male civilians and German soldiers who did succeed in surrendering to the Western Allies. The hunger, the ruins, the prisoner-of-war camps were everywhere, and not much different from one another; only the future was different.

American reports described the Germans who remained in the cellars and bunkers—even in caves—of the cities and towns they came into as dazed or sullen or spiritless. The devastating bombardments, the senseless resistance of the Nazi Army commanders,[2] the years of tension, had left them drained of energy and emotions. If they were males, they were the old or the very

[2] Hitler ordered the execution of officers who retreated without permission, who failed to blow up bridges or blew them up too soon; and if any soldier could not plausibly account for his separation from his unit, the Field Police were to hang him. Nevertheless, many generals and their men succeeded in circumventing these murderous orders.

young, and there were 170 women for every 100 men in
Berlin. There were few signs of the fanatical resistance that
Hitler had called for—rare traces of werewolves, no banzai
charges, no last defense in the redoubt of the Bavarian moun-
tains. The German troops continued to fight bitterly in the
East, but in the West, with the exception of isolated actions of
paratroopers and the Waffen SS, resistance weakened rapidly,
especially after the failure of the German offensive in the Ar-
dennes. The nondescript Volksstürme captured in the last weeks
were reported released as fast as possible when hostilities stopped
so they wouldn't have to be fed by their captors. Hundreds of
prisoners from the regular Army were often guarded by two or
three GI's; there was no fight left in them.

Here and there in the surrendered villages Germans would
show some signs of friendliness, waving or smiling as the troops
came in; but they soon discovered that the American regulations forbade any friendly personal relations. They did as they
were told, cleaning up the rubble, pushing aside the piles of
refuse that clogged the streets. They were fed from the stocks
they still had and, where there was nothing, from Army supplies.
But the Army orders were strict, and there were sharp complaints and reprimands whenever it was found that a unit was
in any fashion going outside the disease-and-unrest formula. An
immediate inquiry was made into a story that DP's who were
supposed to be fed from German supplies were instead being
given food by Americans. The rumor, on investigation, turned
out to be false. Whether the Germans would be fed or given
medical supplies depended largely on the attitude of the individual commander, or on the military government team that
decided which Germans were eligible as non-Nazis to hold
office under the occupation. One tank lieutenant, describing
how he had made his choice for burgomaster before the military-government team arrived, said: "I selected me a mayor who
lived in that big house yonder—and he's doing all right."

The only important American criterion for picking Germans for the job of administering the occupation decrees or running a newspaper or being on the police force was that they be anti-Nazi. A man in one town offered his services and was immediately accepted. He was the judge who had sentenced Hitler to prison in 1923. "Anti-Nazi" of course included the Communists, who undeniably since 1941 had been fiercely opposed to Hitler and all his works. This had little importance during the months of battle when the American regulations were not much different from those of any army; they were designed for the safety of the fighting troops, and nonfraternization at this point was a prudent measure, as was the use of proved anti-Nazis of whatever description.[3]

When the first American troops entered Aachen they found only a scattering of people. One American report said 100 had survived the six-week battle for the city and the Nazi orders to evacuate. The population filtered back slowly; 13,000 returned in the course of a few weeks. It was extremely dangerous at this point for any German to collaborate with the enemy, and the man who was chosen as burgomaster of Aachen was killed by an SS commando squad that made its way back to the city to demonstrate what happened to traitors. Nor would the Nazis confine their vengeance to the victim himself—his entire family was in danger if it came within the power of the party hatchet men.

In Bonn, which was to be in the British zone, the placards of the last resistance were still up when the Americans came in: "Victory or Siberia." All the bridges across the Rhine at Bonn were destroyed; 40,000 of the normal population of 102,000 were left in the city. The Army went to work rapidly to restore the essential services; in a matter of days there was some gas, water,

[3] The Army directive that had preceded JCS 1067 and was in force up to the autumn of 1944 was a nonpolitical, military document dealing with an enemy country "prior to defeat or surrender." This was CCS 551. Providing for a firm but humane administration of occupied territory, it was approved informally by the chiefs of staff and sent to General Eisenhower.

and light in a small part of the city;[4] two months later, in July, streetcars were running; and by November the first lectures were given in the university. Cologne, with some 120,000 inhabitants left out of the 780,000 who had lived on both banks of the Rhine, by the end of March had almost 300 officials and city workers. Konrad Adenauer was given the job of lord mayor by the Americans, but in October he was dismissed by the British commandant and forbidden any political activity.[5] By then there were over 3,000 officials, 6,000 workers, and 1,300 police.

In Frankfurt 35,000 inhabitants out of 500,000 were left; of 177,000 houses, 44,000 were still standing. There were no police, no firemen; the city officials had fled. In the neighborhood of Munich hundreds of "traitors"[6] along with deserters from the hopelessly defeated German Army hung from the trees, and 10,000 forced laborers rose and plundered wine stores and warehouses, celebrating their freedom. The Americans, who had just seen Dachau and its corpses, cared little what the Poles, Russians, French, and Ukrainians did to the city.

The mayor of Stuttgart was nearly shot out of hand by the Nazi gauleiter when he tried to prevent the blowing up of the city's water conduit, which was attached to the bridge crossing the Neckar. The bridge was blown up despite repeated efforts to cut the wires detonating the charge, but the conduit by chance remained unbroken. Hitler's "Nero plan," as the scorched-earth directive was called, ordered that streetcar tracks be torn up, gas mains, power stations, and water supplies made useless. Anyone attempting to prevent such destruction was to be shot immediately. "Who fears death in honor will die it in

---

[4] German resources were to restore these facilities, although American supplies and manpower could be used if they furthered military operations (Oliver J. Frederiksen: *The American Military Occupation of Germany, 1945–1953*, p. 11).

[5] The order was short-lived; at the end of two months Adenauer was again a member of his party's executive committee.

[6] These included the victims of a premature rising against the Nazi commandant of the city by a resistance group, Freiheitsaktion Bayern.

shame" was one of the slogans. By Himmler's order of April 12, every city and village was to be defended to the uttermost. A gauleiter told the inhabitants of one city that they should fight with teeth and nails; another said even with forks. If the party went under, there was no need for the German people to continue to live. "When we slam the door shut," said Goebbels, "the whole world will be shaken."

As the British and American troops came into a town, they rounded up all POW's, and everyone over twelve years of age had to register. Known Nazis whose names had been provided by intelligence officers were arrested. If the town was large enough, a one-sheet Army newspaper was published in German, and the townsfolk were allowed to keep their radios so they could receive instructions from the American authorities, although they were forbidden to listen to music.

There was considerable difference between the tone of the propaganda leaflets urging the German soldiers to surrender and that of the documents after the surrender in May. While staying within the broad terms of unconditional surrender, the leaflets promised good treatment, food, and prompt repatriation. Once hostilities ceased, the Germans were on their own— subject to the unconditional will of the occupier, with no rights whatever. Meetings of more than five people were prohibited; a curfew was imposed; all mail service was stopped; no one was allowed to travel more than six kilometers from his home; no telephones were to be used; and there was to be no repair beyond the essential services of water supply, light, and sanitation.

When the Allied armies were advancing rapidly after the Battle of the Bulge, the mayors and sometimes even the banks of towns that were being overrun were still doing business. In these cases a mayor was often permitted to keep his job, temporarily at least, and, though bank accounts were frozen, the banks were allowed to remain open and new accounts could be started. A limited production was permitted: in one area three creameries were allowed to make butter and a flour mill to run for ten hours a day. Everyone was subject to call for work on the rubble, and where the Army ran into evidence of German atrocities, men and women recruited without regard to their previous political views or activities were ordered to exhume graves and rebury the corpses. In Essen there were 32,000 foreigners, 21,000 of whom were Poles and Russians. The Americans found the bodies of 32 of their number who had been killed apparently by the SS before the surrender of the city, and the Germans were forced to dig their graves.

The DP's—there were more than 4,500,000 who had been brought to the Reich and some few who had come voluntarily —were immediately a problem for the Allied armies. They, along with nearly 2,000,000 prisoners of war, had been forced laborers; they came from all over German-occupied Europe but mostly from the East, brought to work on farms and in factories, often under terrible conditions of malnutrition and mistreatment, although some fared decently in private households. Now they rose in many places from their servitude and in the wild exuberance of the liberation looted and caroused through the streets, impatient of any restraints and a danger not only to their late masters but also to their liberators.

In cities and villages antifascist committees were formed, often under the leadership of former concentration-camp inmates; and of these the American report says: "Some were said to be Communist dominated." [7] The Nazis, while killing or imprisoning all the Communists they could find, had also unexpectedly helped them to keep an organization going when they sent them together to the camps, which the Communists organized with great skill and efficiency. The onrushing troops sometimes emptied all the prisons on the assumption that anyone who was in jail under Hitler deserved to be freed. In one place the Americans were later charged with having appointed as a policeman

[7] Training Packet No. 57, in Occupation Forces in Europe Series, prepared by the Provost Marshal, Karlsruhe (Feb. 7, 1945), p. 89.

a man who had been serving a long sentence as a common criminal.

Since about half the police had been Nazis and could not serve under the occupation, the Germans given the jobs of policing the occupied cities were likely to be poorly trained; they were usually unarmed, although in some places the Americans provided them with weapons against the unruly DP's. During hostilities the police who were permitted to stay on were treated as prisoners of war; they continued to wear their uniforms, which closely resembled those of the Wehrmacht—or they wore civilian clothes and were supplied with armbands.

The orders sent to the American troops on January 1, 1945, which they were instructed to carry inside their helmet linings, remained in force after the fighting stopped. While they said that the situation did not demand rough, undignified, or aggressive conduct, there was to be no entertaining of Germans, no visiting in German homes, no shaking hands, no playing games with Germans, no conversing or arguing with them. Americans could attend a German church, but must sit in separate pews. The Army newspaper *Stars and Stripes* had slogans printed: "Don't get chummy with Jerry" . . . "Soldiers wise don't fraternize." There was a picture of a pretty girl with the warning: "Don't play Samson to her Delilah—she'd like to cut your hair off—at the neck." Another said: "In heart, body, and spirit . . . every German is Hitler! Hitler is the single man who stands for the beliefs of Germans. Don't make friends with Hitler. Don't fraternize. If in a German town you bow to a pretty girl or pat a blond child . . . you bow to Hitler and his reign of blood."

None of this lasted. The simplest impulses in the face of human needs, even the demand for the plainest services—laundering, sewing, merely asking directions—helped break down the unenforceable orders, which crumbled rapidly at the end of hostilities. The official line held for a time; when a proposal was made for the payment of the Allied soldiers in marks, Eisenhower wrote on the margin: "Do we contemplate our soldiers shopping in Germany? If so, how do we even pretend to avoid fraternization?" After the end of the fighting there were nonfraternization patrols of MP's, and regulations forbade assignment of GI's to territory where they had German relatives. An assistant chief of staff on a journey observed that there was fraternization with children; as a result, Eisenhower said that the orders were "obviously not expected to apply to young children." He was asked at what age this exception should apply; ten was suggested, but the general refused to be specific and confined himself to the opinion that it was meant to apply to the very young. An Army observer reported that this relaxation was given a very liberal interpretation. The Negro troops especially were early and enthusiastic fraternizers, and thus were often held in particular esteem by the local population. Under a sign on the Autobahn that read: "Soldiers wise don't fraternize" was written: "This don't mean me, buddy."

Venereal disease in June 1945 was held not to be prima-facie evidence of fraternization, and this generous ruling was widely interpreted as marking the beginning of the end of the order, which GI's, when questioned, thought was being disobeyed by more than 90 per cent of the troops. One thousand cases of fraternization were reported for the Seventh Army, and these were only the cases in which the MP's had made arrests and reported the offenses for court-martial. In July, Field Marshal Bernard Montgomery proposed that troops should be allowed to hold conversations in public with Germans. This caused some consternation among members of Eisenhower's staff; however, there was general agreement that the new dispensation might include standing, walking, or talking with adult Germans but certainly should not permit holding hands, walking arm in arm, or sitting together on park benches. By August, General Eisenhower reported: "Members of my command are now permitted normal public contacts; in this way we will be able to understand better the problems which face us in the coming months." [8] The court-martials, however, continued until September; and not until more than a year later, at the end of 1946, were American soldiers permitted to enter a German movie theater or Germans allowed in American movie theaters or messes except on official occasions.

Nonfraternization was believed to be essential in view of the German character. "It was meant to impress on the Germans the prestige and superiority of the Allies—to show them that they had earned the distrust of other peoples and that they had been completely defeated." [9]

The reopening of schools had to be delayed for lack of non-Nazi texts. The old books were filled with Nazi propaganda. An arithmetic book illustrated the lesson on percentages with the example of a usurer who charged an honest farmer 12-per-cent interest on a loan of four hundred marks for four years. The question was: how much did the Jewish swindler get? Presently texts for the elementary grades were supplied from the United States and England. By chance a good selection of pre-Hitler books was found in New York, at Teachers College. Plates were made in England and shipped to Germany, where the books were printed.

In the West there was misery enough in the last days of the war, but in the Eastern provinces there was no shelter anywhere. Millions—old people, women, and children—fled or were driven west from East Prussia, Poland, Mecklenburg, and Saxony in one of the greatest migrations in history. It was a chaotic movement, slow, painful, unorganized, toward no certain destination, but away from something: the advancing Russians, the fury and vengeance of local native populations. Königsberg was a ruin; its inhabitants perished by the thousands from wounds

[8] *First Year of the Occupation*, Office of the Chief Historian, in Occupation Forces in Europe Series (Frankfurt, 1947), p. 47.

[9] "Historical Report on the Operations of the Office of Military Government," Office of the Military Governor, U.S. Zone, 1947.

or disease and hunger in the city, or while trying to get to the West by sea and land.

The last issue of the newspaper of the German armored divisions, the *Panzerbär,* was published toward the end of April 1945. It told the German soldier that he was the bulwark against Bolshevism and that Berlin would be the mass grave of Russian tanks. Goebbels broadcast to the German people on the Führer's birthday over the bursts of the Russian artillery pounding Berlin; he urged them to victory and the greatness that was characteristic of their leader, who had often been, Goebbels said, in difficult positions before, as indeed he had. A few days later Goebbels and his wife killed themselves and their six children in the bunker where Hitler and Eva Braun had committed suicide.

Toward the end of March, Eisenhower had stood 500 kilometers from Berlin, the Russians only 50; but the Russians were biting on granite and the Western Allies were meeting comparatively light resistance. Churchill and Montgomery urged Eisenhower to press forward and capture the city before the Russians got there, but Eisenhower decided to let the Russians arrive first, and General Marshall and the new President, Harry S. Truman, supported his decision. Here, as at Prague and elsewhere, the Americans held back while the Russians advanced to the predetermined positions, the positions that it was assumed would merely be military lines maintained until the Czechs established their own state, the Yugoslavs and the Poles and the Rumanians held their elections, and the four powers began their collaboration in the occupation of Germany.

But the reports were uniformly disquieting: the Communist-dominated governments were taking over in the areas occupied by the Red armies; there were never to be any free elections, although the forms of voting were carried out. No Allied observers were allowed to function in Russian-held territory, and there were angry interchanges about the treatment of prisoners of war.

The Russians were as reluctant to let Allied representatives into Soviet territory to supervise repatriation [1] as they were for Western correspondents to report on elections, and for special reasons they objected to the treatment of the Russian prisoners of war in Allied hands. In the Russian view, Soviet prisoners of war were dangerous, a reminder of past military defeats—and, more important, the prisoners were open to indoctrination by the West. The Soviet government wanted Russian prisoners to be returned right away and those who had been captured in German uniforms to be separated from the other enemy prisoners for prompt shipment to the Soviet Union. These Russians in German uniform were the remnants of General Andrei Vlasov's army, which the Germans had organized from captured Soviet troops. They were now turned over to the Russians, contrary to the provisions of international law [2] which forbid the capturing power to look beyond the uniform to the nationality of the prisoner.[3] Many suicides occurred among these men before the Americans were able to deliver the remainder, over a period of months, to the Soviet authorities.

Much the same thing happened to the forced laborers and the ordinary Russian prisoners of war. Thousands of them had not the least desire to return to Russia and to the punishment that awaited defectors or anyone whose loyalty the Soviet might doubt. *Stars and Stripes* described trainloads of Russians [4] returning to the homeland with their violins and balalaikas and singing mournful songs, but other reports from Americans did

[1] Only one mission was permitted to enter Poland, and it was not allowed to visit any prisoner-of-war camps (Chester Wilmot: *The Struggle for Europe*, p. 686).

[2] Under Secretary of State Joseph Grew told Stettinius that the repatriation agreement with Russia was illegal, but Stettinius replied that it had to be signed in order to get American prisoners of war back from the Russians. The repatriation of the Russian prisoners was called "Operation Keelhaul."

[3] There were between 500,000 and 1,000,000 of these *Osttruppen* in the German Army at the end of the war. They had been recruited from the Eastern territories the Germans had conquered; a majority were Russian (George Fischer: *Soviet Opposition to Stalin*, pp. 106, 108).

[4] The "Hammer and Sickle Special," the paper called them.

not get into the newspapers: reports about Russians pleading for asylum in the West. Some of them managed to stay in Germany by claiming to be Yugoslavs or Poles.[5]

The Communist *coup d'état* in Rumania, the arrest of the sixteen representatives of the Warsaw Poles despite the safe-conduct that had been given by Moscow, angry charges and countercharges were accompaniments to the sweep of Russian power over Eastern Europe and to the gates of the West. There were few signs of amity at the close of the war. Stalin complained that General Marshall had sent him wrong intelligence reports and that only the quick work of the Red Army intelligence narrowly enabled the Russian troops to escape a disaster in March.

Churchill constantly strove to make Roosevelt and later Truman see what he had come to regard as the mortal peril of the West; but Roosevelt still tried to minimize the differences, saying that most problems straighten themselves out in time, although he acknowledged that firmness was needed. Roosevelt in the weeks just before his death was so obviously not his old self that Churchill thought the cables they were exchanging gave plain evidence of having been written by someone else.

President Truman immediately showed himself capable of acting with firmness and without backward glances. Secretary Morgenthau wanted to go to Potsdam to take part in the decisions on the future of Germany; Truman told him that the Secretary of the Treasury was more needed in Washington, and when Morgenthau said in that case he would resign, Truman promptly accepted the offer. The President was in the center of a tug-of-war of his advisers. Forrestal and others were urging a harder policy toward Russia. Stimson thought that from the point of view of the United States it mattered little who ruled the Balkans, and he wished to continue the policy of attempting to get along with Russia by making as few demands as possible. On the question of Germany, Truman was inadequately briefed.

[5] Testimony before the Eastland Committee, June 11, 1957.

Although he looked forward to a Germany that would in due course take its place in Europe, he carried with him Roosevelt's dismemberment plan when he went to Potsdam, unaware apparently that by then both Churchill and Stalin had abandoned the idea of breaking up Germany. Stalin said in a speech on May 9, a day after the signing of the surrender in Berlin, that Russia wanted neither the dismemberment nor the destruction of Germany. For Churchill a divided Germany would only further weaken Western Europe and remain an invitation to Russian penetration; for Stalin it could hardly provide the reparations Russia was demanding. Stalin told Hopkins in June that he had given up the idea because of British opposition, though he still favored it; but that was one of his innumerable jests. Neither he nor the Soviet representative in London, F. T. Gusev, took any serious interest in the subject after Yalta.

Now there was no one left favoring dismemberment except the French, who were not invited to Potsdam, and the Americans, who had no urgent political reasons for supporting it; and the subject was dropped, although a dismemberment commission was actually at work in London. It had only two meetings before it ceased operations.

Truman continued to share his predecessor's high opinion of Marshal Stalin. He liked the way Stalin looked him in the eye, and he too thought that when things went wrong they were the result of matters outside the control of the Marshal. The Potsdam conference, which lasted from July 17 to August 2, was the high point of Russian power, the low point of British. Churchill had to depart in the middle of the conference, cheerful but defeated in the British general election, to be replaced in the negotiations by Clement Attlee. That left only the Russians with the full complement of the men who had been present at Teheran and Yalta. Byrnes and Truman were new to these discussions. But the good humor that had impressed everyone at the other conferences continued; there were dinners and splendid entertainments, and the clashes as the underlying differences emerged were still muffled with wit.

Truman wished to have the straits of the world—Suez, Panama, the Black Sea straits, Kiel, and also the Rhine-Danube passage—internationalized, and Stalin remarked that he did not favor it, whereupon Truman said that he would have to report the matter to Congress. "That is your privilege," replied Stalin. There were other interchanges on the same subject. At one point when there was talk about internationalizing the Black Sea straits, Molotov asked Eden why, if it was such a good rule, it shouldn't be applied to Suez. "The question has not been raised," said Eden. "I am raising it," Molotov told him. Churchill then added that the British were satisfied with the present arrangements and that the canal had been operated that way for seventy years. Molotov replied: "There have been lots of complaints. You should ask Egypt."

When the time came to discuss the disposition of the German fleet, Stalin asked Churchill what had become of the one third of it which was to go to Russia. Churchill said that weapons of modern war were so terrible that in his opinion the fleet should be sunk. "Let us divide it," replied Stalin; "if Mr. Churchill wishes he can sink his share."

Potsdam was also the occasion of another historic remark by the Marshal. The matter of religion in Russia had always deeply affected the Western Allies. Even in the 1930's prominent Americans and Britons had seen the essentials of Christianity in the Russian experiment, and in 1945 an American Roman Catholic priest of Polish descent had been invited to visit Moscow to see and tell how religion was flourishing in Russia. Now Churchill again raised the question of the treatment and rights of religious groups. It was then that Stalin asked: "How many divisions has the Pope?"

The Protocol of the Proceedings of the Berlin Conference, which summed up the accomplishments at Potsdam, was a stiff document. Like JCS 1067, it foresaw a Germany with severely reduced industrial capacity—the lessons of the defeat brought home to every German; an agricultural, denazified, demilitarized, deconcentrated Germany. It declared that the German people had begun to atone for the terrible crimes committed under the leadership of those who in the hour of their success the people had openly approved and blindly obeyed. It repeated that German militarism and Nazism were to be extirpated, although it was not the intention of the Allies to destroy or enslave the German people and they were to be given an opportunity to prepare for the reconstruction of their life on a democratic and peaceful basis. Supreme authority was to be exercised in each zone by its commander in chief, and in matters affecting Germany as a whole by the commanders acting jointly as members of the Control Council. So far as practicable, there was to be uniformity of treatment of the German population throughout the country. The purposes of the occupation by which the Control Council were to be guided were:

"The complete disarmament and demilitarization of Germany and the elimination or control of all German industry that could be used for military production. . . .

"To convince the German people that they have suffered a total military defeat and they cannot escape responsibility for what they have brought upon themselves, since their own ruthless warfare and the fanatical Nazi resistance have destroyed the German economy and made suffering and chaos inevitable. . . .

"Productive capacity not needed for permitted production shall be removed . . . or if not removed shall be destroyed." The German economy was to be decentralized, to eliminate the "present excessive concentration of economic power as exemplified in particular by cartels, syndicates, trusts and other monopolistic arrangements."

"In organizing the German economy, primary emphasis shall

be given to the development of agriculture and peaceful domestic industries. . . ."

Germany was to be treated as a "single economic unit" and "common policies" were to be established for mining, agriculture, wages, and prices.

"German industry and all economic and financial international transactions" were to be controlled to prevent "Germany from developing a war potential," as were all "public or private scientific bodies, research and experimental institutions."

German living standards were not to be higher than the average in European countries, excluding the Soviet Union and the United Kingdom.

In accordance with the Crimean decision Germany was to be compelled to pay for the loss and suffering that she had caused to the united nations. Russia was to be compensated by removals from her zone and from German external assets; the shares of the United States and the United Kingdom and other countries entitled to reparations were to be met from the Western zones and external assets. In addition Russia was to get 15 per cent of German machinery to be "removed from the Western zones of Germany, in exchange for an equivalent value of food" and raw materials, and other commodities. An additional 10 per cent was to go to Russia without any balancing payments.[6]

The conference noted "with pleasure the agreement reached among representative Poles" which had made possible a "Provisional Government of National Unity." Recognition of this government by the United States and Great Britain had resulted in withdrawal of their recognition from the former Polish government in London, which no longer existed. Poland, it was repeated, was to hold "free and unfettered elections as soon as possible on the basis of universal suffrage and secret ballot, in

[6] 81st Congress, 1st Session, Senate Document 123: *A Decade of American Foreign Policy*, pp. 34–50.

63

which all democratic and anti-Nazi parties" were to take part, and representatives of the Allied press were to report in full freedom upon developments in Poland before and during the elections. The final delimitation of the western boundaries of Poland was to await the peace settlement, but meanwhile the Oder-Neisse boundary was drawn from the Baltic to the Czech frontier. Danzig was to go to Poland and not be part of the Russian zone of occupation. It was agreed in principle that Königsberg would ultimately go to Russia; the United States would support Russia's claim to this city at the peace conference.

Finally there were to be transfers of German populations from Poland, Czechoslovakia, and Hungary: nine million people were to be moved in an "orderly and humane manner," though no one said how this was to be done; and the migrant Germans were to be "distributed equitably" among the zones.[7] Churchill at this point said that public opinion in England was disturbed by these transfers, to which, however, he had agreed as early as Teheran.

Potsdam, despite the absence of Churchill after the first meetings, had much the same warm and friendly atmosphere that had characterized all the gatherings of the Big Three. President Truman played the piano—the "Missouri Waltz." He thought that Stalin's missing a meeting was not really due to illness as reported, but to his disappointment at the outcome of the British elections. Still, he had his doubts—he had said at the beginning of the conference that the one language the Russians understood was that of force, and he wrote to his mother: "You never saw such pig-headed people as are the Russians. I hope I never have to hold another conference with them—but, of course, I will." [8]

Stalin was as wary as always. When Churchill had suggested

[7] The German Red Cross reported in September 1945, two months after Potsdam, that 13,000,000 refugees had come into Germany. *Keesing's Contemporary Archives*, V (1943–6), 7519.

[8] Harry S. Truman: *Memoirs*, I, 402.

the phrase "responsible governments" for the new governments regarded as legitimate by the Allies, he had insisted on the substitution of "recognized governments"; that was something he could defend in the days to come. And when Hopkins had spoken to him in June about freedom of the press and of elections in Poland, he had said that such principles of democracy were well known to him; but, urged at Potsdam to permit freedom of the press in Poland, he said that the Poles were too sensitive to receive suggestions from outsiders in such matters.

Churchill had wanted to call the Potsdam conference a month before it was held, while the Allies still had bargaining power in the positions of their armies; he had stopped the demobilization of the British Air Force and ordered the British troops not to give up ground even inside the Russian zone. He had even considered rearming German troops before the huge looming danger of the Russian mass. But this found little American support despite the group around Truman which was almost as dubious of Russian intentions as was Churchill. General Eisenhower, Truman said, couldn't understand why Churchill was so determined to mix political and military considerations. Two weeks before the conference opened, Justice Hugo Black of the Supreme Court told an audience at the Hollywood Bowl: "It was Hitler's diabolic exploitation of the fear of bolshevism which kept nations divided within and suspicious of one another. . . . Some clamorous voices have been prophesying a war with Russia. . . ." The *Stars and Stripes* declared that the speech found a quick response among American fighting men: "There is nothing in the actions of either Russia or America to indicate that these two powerful countries desire anything but the friendliest of relations. Critics are playing directly into the hands of the warmongers." [9]

Truman, in the perplexities of his new responsibilities, turned to the men Roosevelt had trusted. He sent former Ambassador Davies to London, and Davies later joined him at Potsdam. In

[9] *Stars and Stripes*, June 18, 1945.

London, Davies listened to Winston Churchill voice his anxieties over Russia and asked Churchill why he had not made an alliance with Hitler. Truman sent the ill Hopkins to visit Stalin just before Potsdam; and Hopkins, although disquieted by the turn of events since Yalta, assured Stalin that the United States too desired only friendly powers on Russian borders, that it opposed the *cordon sanitaire* which Stalin thought the British were constructing, and agreed that there were no reasons for major difficulties to arise between Russia and the United States. The two countries, he continued to believe, were mutually dependent; Russians were like Americans, and their socialism was their business. Truman continued in the Rooseveltian search for the postwar United Nations that would solace the world. When Churchill, trying to quiet American suspicions of British intentions, offered to share British bases with the United States, Truman said this could be done under the international organization.

In Berlin, Truman mused on the vast desolation and the plight of the civilian population, the disaster one "crazy egotist" had brought upon Russia, Poland, England, and the United States. "I never saw such destruction," he wrote, as he saw the processions of old men and women and children making their way over the shards of the city, "I don't know whether they learned anything from it or not."

What he saw was a city that had been hit with one tenth of the bombs dropped on Germany—and that had been captured by block-to-block fighting which lasted for weeks. The destruction in the center was 95 per cent; in the city as a whole, 65 to 75 per cent. Only about one quarter of the houses were somehow habitable, and only one person in ten was under thirty. What machinery remained when the fighting was over had been gouged out by the Russians as reparations: 90 per cent in the iron-and-steel industry, 75 per cent in the printing industry, 70 per cent in the vehicle industry, 85 per cent of the machines producing electrical and optical equipment.

Potsdam ended with the customary formulas. Truman thought that, though much remained to be done, a good deal had been accomplished, and the ground laid for future collaboration.

The twenty-five thousand American troops who had entered early in July were left in Berlin, after some preliminary confusion as to their quarters, a circumstance shared by the British. The Russian preparations in regard to these matters had been less than adequate. The terms under which the Americans stayed were in the hands of the deputy military governor, General Lucius D. Clay, to whom full authority was given by General Eisenhower. General Clay did not make any formal written arrangements about the right of the troops of the Western Allies to use the roads and railways into Berlin independent of Russian supervision. He thought it unnecessary, although the matter was discussed both at the meetings of the Russians, British, and Americans in Berlin and by the American advisory group in London. One champion of dealing softly with the Russians, the American ambassador to England, John G. Winant, who had strongly opposed giving the Russians cause for suspicion by holding the forward positions in the Soviet zone as Churchill was advocating, wanted to spell out the right of the Allied troops to free access to Berlin without Russian controls. This, however, the Army failed to provide, believing that the co-operative venture of Berlin was dependent on larger issues of collaboration and that the details were relatively unimportant in the light of the great purpose.

The Army was doubtless affected in part by the amiable relations between individual American commanders and their Russian colleagues. Generals on both sides exchanged medals, horses, jeeps; Marshal Gregori Zhukov presented Eisenhower with a decoration of a star, ninety diamonds surrounding a group of synthetic rubies. Like their civilian chiefs, the generals got along with immense cordiality. There were annoying difficulties about billeting and permission for the Allied troops to use the roads to Berlin, but these could be attributed to the innumerable requirements of two armies coming together in the common task of redeploying their troops and governing the defeated enemy. The soldiers, however, maintained their camaraderie longer than the statesmen, perhaps by virtue of their secondary position in both countries. So long as official relations were friendly, if only on the surface, they met and drank together in an atmosphere of relaxation after the defeat of the enemy, and would cheerfully do so until otherwise ordered.

At Potsdam the American aim continued to be satisfaction of legitimate Russian demands for security and bringing Russia into the war against Japan, with due regard for her needs in the Far East and her losses in the Russo-Japanese War of 1904–5. But although Japan, like Germany, was regarded as an example of the classic aggressor, there was one important difference in the Far East. No arrangements were made for four-power collaboration in administering Japan after the defeat.

Senator Arthur H. Vandenberg thought there was no reason why the United States should not sign a hard and fast treaty to keep Germany and Japan permanently disarmed, to remove Russia's only reason for appropriating the border states. This point of view had its adherents in the highest circles; in fact, the Truman administration believed it desirable for the Russians to have friendly states on their borders and at the same time proposed treaties that would provide American guarantees of German disarmament. Secretary Byrnes was to offer such guarantees for periods of up to fifty years.

This was the picture as the American delegation to the Potsdam conference returned home and the Army set about its task of governing Germany. The ruins of Germany were awe-inspiring, but did not evoke much sympathy; people reminded one another of the ruins the Germans had left behind them—Warsaw too was more than 80 per cent destroyed, and some of the towns the Germans had occupied would never rise again. There were only some thirteen thousand Jews left in Germany. The

Chief Rabbi of Berlin, who had refused all offers to leave Europe during the war, said now that there would never again be a Jewish community in Germany, as the losses had been too overwhelming. But he said too that there were decent, honorable Germans and that they should be given an opportunity to win their way back to the community of civilized nations.

IV

BERLIN AND THE FOUR POWERS

As THE British, French, and Americans entered Berlin in July 1945, they found a complete apparatus of government at work. In the midst of the ruins of the city, while bodies were still being fished out of the flooded subway and rowboats moved among the stranded trains, the Communist organizers had swiftly and according to plan recruited the cross-section of the population which was to be used in the administration of the city. They had orders to appoint people from the middle classes—doctors, lawyers, trade-union men, liberal and conservative citizens—to head the new departments, with Communists being appointed to the less spectacular but more strategic posts under the nonparty men. In the Berlin Magistrat, the executive part of the city government, there were seven from the middle-class parties along with six Communists and two Social Democrats. The Communists, most of them returning to Germany after a long exile, worked with impassioned energy and conviction fourteen hours a day, seven days a week. The Russian commandant of the city chose a non-Communist, Arthur Werner, an architect by profession, as lord mayor. Werner was sixty-seven years old—the men appointed to the new regime were likely to be sixty or over—with no political experience but with an anti-Nazi record. The same techniques were used throughout the districts. The conspicuous positions were given to non-Communists, but education and police were always safely in Communist hands.

The organizers had been told in the party directives that

communism would now be adapted to the conditions of countries outside Russia. Thus the great issue that was to shake the foundations of the movement in 1948, when Tito would break with the Kremlin, and to reappear in 1956, when Poland and Hungary would attempt to do the same thing, seemed at this time to be resolved in favor of a decentralization from Moscow. So the antifascist front could be formed with strong faith on the part of some of these men that Germany, at least East Germany, could develop along what they believed to be broadly based democratic-socialist lines. German speakers at political meetings referred to these new doctrines designed to attract men and women of all the postwar parties. Wilhelm Pieck, leader of the German Communist party, on June 25 said: "Germany needs an anti-fascist democratic regime, free trade and private enterprise on a basis of private ownership, free trade unions, no racial or other discrimination." The "United Front of the Anti-Hitlerites" was the unshakable platform upon which the parties were founded.[1] The first to be licensed was the small band of Communists who had survived the concentration camps and the Gestapo searches; 120 of them were present in June at the refounding of the Communist party. The Communists were to unite with the other authorized parties in an antifascist alliance dedicated to the rebuilding of Germany and the destruction of any Nazi elements that remained. Before the Potsdam conference four parties were approved in Berlin and the East zone by the Russians: the Communist party; the Christian Democratic Union; the Liberal Democratic party; and the old Socialist party of Germany which had long dominated Berlin before the Nazis came into power, and was now christened anew the Social Democratic party or SPD. On July 16 the four parties, at a meeting in Berlin, made a joint declaration on the need for a radical reorientation of the German people and the creation of an antifascist and democratic political order. The

[1] Richard Lukas: *Zehn Jahre*, pp. 92, 94; Wolfgang Leonhard: *Die Revolution entlässt ihre Kinder*, pp. 393, 394; *SBZ von 1945 bis 1954*, p. 8.

parties would keep their independence, but were united in what they opposed and in the general goals they sought. By the end of 1945 the Russians felt that the Free Germany Committee could be dissolved and its functions be taken over by the anti-fascist organizations.

The plan was simple and intelligent. Germany, wherever the Russian writ ran, was to be reorganized from the top down and the bottom up. It was to be reconstructed in its land tenure and its industrial life, but it was to produce. Where the owners of a plant had fled, the workers were urged to take over and run it themselves. Factories such as Siemens in Berlin [2] which still had some working machinery were praised in the party press for manufacturing, despite all the difficulties, out of odds and ends of materials, shovels and pots and pans that could be used against the debris and—if there was anything to cook— against the hunger. For the Russians brought nothing and gave nothing, and in fact they had little to spare.

In the case of the Communists the party was headed by Germans who came directly from Moscow or from Hitler's concentration camps. The leaders of the other parties either had been under arrest or had managed to stay alive in hiding or awaiting in an obscure job the day of liberation. Kurt Schumacher, who became leader of the Social Democratic party, had survived the concentration camps, although broken in body; Konrad Adenauer of the Christian Democrats had been imprisoned; Jakob Kaiser, who for a time would be head of the CDU in the East zone, had been a fugitive from the Gestapo. Such records were common among these men in Berlin and throughout Germany who had "risen from the catacombs." Disgrace under the Nazis was a passport in 1945 to political activity. The eighty-year-old Social Democratic party was re-established as a socialist, workers' party; the new Christian Democrats and the Liberal Democrats, intending to appeal to the former

[2] Siemens was one of Europe's chief producers of electrical equipment.

72

middle-class voters, spoke of individual liberty and responsibility.

But party lines were indistinct. Former members of the Weimar Liberal party helped found the Christian Democrats, among whom were men who wished for an alliance with the Social Democrats. The idea of them all was to sweep the past clean, to overcome the errors and division that had led the anti-Nazi parties and the nation to destruction. "Democratic" appears in the name of every party except the Communist, where it was taken for granted. Under this aegis the People's Democracy of the East zone would be founded.

As individuals the Russians were friendly to the Germans by comparison with the Americans; they shook hands, they offered the new German functionaries drinks and cigarettes, and they followed instructions to the letter. One Russian commandant asked his political adviser what had happened to the delegates to the Liberal Democratic party, the Socialist party, and the Christian Democratic Union, and when told they had not yet been appointed in his area, he ordered that branches be founded right away; his instructions said there were to be non-Communist parties, and if they didn't exist they had to be created. The Russians did not believe, they said, in collective guilt, but the Germans bore a responsibility for Hitler and in any event they had to work and to be brought into approved political organizations.

The job of the German was to co-operate with the new order. Woe to him, whatever his station in life, if he failed for whatever reasons. The Communist papers did not hesitate to name names—the mayor of a village, a farmer, a woman worker who took a day off to get her hair curled could be and were denounced as saboteurs if the party found them wanting. If a man collaborated, whether landowner or former Nazi, there was a place for him, as there was a place for the war factories. Those factories not dismantled for reparations continued to produce goods which in the West were forbidden but which in the East could work for the benefit of the Russians too.

The Russians had made an indelible imprint of another kind on Berlin. Here too they had run wild, raping and plundering, celebrating the victory and the end of the years of merciless battle. By day they had put the Germans, both men and women, to work in dismantling commandos, clearing up rubble, removing tank barricades; and by night they terrorized the city. No woman was immune, no matter what her age. Alarm systems were arranged, to warn of the approach of Russian soldiers; Berliners rattled the letter boxes when they visited friends, so they could be quickly distinguished from the Russians, who hammered on the doors or burst them open. Women climbed onto roofs, pulling their ladders up after them; they hid in cellars or in the wobbly, precarious, bombed-out upper stories of buildings; they smeared their faces with dirt to make themselves unattractive. But few evaded the soldiers by any stratagems, and a regulation provided that any woman who had been "visited" by the Russians had to report for medical treatment.

The barbaric behavior of the Red Army made the job of the political organizers more difficult and had a part in the failure of the Communists ever to gain a mass following in Berlin. The Army's political program for the city ignored small human considerations, concentrating on the ideological sectors that had to be conquered with the help of the Germans. Here the reconstruction was astonishing. The fighting stopped in Berlin on May 2. There were immediate orders for cabarets and restaurants to be reopened. On May 22 the first Russian film was shown, on May 26 the first concert was given, under Leo Borchard of the Berlin Philharmonic, on May 27 the Renaissance Theater was opened, on June 1 the first pension payments were made, on June 3 there were bicycle races and a football game between the Red Army and Berlin, on the 5th swimming pools were reopened and the first Berlin telephones were usable again, on the 10th the Deutsches Theater was opened, on the 15th

Marshal Zhukov gave permission for the four antifascist parties to be started, on the 22nd the Christian Democratic Union was founded. And by July 3, before the opening of the Potsdam conference, the Social Democratic party and the Communists had formed a united front that was to end in the spring of 1946 with the merging of both parties in Berlin and the East zone as the SED, the Socialist Unity party. On June 22 the city library opened, and the Berlin radio station started operation at six o'clock that morning; the Commerce and Dresden banks reopened along with the Deutsche Bank and the Stadt Bank. By July 10 there were 11 theaters and 150 moving-picture houses operating; there were 5 Soviet-controlled newspapers, including an organ of the Red Army, the *Tägliche Rundschau,* before any paper representing the West was started.

On July 1 the first American troops entered Berlin to find everything important to the running of the city already organized. The only difficulties were in arranging for their own billets and supplies, and the delay in getting across the Elbe, where the advance American party had been held up by the Russians for ten days. When they marched in, the troops were confined to the use of one road, and the number of planes that could land at the Tempelhof field was limited. The Russians took everything of any value from the quarters they turned over to their Allies, leaving bare, often filthy floors. But there was a city government; there were newspapers and other clear signs that a well-planned occupation was at work.

There was humor along with the cultural revival. Stories were printed that had been long suppressed. One written in 1934 and printed in the *Tägliche Rundschau* in August 1945 was about Little Red Riding Hood. In this account the little girl was looking for an Aryan grandmother; a lot of people, the narrator said, are looking for her now; and the dialogue went on with patent references to the new order of 1934. The answer to the question about the grandmother's health was: "Ah, my dear, things were fine a while back, today they're even better; but it would be better if things were just fine again. . . ." "What a big nose you have." "I beg your pardon: I have my Aryan credentials." Goering then comes by with I. G. Farben, and the Reichsmarschall would like a few cannon changed to butter—just for his own use, he says. Hearing a loud noise, he asks: "How can an Aryan grandmother snore in such an unracial fashion?" [3] This was the first appearance of what was expected to prove a huge accumulation of manuscripts unpublishable since 1932. Bookstores were opened too, in convenient locations, so that the busy housewife, the *Tägliche Rundschau* pointed out, could market and keep up with her reading at the same time.

The Russians had a formula for everything, including the time on which Berlin ran; from June 20 on, it was Moscow time, and since the sun could no more be ordered in its course than Lysenko's plants, Berliners found the city light at midnight and dark at seven o'clock in the morning. No plot of land was unplanted in the summer of 1945; the barren Tiergarten with its stumps of trees and toppled statues was divided into innumerable garden plots with bits of debris to mark the limits of each. Bomb craters were filled in and planted, as were athletic fields and parks.

At the first meeting of the Berlin Kommandatura, the Allied governing body of the city, the British and American representatives were confronted by a Russian demand that they provide food for their respective sectors.[4] Since they had just entered Berlin they asked for more time, pointing out that the Russians were already established in the city and in a position to make supplies available. The Russian commander's reply was that the Americans and British had had since the Crimean conference to prepare for this operation. He did agree to supply the Allied sectors temporarily, but the Russians never brought

---

[3] *Tägliche Rundschau*, Aug. 18, 1945.
[4] "Historical Report on the Operations of the Office of Military Government."

food of their own to Berlin. What food came in was from the East zone and from stocks taken from the Germans. The Americans and the British, on the other hand, brought food from their own stores. It was obvious that Berliners were going hungry, and despite the grim provisions of JCS 1067, the first distribution of food, two hundred thousand tons, was ordered by General Eisenhower to tide over the population in the Western sectors until the harvest. It was desperately needed; refugees were pouring into the city at the rate of twenty-five or thirty thousand a day. Berlin had scant supplies of its own; the death rate of children and old people rose to heights not matched since the Thirty Years' War. More than half the babies born in Berlin in August died, mainly of malnutrition, a United States government report showed some months later. There were 1,448 deaths out of 2,866 births—ten times the death rate of the United States. There were no coffins in which to bury the dead, who were trundled circuitously around the blocks of rubble in carts or wheelbarrows, covered with whatever could be spared—sometimes with paper.

Since the Americans, unlike the Russians, had no clear plan for Germany, they issued statements and directives of a confusing and contradictory nature. General George S. Patton, having fought a swift and bold campaign against the German armies, told reporters that he was using Nazis in military government, adding that there wasn't much more difference between German parties than between the Republicans and Democrats back home. A violent storm broke out that ended with his being relieved of command. "The chief goals of the occupation," said *The New York Times*, "are being thwarted." A writer on *PM* said he didn't know how many demobilization points Patton had, but enough certainly to send him home. While the Russian-controlled papers joined heartily in the denunciations, all over the Russian zone and in the Russian-occupied countries former Nazis were being used in the Soviet-controlled governments—as, indeed, they were in the French and, to a lesser degree, English zones. Americans went at denazification with a puritanical intensity that followed the letter of the law and moved well beyond it; as a result of the American investigations into millions of party members, it inevitably happened that innocent people were jailed, some of them for considerable periods. The Russians used the Patton case, however, as an example. The *Tägliche Rundschau* said Patton's beliefs were typical of those of American officers, who everywhere were being friendly to former Nazis, keeping them in important industrial and administrative positions and failing to carry out the agreed-on denazification. American officials were attacked for their benevolent attitude toward German industrialists, although the American military government was zealously rounding up German businessmen—anyone, in fact, who had been on the board of directors of a firm that had earned as much as a million marks, or $250,000, a year. The United States, the Soviet press charged, was rebuilding I. G. Farben instead of dismantling it. The *Tägliche Rundschau* denounced those too who denied that there were democratic governments in Rumania and Yugoslavia. There were two danger signs, an article said, that had to be watched for carefully: one was any attempt on the part of the Western powers to use communism as a stalking-horse; behind such deception would lurk German rearmament. The other was the attitude of the Church; a pastoral letter from a bishop in Munich opposing a peace of force was quoted. This, the article charged, was a revisionist view that, as in the aftermath of World War I, might lead to a revival of German militarism.

In some areas under their control the Russians put everybody to work clearing the debris; in others only former Nazis were assigned the jobs of heavy labor. An article in the *Tägliche Rundschau* asked whether there were unemployed in Berlin. It was, the writer said, a ticklish question. All sorts of workers were needed, but of course many white-collar workers did not want to perform the hard physical labor that had to be done. Criticism of the new administration was permitted up to a point—if it affected the German officials; no criticism of the Russians themselves was tolerated. In one town, a paper reported, the burgomaster had been keeping supplies for himself, and since he had been unmasked there was food enough to go around. There were also attacks on the bureaucracy: the long waiting, the rudeness of the clerks—a man could get lice, an article declared, before he could legally become a Berliner.

Very little that could be turned to the uses of Communist propaganda was missed. In August there was a ceremony for those who had suffered or died for spiritual freedom under the Nazis, and there were articles on artists such as Käthe Kollwitz telling of her love and sympathy for the workers.

All the Berlin papers ran accounts of how the Germans could make do with the odds and ends that remained to them. Glass, it was explained, could be cut down where necessary to fit smaller window frames; there were pictures showing a builder demonstrating to two women how to repair a roof; moth-eaten sweaters could be unraveled and the wool used again. Fresh vegetables could be dried and fuel thereby be saved—"only work makes values." Stories were told of the Germans' ingenious use of the fragments and the energy that were still theirs; how a burgomaster improvised care for refugees, how the workers and management of a plant somehow got production started, how women were coming into their own—they were mayors of towns now, active in political life, and extremely busy too on the ruins of Berlin, where they greatly outnumbered the male workers. War prisoners sent greetings to their relatives through the Communist newspapers; and the Germans were told that all during the war letters had been sent by the prisoners, but that Hitler's censorship, in an effort to suppress the news that German soldiers were being well treated in Russia, had not let the communications be delivered. A fifteen-year-old boy had his picture taken running a tractor—he was said to work all day beginning at five a.m.; and there were many more such stories showing how the Germans must throw themselves into the task of growing food or rebuilding. This included the entrepreneur, for private industry was to be encouraged in Germany, the Russians repeated; and there were articles on the theory of the free market and how it must be really free to function as it should. From August 15 on, Marshal Zhukov ordered, German industry was to be rebuilt with all energy and speed, including plants that could manufacture artificial fertilizer, a commodity that was viewed with suspicion by the West because it could also produce explosives.

In mid-August the leaders of the four antifascist parties made a common declaration that it was the will of the German people in these hard times to carry their burdens in worthy fashion, to get rid of militarism, to rebuild the economy, to establish freedom of the spirit and conscience, to rewin the confidence of other peoples. Berlin would rise again, the Communists told the population, the ravaged Tiergarten more beautiful than ever, and larger; Unter den Linden would be made free of traffic, and two- and three-story houses would be built on it—this was near the future site of the Stalin Allee.

There were also some actual improvements. Rations were raised in October for people doing heavy work as well as for those in key industries, and for professors, doctors, teachers, writers, artists and nurses. Although German soldiers were forbidden by the Allies to wear their old uniforms after August 31, many of them had to, having nothing else. A firm of tailors in Berlin specialized in dyeing uniforms dark blue, putting on patch pockets, and making use of the knee pads of parachutists and other stray bits of material for linings and belts and boys' pants and coats of all sizes.

There was a blacklist of German authors who could not be published, but it was announced that there would be a large supply of books in the new East Germany, since they were essential to political activity and education, and schoolbooks were soon provided in large quantities—far greater than in the West.

While the Russians were accusing the Americans and British of failing to cleanse their zones and sectors of Nazis and industrialists, the Americans continued to fight the war in their instructions to the troops. A *Post Hostility Pamphlet* issued by the Army for troops bound for Germany was described as "written by men who know Germany today" and was as belligerent as anything written during the war. It said, in fact:

> You are a soldier fighting a war . . . the shooting is over but there is a lot to be done. Sudden raids have developed as the best way to be sure that the Germans aren't concealing weapons, Nazi literature, or Army property. These surprise swoops . . . quickly discourage the German burgher from trying to play games with the laws laid down by the Allies. Russia cannot afford to wreck factories which she needs. . . . Towns look clean and bright. . . . Look out, the people are still a formidable enemy. . . . There are children who shuffle from one foot to another outside your mess hall; they'll be too polite or too scared to ask for food but you can see in their eyes how hungry they are. . . . Old men and women pulling carts, young girls in threadbare clothing . . . are still better off than thousands of the Greeks and Dutch and Poles they enslaved. The "little" Germans are the people who accepted slave labor and were glad to get it. Along with the industrialists and the munition makers, the Nazi farming and working classes shared in the profits of Germany's inhumanity. And you have to be tough about it in terms of the individual people you meet. The ragged German trudging along the street with a load of firewood may not look vicious but he has a lot in common with a trapped rat. . . .

The pamphlet quoted the editor of *Foreign Affairs*: "Nazi behavior is not a flash in the German pan but the reflex of an old strain of endemic barbarism methodically kept alive and developed. The German in Germany is forever a prey to that mad delusion." [5]

Among the Western Allies the French view of the Germans was closest to that of the Americans. The French too had a program that was almost entirely negative. Any central German agency was an offense and a danger in their eyes, and they were the first to use the veto in the Allied Control Council when a proposal was made to establish a central German postal administration. Stamps issued in their zone had imprinted across them "Zone Française." The French saw no point in distinguishing Nazis from other Germans—who had marched into France, General de Gaulle pointed out, three times in one man's lifetime. "I do not want ever to see the re-establishment of a Reich again," he said in October.[6] And the French in the same month refused to permit the amalgamation on a national basis of German trade unions. The first serious disagreements in the Allied Control Council were with the French: the Americans, who wanted the administrative arrangements for governing Germany to run smoothly and so favored the establishment of German central agencies, as did the British and Russians, threatened to establish three-power machinery in the Russian, British, and American zones if the French persisted in their obstruction. The Russians, too, were critical of the French tactics. One of them said to the French delegate at the meeting where the French vetoed a central German postal authority: "You are wrong. At the end of ten years there will be sixty million Germans and forty million Frenchmen. You cannot change these facts with your vote."

But the French were obsessed by two purposes that had long played a role in their political decisions. One was the drive for a security which could be gained only by returning to a Europe of Richelieu through the fragmentation of German power, through dismemberment, occupation of the Rhineland, and

[5] *Post Hostility Pamphlet.*
[6] Oct. 13, 1945. "U.S. Group Control Council for Germany."

separation of the Ruhr and Saar from German control. The French might recover a sense of security if Germany was weakened by such devices and France was supported by a system of alliances and an international organization that would guarantee her territorial integrity.

There was another French goal, more difficult to attain: it was to regain the prestige of a great power. The failure of the Big Three to invite France to Yalta and Potsdam was bitterly resented. The French claimed a voice in all negotiations now and asserted their equal status. When French troops captured Stuttgart, they refused to move out, although General Eisenhower ordered them to leave and occupy the zone that had been agreed upon.[7] A similar episode occurred in Italy, in the Val d'Aosta; and in both cases the Americans succeeded in getting the French to accept the evacuation order only by threatening to cut off supplies. In the Far East the French wanted to have a token force in the final battles against Japan, although here, as in Europe, the equipment they would use would have to come from the Americans.

One other thing the French shared with the Americans: belief in the need for German re-education. To this end they were to emphasize cultural exchanges with the Germans on a scale that was equaled only by the Russians. They reopened the University of Mainz, which had been closed since the time of Napoleon; they sent excellent lecturers; they permitted the establishment in their zone of a German newspaper which the Americans had not been willing to license because of its dubious personnel—a paper that was to become, as the *Frankfurter Allgemeine Zeitung,* one of the best edited and most influential in postwar Germany.

In Berlin—especially in the area that lay behind the old Reichschancellery—there was lively collaboration, not only among the Allies but with the Germans. This was the main site of the black market, and it was to flourish in Berlin and all

[7] Dwight D. Eisenhower: *Crusade in Europe,* pp. 412–13.

over Germany until the currency reform put an end to most of it in 1948. In the summer and autumn of 1945 it was at its height. The Russian soldiers had not been paid for months, some of them not for a year and a half. They were paid now in occupation marks, the plates for which had been furnished by the American Treasury Department. The Russian marks differed from those used in the West only in having a hyphen before the seven-digit number while the Western marks had a zero. Although the pay of the Russian soldiers was small compared with the Americans', it had accumulated so long that the men often carried their marks in satchels.

The Russians were passionate collectors of wrist watches, clothes, and Western artifacts of all kinds; and since their marks, like the American ones, could be converted by the GI's into dollars at the rate of ten to the dollar, the trading was brisk and the sums collected by the Americans were prodigious. During the first months of the four-power occupation, the American troops stationed in Berlin sent home more money than they were paid. A spot check of Frankfurt, center of the American zone, showed that more than half the marks there were of Russian origin. In August the Army ruled that only a man's pay plus 10 per cent could be mailed home, and $3,154,518 was sent; the pay for that month was $3,044,224. In July the troops sent home a million dollars more than they had been paid. When a ceiling of $100 was put on single money orders, the mail clerk of one small unit brought in 512 applications; informal syndicates were formed, men brought cots to sleep on in front of the Army post offices to wait for the nine a.m. opening; a lieutenant reported that the post office workers had had only eighteen meals in seventeen days. The arrangements for cabling flowers were made use of; $25 worth could be sent with each message, and cash instead of flowers would be delivered to the fortunate relative in the United States. In all, it was calculated, some $250,-000,000 worth of Russian occupation marks was converted to dollars and the bill was paid by the American taxpayer. In addition there was trade with the Germans, as well as a good deal of "liberated" booty. One man sent home a dismantled motor-cycle in three shipments. In the packages, for which no declaration was required unless they contained firearms, were such trophies as Leica cameras, Zeiss binoculars, Meissen china, silver, jewelry—whatever was not too hot or too heavy. In return the Germans, or some of them, got food and coffee, and occasionally they even smoked, although cigarettes were usually much too valuable as currency to be consumed.

If every corporal in Napoleon's army carried a marshal's baton in his knapsack, each American carried a golden key. Either by force or by trade a man could do well for himself in the Army if he chose, and help hungry people too if he traded the cigarettes or coffee or C rations to those Germans who had something to sell. The opportunities for the improvement of a soldier's finances were to last in the American Army for a long time. A package of cigarettes in 1947 was worth about 135 marks—almost a month's wages for a laboring man, who could not buy much with his German marks in any case. One cigarette bought twice as much as a hard day's work clearing the rubble of Berlin. A WAC corporal was reported to have sent home $100 weekly from the sale of her PX cigarette allowance. According to the *Stars and Stripes*, the Germans were becoming a nation with bowed heads—looking for cigarette butts—and any job with the Americans was eagerly sought after, even though American orders not to share food with the Germans extended past the time when American wives came to set up housekeeping. They were told never to allow leftovers to get into the hands of their maids—the food was to be destroyed or made inedible. Actually, of course, few American women or men followed the regulations in the face of a starving population, and the German household help had marvelous access to ash trays and coffee grounds and bread ends, along with what bounty might be bestowed upon them.

It was not only the Germans who were hungry and in want of everything. In Holland infant mortality was up 400 per cent, in Poland a million people were homeless, more than a million in

Greece were without shelter, and in France and Italy and throughout Europe the situation was much the same. In 1945 Europe produced only 30 per cent as much of the bread grains as had been raised in 1938, half as much food and milk fats—and even if the food had been available the bombed and blown-up transportation systems would have been unable to deliver it. But help on a large scale was on its way for all the countries of Europe with the exception of Germany. The Nazis had stirred up emotions of hatred and vengeance quite equal to their own, and people who normally would have been appalled at German suffering not only accepted it but approved of it.

A cartoon by Bill Mauldin in *Stars and Stripes* showed a GI feeding a hungry little girl. The caption said: "Careful, Pete, Congress might hear about this." On the wall was a sign: "Notice to U.S. Troops. American taxes pay for your food—it is forbidden to give, sell, or trade it to natives." An American intelligence survey reported a German university professor as saying: "Your soldiers are good-natured, good ambassadors; but they create unnecessary ill will to pour twenty litres of left-over cocoa in the gutter when it is badly needed in our clinics. It makes it hard for me to defend American democracy among my countrymen."

The Germans had no rights of any kind. General Eisenhower's first proclamation, issued on July 14, told them they were to obey orders "immediately and without question." It followed the Allied proclamation of June 5 placing all Germans and what remained of their country under the control of the victorious powers. Nazis were dumped into jails or camps by the thousands —a complete list of party members had been captured—and so were militarists and industrialists and people who violated the curfew or any other of the Allied regulations. People denounced by anonymous informants were imprisoned; [8] some were arrested

[8] Denunciations were widespread and often the result of nothing more than personal malice. When the future president of West Germany, Theodor Heuss, applied for a license to start a newspaper in Heidelberg, dozens of letters attacking his character were received by American authorities.

by mistake because their name or status was misunderstood or because they had worked for some German agency that was now regarded as criminal. One woman who had been a secretary in the office of the German admiralty was held for six months with no charge brought against her in any court; no word from or about her came to her family. A man was thrown into jail as the adjutant of Minister Speer, who had organized German production; actually he had only been part of a work detail called "Adjutant Speer," which was confused by the Americans with the Nazi minister who was charged with being a war criminal. Even anti-Nazis might be arrested—through error, of course; but since the arresting officers were soldiers following orders and were to pay no attention to such matters as habeas corpus and the refinements of the law as the West knew it, the accused could lie in jail for months ignorant of the charges brought against them. The Americans immediately arrested 70,000 former Nazis and suspect persons, and in two raids in November added 80,000 more. General Clay announced that there were 100,000 dangerous Nazis in jail; these included the major war criminals who were to be tried at Nuremberg and elsewhere, men who had run the concentration camps, high officers in the SS—men who undoubtedly belonged in jail. But among them were many who had done far less for the German war machine than the technicians who had worked on the V-1 and V-2 weapons and who were being eagerly rounded up by both the Russians and the Americans, not for imprisonment but for the amenities and special treatment that would enable them to pursue their research in either the East or West.

For the Russians, who brought no ideas of habeas corpus among their ideological assortment, the anti-Nazi proceedings were an important part of the construction of the new socialist order. "Nazis" or "reactionaries" or "fascists" were terms applied equally to Junkers or to Social Democrats who refused to join the SED—the Socialist Unity party—or to any political, labor, or other leaders who resisted Communist attempts to take over the direction of the parties. The Russians permitted a Catholic, Andreas Hermes, to become head of the Christian Democratic Union in Berlin; but as soon as it became apparent that Hermes would oppose such measures as expropriating any farm of more than 250 acres in the East zone without compensation to the owner, he and everyone else who opposed the decrees were called fascists, reactionaries, or warmongers and were dismissed from their posts. Nor, indeed, were the Western Allies long immune; it was a matter of no more than weeks before they were accused of keeping fascists in power and of plotting to join them in creating a bloc against the Soviet Union.

The Russians had done their preliminary work well in Berlin. They had taken over and run the Berlin radio station and continued to do so, although it was in the British sector. They never let the Western Allies use it, although they made frequent promises that it would soon be available.

The Americans started a newspaper, the *Neue Zeitung*, in October; like the *Tägliche Rundschau*, it was the organ of the Army, a professional, well-written paper with news services from all over the world—an enormous boon for the Germans, who had long been cut off from any outside communication. In its first issue on October 18 General Eisenhower wrote:

The *Neue Zeitung* will be a factor in demonstrating to the German people the necessity of the tasks which lie ahead of them. These tasks include self help, the elimination of nazism and the active denazification of German government and business. The moral, intellectual, and material reconstruction of Germany must come from the people themselves. We will assist them in this reconstruction but under no circumstances will we do the actual job for the Germans. The German people must recognize that to survive the coming winter they must rid themselves of the herd spirit in which they were steeped during the last twelve years.

... Militaristic ideas must be eradicated from the German mind. For all civilized nations on this earth aggression is immoral; the Germans have to be educated to this self-evident truth. . . .

Despite the appearance of the *Neue Zeitung,* the Germans remained sealed off from the world except for what the occupation forces permitted them to learn; books, newspapers, and magazines from outside Germany were forbidden to them. It was a crime for a German to be in possession of a publication from the West, for he had no means of obtaining it except from Allied sources, which were closed to him. Instructions posted at the German-Swiss border told the Germans it was forbidden to attempt to communicate with the people on the other side of the frontier whether by words or by making signs.[9]

The country in effect became an immense concentration camp. In October an arrangement was announced by which 350,000 more German prisoners of war were to be turned over to the French at the rate of 50,000 a month to help French reconstruction. Ninety thousand prisoners were to be returned by the French to the American authorities because of their poor physical condition, and it would not be long before many of the healthy prisoners of war going to France would be in the state of the 90,000.[1]

American newspapers such as the *Neue Zeitung* were the most successful of the early projects of military government. The *Neue Zeitung* started with a circulation of 500,000 copies, which rose within three months to 1,500,000. Copies had to be rationed, and their black-market price was eight marks. The paper considered boldly the major problems with which the Germans were struggling, including those of naked survival; collective guilt for the crimes of the Nazis, for example, it rejected,

[9] Kurt Zentner, ed.: *Aufstieg aus dem Nichts,* I, 269.
[1] The French said they had been promised more than 1,000,000 Germans for labor service that was planned to continue over a period of years; 700,000 were already in their hands (*The New York Times,* Oct. 13, 1945).

and it printed exchanges on the subject by Sigrid Undset and Karl Jaspers. Jaspers held that the Germans were certainly responsible for what had gone on, but he denied the imputation of collective guilt that was charged by Sigrid Undset. Every question for the Germans was like an outstretched hand; they had to be given a chance for life. "We are indeed guilty," he said, "in so far as we suffered this regime and failed to risk our lives to get rid of it. Re-education must be accomplished through self-education. The facts must be met. Four million German soldiers died for a regime that killed four million Jews. Hitler's Germany was not ours but we suffered it. The Western tradition must be regained; we have to understand history and to make it contemporary; to awaken the self-responsibility of the individual which comes through self-education." [2]

For a long time the American papers printed nothing that might jar Russian sensibilities; there were no parallels in their columns to the references in the Russian-controlled papers to Allied imperialists who consorted with Nazis and militarists and ignored the agreements of Potsdam. The *Neue Zeitung* and the others resolutely ignored any suggestion that all was not well among the Allies. The *Neue Zeitung* was nevertheless a good paper, far better than the Germans had been getting for many a year—even though it described the migration of the millions of Germans who were being driven out of Czechoslovakia, Poland, and other countries where their families had lived for centuries in a headline "Six Million Return Home."

The Americans licensed newspapers with an eye to the representation of the antifascist parties on the newspaper staffs. Among these, of course, there were Communists. Two were on the *Rhein Neckar Zeitung* as well as two on the *Frankfurter Rundschau*, and they were represented on other papers in the American zone either under the protective coloration of "Leftist" or as known party members. The American licensing board of fifteen which made the decisions on whether or not a paper

[2] *Neue Zeitung*, Oct. 25, Nov. 4, 1945.

would be permitted to publish also included two men who were later to have difficulty when American authorities became more critical of Communist influence in these positions.[3]

The Russians had established a single trade union in Berlin and they made essential supplies available to it on a large scale. As was the case with the political parties the Russians supported, the Communist trade-union organizers were provided with cars and typewriters and printing facilities, while the AF of L and other American labor men who were attempting to set up free unions in accord with the American directives had neither funds nor materials to aid non-Communist Germans. And while it was by no means unusual for a Russian or Communist organizer to be critical of his Western colleagues, no similar attitudes were tolerated by the Americans. General Clay became angered with an AF of L representative, threatening him with exile from Berlin because he described the methods by which the Russians were controlling the union movement. The American trade-unionists were reduced to importing cigarettes from the United States and selling them on the black market to help pay the expenses of the non-Communist German union they were trying to organize and to get for it the typewriters and office equipment they could not obtain from official sources.

The results of the Austrian elections of November 1945 were an unexpected blow to the Communist leaders in Berlin and necessitated a change in the party strategy. Henceforth the unity of the Social Democrats and the Communists would be preached; the Communist party would submerge its identity in the SED. The Communist leaders up to then had deluded themselves into thinking that what their own propaganda said was true—that the workers of the former Nazi-dominated countries would welcome the promises and haven of the party. Nothing of the sort happened; in Austria the Communists elected only 4 deputies, the Socialists 76, the People's party 85.

[3] One of them, Cedric Belfrage, was to be deported from the United States.

Berlin too, it soon became clear, was overwhelmingly anti-Communist. Some of the party leaders might agree on the union of the Social Democrats and the Communists, but the rank and file of the Social Democrats would have none of it. The old trade-union men, the Social Democrats of the 1920's, knew Communist tactics from the days before Hitler came to power and also from the concentration camps where the Communists had often organized the prisoners with professional skill and ruthlessness. Leaders such as Kurt Schumacher of the Social Democrats, and many in the CDU and the Liberal Democratic party as well, had no illusions about what working with the Communists meant.

On the other hand, Jakob Kaiser of the CDU, Ernst Lemmer, who had belonged to the Liberal party in the Weimar Republic, and many others hoped earnestly to build a bridge between East and West Germany and between the two worlds of East and West. In the early months of the new parties there was a genuine and widespread belief that a successful collaboration of the antifascist forces in Germany was possible. In addition there was a sense of guilt toward Russia because of the unprovoked German attack. Many of these men who had been opposed to both Hitler and his war felt a grave responsibility to attempt a reconciliation.

The four parties that had been approved in Berlin by the Russians and later by the Allied Kommandatura were united only in so far as they were by origin, definition, and conviction antifascist and were led by men who had been old and known opponents of the Nazis. The two middle-class parties—the Christian Democrats and the Liberal Democrats—had a historical relationship to the Centrist and Liberal parties of the Weimar Republic: the one with Christian principles as part of its program but, as its leaders emphasized, socialist purposes too; the Liberal Democrats also aiming to recruit the former non-Marxist voters, but on a platform without religious implications.

The Liberal Democrats favored free enterprise, education for all according to their ability, a social and political program based on broad humanistic principles. This philosophy was formulated by direct descendants of the Manchester Liberals, among them Theodor Heuss, a journalist who would later become president, and Reinhold Maier. In Berlin the summons to ratify the founding of the party was issued on July 7 by a small group that included two former ministers of the Weimar Republic.

The Christian Democratic Union was founded in Berlin by Andreas Hermes, who had been a minister during the Weimar Republic, and, among others, by Jakob Kaiser and Josef Ersing, who had been involved in the plot of July 20. Hermes and thirty-four signers issued the summons to approve the founding of the party on June 26. The declaration of principles stated that for the Nazi view, "Right is what is useful to the State," should be substituted "The people require only what is just." The state was to be subsidiary to the needs and purposes of the individuals who formed it and to the family, which is the center of the community. The right of parents to see to the education of their children was affirmed. The ownership of private property was approved, but property was to be held only with due regard to the public welfare, and the party favored a modified land reform. Workers were assured the right to work; they were held equal in status to employers, as were women to men. With an eye to the past electoral weakness of the Catholic Center party even in Catholic communities, the separation of church and state was emphasized. The CDU was intended to be and has largely remained an alliance of Catholics and Protestants.

The Social Democrats had by far the biggest representation when the party summons was issued in Berlin by Max Fechner, Otto Grotewohl, and twelve others, some of whom, including Erich Ollenhauer, later leader of the party, had returned from exile. Grotewohl favored close relations with the Communists, agreeing with them that the tragic division of the workers during the Weimar Republic had enabled Hitler to come to power. Grotewohl would soon be one of the founders of the SED, the Socialist Unity party, which, despite the elaborate ceremony of integration, was in effect the old Communist party. The Social Democratic party in general continued its former socialist program, although socialism was mentioned only three times in the party summons and Marxism had undoubtedly lost its appeal to many members. The program aimed at land reform and the nationalization of banks, insurance companies, and mineral resources. Kurt Schumacher, a dedicated opponent of communism as of Nazism, was reluctant to formulate any program because of Germany's inferior status as an object of government of the victorious powers. Schumacher had been anti-Hitler long before many in the Allied camp and was as openly contemptuous of their authoritarianism as he had been of Hitler's.

The two workers' parties, the Socialists and the Communists, were, as we have seen, the first to be licensed by the Russians; and of these two the Communists had considerable material advantages. These became liabilities, however, because the party was so evidently dependent on the Russians for them. While the Americans freely permitted the four parties to operate in their zone, they gave no support to the Christian Democratic Union or the Liberal Democratic party or the Social Democratic party against the Communists. On the contrary, under the banners of the antifascist front, Communists were well represented in important positions in the occupation; they were appointed by the Americans to local administrative posts as well as staff jobs on newspapers and in radio stations.

The Americans were the next after the Russians to stir the embers of political life in their zone. The British followed, but elections in the British and French zones were not held until the fall of 1946. By October 1945, General Clay, as Eisenhower's deputy, announced the formation of a council of ministers of the states, or *Länder*, of the American zone. He said that voting soon would take place in the villages and that there would be a free press and radio before long. By "free" he meant, of course, under Allied control; the German press would be free to express itself only in so far as it did not criticize any of the Allies or the dismantlings, requisitionings, or other programs which accompanied their governing of Germany. He repeated that the Allies did not wish to destroy Germany as an economic entity or to destroy the German people. The United States wanted demilitarization—including the destruction of German heavy industry and its war potential, and decentralization of industry. After these steps had been taken, the job of governing could be turned over to the Germans under the Allied military governments.

Beyond this, the Americans had few political prejudices. They would authorize the beginning of democratic government in a small and local way; they wished to show their good will to Soviet Russia, and it was the Left, they believed, that had emerged in virtue and triumph out of the war, as against a reactionary Right. Thus, they would not permit the establishing of a monarchist party in Bavaria, although it too would have been strongly anti-Nazi.

On October 28 the *Neue Zeitung* reported that party life was beginning again in the American zone and that there was especial activity on the Left. Socialist and Communist parties had been licensed, and Communist speakers were urging the antifascist parties to work together and get rid of the real fascism that still remained in Germany. In Munich, the paper reported, co-operation between the four parties had been decided on; in Darmstadt a common program had been announced for the Socialists and Communists. In Berlin six hundred members of the Socialist party wanted the communalizing of everything needed to provision the city; but it was doubtful, the *Neue Zeitung* said, that all the parties would be brought under one banner, and a declaration of independence for each was to be expected. The semimonthly report of the American military government declared that the Communists were unlikely to keep their present supremacy, that although the four parties were united in Berlin, such solidarity would not be demanded in the American zone. The Americans wished—despite the hunger, the dismantling, the requisitions, the arrests—to see the green shoots of a beginning democracy. But there were to be no trappings for the parties, not even armbands, and no parades.

Any party leader who came under the ban of the Russians was also an enemy of the Western powers. When the Russians forced one of the CDU leaders from his party post in Berlin, the British refused to let him undertake any political activity in their zone. Two German Communists were sentenced in the American sector for having acted against the interests of the American military government; they had been detected in efforts to further the Communists' control of the appointments and dismissals of German personnel. The Communist press burst forth with denunciation of the persecution of antifascists, and the sentences were commuted by General Clay.

American policy continued to point in two opposite directions. On the one hand, the Americans fed their enemy; they brought into Germany 500,000 tons of food in the course of the summer and autumn; they called for elections and proclaimed the responsibility of the Germans to govern themselves. There were innumerable acts of individual kindness along with brutal looting that, although on a much smaller scale, matched what the Russians were charged with. On the other hand, in the Allied discussions of the German level of industry in December, the American State Department's suggested quota on steel production was the lowest recommended by any of the four powers. The British proposed 9,000,000 tons a year, the French 7,000,-000, the Russians 4,500,000, and Washington 3,500,000. The decision in December was for 5,800,000 tons, and General Clay reports that he was rebuked by the State Department for having accepted that figure.[4]

[4] Lucius D. Clay: *Decision in Germany*, pp. 108–9.

V

THE TRIALS

As THE Nuremberg trials were about to start, the Russians moved swiftly on many fronts. The first meeting of the foreign ministers' council in September 1945 in London, which it was hoped would prepare the way for the peace treaties in Europe, failed to reach any agreement, as Moscow demanded that a control council be established for Japan similar to that in Germany. The United States, with experience of such councils in Hungary and Rumania and now in Germany too, was unwilling to repeat the experiment in the Far East. President Truman, still hoping that Stalin would be easier to deal with than Molotov, sent Harriman on a mission to see him while he was vacationing in a Black Sea resort. Stalin paid no attention to the President's inquiries about the Balkans. His first comment on Truman's letter was: "The Japanese question is not touched upon." [1]

British and American observers were barred from Yugoslavia, and there were reports that the two governments would end their recognition of the Tito regime. In Poland, although the Government of National Unity included five members of the former London Polish government, the population was reported "cowed" and the country under the complete domination of the Communist forces. By the end of October President Truman said the United States would not recognize imposed regimes,

[1] David Dallin: *Soviet Russia and the Far East*, p. 240.

and Britain's foreign secretary, Ernest Bevin, was saying the same thing on behalf of the British. In November, the month in which the trials of the major German war criminals began, there was a meeting in Madison Square Garden in New York of the National Council of American-Soviet Friendship. The speeches reflected the hope that Russia might still be persuaded of the peaceful intentions and good will of the West, but they also reflected some concern over what the Russians were doing. The meeting was attended by the Dean of Canterbury Cathedral, who had flown to New York for the occasion, by Joseph Davies, and by Under Secretary of State Dean Acheson. There were messages from Secretary of War Robert P. Patterson, Admiral Ernest J. King, General Eisenhower, and President Truman. The Under Secretary of State said what had been often stated before—mainly, no doubt for the benefit of the puzzling men in the Kremlin: that there had never been a place on the globe where the interests of the United States and Russia had clashed and there was "no objective reason to suppose that there should now or in the future be such a place." The paramount interest of both nations was peace, but this was complicated by the desire of both nations for security. The United States, Acheson said, understands "that to have friendly governments along their borders is essential both for the security of the Soviet Union and for the peace of the world. But it seems equally clear to us that the interest in security must take into account and respect other basic interests of nations and men, such as the interests of other peoples to choose the general surroundings of their lives and of all men to be secure in their persons." [2]

Acheson thought there was no greater opposition between the two countries today than in the time of Jefferson and Tsar Alexander. Both were continental countries with space for development. The goal of both was to raise the living standards of their peoples to the highest possible level.

To these words Joseph Davies added that no government or

[2] *The New York Times*, Nov. 15, 1945.

people has had a better or more consistent record of effort to preserve peace and security for mankind than the Soviet Union.[3] And General Eisenhower said that Russia was seriously trying to better the lot of the common man and that the Russians wanted the friendship of the United States.

While the Soviet was consolidating its positions in the Balkans and giving direct aid to the Greek Communists, the Moscow conference of foreign ministers which followed the London meetings was convened in December at the suggestion of the American Secretary of State. In Moscow a compromise was reached on Russian demands in the Far East. The Russians had been asking what the American troops were doing in China, where they were stationed with the full consent of the Chinese central government, while Russian troops, following the surrender of the Japanese armies, were in complete control of Manchuria and dismantling its industries. Both countries now agreed to withdraw their forces at the earliest possible moment. Russia was not to send troops to Japan, but was to have a place on the advisory commission, leaving General MacArthur's authority substantially unimpaired. A Korean government would be formed on the model of Yugoslavia and Poland—by a union of the "democratic parties"; the Soviet government could not permit free popular elections there any more than in Europe. There would be a trusteeship under Russia and the United States for five years. The Russians rejected an American proposal that the two zones above and below the 38th parallel be merged. They were kept separate and, as was the case in East Germany, Communist control was swiftly and efficiently organized in the area under Russian occupation.

Russia moved now on a world-wide front. In the Middle East a Communist uprising in Iran threatened to spread to neighboring Iraq. Germany was merely one sector of the front.

In the midst of these first reshapings of the structure of power, the four Allies met in Nuremberg in what the Americans

[3] Ibid.

especially saw as a vast symbolic act of collaboration to declare a new law for the world society of nations.

The Nuremberg indictments may be divided into two parts, different in kind if not in purpose. One part, charging the defendants with having committed war crimes and crimes against humanity, had to do with acts of violence of a monstrous kind and on a vast scale, crimes that would be punishable in any court in the Western world except perhaps those of the late Third Reich, where whatever served the cause of the race and its leader was regarded by the National Socialist judges with a benevolent eye. The other part accused the defendants of something quite different: waging aggressive warfare or conspiring to wage it.

It was by no means new in history for the victor to accuse and then kill the enemy he had defeated; there had been many such occasions, and it would not have been difficult to cite precedents, although in the West one would have had to go ba⌐k some centuries to find them. Of the two who had been called war criminals most recently, Napoleon had been neither tried nor executed, although the allies had had some hope that the French or he would take matters into their own hands; and Wilhelm II, despite being publicly charged with "supreme offences against international morality and the sanctity of treaties," had been allowed to escape punishment through asylum in Holland. But neither Napoleon nor Wilhelm could properly have been charged with methodical slaughter and tortures like those inflicted by Hitler and his men, although they might be and in fact were often accused during the course of hostilities of assaulting peaceful nations—of crimes against peace. Men charged with violating the rules of warfare had often been brought before the victors' courts,[4] but this was the first time—as Robert

[4] After World War I the British wished to try Admiral von Tirpitz, and the Belgians had Bethmann Hollweg on their list of war criminals. Altogether the Allies had some 900 names of Germans to be tried, among them Hindenburg and Ludendorff, and the right to try them in Allied courts was stipulated in the Versailles Treaty. But in fact none of these men appeared

Jackson, the chief American prosecutor, and his colleagues pointed out—that the responsible heads of a government were to be tried in court for the crime of plotting and waging war— for having committed war. This event, they said, represented moral issues of the most compelling kind, evidencing the determination of the "peace-loving" people of the world at long last to punish the international lawbreaker as they would any local marauder. The trials were the very symbol of the new international order, a United Nations in miniature, but for all the world to see and take hope from. The machinery of law was fashioned out of the disparate systems of the four powers, each yielding a measure of sovereignty and co-operating in stern but just deliberations so that the guilty would be punished and any like-minded lawbreakers would be deterred in the future.

The slow climb of mankind from violence to community, the triumph of Eros over the arrows of the destroyer—men of good will had been writing such phrases for many years, and Cordell Hull had said approximately the same thing when he denounced "treaty breakers." [5] A new law had to be stated giving effect to the world conscience of the twentieth century—a landmark in international co-operation, Jackson called it.[6]

Early in 1945 Roosevelt had asked the Secretary of State for a report on preparations for the trials that he had foreseen for

---

before any court; sixteen defendants were tried in a German court in Leipzig, six of whom were found guilty and given what was generally regarded as light sentences. All the trials involved violations of the rules of war.

[5] While there was no precedent for the criminal charges against individuals for having "committed war," there was a large body of literature on the subject of "just" and "unjust" war, beginning in antiquity and ending with Russia's being expelled from the League of Nations in 1939 for having attacked Finland in violation of the Kellogg-Briand Pact.

[6] There were elements of this kind of thinking after World War I. For example, under the terms of the Versailles Treaty, Germany paid not a war indemnity but reparations—that is, payments for illegally caused damages. The war of 1914 had been, the theory went, a war imposed upon the Allies; there had been insufficient cause for the German attack. Needless to say, this was a position that became a matter of long and inconclusive debate, but in fact few historians in the United States any longer took this view before the rise of Hitler again colored historical thinking.

many years, saying the charges should include waging aggressive warfare in violation of the Kellogg-Briand Pact. The alliances of the war were to be transformed into the peaceful co-operation of the United Nations, and, in fact, admission to the United Nations was open only to the countries that had gone to war. Thus would begin the construction of the new world order of the peace-loving nations, to which the countries that had remained at peace would later be admitted.

The Nuremberg trials were part of this grand design. Although it was the Moscow conference of 1943 which had prepared the formula, the ingredients had been brewing for a long time. In the Pact of Paris of 1928, in the Quarantine Speech of Roosevelt in 1937, in the press conferences and addresses of members of his Cabinet, the crusade against aggression was preached, the criminal nature of taking recourse to war was stated, and its perpetrators were threatened. In 1932 Stimson had declared war "illegal throughout practically the entire world. . . . It is an illegal thing." [7] Jackson in 1945 echoed the sentiments: "No political, military or other considerations justify going to war. . . . The law . . . requires that the *status quo* be not attacked by violent means." The trials, he said, were "mankind's desperate effort to apply the discipline of the law to statesmen who have used their powers . . . to attack . . . the world's peace, . . . part of the great effort to make the peace more secure." [8] The British prosecutor, Sir Hartley Shawcross, expressed the same views. "It is a fundamental part of these proceedings to establish for all time," he said, "that international law has the power . . . to declare that a war is criminal. . . ." [9] And the President of the court, Lord Justice Lawrence, one of England's foremost jurists, declared: "The trial which is now about to begin is unique in the history of the

[7] *The New York Times*, Aug. 9, 1932.
[8] *Trial of the Major War Criminals* . . . , II, 154; XIX, 399.
[9] Ibid., XIX, 448.

jurisprudence of the world and it is of supreme importance to millions of people all over the globe." [1]

Who had committed these crimes which had "no particular geographical location"—that is, were confined to no one country—and so were to be tried by an International Military Tribunal of the four powers? The German people as a whole were not guilty, said Jackson and his colleagues of the American prosecution. The concentration camps and the apparatus of coercion had been used to keep them in order too. "We know that the Nazi Party was not put in power by a majority of the German vote. We know it came to power by an evil alliance between the most extreme of the Nazi Revolutionists, the most unrestrained of the German reactionaries, and the most aggressive of the German militarists." [2] Who were the criminals? Hitler, of course, but he was dead (although Stalin told Truman he had his doubts of this). Himmler and Goebbels, too, had committed suicide, but there remained such men as Goering, Rosenberg, Ribbentrop, Streicher, who would represent the party well enough, and there were also the heads of the armed forces, the chief of propaganda, and so on. But not only those who had run the apparatus of government were to be tried; the representatives of industry and banking too, such men as Schacht and Krupp, who by producing the money and guns had also conspired against the peace, were in the dock, and the death penalty was asked for them. It was American policy to destroy German and Japanese militarism and its foundations in the large landowners and big industry as well as in the Nazi formations and the General Staff.

So the indictments of Nuremberg included the General Staff and the high command of the armed forces arraigned as criminal organizations along with the Gestapo and the SS, and they also named Gustav Krupp von Bohlen und Halbach. When a

[1] Ibid., II, 30.
[2] Ibid., pp. 102–3.

medical commission of six appointed by the court reported Herr Krupp too ill and senile to defend himself, Jackson proposed that he be tried *in absentia*, and if that proved unfeasible, that a son, Alfried Krupp (who had not been named in the indictment), be tried in his place. "Public interests, which transcend all private considerations, require that Krupp von Bohlen shall not be dismissed unless some other representative of the Krupp armament and munitions interests be substituted," he said.[3] Mr. Jackson added that he realized he might be criticized for taking this position but he was reconciled to criticism if a member of the family faced trial. "The United States respectfully submits," he said, "that no greater disservice to the future peace of the world could be done than to excuse the entire Krupp family."[4] While the British prosecutor took a more moderate view, mildly urging the trial of Gustav *in absentia*, and the French preferred to substitute Alfried, the Russians adopted the American formula: try either one. The President of the court, however, a man of great learning and conspicuous probity and fully aware of his responsibilities, questioned the prosecutors closely on the propriety of trying a man who could not understand the nature of the proceedings whether in the court or out of it. Both Jackson and Sir Hartley Shawcross admitted that Gustav could not have been tried in the United States or in England under the circumstances, but the rules of Nuremberg were different in their opinion. A Krupp was needed, senile or not. In the end Gustav was not tried, although the Tribunal held the possibility in reserve should his health improve, and Alfried was brought before a later American court, where he was sentenced to twelve years in prison and confiscation of his property.

This view of guilt by category was deeply, and no doubt honestly, shared by Stalin, who, to Winston Churchill's surprise, wanted trials for the major German war criminals. For Stalin

[3] Ibid., I, 134.
[4] Ibid., p. 138.

the successful revolution could come to Germany or any other country only by rooting out the representatives of the old order and their sources of power in industry and the land. One of the great public trials, whether at Nuremberg or Moscow or Belgrade, merely dramatized these necessities—there could be no question of the guilt of the accused, only of what use could be made of it as propaganda.[5]

Men like General Vlasov were hanged without ceremony or visible preliminary; it was only in the satellite countries, *de facto* or to be—in Yugoslavia, where Draza Mihailovich was sentenced to death, in Poland and Czechoslovakia—that long, well-publicized public trials were held.[6] For the Americans, though, the trials had a conspicuous place in the character of the one world they were intent on building. The United States was not only the host nation at Nuremberg; newly converted to the doctrines of collective security, American spokesmen were far more zealous than those of any other country in expressions of faith and hope on its behalf and in praise of the moral virtues of the trials.[7] Up and down the land it was said that now at

[5] In June 1945, months before the start of the trial, the Soviet judge-to-be, Nikichenko, told his Western colleagues: "We are dealing here with the chief war criminals who have already been convicted and whose conviction has been already announced by both the Moscow and Crimea declarations" (Whitney R. Harris: *Tyranny on Trial*, p. 16). All the Tribunal needed to do was to determine the measure of guilt and pass sentences. Nor were the British always as aloof as the proceedings of the trials might indicate. A British *aide-mémoire* to Judge Rosenman before the trials were agreed upon said that Hitler and Mussolini should be killed; there should be a preliminary trial, but there were dangers in a long and elaborate trial to which the British public would react adversely. "Our work," said the British representative Sir David Maxwell Fyfe, "is to see these top-notch Nazis tried, condemned, and many of them executed" (Robert H. Jackson: *Report*, Department of State Pub. 3080, pp. 340–4). Sir David was later on the prosecution staff.

[6] In 1943 the Free Germany Committee, as one of its goals, had announced from Moscow the trials of war criminals but amnesty for all those who broke with Hitler in time to aid the liberation of Germany; whether a German general was a danger to the state depended solely on his attitude toward the Soviet.

[7] Walter Lippmann compared the trials to the Magna Carta, *habeas corpus*, and the Bill of Rights; *The New York Times* wrote editorials that

last the United States was where it belonged; not only was it to be a pillar of the United Nations, but also a law was being proclaimed which would make plain even to the blindest isolationists the iniquities of the past. These were the black deeds of the men on trial and, in a sense, of the United States itself, which had let Nazism flower when it had withdrawn from Europe and repudiated the League. The trials were a visible sign that gas ovens and aggressive warfare were of the same essence, and also that this time the United States was in Europe and in the world as a mighty force to keep the peace against any rising of Germany or Japan. A peace under law.

In June 1945, meeting with his staff and British colleagues in London, Jackson proposed the agenda of Nuremberg, and the court procedures that would have to take account of continental law and Anglo-Saxon law were worked out. The Russians joined the later meetings and made a number of suggestions that the others found useful about the division of labor among the prosecution, and one of their number and a member of the French staff became judges of the court they had helped to establish. Lord Justice Lawrence was appointed President of the Tribunal; the American judge was a former Attorney General, Francis Biddle; the alternate, John J. Parker, was a judge from North Carolina. There were four justices, one from each of the main victorious powers, with four alternates. For a death sentence three votes were required.

There were twenty-one defendants in the Nuremberg prison —the Palace of Justice. Twenty-three had been scheduled to be tried, but Robert Ley, leader of the German Labor Front, killed himself before the trial started, leaving a letter in which he said that anti-Semitism had been the undoing of them all and asking for a reconciliation with the Jews. Bormann, who could not be

---

repeated the sentiments of Jackson; President Truman thought the trials were blazing a new trail to international justice; the Attorney General felt that they represented the highest level of objective justice; one admirer called Jackson's presentation "one of the great state papers of history."

found, was tried *in absentia*. The military men were deprived of their rank and status because the Geneva convention stipulated that officers could not be put in solitary confinement. All the prisoners were kept under strict discipline: no talking was allowed during the noonday meal; they had to sleep at night so their hands and faces were always visible, and their guards were to wake them up if they turned. There were extraordinary security regulations; the prisoners marched in groups of four from their cells to the court; at two check points their arrival was telephoned ahead; and every spectator in the courtroom was screened and searched by the MP's.[8] The prisoners were defended by German lawyers, not by Americans as in Japan. There were one lawyer and an associate for each, but, again for security reasons, they were not allowed to be alone with their clients (this regulation was relaxed in the case of the German doctor who visited each man daily); the accused and their counsel had to meet, at first twelve or fourteen at a time, in a small room where concentration and privacy were hard to come by. Later a second room provided with a typewriter could be used, where the lawyers talked with their clients seated on opposite sides of a heavily wired window. For the prosecution the Americans had a staff of 634, the British, French, and Russians each about as many. The German lawyers appeared in legal robes,[9] as did the judges, except for the Russian, who wore his Army uniform. The prosecution dressed in civilian clothes or Army uniforms. One of the Russians first appeared in the uniform of the Red Army, but as the trial progressed he gained weight and changed to civilian clothes. The translation system enabled the defendants to hear testimony even in foreign languages almost simultaneously through earphones. Once at the start of the trial

[8] Some of the wives of the prisoners succeeded in getting into the Palace of Justice—Frau Jodl as a lawyer's assistant, and two others, one of whom got into the courtroom itself and with an almost imperceptible motion of her umbrella sent a greeting to her husband.

[9] There was one exception, Otto Kranzbühler, who wore his German naval uniform. He was a career officer and a judge in the Navy.

these were connected with the microphones at the judges' bench; this was soon discovered and the circuit turned off.

The prisoners were fed plain fare by ordinary standards—certainly by the standards they had been accustomed to in their days of power—but it was more substantial and nourishing than what the ordinary Germans were eating outside. A watery soup, vegetables, potatoes, sometimes even powdered eggs and coffee. Goering lost weight, and his operatic figure became shrunken under the plain uniform he wore. Civilian clothes were made for all the prisoners who needed them. These were put on an hour before the men marched to trial and taken off as soon as they returned to their cells.[1]

The court was in session from ten a.m. until five p.m., with two ten-minute breaks and a lunch hour; in the dock the prisoners were allowed to talk together as long as they did not disturb the proceedings. At first they had to be in bed by ten o'clock; later the hour was changed to eleven. For exercise on the first day of the trial they were taken to the dusty, unused prison gymnasium with its basketball hoops and other incongruous paraphernalia of sport. It was there that the executions of those condemned by the court would take place some ten months later. On fair days they walked in the prison courtyard, but were not allowed to converse. Talking between the prisoners was forbidden at all times, even in the showers, where they went two at a time. The one exception was the courtroom. They had to keep moving during their periods in the prison yard;

[1] The prisoners were at first objects of great curiosity to visitors as well as to Allied authorities (one American general sent Goering a present of cigarettes). They were asked for their autographs; Fritzsche reported that he complied but not until his callers wrote "nonsense" across the copy of the indictment that appeared on the souvenir folder they brought. The defendants were given psychological examinations that included intelligence tests. On these Streicher, who had made a career as a professional anti-Semite, was low with 106, and Schacht highest with 143. Goering and Doenitz had scores of 138. (G. M. Gilbert: *Nuremberg Diary*, p. 31.) They were allowed all the writing materials they wanted, and Hess, who thought the sugar given him was poisoned, was seen to write endlessly but always destroyed what he had written.

when one of them spotted a four-leaf clover in a patch of grass and stopped to pick it, it was taken away by a guard.[2]

The emotions that the barbarism of the Nazi government had aroused in every country, including the neutrals, were powerful witnesses at the trials.[3] With the end of hostilities a great weight had been lifted from the conscience of the entire world. The Swedish foreign minister congratulated the Allies, expressing the gratitude of his country for their victory. Now not only were the guns silent, but also the apparatus of terror—of the concentration camps and the ghetto cities—was smashed; and the trials brought the whole nightmare story to light.

More than 6,500,000 foreigners had been brought to Germany as forced laborers; there had been slaughter and plunder on a scale to match the huge armies and technical apparatus that made the war itself unique in the speed and mass of its destruction. Some 12,000,000 people had been done to death, it was estimated, 2,500,000 men, women, and children at Auschwitz murdered or starved, killed in gas ovens or motor vans especially designed for the purpose; 1,500,000 at Maidanek.[4] So great was the press of these enemies of the Third Reich bound for the slaughter pens that they often had to be lulled into a sense of security so that they could be handled

[2] These restrictions can undoubtedly be ascribed to the security requirements for major prisoners on trial for their lives. There is no evidence of physical mistreatment of the accused while they were in this prison, although some of the guards played practical jokes. One of them fashioned a toy gibbet, which he showed each prisoner in turn; another, who admired Goering's boots and wanted to buy them, told him he wouldn't need them where he was going.

[3] According to polls, the German people overwhelmingly thought the defendants guilty, and so even did many of the accused. Ley in the note he had left spoke of their guilt. Frank, who had been governor general of occupied Poland, said: "A thousand years will pass and still this guilt of Germany will not have been erased" (Trial, XII, 13).

[4] These figures were scaled down by later estimates. The Auschwitz killings were calculated at under a million; those of all the exterminations between 4,194,200 and 4,581,200 (Gerald Reitlinger: The Final Solution, pp. 460, 501).

expeditiously. At the railroad station at Treblinka outside Warsaw, signs were put up to suggest that it was some central ship-
ping-point—to Vienna, Berlin—but the prisoners were going no
farther, for this was an extermination camp. At another camp
the transports were met at the station by an orchestra dressed in
costumes of white and blue and playing romantic music—the
"Barcarolle," the "Merry Widow"—and then the prisoners were
marched to the gas chambers. Of the estimated 2,500,000 to
3,500,000 Jews in Poland at the beginning of the war there
were 100,000 left in 1944; of the 9,600,000 Jews in Europe, 60 per
cent were dead, Jackson said—4,000,000 of them in the concentration camps. And the fury of the Nazis had not been confined to the Jews; the Russians and the Poles too had been
slaughtered—for sabotage, in reprisal for partisan attacks,
for being alleged Communists. Here is Himmler on the subject
—part of a speech he made in Posen on October 4, 1943, to the
SS generals:

> What happens to the Russians, the Czechs, does not inter-
> est me in the slightest. What the nations can offer in the
> way of good blood of our type we will take, if necessary, by
> kidnapping their children and raising them here with us.
> Whether the other nations live in prosperity or starve to
> death interests me only so far as we need them as slaves of
> our culture; otherwise, it is of no interest to me. Whether
> 10,000 Russian females fall down from exhaustion while
> digging an anti-tank ditch or not interests one only insofar
> as the anti-tank ditch for Germany is finished.[5]

[5] *Trial,* III, 406. German experts on the Eastern territories were appalled
at the stupid savagery of the Gestapo, the SS, and the Einsatz Commandos
(a murderous special service). Seventy-five per cent of the Russians, one observer said, had welcomed the advancing German troops as liberators in the
first year of the war, but after experiencing the occupation, the public beat-
ings that Bormann and the Führer said were necessary to keep the population in subjection, they fled to the partisan bands or gladly joined the passive
resistance of an enemy population (*Trial,* XXV, 344). The NKVD, these
people said, had done their murdering in the cellars—the Russian population accepted the brutal facts of life in a police state—but this public butch-

One order in the Ukraine had read:

> To Sicherheitsdienst officers: When searching villages, or when it becomes necessary to burn down villages, the whole population will be put at the disposal of the commissioner by force. As a rule no more children will be shot. . . . If we limit harsh measures . . . for the time being it is only done for the following reason . . . The most important thing is the recruitment of workers.[6]

Frank had said: "Gentlemen, I must ask you to arm yourselves against all feeling of pity. We must annihilate the Jews."[7] The entire Polish economy, he had confided to his diary in 1939, was to be run at the absolute minimum for existence. The Poles were to be the slaves of the Greater German World Empire. Any non-Germans hindering the reconstruction necessary for the prosecution of the war would be killed. . . . And so they were; on the grounds that all Jews were the deadly enemies of the Reich, the Einsatzgruppen had killed 135,000 in the Baltic states in three months. In 1941 the Gestapo ordered the execution of all Russian POW's who were dangerous to the Nazi overlords or who might become so. As Bormann said, "The Slavs are to work for us. In so far as we don't need them, they may die."[8]

There was a German report in September 1942 on the destruction of the "partisan-infested" village of Borysovka. All the inhabitants were shot with the exception of five families; in all, 49 men, 97 women, and 23 children were killed. By far the most

---

ery and degradation made them look back even on Bolshevism with nostalgia. Hundreds of thousands of people were homeless in the East not because of the tides of battle but because they were being punished.

[6] *Trial*, I, 245.

[7] Ibid., III, 538.

[8] Ibid., V, 332. Prisoners and foreign workers were used as hangmen, and for this the going rate was three cigarettes. The Einsatz Commandos, who were sometimes depressed after their return from an expedition, were given light therapy through explanations that their deeds had been for the benefit of their own people (ibid., XXVIII, 46, 47).

difficult part of the action, the report said, was getting the cattle away to be driven to the neighboring village—that had taken a lot of time.[9]

A decree of February 6, 1943, called up all inhabitants of the Eastern territories between the ages of fourteen and sixty-five for forced labor.[1] Sauckel, one of the defendants who had had charge of the forced labor, was quoted as having said in 1944 that of 5,000,000 foreign workers not 200,000 had come voluntarily.[2] Work as the war progressed became even more important than the "final solution" of the racial problem; Himmler came to admit that the leadership had underestimated the importance of labor in the early days of the war. Now this miscalculation was corrected. But those marked for forced labor who couldn't work were killed. That is one of the reasons why so many children were sent to the gas ovens—they had little to contribute to the war effort or to the economy. Many of their elders were, on the other hand, reported as making useful suggestions for improving production in the factories where they worked.

If Russian POW's couldn't work, they might be executed too —at Mauthausen 4,000 were killed as unfit for labor. According to an order of the Führer, political commissars serving with the troops were not to be recognized as POW's but were to be killed (the Army generals testified they had disregarded this order),[3] and where partisans appeared all the people of the neighbor-

[9] *Trial,* XXXIX, 374.

[1] According to one directive, children as young as 8 years old were to be sent to forced labor in Germany and some 50,000 between the ages of 10 and 14 were brought to the Reich to be allotted to German tradesmen as apprentices; at the end of two years they would be skilled workers—and in addition, the official statement pointed out, the biological potential of the enemy would be reduced (*Trial,* III, 407).

[2] Ibid., II, 139.

[3] Later inquiries have disclosed that the troops, for the most part, knew nothing of the order. The high command, however, issued this "Commissar Order," as it was called, on direct command of Hitler. When it was ignored or sabotaged, it was because of the revulsion of the field commanders. Hitler was obliged to countermand it in May 1942 after it had been in force for a year.

hood were held accountable; their houses might be burned down, and the population transported or killed.[4]

Next to the Russians the French were most numerous among prisoners of war and forced laborers in Germany. And of 250,-000 French men and women deported for racial or political reasons only 35,000 survived, according to the French prosecutor François de Menthon. The German decree for forced labor in France and Belgium was issued on October 6, 1942, for men between the ages of eighteen and fifty and for spinsters between the ages of twenty-one and twenty-five. In 1944 men between sixteen and sixty and women between eighteen and forty-five were subject to call. In 1943 there were 1,340,000 French workers in Germany: 605,000 from the civilian population—of whom 44,000 were women—and 735,000 prisoners of war. Up to 1945, 722,950 French had been deported to Germany.

The Dutch deportations, which amounted to 99,600 in 1940, were 99,900 in 1941; 162,800 in 1942; 148,900 in 1943; and went down to 20,000 in 1944—a total of over a half-million. The stories were much the same for the other occupied countries; hostages were killed at rates that varied between five to one and one hundred to one for the killing of a German soldier by the Resistance; in addition, especially as the German military situation worsened, there were wholesale reprisals against entire communities.

Neanderthal man had stepped out of his glass case at the Bonn museum, and he and his tribe had taken over the weapons and techniques of modern Europe. The trials disclosed brutal experiments that tested how far oxygen could be reduced before a man died, how much cold a man could endure, tests of the speed and efficiency of killing with bullets containing aconite, blood-clotting tests made by amputating or shooting.

[4] There was to be no possibility of any but German military power up to the Urals. West of this range there was to be no heavy industry in Russia, and not even technical training was to be given the Poles—these people were the creatures of the master race.

Not one of these, with the possible exception of the freezing experiments (which were followed by a variety of bizarre methods of warming up the victim again by means of water and animal heat), had the slightest scientific value. Like the Hitler state itself, they gave sadists opportunities they would not have had in other societies and times. But here the race alone counted, and the race, its purposes, and its laws were what the Führer said they were. German TB patients, people suffering from chronic diseases, the allegedly insane were subject to the same laws of extermination which governed the decisions on the Russians, Poles, Jews, and the others.

And nothing was too good for the party leaders. For Goering's sake the art collections of the Jews were ransacked—the plundering of the Rothschild collection was even declared to be a boon for Europe, since the treasures were thus kept from going outside the continent. The loot poured in from France, Holland, Russia—there were paintings by Rembrandt, Frans Hals, Goya, Velazquez. One report mentions 29 shipments consisting of 137 freight cars, with 4,174 crates brought to the Reich. The inventory was incomplete, but so far 21,903 *objets d'art* had been counted: 5,281 paintings, 684 miniatures, 2,477 pieces of furniture of historical value, 5,825 pieces of porcelain, bronze. . . . Books were brought in by the carload, 40,000 from their Jewish owners in Paris, 160,000 from Amsterdam. It had been a special duty for the Rosenberg Einsatz Commando charged with collecting and "safeguarding" art to call to Goering's attention any objects that might interest him. In all, 674 trains had been needed to move the plunder, including 27,000 freight cars.[5]

There was plundering of a less aesthetic kind too. The so-called Reinhardt Action in Poland yielded from the Jews before they were taken to the extermination camps over thirty pounds of platinum, tons of gold and silver, thousands of watches, rings, over a million dollars in American money—all that a

[5] *Trial*, XXVI, 527; VII, 64.

harassed people had managed to salvage after the years of war; and after they were killed the gold teeth were pried out of their mouths. Nothing had been overlooked; the so-called Nacht und Nebel decrees had been designed to keep the families of prisoners in a state of constant anxiety—the prisoner simply disappeared, and his family was not told where he had been taken, or if or when he had been killed. *Angst* for everyone, everywhere, day and night. When Dutch railway workers struck, Hitler wanted them killed along with any other passive resisters among the population.

"A thousand years will pass and still this guilt of Germany will not have been erased. . . ." [6] This was the story of half the indictment, a story of vast and unimaginable criminality, and the court heard it from the lips of eyewitnesses, from the methodical records kept by the Nazi bureaucracy, from inmates who had survived the camps, and from their guards; they saw it in photographs and moving pictures. Millions of words of testimony were heard; the proofs were unassailable. For those who had carried out these crimes—the actual perpetrators—trials were already going on or were soon to come at Dachau, at Belsen, in Prague and Warsaw and many other places. There was evidence, there were witnesses enough to hang them twenty times over. And as for those in the dock at Nuremberg, Sir Hartley Shawcross, the British prosecutor, wanted all twenty-one of them hanged as common murderers, and in this view he was joined enthusiastically by his colleagues.[7] But Jackson, who had opened the case of the prosecution with a speech lasting five and a half hours, accused the defendants of the gravest crime of all. He made the charge of conspiracy to commit ag-

6 Ibid., XII, 13.
7 The death penalty was asked for all of them: for Hess, who had made his insane flight to England in 1940, and who, although he told the court he had been feigning amnesia, told also of the conspirators still pursuing him, of the strange eyes of his doctor and visitors; for Schacht, who had been in a Nazi concentration camp; for von Papen, who had been in Turkey during the war; for the admirals; and for the relatively unknown Fritzsche, who had been head of German broadcasting.

gressive warfare—the crime that, in his opinion, underlay all the others—and this crime he thought had been committed not only by the men in the dock but by organizations such as the General Staff and the high command, which time and again had plotted against the peace and independence of other nations and now at last would meet their judges and their punishment in the grim resolution of the aggrieved and also the victorious powers. To find the General Staff not guilty, he said, would be a graver miscarriage of justice even than freeing the defendants; it was the center, the kingpin that held them all together. The German war plan antedated Hitler; it was the means of imposing Germany's will on the world.[8] So the Army was on trial along with purely party organizations—the Gestapo, the Sicherheitsdienst or SD, the SS, the SA, ranging in their membership from forty in the Reich cabinet to millions who had been in the major party formations. Altogether the German counsel calculated that seven million Germans were involved; the prosecution, allowing for duplications, said only two or three million.

Jackson was developing the proposition that war had become illegal during the twenties and thirties, that the court was merely stating the law which already existed in treaties and in public opinion. He had to point out, however, at the very start of the proceedings, that naming Latvia, Lithuania, and Estonia in the indictment as being within the boundaries of the Soviet Union did not mean that the United States recognized this state of affairs. Such recognition would clearly have violated the Stimson doctrine as well as other essential articles of faith of the American case against the Germans. Then there was the matter of defining the aggressor; the ugly term had long been used against

[8] Telford Taylor, of the American prosecution staff, summed up this view: "Characteristics of German military leaders are deep and permanent. Their philosophy is so perverse that they regard a lost war and a defeated and prostrate Germany as a glorious opportunity to start again on the same terrible cycle. We are at grips with something big and evil and durable that was not born in '33 or even in 1921" (*Trial*, XXII, 294, 295).

one of the powers on the Tribunal and would soon be used by the same power against the other three now sitting in judgment. The Russian prosecutor had a characteristically forthright solution for the problem: simply call the criminal acts "aggression . . . carried out by the European Axis." But since this expedient was too plain for the sensibilities of his colleagues, "aggressor" was never defined.[9] Yet in effect it was the Russian definition that was adopted. Aggression was precisely those acts which the Axis had committed—although the definition was never written down.[1]

The Russians themselves used the word freely. "On September 1 the Fascist aggressors invaded Polish territory, in treacherous violation of existing treaties," declared the Soviet prosecutor. Questioning Fritzsche, he asked whether he thought Germany justified in this, and Fritzsche was able to reply that at the time he took the same view of the matter that the Russian government then had, a view which had been thoroughly represented in all the Russian newspapers. This was the only way that

[9] Jackson: *Report*, Pub. 3080, p. 327.

[1] In the meetings preliminary to the start of the trial the Russians and French took a view quite different from Jackson's. The French delegate to the London meetings, Professor Gros, told him bluntly: "We do not consider as a criminal violation . . . a war of aggression. If we declare war a criminal act of individuals, we are going farther than the actual law" (Jackson: *Report*, Pub. 3080, p. 295). Jackson replied at some length, summing up the American position in the course of the long discussions over aggression and its definition: "Our attitude . . . ," he said, "was based on the proposition that this was an illegal war from the moment that it was started, and that therefore, without losing our rights as neutrals or non-belligerents, it was our right to extend aid to the nations under illegal attack, and the lend lease program, the exchange of bases for destroyers, and much of American policy was based squarely on the proposition that a war of aggression is outlawed (Jackson: *Report*, Pub. 3080, p. 299). . . . And throughout the efforts to extend aid to the peoples that were under attack, the justification was made by the Secretary of State, by the Secretary of War, Mr. Stimson, by myself as Attorney General, that this war was illegal from the outset and hence we were not doing an illegal thing in extending aid to peoples who were unjustly and unlawfully attacked. . . . We want this group of nations to stand up and say, as we have said to our people, as President Roosevelt said to the people, as members of the cabinet said to the people, that launching a war of aggression is a crime and that no political or economic situation can justify it" (ibid., p. 384).

historical facts known to everyone in the courtroom could be referred to.

There could be no inquiry into British plans for invading Norway, nor into possible American acts of aggression in the Atlantic before the United States entered the war, nor into the landing of American forces in Africa against the garrisons of the French, with whom the United States was not at war—in order, as Mr. Roosevelt said at the time, "to forestall an invasion of Africa by Germany and Italy, which if successful would constitute a threat to America across the comparatively narrow sea from Western Africa. . . ."[2] The defense counsel could not ask whether the Russians had joined the Germans in Poland a few days after September 1, 1939. Witnesses could refer to the secret clauses of the German-Russian agreement of August 23, 1939, but these could not be introduced as a document. No questions could be asked Paulus, coming from his captivity in the East, about the treatment of German POW's or of the forced laborers. When the Russian prosecutor said that there had been systematic plunder of private property by the Germans, which was true, the German counsel were not able to ask him about Russian practices in such matters. There could be no quotations from a report of the German embassy on the mistreatment of Germans in Poland before the war. "We are here to try the major war criminals; we are not here to try any of the signatory powers," said the President of the court when the German counsel attempted to bring in evidence of this kind.[3] Any Allied paper was a document for the court, as was any German paper that had been captured by the Allies. But things were different for the Germans.

Aggression was what the Germans had committed. In Jackson's and the court's thinking, it could have no historical background. The defense was not allowed to go into details about

[2] Quoted in Wilbourn E. Benton and George Grimm, eds.: *Nuremberg: German Views of the War Trial*, p. 115.
[3] *Trial*, IX, 685.

the Versailles Treaty, or about any Allied blunders and mis-
calculations that might have helped bring Hitler to power. It
could make no case against England for the mining of Norwe-
gian territorial waters before the German invasion, although
Winston Churchill had called that a major offensive operation
of war. It could not go into Allied plans for the invasion of
Greece, or the bombing of the Ploesti oil fields before Rumania
was a belligerent, nor take up any Allied breach of the customs
of war. Hitler's orders to shoot captured commandos, and their
subsequent executions, were carefully gone into, but the Germans could not ask what had happened to German commandos
captured by the Allies. The German bombing of Belgrade could
be testified to, but not the American bombing of Dresden in
1945, a city hitherto unscathed and therefore filled with refugees,
where in a single night twice as many had been killed as at
Hiroshima. The Russians a few years later were to use this episode as evidence for the Germans of the brutal kinds of war
crimes to which the Americans were prone.[4]

The trials were conducted with remarkable fairness, given the
circumstances, but the inner contradictions bobbed to the surface on many occasions. When the Chief Justice of the United
States Supreme Court died, the President of the Tribunal asked
Jackson if he would not like to say a few words; he was sure that
Jackson's American colleagues on the bench, Justices Biddle
and Parker, would like to observe the occasion too.[5] On the

[4] Since politics are more important than law in determining an aggressor,
no one in the courtroom could have dreamed of accusing the Russians of
attacking Japan a few months earlier without visible cause. Yet Japan had
repeatedly asked Russia during the last year of the war to act as intermediary
in arranging for the discussion of peace terms with the United States and
Great Britain. Stalin casually mentioned the overtures at Potsdam and then
joined the war, giving as his reason the obligations he had to his Allies and
the charter-to-be of the UN. Nor, as has been suggested, was anyone in the
courtroom likely to be concerned with the legal question of aggression arising
out of the convoying of Allied ships and the attempted sinkings of German
submarines by American destroyers while the United States was still at peace
with Germany.

[5] Ibid., XII, 97.

other hand, Lawrence was bleakly courteous toward the defense lawyers and toward the defendants; to the counsel for Papen he said: "As you know perfectly well, this is not the time to put questions on behalf of Von Papen. You have had your opportunity, and you have not done it"; [6] of Ribbentrop he remarked that "this exaggerated going into detail" wouldn't help the defendant's case, in his opinion; [7] to the counsel for the SA, Hitler's former brown shirts: "We will hear no more from you"; while to the French prosecutor he explained: "I mean, of course, we do not doubt for an instant what you say is true, but at the same time it is not the correct way to do it." [8] He was equally courteous to Jackson, asking whether he would mind letting the defendant's counsel have a look at some documents: "If you tell the Tribunal that there was no such agreement, the Tribunal will of course accept that." [9] Toward the Germans he was polite, but there was an edge to his correctness. And he patently wished the trials to move along. One of the German counsel pointed out that the court had granted two days for the Americans to present their side, and one day for the Russians, while he was given one day to answer both.[1] But Lawrence allowed Goering to testify at considerable length and over Jackson's vehement objections that Goering was turning the proceedings into a forum for Nazi propaganda.

Jackson was very quickly a prisoner of his own formulas of

[6] *Trial*, X, 221.
[7] Ibid., p. 278.
[8] Ibid., VII, 30.
[9] Ibid., II, 436.
[1] Outside the walls of the Palace of Justice things were more summary. A German witness called by the prosecution to testify against one of the defendants testified instead in his favor, and was promptly clapped into jail although he had come to Nuremberg a free man. Relatives of the men on trial were arrested. Prisoners were held incommunicado, in many cases without knowing the charges against them. They were subject to ethnic if not racial laws: "No German may do this . . . Germans may only do this. . . ." But they were helped, too. Some food was supplied by the Allies, some encouragement. The crime of being a German was not so long-lived nor was it ever so hopeless as the crime of having been a Jew.

lawbreaking, and Goering had little trouble pointing out the inconsistencies. For example, there was Jackson's cross-examination on German mobilization plans. These included in the mid-thirties what the Germans called clearing the Rhine—i.e., getting the Rhine free of commercial traffic so that war supplies and troops could move freely. Jackson thought this operation referred to the freeing not of the Rhine but of the Rhineland, and asked Goering why, if he was opposed to war, he had not made these German plans public. Goering replied by asking whether the United States customarily made its mobilization plans a matter of general knowledge. Again, Goering testified that he had been opposed to the attack on Russia, and Jackson asked him why, if that was true, he had not either broken with Hitler or appealed to the German people. Goering replied that if he had resigned every time he and Hitler had disagreed their relationship would have ended years before, and he asked Jackson when in history a soldier in time of war had made an appeal to the people over the head of his commander in chief. When Jackson alluded to the iniquities of the V-2, Goering, referring to the Allied devastation of German cities, said: "Thank God, we still had one weapon that we could use";[2] and when there were references to the depredations of the Germans, Goering could point at the dismantlings and confiscations then going on in Germany.

During the days when the trials were being held the Russians were busily consolidating their hold on the countries they had occupied, were gutting German factories, transporting German technicians from Berlin: three thousand it was estimated were seized, given two and a half hours to pack, and sent off to the East. In accordance with the Yalta agreement, the Russians were using slave labor of millions of German and other prisoners of war and civilians. And not only the Russians. In Czechoslovakia all Germans over ten and under sixty were to do forced

[2] *Trial*, IX, 431.

labor. Millions of Germans who had no part in the creation or maintenance of Hitler's Reich were being driven from their homes, where their families had lived for centuries, for no other crime than being of German descent. The French were getting thousands of Germans from American POW camps, and these men were treated in such a fashion that American officers compared them with the emaciated inmates the Allies had liberated from Dachau. If this was related to the actions of the Nazis, that was a defense the German counsel were unable to make on behalf of their clients. None of these questions could be investigated. *Tu quoque* was no answer, the court said.[3]

Jackson was to say some years later (1948) that the trials showed that an international criminal trial can be successfully conducted. That, he had come to believe, might be more important than any other feature of the Nuremberg experience. This was something, but something less than Magna Carta. In so far as the court continued an operation of war by peaceful means against the common enemy, what Jackson said was undoubtedly true. Even the murders in the Katyn forest could be solemnly laid to the Germans by the Russians, and witnesses produced, although there were people on the Allied side who knew how flimsy the Russian case was and how strong the evi-

---

[3] It was hard for the Germans to find answers. The predominantly Anglo-Saxon legal procedures were unfamiliar to them. Under German law, defense counsel are supposed to be seeking for the truth of the matter, as are the prosecutors and the judges—and one of the German counsel explained to the court that he, too, had lost everything in the war, his family, everything he owned; what, he asked, would be his motive in shielding the guilty? The records of the trial are filled with protests against the Allies submitting documents and quoting from them without the German defense counsel being able to get copies. Even when the court intervened, they were often unable to get the material—perhaps owing to the enormous technical job of translating and mimeographing which had to be done by the Allies. But the submission of documents from the German side had to be approved either by the prosecution or by the Tribunal before they could be translated into four languages and mimeographed. So it was difficult for the German lawyers to surprise witnesses appearing against their clients with unexpected disclosures —something that was not true for the prosecution. The Germans were being constantly surprised by documents they could not see beforehand.

dence against them.[4] But neither Russian responsibility for the Katyn murders nor the crimes of anyone save Germany troubled the court. The French prosecutor, too, praised the perfect collaboration.

Until the verdicts came in. Three of the defendants got away, to the intense indignation of the Russians and Jackson: Schacht, who was denounced but found not guilty because he had broken in time with Hitler; Fritzsche, who had replaced the dead Goebbels in the dock because he was the chief of German broadcasting; and Papen, who had been out of the country during most of the war. In addition the SA was found to be no criminal organization because it had largely ceased operations by the mid-thirties, the Reich cabinet because it had met so seldom, and the General Staff and the high command because they were not organizations in the technical sense. The court upbraided the men who had disgraced the profession of arms, and it called the General Staff a ruthless military caste—but that was all.[5] Eleven of the defendants were condemned to death

[4] Roosevelt had been informed of the materials the Poles had collected on the subject and had waved it aside as German propaganda. The Polish government in London had known who the executioners were, and Churchill too had been told the story but had merely remarked that if the Poles were dead, nothing that could be done now would bring them back to life. In January 1946 General Clay sent Jackson a confidential report that had come from the American embassy in Warsaw telling of the doubts Poles were expressing about German guilt. But Jackson took the position that "we would keep hands off and leave the entire contest to the Soviet and German lawyers" (Harris: *Tyranny on Trial*, p. 252).

[5] The total state here, as in Russia, had protected itself against all comers. Among 800 General Staff officers the mortality off the field of battle was very high; some 150 died on the "inner front" of Germany. Of the field marshals, only 2 lasted for the entire war; 3 were executed or committed suicide, 2 were killed in action, and 7 were dishonorably discharged. Of 36 colonel generals, 22 were dismissed, 3 hanged, and 21 discharged with ignominy. In many—though not enough—ways the Army had been Hitler's most powerful opponent. Although an order of the high command in 1941 had said that the enemy was not the Russian people but the Jewish Bolshevik conspiracy, on the whole the German Army had behaved as decently as any other toward enemy populations. In later years General Eisenhower was to announce formally to the German people that the Army had retained its honor.

The shooting of hostages, as was to be made clear in later trials, was a

and seven to long terms of imprisonment. Of these the mildest sentence was ten years; the longest, life. Hess, who had been indicted on only two of the four counts—conspiring to wage aggressive warfare and waging it—got life. He said some words about the conspiracy against him and the strange eyes looking at him, and then was taken off to Spandau with the others who were neither executed nor freed by the court. At Spandau the four powers continued to collaborate formally in running the prison, each taking its turn as jailor of the month, keeping guard over the men who committed the crimes of which the Western powers and the Russians each have accused the other over many years. Spandau is all that is left of the perfect collaboration. Of the others found guilty, Goering succeeded in committing suicide, and ten were hanged.[6] The trial had been one of the longest in history—it had lasted 216 days, ending on October 1, 1946; ten million words had been printed in the record, there were five million words of testimony, tons of documents had been processed. All this as befitted the landmark in history it was claimed to be.

What kind of landmark was it? To assert a new international law unrelated to the political facts of the postwar period, to project in the figures of impartial judges the features of the four policemen—with France replacing China; to pronounce upon acts of which at least one member of the Tribunal was itself conspicuously guilty, and, what is perhaps worse, whose guilt was known to everyone in the courtroom, was not to deal with the

---

terrible but legal expedient. Counsel for German defendants were eventually able to cite British and American military manuals on the subject, declaring the killing of hostages indispensable as a last resource. And even the methods of fighting submarine warfare were not specifically German. The *Judgment* of the Tribunal pointed out that British orders had called for the sinking on sight of any ship in the Skagerrak, and Admiral Nimitz testified that American submarines had been ordered to sink any Japanese ship without warning from the very first day of the war. There was, in fact, a good deal of evidence that German submarine crews, in the early days of the war especially, had tried to rescue enemy crews at considerable risk to themselves.

[6] On the day the sentences were announced *The New York Times* reported a Russian charge that the United States was planning an atomic war.

real evil that had been made known in the course of the trials, but rather to evade it and suggest that the real crime, in the words of Field Marshal Montgomery, lay in waging unsuccessful war. Yet the trials had shown that there were crimes which demanded punishment, and to have been a willing participant in the upper echelons of the party was sufficient reason for it. The International Military Tribunal freed three of the defendants, but the German courts investigating their past connections with the party did not. They were all given heavy sentences of fines and imprisonment: Schacht and Papen eight years, Fritzsche nine.[7]

Who were the criminals? For the Russians, they were those who couldn't be used or who would not collaborate in the new Soviet order. Otherwise, whether general or marshal or gauleiter or capitalist, if they would cooperate they too could help revolutionize Germany. For the Russians the men in the dock were useful only as symbols of the Hitler period, and as such they had to be destroyed; whether as aggressors or common murderers made not the slightest difference. For Jackson too they were symbols—the loyal Nazis he thought were just lying low, biding their time. When Goering committed suicide, Jackson said it showed his lack of character, and thought this deed would rob him of his chance for martyrdom. The failure to indict a Krupp would be a world calamity, as would the failure to find the General Staff guilty. Everything was blown to the proportions and simplicities of a Hollywood screen.

But the live history constantly eluded him. Even while the trial was going on, Jackson admitted that there was nothing in Europe which could be called peace, that the underlying conflicts which had set Europe fighting were not solved.

Had a beginning been made at Nuremberg toward controlling these acts of armed force? It might be said, on the con-

[7] But these sentences, too, had their political significance; they were revised by the German courts, no doubt in the light of the new international climate that was rapidly developing; and by 1949 all three were free.

trary, that the trial was a disservice to the cause of international or any other kind of morality. In proclaiming the lofty purposes of the victors, at least one of whom had committed all the crimes imputed to the defendants, in declaring a law that had no roots in the past or in the thickets of contemporary life, with the same nations ceremonially sitting in judgment and prosecuting their enemies, it gave evidence against the very order, impartiality, and renunciation of violence which were its stated aims. Even the freeing of the three men became suspect; did they serve the Western members of the court as comforting evidence that it was a legal body rather than an instrument of vengeance of the victorious powers?

Confronted with great evil, the architects of the new world order could all too readily feel an uneasy virtue. Much as Goering had helped Europe in keeping paintings from going abroad, Stimson served humanity with new weapons. Writing in *Foreign Affairs* in 1946, he said: "We used submarine and atom bomb for winning a quick victory over the aggressors and to save not only our troops but the enemy as well." The great crime, he felt, still was war, not its methods.

It was also in 1946, after Churchill's speech in Fulton, Missouri, that the Soviet-controlled press all through Russia and the satellites, including East Germany, called Churchill, along with other critics of Soviet policies, "Hitlerlike" warmongers and "imperialist aggressors," accusations that were soon to spread to Truman and Acheson and innumerable others who had repeatedly assured the men in the Kremlin there was no cause for conflict between the peace-loving nations.

VI

LEARNING BY DOING

Twelve million *Fragebogen* [1] with 131 questions were distributed by the American military government to all Germans over eighteen. They dealt not only with membership in the various party organizations but with whether a man or his wife or their parents or grandparents had ever had any titles of nobility (military-government instructions were to look out for people with "von" or "zu" before their names). The *Fragebogen* asked whether the person questioned had ever belonged to a university fraternity, how much money he had earned, how much land he owned. The classifications were designed to catch the Junkers, the nobles, the industrialists, who were believed to have sustained and nourished militarism and Nazism for many long years. Few if any of the men who were ready to risk their lives to overthrow Hitler in 1938 or in the rising of July 20 could have escaped such a net. To have owned more than 250 acres of land, to have been a director of a firm that employed 3,000 people, were circumstances as suspicious in the American zone as in the Russian. To have been a member of the German General Staff was reason enough, despite the decision of the Nuremberg Court, for mandatory classification as a major

[1] In March 1946 the *Länder* of the American zone enacted the "Law for Liberation from National Socialism and Militarism." Four classes of persons were defined: "Major Offenders, Offenders, Lesser Offenders, and Followers"—all subject to penalties. The questionnaire was designed to determine who was to be tried.

offender, subject to stiff penalties of imprisonment, fines, and other disabilities.

The Americans concentrated on destroying any traces of a German army. Military Government Law Number 154 prohibited the teaching directly or indirectly of any military principles, techniques, or mechanics, any veterans' organizations, any parades, civil or military, any singing of military songs. A violation of these regulations could be severely punished—even with the death penalty.

The intensity with which the Americans went at the task of disinfecting Germany may be seen by a comparison with the statistics of the French and British zones. In the American zone 35 to 50 per cent of the teachers were dismissed, compared with 12 to 15 per cent in the British zone and 10 per cent in the French. Of those arrested for Nazi or militaristic activities, the British tried 2,296, the French 17,353, the Russians 18,328, and the Americans 169,282.[2]

The Americans could be so zealous that they sometimes went beyond what the *Fragebogen* could turn up. A Munich publishing firm was forced to change its name, and its chief officers were barred from their posts, merely because it had stayed in business during the Nazi period. There had not been a party member among its directorate, but the Americans were unimpressed by this or by testimony that it had been anti-Nazi and that the Nazis had in fact wanted to shut it down for that reason. The firm had managed to keep going only because it published technical books and some of its products were important to the war effort. Now the Americans were as skeptical of it as the Nazis had been, and refused it a license to publish books.[3]

[2] Harold Zink: *The United States in Germany, 1944–1955*, p. 165, quoting W. Friedman: *The Allied Military Government of Germany*.
[3] General Clay said that it was difficult to prove that an industrialist had provoked war but that it was commonly assumed that anyone who had successfully engaged in business under Hitler was part of a conspiracy to wage aggressive warfare.

The American passion for denazification was used by the Russians as a propaganda device against the United States, despite the constant attacks of the Soviet press on the Western Allies for being too lenient in the denazification processes and for harboring industrialists and German military formations in their zones. In the spring of 1946 an American general forbade the return to Berlin of Wilhelm Furtwängler, director of the Berlin Philharmonic Orchestra. The grounds were that he had performed during the Hitler period and so had been a tool of the Nazis—the charge, in effect, was that he had kept his job. The Russian-controlled newspapers, on the other hand, compared him with Beethoven and Brahms; and when the Allied Control Council decided some weeks later to permit Furtwängler to conduct, this was a clear victory for the Russian devotion to culture and enlightenment in postwar Germany as against the narrow, philistine American incomprehension.[4]

The Russians were alert to take advantage of such opportunities. An American correspondent visiting Dresden reported that the Soviet commandant, pointing to the ruins, said in a friendly but rueful manner: "That was your work and now it's our job to clean it up."[5] They compared the beginnings of reconstruction in their zone, the drop in unemployment, the higher food rations, the firmness with which they dealt with the "real" Nazis and militarists, with the West zone's poverty and hunger and plots against a German democratic state.

The Americans, with the mountain of hundreds of thousands of cases before them, turned over the denazification proceedings to German tribunals in June 1946; from then on, too, the German court system was to deal with the cases of Germans which did not directly affect the Allies. The judges, like the members of the denazification tribunals, were subject to Allied supervision and had themselves emerged unscathed from the denazification investigations. In the American view a free Ger-

[4] *Tägliche Rundschau*, March 9, 1946.
[5] *The New York Times*, Jan. 3, 1946.

man society would have to learn its lessons in democracy from the ground up, and denazification began the process. When the Americans alone had administered the denazification, Military Government Law Number 8, which became effective in September 1945, made it mandatory to dismiss anyone who had ever been a member of the Nazi party for whatever reason from any position save one of ordinary labor. "However slight the apparent extent of nazi party participation, a member's continued employment except in ordinary labor is unlawful." [6] He could appeal, but until he did and won he could have no position of influence anywhere.

The assignment was overwhelming, beyond the capacities even of the formidable bureaucracy that was called upon to perform it. To simplify it, a so-called youth amnesty was proclaimed in July for Germans born after January 1, 1919, and in December—on the assumption that the less well-to-do were more virtuous—it was extended to those who had earned less than 3,600 marks (roughly $900) between the years 1943 and 1945, and whose taxable property was not more than 20,000 marks in 1945. This youth amnesty affected some two million young men. The weight of the program still bore heavily on a large proportion of the population. Three million were chargeable, 72,000 were in jail awaiting trial.[7]

Soon after the German tribunals began to operate, the Americans charged that they were far too lenient. General Clay reprimanded them for the slow pace and laxity of the proceedings; denazification must come first regardless of the effect on the economy. It was a common criticism of both Germans and Americans that the system was harder on the little Nazis than

---

[6] *Weekly Information Bulletin*, HICOG (Oct. 13, 1945), p. 5.

[7] In Munich 1,900 firms, employing 135,000, dismissed or demoted 5,000 employees as a result of denazification requirements. In Stuttgart 5,921 firms, employing 13,921, dismissed or demoted 1,528. In the Robert Bosch works 200 out of 700 lost their jobs, as did some of the people who had been employed for 25 to 30 years in a porcelain factory in Arzberg; a man who owned a clothing factory and, according to German testimony, had joined the party to prevent its being closed was forbidden to enter it.

on the big ones. Hearings generally lasted two hours, after which there was a recess and then the verdicts would be announced. Often money fines were assessed which were important in the average budget but not at all in those of the black marketeers. Another criticism was that the big ones could move on—to another *Land* or zone where they were not known—and so wait out their time until public opinion had a chance to cool.

While the Americans turned over local political and administrative authority to the Germans at a rapid rate, more rapidly at times than the Germans were prepared for,[8] the daily life of the German people remained as miserable as before. The burgomaster of Stuttgart reported that in the city's supplies there were 60,000 pairs of shoes, 71 overcoats, and 220 suits available for a population of 330,000.[9] An American correspondent wrote that in Frankfurt there were 900 overcoats for 400,000 people and those were earmarked for DP's. Eight million refugees were to come in from the East between 1945 and the end of 1946, at the rate of 5,000 to 10,000 and more a day, to a part of Germany that had for the most part produced manufactured goods, not food. They came to a West Germany that had only 60 per cent of its former dwelling space intact, that manufactured in 1946 a third as much as in 1936, and to which the food stocks of the Eastern provinces were no longer being delivered. The Russians, in return for the reparations from the West zones, never made the promised deliveries of food; these had to be arranged on an occasional barter basis.

The land was exhausted in both East and West Germany after the wartime lack of fertilizers; seed was scarce, equipment as worn as the people. The faint stirrings of political democracy were praised by German and American speakers as the preliminary parliaments began their deliberations; but there was not enough to eat. The target ration of 1,550 calories, about half of

[8] The ministers president thought it too early to hold elections for the constituent assemblies of the *Länder* in the American zone in May or June—a year after the end of hostilities.

[9] *Report* of the Oberbürgomeister, Jan. 30, 1946.

131

what was needed in a day of normal activity, was rarely reached; there was no fuel for heating, nothing to repair the damage with except the debris that could be salvaged from war wreckage. Firms specialized in this business; one in Berlin used broken parts of airplanes; bricks from the rubble were cleaned by hand, mostly by women at a cost ten times the price of new ones.

In the East zone the Junker estates were broken up quickly and methodically. This was, of course, a matter of basic policy that had been followed in every country under Soviet control— the poor peasants and the landless and the refugees were to be given the estates of the exploiters. The Russian papers told of projects to send 3,000 children to the country, where they would be adequately fed, and of the delight of the land-hungry peasants and the dispossessed at being given farms that had belonged to the great estates.[1] It is true that the average size of the farms acquired in this way was not large—they ranged from 17 to 22 acres, including woodland—but it was larger than in the satellite countries; in Hungary and Poland, for example, the farms averaged 7 acres. In a state such as Mecklenburg, where almost two thirds of the arable land had belonged to estates of over 250 acres, ownership was transferred to thousands of small farmers; in the entire East zone about 400,000 got farms.[2]

There was little jubilation, however, on the part of the peasants in the bleak atmosphere of the East zone, where quotas for delivery of farm products to the authorities and the costs of renting farm machinery from the tractor stations would always be too high. Nevertheless, there were dutiful resolutions of approval by local farmers' organizations, and a large majority of the population of the East zone voted for the confiscation of property of "war criminals and other antisocial elements." The land was divided among "new farmers," refugees, farmers who held less than twelve acres, co-operatives and townships; and production went down rapidly because the small holdings, with

[1] *Tägliche Rundschau*, May 13, 1946.
[2] Richard Lukas in *Europa-Archiv*, I (1946), 116.

their depleted soil and worn equipment, could not be worked efficiently. At the same time the agrarian reform was being pressed, businesses and factories were taken over, only instead of being decentralized they were formed into a large trust. The Russians transplanted the ingenious scheme of mixed S.A.G. companies (Sowjetische Aktiengesellschaften) they were using in Manchuria and the Balkans. Fifty-one per cent of the stock was held by them and 49 per cent by the Germans; thus the factories could produce for the Russians without giving the appearance of confiscation. In all, 200 enterprises of the East zone were appropriated in this fashion, of which 74 were returned to the Germans as being insufficiently profitable, but not before they were stripped of their most valuable equipment. Other firms were administered wholly by German functionaries; their products were shipped to the Soviet Union as reparations, and a small share went to the East German economy.[3]

In the American zone there was also a powerful drive to change the ownership of German industry and to break up any Junker estates. However, there were few large landholdings there. In Württemberg 0.1 per cent were over 250 acres, in Baden .23 per cent; there were few or no large estates in Hesse, and they were rare in Bavaria.[4]

There were, however, some surviving businesses and industries, 2,264 in all in October 1945, of which military government reported "only 995 . . . can properly be called industrial plants, the rest being sawmills and utilities installations."[5] By early 1946 these had doubled, but they continued to produce just a trickle of goods—the fuel and raw materials were lacking. Any one of them which employed more than 3,000 workers or

[3] By mid-1946 7,000 factories had been given to the *Länder* authorities, to co-operatives, or to "suitable democratic persons" to run.

[4] Nevertheless, General Clay thought that many large holdings were kept from the market by the system of land tenure, thus depriving people of the right to own land or to improve their economic status. He asked the ministers president to discuss the problem and make recommendations. (Letter from Clay, U.S. Army Document Center, Kansas City.)

[5] *Weekly Information Bulletin*, HICOG (Oct. 6, 1945), p. 11.

had done more than 25,000,000 marks' worth of business annually had to be broken up.[6] To have done more than 25 per cent of the business in a particular market was also prima-facie evidence in the American zone of the need for decentralization.

While these efforts were being made to change the face of what remained of the German economy, production throughout the Western zones stagnated at uniformly low levels. Although an output of 5,800,000 tons of steel was authorized, the actual production in 1946 was only 2,000,000 tons. And this was owing in part to the low rate at which coal was mined, which in turn was linked to the lack of consumer goods with which to provide incentives, the lack of adequate housing in the industrial areas, and the lack of tools to work with.

It was hard to do any useful work in the Western zones. There was growing unemployment, and if people had jobs their marks bought a starvation diet. A cartoon in a German paper showed a man starting out for his day's work and the neighbors saying: "They must have an extra income—he can afford to work." It was far more rewarding to go out into the countryside to trade clothing or pieces of furniture or jewelry to the farmers for food than to work at a daily job, even at coal-mining, for which special benefits were given in the form of increased ration allowances. The American Army, attempting to increase production, gave a priority for the release of prisoners of war who had been coal-miners. One of the many unexpected results of the occupation was the advantage their sentences gave those convicted Nazis who were debarred from all but physical labor and who could join the food-hunters without troubling themselves to work on the rubble removal.[7]

[6] The British, on the other hand, required only the decentralization of firms that had employed 100,000 or more people.

[7] A military-government regulation made it mandatory for every male between the ages of 14 and 65 and every woman between 15 and 50 to register for work. Compulsory labor could be ordered when necessary, but it could also be evaded. (Manpower, Office of the Military Governor, Jan. 1946, pp. 3, 5.)

As for the ordinary Germans, people were too exhausted to work more than a few hours, and men fainted on their jobs in the cities. There were American reports that hunger typhus—which, like all typhus, is spread by lice—was beginning to appear among Berliners who were too weak and dispirited to be clean. There were few stout Germans now; the Americans weighed and measured them and found them, especially the young and old, dangerously undernourished. Children were given a warm meal in the schools and they were also likely to be given a share of their parents' rations, but they were seriously underweight, as the Hoover report would show. A special representative of President Truman reported in November 1945 that food must be sent to Germany, but American newspaper accounts said the Germans were not greatly in want; some declared they looked a good deal better than Americans had during the depression years. On February 8 *The New York Times* reported in a dispatch from Raymond Daniell that the Army denied that Germans were starving: in fact, they were gaining weight. Daniell wrote that the Army was puzzled by agitation in the United States for sending food.

In March the British military government announced that it would have to cut rations in its zone from 1,500 calories to 1,040; in Hamburg, which was in the British zone, thirty-three workmen collapsed from hunger. Rations were cut in the American zone, too, to 1,275 calories by April 1. On April 14, 1946, General Joseph T. McNarney reported to Herbert Hoover, who had gone to Europe to investigate the food situation, that there was not enough food available to support the Germans even on their present famine rations.[8] He foresaw a ration of 915 calories a day until the harvest, and rations were reported even lower in the French zone, where an American observer re-

[8] Hoover said that food conditions in France, Italy, and North Africa were difficult but not intolerable, that Poland was the hardest hit, with 2,600,000 children suffering from undernourishment. He estimated that there were 20,-000,000 children who were diseased or in subnormal health on the Continent.

ported "a frightful public health situation." [9] At a meeting of the ministers president of the American zone in April it was reported that 300 out of 1,000 children had died in their first year.[1] An article in the *Christian Century* asked if the Christian church was to be an accessory to murder, saying that millions of Germans were starving and quoting the anti-Nazi Bishop of Berlin, Wilhelm Dibelius, who wrote: "By no stretch of the imagination can these doomed babies, their mothers, and the aged be called war criminals. . . ." [2] On May 17 the German Council of States [3] announced further ration cuts to 1,180 calories, and in June the first signs of hunger edema were reported. Clay promised the ministers president 65,000 tons of grain, and the ration went up from 1,180 to 1,225 calories. In July a *New York Times* correspondent wrote that Germany was getting closer to starvation every day. (In September, at the time Secretary of State Byrnes spoke in Stuttgart, General McNarney reported the weight of the Germans at its lowest since the occupation began.)

In January 1946 General Eisenhower had given permission to the Swedish Red Cross to send food to German children, and by summer the first American private aid was allowed to go to Germany. Earlier attempts to send food—by the Lutheran churches in the United States, for example—had been unsuccessful, as the Treasury Department rejected applications under the Trading with the Enemy Act.[4] The shipments were the be-

[9] Pollock to Clay, June 8, 1946, U.S. Army Document Center, Kansas City.

[1] April 13, 1946, U.S. Army Document Center, Kansas City.

[2] There was the same prospect of high infant mortality as when the American military-government authorities had reported on October 13, 1945, that half the babies born in Berlin in August had died. (U.S. Army Document Center, Kansas City.)

[3] This had been established in the American zone in October 1945. It was headed by the ministers president of the states. It could only make recommendations, which had to be approved by the military government.

[4] President Truman was reported at first to have denied that there was starvation and then to have agreed that there was and that food could be sent.

ginning of a flood of private relief that had already started with GI's and American officials in Germany, who paid no attention to the orders against sharing American rations; and now it poured from the United States, from Switzerland, from Sweden, from Quakers and Catholics, and people of no religious affiliation who responded to stories of what was as great a concentration of human misery as had been brought to any nation of the modern world.[5]

Both cities and countryside had returned to savagery. As in the period after the Thirty Years' War, when wolves roamed the streets of what had been thriving villages, now again wild creatures invaded once-cultivated places. There was the wild-pig plague, as the Germans called it. These animals had prospered, since farmers were not allowed to have rifles or shotguns and there was no adequate defense against their depredations. In herds of fifty or sixty the pigs uprooted potato and other crops, and did great damage, despite efforts to fence off fields and farmers arming themselves with bows and arrows. The Americans hunted the pigs for sport but liked to use jeeps on these expeditions and the animals, which moved by night, had little difficulty avoiding the hunting parties.[6]

Delinquency and crime rose steadily. The nourishment coming from the black market and the wonders of the PX's were not to be had by good, solid, hard-working people. They were for the smart lad who traded, or for his sister. There were 80,000 to 100,000 young people without fixed homes or jobs in the British zone, 150,000 in the American zone. Illegitimate

[5] By October 1946, 180,585 CARE packages as well as other private gifts of food and clothing had gone to Germany.

[6] An American medical officer in a long letter that reached General McNarney blasted the hunting habits of his countrymen. Game, he said, was being crippled by the hundreds with carbines and other nonhunting weapons, including burp guns; one man boasted of having killed 64 deer using a Garand rifle. The devastation of the wildlife was estimated—with the exception of the pigs, which were harder to shoot—at 90 per cent. (Letter of Col. F. T. Chamberlain, Dec. 7, 1946, U.S. Army Document Center, Kansas City.)

births went up from 6.5 per cent in 1938 to 16.4 per cent in 1946. Cases involving juvenile delinquents went up 400 per cent.[7] In Berlin 2,000 people were arrested every month, as compared to 3,000 for the entire year of 1935. Divorce petitions increased. Stealing became respectable. In the city of Bremen the number of boys who came before the courts for theft increased sharply; the report wryly says that there were fewer girls because they had other means of obtaining food and shelter. In Hesse over 30 per cent of the children had an abnormal family life—one parent or both were dead—and out of 35,000 young people leaving school in 1946 only 1,500 could find jobs.

Prisoners of war were returned by the Americans as soon as they were no longer needed for work. Seventy-four per cent, they hopefully believed, had been re-educated under American indoctrination and would be sources of democratic ideals when they returned to civilian life. Sixteen per cent were still not favorable in their attitude toward the United States and toward democracy, and 10 per cent remained militant Nazis.[8] Thousands of prisoners were kept by the British and French until late 1947. The British were apologetic about the slow pace of discharges, but said they needed the prisoners for work, especially on the farms; they paid them eighty cents a day. The Russians allowed a few thousand of their prisoners to return; but—in part because many of them were in wretched physical condition, and in part because the Russians, too, needed manpower—they released them very slowly over a period of years, and some have never been freed.[9]

American mobile discharge units sped the return of prisoners

[7] *Deutschland Heute*, p. 381.

[8] *The New York Times* reported on August 19, 1946, that the British found 70 per cent of their prisoners neutral toward Nazism; the remainder split into those for and against.

[9] Former German prisoners of the Russians who survived the forced-labor camps in the postwar years have said that the food was wretched but not much worse in quantity or quality than what the civilian population was getting.

to civilian life, although thousands more were kept at work on such projects as the building of the sparkling American suburb behind barbed wire in Frankfurt. This housed the 845 members of the American community, including wives and children, with beauty parlors, movie theaters, a community center costing a half-million dollars, along with the other utilities of the good life for the expatriates who found themselves unexpectedly on foreign soil. Outside this magic world there were 450,000 Germans living in the ruins of the city.

The American reform of the German school system began with the goal of making it more democratic, of seeing that the Germans provided free books and tuition and compulsory schooling up to the age of fifteen. The Americans wanted to break up the caste system that had kept the children of workers from going on to the *Gymnasium* or the university. Private schools were to be permitted, but the principal aim was the "socializing and enriching of the curriculum of the public school." "The research point of view," the American educators said, "should be emphasized at all levels of the school program." For the attainment of such lofty goals the immediate situation was unpropitious. There were often eighty children to one denazified teacher, and few of them had shoes or proper clothing. The children of some families took turns going to school, sharing what there was to wear. In Bavaria, because of the classroom shortages, pupils could attend school only two hours a day; and all the children in the cities were undernourished.

While Germans were being re-educated in the schools and in the Army camps, the formal processes of democracy were beginning. Throughout the German *Länder* of the American zone in the winter of 1946 there were elections, which with American aid and approval would determine the kind of parliamentary democracy the Germans were to be allowed to aspire to.

The first local elections were held in January and resulted, as they would everywhere in the Western zones, in an overwhelming victory for the non-Communist parties. The Christian Democratic Union (CDU) got 1,484,713 votes, the Social Democratic party (SPD) 980,000, the Communists 136,788, and the Liberal Democratic party (LDP) 99,280. In the West former Nazis were not allowed to vote, in contrast to the campaign of the Socialist Unity party in the East zone, where they were urged to join the party and one enthusiast coined a slogan: "The SED, the great friend of the little Nazi." [1]

Here, as on other fronts of the postwar political struggles, Russian propaganda set out to recruit a following, using generous and broad appeals. Everyone was eligible to take part in the new order, everyone could help, everyone had a place in the reconstruction. What was needed was unity and cooperation. The split between the workers' parties in the 1920's had helped bring Hitler to power. Now the SED, as the center of a unified movement, would defeat the reaction, and those who had belonged to the reaction could purge themselves by joining the party. Nevertheless, the Communists had little success wherever Russian military strength was lacking. The Russian Army could announce that henceforth it would take over the care of German orphans in the East zone; military government established a youth organization and saw to it that the young Germans were invited immediately to international conferences, something that would have been unthinkable for the Americans to do; confiscated property was returned to some two thousand "followers"—small-fry Nazis; but the results were unfailingly the same. The rank-and-file members of the Social Democratic party in Berlin voted overwhelmingly on March 31 against the merger of their party with the Communists—82 per cent opposed it. Even in the East zone, despite the full control over the voting and all the material and strategic aid the Soviet authorities could give the SED, the additional voting strength of the so-called mass organizations—the women's Communist guilds, farmers' Communist organizations, the trade unions and

[1] Wolfgang Leonhard: *Die Revolution entlässt ihre Kinder*, p. 448.

such—was needed to give the party a majority in the East-zone parliaments when the elections were held in September.[2]

The Christian Democrats and Liberal Democrats were tolerated and to some degree encouraged in the East zone because the presence of the middle-class parties was essential to the Communist formula for democracy in East Germany as it was in Poland. Some of the members of these parties accepted the Communist view of their role—Otto Nuschke, for example, of the CDU. He favored collaboration with the Russians as against the West, believing it indispensable for Germany as well as for his party. The Communists therefore ruled with a wide variety of appeals for the cross-section of the population of the East zone. There was the party of united workers, socialists, and Communists—the SED. There were the middle-class parties, designed for non-Communists, and the well-developed mass organizations of Communist workers grouped by vocation or special interests. Although there was a considerable imbalance in the resources allotted the parties, the counting of the votes seems to have been conducted with reasonable fairness—in contrast to Poland, for example, where thousands of anti-Communist votes were not recorded. In East Germany too, however, meetings of the middle-class parties were broken up by Communist bands—these parties were to be tolerated but reminded of their weakness.

The Socialist Unity party was recognized by the four powers in Berlin but not in the zones of the Western powers. Everywhere outside the authority of the Russian occupation the Socialists refused to merge; and while General Clay in a broadcast from London in April announced that he favored a Unity

---

[2] There were 11,623 communities in the East zone where local branches of the parties could be organized. The SED was registered in all, the CDU in 4,200, the Liberal Democrats in 2,200. When the time came for voting, the Soviet authorities again permitted the SED to be registered in the 11,623 communities, but only 2,082 CDU branches and 1,121 of the Liberal Democrats were registered. The SED received 80 tons of paper as against 9 tons for the other two parties. (Richard Lukas: *Zehn Jahre*, p. 17.)

party as long as it held to the tenets of democracy, none of the enormous pressure that could be exerted in Berlin and the East was possible in the Western zones; the party and its influence stopped with the Russian bayonets and rewards.

There were other causes of the strengthening of pro-Western sentiment. In March 1946 Winston Churchill made his "iron curtain" speech in Fulton, Missouri; and, while the international caldron seethed and bubbled, public and official opinion in England and America was stirred by the disclosures of the widespread and successful Russian spy apparatus on the North American continent when in Canada the Soviet code clerk Igor Gouzenko asked for asylum and brought his files with him. In Germany it was evident that the Americans and the British were, in effect, paying for the Russian occupation. Nothing much was coming into the Western zones although a good deal continued to go out. Germany was not being treated as the economic unit that had been decided on at Potsdam; the Russians were not making the promised deliveries of foodstuffs from their zone, although the reparations due them were coming to them from the West zones and from the dismantlings and current production in the East. In Yugoslavia, American planes flying off course were shot down, and in one of these attacks five men were killed. Just before this there was the trial of the formerly highly esteemed patriot Draza Mihailovich; it was in part, according to the Soviet press, a trial of the British and American forces, too, who had attempted to organize an opposition in Yugoslavia. In Greece, in Malaya, in Vietnam, in Iran, there was the smoke and fire of struggle. American officers were arrested in the East zone of Germany as spies and held for twenty-six days, their offense having been to enter the Russian zone without passes. Three Communists were arrested in the West zone as spies. The foreign ministers met and parted in Paris without being able to agree on a program for an exchange of products of East and West zones. There were still no Russian deliveries, and in May General Clay temporarily stopped sending reparations. Clay suggested in a memorandum to Byrnes that if the Russians would not take part in the exchange of commodities Western Germany should be federalized and the zones of the three powers merged.

In July at the meeting of the foreign ministers in Paris Molotov read a statement directly challenging the United States and its German policy. He attacked the whole notion of the Morgenthau plan and of JCS 1067; he opposed separating the Ruhr, Rhineland, and Saar from Germany, making her an agricultural country, or federating the German states. Russia wanted a strong central government, a revival of German light industry, and an increase in industrial production; she also wanted the $10,000,000,000 in reparations which had been promised at Yalta and Potsdam. The West, he repeated, was trying to split the country, using Germany as a pawn in its power politics. While emphasizing the need for the long-term disarmament of Germany, he also set Russian policy squarely against the French, who were still opposing the establishing of central German agencies and urging the separation of the Ruhr as well as the Saar from the German economy. He was opposing, too, the hard-peace advocates in both England and the United States, many of whom had been previously identified with what were regarded as the Russian aims. Russia needed German reparations; Molotov's call for a central government and increased production was designed to get them, to encourage the Germans to look forward to political independence, to provide the incitements for German co-operation in Soviet control of the East zone, and to prepare the way for advances beyond it.

Byrnes replied that the United States, too, rejected the idea of an agrarian Germany, and he denied the Russian charge that federalization was a return to the earlier plan of splitting up Germany and imposing on her a peace of vengeance. As for reparations, he said the Russians had already taken $14,000,000,000 worth from their own and the Western zones. On his return to the United States from the meeting of the foreign ministers, Byrnes proposed a merger of the zones; the United States zone, he said, was costing the American taxpayer $200,000,000 a year, and only central German agencies—which the French would accept if the Saar was excluded—and economic unity would reduce this figure. His offer of a merger of the zones was repeated in the Allied Control Council, but was to be accepted only by the British, who were also paying out large sums for the support of their zone.

The Communists' appeal to the Germans was weakened by the necessity the SED was under to accept the Polish-German border as final, while the spokesmen of the West could argue that the decision must await the peace conference. The Soviet's political strategy could to a degree offset this by opposing the continued French demand for separation of the Ruhr, Rhineland, and Saar from Germany.

The Russian propaganda attack on the West swept from one sector to another. Russian papers charged that the British and Americans were training thousands of anti-Soviet troops among German prisoners of war and the men in the labor services they were recruiting from the Poles and others who did not wish to return to their native countries.[3] Vyshinsky declared in the United Nations that an antirepatriation organization controlled the repatriation centers, although the United States pointed out that 1,000,000 Russians and 3,000,000 Poles had been returned. The United States authorities had ordered that no Soviet citizen subject to repatriation under the Yalta agreement would be provided for in the refugee camps after December 1945, except in those under Russian administration. This order was suspended in January 1946; and the new directive provided for the forced

[3] The Russian charge that the British still had 120,000 armed German soldiers, including an air force, was indignantly denied by the British, who offered to open their zone to Russian inspection if the Russians reciprocated. Soviet papers described a German admiral in full-dress uniform appearing at a British dinner, and German formations with decorations and arms—fanciful and picturesque accounts that were continually denied by the British and repeated by the Russians.

repatriation of all Russians captured in German uniforms; of those who had been members of the Soviet armed forces on or after June 22, 1941, and had not been discharged; and of those charged by the Soviet with having given aid and comfort to the enemy. In July there were still almost 200,000 Poles in the DP camps. As an incentive to return, a sixty-day ration was offered them, and 48,000 went from the American zone. In the autumn the Warsaw government invited a delegation from the camps to visit Poland, and they came back with a favorable report. As a result some 18,000 returned to Poland.[4]

Byrnes's speech in Stuttgart in September 1946 had something for everyone. It was an acceptance of the Russian challenge, but it was also designed to assuage Russian fears of German aggression. Clay had proposed two months earlier that the State Department define American policy in Germany, but *The New York Times* reported that the decision to make the speech had been arrived at only four days before it was given—the second foreign ministers' meeting in Paris having come to another dead end. A week earlier seven American warships had been ordered to Greece on what was described as a courtesy visit, while the Russians charged the Greek government with terrorist activities and demanded a UN investigation of the fascist bands which it said were spreading death and destruction there. The British were called accomplices in these depredations and the Americans were assailed for having sent the war vessels to the Mediterranean.

Byrnes rode through the streets of Stuttgart past the ruined buildings in Hitler's own Mercedes. The crowds watching the Americans go by, although they had been waiting since early morning, were undemonstrative: this was another speech, as

[4] Late in June, General Sir Frederick Morgan, British chief of UNRRA operations in Germany, announced that no further supplies would be given non-Jews who did not return to the countries of their origin, unless they were in danger of persecution. This was directed particularly at Poles and Yugoslavs who were slow to return. But here, as later in Korea, the Communists held that all these people would wish to go back to their homelands if they were not interfered with. (*The New York Times*, July 1, 1946.)

far as they knew, by another of the conquerors. Some 1,500 American military-government officers heard Byrnes; among them were a scattering of Russians and some 150 Germans— the ministers president of the American-zone *Länder* and others working under the American administration, all a little frayed and elderly. On the platform with Byrnes were Senators Vandenberg and Connally, Robert Murphy from the State Department, and General McNarney. Byrnes spoke in English, but the speech was translated into German, and when he had finished, the Germans present were deeply moved. This was the outstretched hand for which some of them had been waiting for years—ever since Hitler had come to power in 1933.

It was not a soft or forbearing speech, but the Secretary held out the hope of a revived, peaceful, independent Germany, the possibility of recovery both physical and moral; at the same time he held wide open the door of cooperation to the Russians, and to the French (to whom he promised the Saar, although refusing to permit the detachment of the Ruhr and Rhineland). The speech was designed to be as much as possible to all the countries involved: to give hope to Germans and to put the country on something approaching a self-sustaining basis; to assure the French that, despite the desire of the British and Americans for increased German production and centralized German agencies, French security and welfare were being scrupulously safeguarded. And to the Russians the speech reiterated the promise of American support for Russia's acquiring the German city of Königsberg. Mr. Byrnes still held out to the Russians the sticky candy of American assurances that the United States would not forsake Europe—he referred to the American proposal "for a treaty with the major powers to enforce peace for twenty-five or even forty years"; he said again that the United States was prepared to see to it that the Germans remained disarmed, and would keep American troops on the Continent for the long period that would require.

"I want no misunderstanding," he said. "We will not shirk

our duty. We are not withdrawing. We are staying here. . . . In 1917 the United States was forced into the first World War. After that war we refused to join the League of Nations. We thought we could stay out of Europe's wars and we lost interest in the affairs of Europe. . . . We will not again make that mistake. . . . We have helped to organize the United Nations. We believe it will stop aggressor nations from starting wars. . . . Security forces will probably have to remain in Germany for a long period."

The United States wanted Germany administered as an economic unit. "If complete unification cannot be secured, we shall do everything in our power to secure the maximum possible unification. . . . The American government is unwilling to accept responsibility for the needless aggravation of economic distress that is caused by the failure of the Allied Control Council to agree to give the German people a chance to solve some of their most urgent economic problems.

"So far as many vital questions are concerned, the Control Council is neither governing Germany nor allowing Germany to govern itself.

"Germany is a part of Europe, and recovery in Europe . . . will be slow indeed if Germany with her resources of iron and coal is turned into a poorhouse."

The United States favored the early establishment of a provisional German government that would not be the satellite of any power. Of the Saar he said: "The United States does not feel that it can deny to France, which had been invaded three times by Germany in 70 years, its claim to the Saar territory, whose economy has long been closely linked with France . . ."; but although he gave with one hand, he withheld with the other, adding "except as here indicated, the United States will not support any encroachment on territory which is indisputably German or any division of Germany which is not genuinely desired by the people concerned. . . ." He repeated the willingness of the United States to unify the economy of its zone

147

with any or all of the other zones willing to participate in the unification. The offer, he said, had so far been accepted only by the British.

Finally, after repeating that the German people were suffering from the effects of the war that Hitler had brought on them, he said: "The American people want to return the government of Germany to the German people. The American people want to help the German people to win their way back to an honorable place among the free and peace-loving nations of the world." [5]

Thus Mr. Byrnes. The 150 Germans rose at the end to applaud, and some of them were weeping. Here was a promise not only of a measure of reconstruction, of a political and economic future, and of the right of Germans to rule themselves, but also, and most important, of the readmission of Germans to membership in the human race. A newspaperman asked the minister president of Württemberg-Baden, Reinhold Maier, what he thought of the speech. "It was magnificent," Maier said, "a wonderful turn in a new direction." "Do you agree," the correspondent asked, "with Mr. Byrnes on the question of the Saar?" Maier said he did not. "Do you presume," the newspaperman asked further, "to disagree with the Secretary of State of the United States?" The Saarland, said Maier, in a free election supervised by the League of Nations in 1935, had voted nine to one to return to Germany. This was the expression of the will of the people of the Saar, which had been and was German. There was a silence around the two men, and Maier went home. Soon afterward he was called on by a high-ranking American officer of the military government. Word of the exchange had got around, and the officer had come to congratulate the minister president on his courage and forthrightness and to add that he agreed with every word.[6]

[5] James Byrnes: "Restatement of U.S. Policy on Germany," in *Germany, 1947–1949*, pp. 3–8.
[6] Personal interview.

Speech and visit together summed up many of the perplexities of the American occupation. The speech was, on the whole, sensible and useful despite the hectoring platitudes and the lavish hand that gave France purely German territory which she could keep only with the help of foreign armies. But the officer too was representative of many Americans. It will never be known how many of the military men and the civilians of the occupation who were trying to help guide the Germans back to the civilized world made the same kind of visit to the Germans. The broad policies laid down in the Byrnes speech would help them in their self-appointed task. Sufficient aid, in the shape of large imports of food and raw materials and the establishment of a sound currency, was still two years away. Not until 1948 would that appear. Until then the speech brought mainly hope; the lot of the Germans remained substantially the same.[7]

Byrnes was promptly attacked by the French, the Russians, and his own countrymen. The French said the speech was pro-German; Soviet spokesmen said that Byrnes favored the division of Germany and that the offer to merge the zones was really a move to that end. Stalin wanted no treaty with provisions against an armed Germany; the East zone, having become the People's Democratic Republic, would soon have its own "barracks police," which could be used as were the Communist formations in Korea against the non-Communist areas. In the United States there was confusion in and out of the Truman administration. Henry Wallace, Secretary of Commerce, made a speech a few days after Byrnes's and said the President had approved it. In it he again praised the Soviets, warned the United States against being a pawn in the service of the British

[7] The United States and Britain sent $64,000,000 worth of aid to Germany in 1945, $468,000,000 in 1946; without this, thousands of Germans would have died. But, as we have seen, only rarely did the food sent permit maintenance of the minimum ration. The RFC announced that it would make a loan to pay for raw materials and that every dollar would produce $9.00 worth of goods. This aid, however—designed to help light industry and thus pay for imports of food—was only a token of what was required.

Foreign Office and British imperialism, and said the most important peace treaty would be one between the Russians and the United States. His sentiments were shared by Senator Pepper, who at a mass meeting of the Political Action Committee warned against foolish people who wanted a Hitler blitzkrieg against Russia; by Harold Ickes; Sumner Welles; and the son of the late President, Elliott Roosevelt, who attacked Winston Churchill's Tory imperialism and extolled the friendly relations that had existed between Russia and the United States when his father was President. Wallace, after charges and counter-charges of bad faith, resigned, and Byrnes and his policy were triumphant. That was a step forward politically, but the German people remained where they were.

In November the London *Economist* pointed out that there had been no recovery in Germany—after eighteen months. American statistics showed that German production had doubled in the period 1945–6, but the base rate was so low in those first months after the end of hostilities that the increase had little meaning. Production in 1946 was one third of 1936; the population, with the refugees from the East, was up by 25 per cent.

It was calculated that at such a rate of production each inhabitant of the British zone would receive one suit in forty years, a pair of socks every four years, a shirt every ten years, a pair of shoes every three years.

In England as well as in the United States there were influential people who believed that the Germans were contriving to divide the Allies, and they warned against the resurgence of German power. The International Committee for the Study of European Questions, which counted Sir Robert Vansittart among its members, issued statements showing that Germany was more powerful now in comparison with her neighbors than in 1939, her increase in population during the war having been greater than that of the countries she had attacked and occupied.

This calculation was made possible by adding the number of refugees who were being forced out of the Eastern countries into the shrunken territory (little more than half of the former Germany) that lay in the hands of the Western Allies.

American correspondents reported Germans secretly drilling in the woods; meetings of Nazis plotting to get back into power; the writing of "88" on walls of German cities (the letters stood for Heil Hitler—*h* being the eighth letter of the alphabet). An American general thought the Germans were planting rumors in an organized fashion in their efforts to sow discord, and an antirumor committee was set up to checkmate such activities.

Correspondents also echoed the Russian charges on the use of DP's in Allied military service. As the Americans and the British too clamored to get their soldiers home in 1945 and 1946, there were "We want to go home" parades and demonstrations of American soldiers from Frankfurt to the Far East. Poles and other displaced nationals, dressed in American Army uniforms dyed black, could be used as replacements in some of the routine military tasks, such as guarding American installations, and at the same time be given jobs instead of idling in the DP camps, which continued to be centers of violence throughout the Western zones. These men were far from being tactical bodies of troops, but their presence was the cause of virulent Russian charges that equated their effectiveness and malign purpose with that of the Polish contingent of General Vladislav Anders which had fought in Italy against the Germans and been disbanded.

All four German parties had joined in begging the help of the Allies early in 1946 in controlling the bands organized from among the displaced persons which were roaming and plundering the countryside. There were 50,000 of these marauders, the Germans said. The initial Allied attitude of forbearance toward all the DP's had hardened considerably as a result of the excesses of this lawless minority, whose malefactions included murder as well as heavy dealings in the black market.[8]

It was a time of lawlessness, with riches at hand for those of flexible morality and nimble wits. There were prosecutions [9] of officers in the American zone and Berlin, where the black market was called vast and organized and included, it was said, radium, jewelry, perfume, automobiles, and even paintings.

That was the debit side of the ledger. On the credit side, American women in Berlin bought shoes and stockings for German children who were recovering from tuberculosis in a hospital they could not leave because they had nothing to walk out in except their bare feet. But it was not so much the American women who brought their bounty to the Germans as the American men. There are no records of the tons of food coming from American Army supplies and PX's that went to the German civilian population because of the relationship of a GI with an attractive Fräulein, but the supplies flowed in munificent streams for years; the Army personnel changed; the streams never subsided. In addition, the German secretaries and clerical workers in the American occupation got one meal a day from their employers and so could give a portion of their ration cards to their families.

All was not friendship, however. The relationships were likely to be resented by the German males who saw their girls going off with the opulent Americans. German girls had their hair shaved for being friendly with the conquering troops, and there

[8] There were now between 830,000 and 850,000 DP's in Germany, well fed but in poor quarters and lacking clothing; 20 to 25 per cent were Jews, some of whom were still migrating from Poland and most of whom wanted to go to Palestine. Thirty-five per cent of the crimes committed by DP's involved violence. In Bavaria there were 1,300 raids by the American constabulary in one week; 2.5 tons of army margarine were found, along with English, American, and occupation currency, including $290,000 worth of marks. (*Report* of the U.S. Constabulary, Karlsruhe, 1947.)

[9] One of them was a result of robbery by two American officers—a man and a woman—of the Hesse crown jewels, worth, it was said, $3,000,000. The jewels were recovered, the culprits tried and sentenced.

were other signs of displeasure on the part of the young men.[1]

Isolated acts of resistance occurred, too, as when in Stuttgart a bomb exploded in an American office and another was thrown through the window of a room where denazification records were kept. No one was injured; the bombs turned out to be crude and amateur devices. But the Stuttgarters took them seriously: 75,000 of them held a parade, and the streetcars stopped in protest against the bombings.

Unemployment rose in the American zone by almost half a million, while it dropped in the East zone from 372,000 to 182,000. In the face of these figures the dismantling of industries that might have been producing goods for the Germans and the rest of Europe continued; steel bearings that were essential to the battered German railroad system could not be manufactured because the Kugelfischer factory, with only 20 per cent of its capacity left, was still being dismantled as a war plant. There were protests among workers and in the new parliaments, but no violence developed. A deputy in the Hesse parliament late in 1946 rose to say:

> Today's misery comes from the shutting out of democracy. The spirit of militarism and of National Socialism must die if Germany is to live. . . . The Germans must feed themselves and pay for their own goods or every word about democracy is meaningless and a nation goes under. Not every German is guilty but the majority made great mistakes. Collective guilt is to be rejected. . . . The German people have contributed much to the world, and Germany freed from the ideology of the past should have a place and

---

[1] One letter written in English to a girl in September 1946 read: "You are a very filthy creature. An American whore such as you can't be found so quickly again. Don't flatter yourself by thinking you are pretty. When one looks at your rouged-up puss one thinks they are seeing a worn-out cow." On the back was added: "just like you the following girls are hated," and five names followed. Two girls, the letter said, giving their names, "are not as big pigs. We know them all."

a change in its unbearable fate. The Byrnes speech was a ray of hope for the possibility of a state, a community for Germany. . . . It breached the iron ring of helplessness. . . . Without the food the United States has given Germany it would have starved. This is the first time in history that a conqueror has given such help to the conquered. We stand before the winter solstice.[2]

Many solemn and carefully weighed statements of this kind were made in the parliaments and in the public press. There was widespread recognition of Germany's obligation to pay for the damage done other peoples, but it was pointed out that restitution could not be made while no means were available. In fact, with the influx of refugees, more industrial capacity was needed than before if Germany was to reach the average of the European standard of living. Raw materials were required, not the destruction of plants. The German failure to produce was plainly hurting the European economy, and this was pointed out not only by Americans but also by Germany's neighbors.

The Dutch complained that half their industrial equipment had come from Germany and that now they were unable to get parts for their machines or sacks for their dikes; they were importing only fractions of the amounts they had formerly, and as a result their own factories were running at half-time or less.

Despite the failure of economic recovery, the German elections in the autumn showed the effects of the Byrnes speech. Hesse could socialize the iron-and-steel industry, Bavaria could favor private enterprise, the British representatives of a Socialist government could press for the nationalization of key industries; but the sentiments of the Germans were anti-Russian and antitotalitarian, whether they voted for the Social Democrats or the bourgeois parties.

The main job of the Germans at the moment, as many speak-

[2] *Drucksachen des Hessischen Landtags.*

ers pointed out, was to stay alive; but although in Berlin, as the elections approached, liquor and coal briquettes (stamped with their Communist origin) were given away, Germans stoically preferred the fare of the West, however thin, to any more experience with a totalitarian brew, no matter what the label or the promises. The SED could do more than electioneer: it could provide evidence of the esteem in which it basked. For example, it asked for aid for the repair of Berlin houses. When the Allied Control Council was slow to provide it, the Russians sent 4,000 tons of cement, 27,000 cubic meters of wood, roofing supplies, and other materials. But the SED was badly defeated in the city elections. The Social Democrats polled 48.7 per cent, the Christian Democratic Union 22.1 per cent, and the SED 19.8 per cent of the votes; the Liberal Democrats got 9.4 per cent.

As Christmas approached, there were for a few days two German administrations in Berlin; the Social Democratic mayor elect, Otto Ostrowski, was prevented from taking over his office by his Communist-appointed predecessor. The new government was finally seated, although the Russians wished to examine more closely, they said, the credentials of Ernst Reuter as minister of utilities before approving him. The Russians reported that they were bringing in 900,000 bottles of vodka; the French were planning to get along on 100,000 bottles of wine; the British were importing whisky, and also sweets for the German children; the Americans virtuously said they were bringing food and candy for the children and fruit juices for themselves. The first warming-centers were fitted out, where Berliners who had no heat in their houses could keep from freezing. Crude wooden toys were put on sale for the children.

As 1946 drew to a close the French marched in 1,200 troops, who put up customs barriers around the Saar. General Clay protested against the unilateral action, maintaining that such a decision should have been made by the Allied Control Council; but the French replied that the measures were taken against the black market, and the Saar became part of the French economy.

The announcement that German children would be getting American food and candy for the holiday aroused indignation among some of the correspondents. One reporter said that German children were going to have a big Christmas while DP's were being overlooked: Christmas parties were planned for 500,-000 children while $14 had been collected for the DP's.[3] Another reporter from the same paper said the Americans were having a hard time teaching young Germans new ideas in the discussion groups; the German character was peculiar, and the young apparently suffered from its congenital defects.[4] In addition, the Bavarian Landtag, meeting for the first time, elected as its president a man who had voted for Hitler's assuming dictatorial powers in 1933 and who had a denazification trial in prospect. He denied the allegations, saying he had been anti-Nazi and in a concentration camp; but the Landtag decided against him and he was deprived of his office.

Along with other signs of the season's good will, it was announced that German women might marry American soldiers, and there were pictures of a merry group of them on their way to the United States, buxom and well fed. Their appearance, in a land where the prevailing color of complexions was described by American observers as green or yellow, was proof of the devotion of their American fiancés.

Any German, whether former concentration-camp inmate or Nazi or employee of military government, might be summarily turned out of his home; but for the holiday season General McNarney stopped requisitions of German houses. Each incoming American family displaced eight Germans—the requisitioning of only 125 houses in the Grunewald would dispossess 1,000 Germans.[5] But for the holiday everyone could stay where he was.

[3] Dana A. Schmidt, *The New York Times*, Dec. 16, 1946.
[4] Delbert Clark, *The New York Times*, Dec. 16, 1946.
[5] In Bavaria, *The New York Times* reported, 25,000 had been evicted from their homes.

VII

THE DEAD CENTER

THE WINTER of 1946–7 was one of the coldest in the history of Europe. In Germany temperatures went down to fifteen and twenty degrees below freezing and there was no fuel. Sticks of wood that could be found in the parks and what coal had been saved or might be picked up on the black market or fell off the carts delivering fuel to the occupiers provided such warmth as there was in the cities; nothing had been delivered for heating since October. One American report said food conditions were best in the Russian zone, where rations were being dispensed on schedule. In the West there were plans for increasing industrial production—over $1,000,000,000 worth of raw materials was to be provided—but these lay in the future, and for this winter there was little of anything. Two hundred people froze to death in Berlin. People slept on the floors of railroad stations, paying three pfennigs for a night's lodging, and in "bunker hotels," which were former air-raid shelters; twenty thousand were reported living in the cellars of Hamburg. Seventy-five per cent of the industries in the American and British zones had to be shut down because of the cold. Production in January fell to 31 per cent of 1936 and in February it was 29 per cent. The schools were closed.

The cold slowed the wheels of justice as well as transport. General Clay reported that the demolition of plants in Bremen had been affected; and only 28,323 denazification trials were held in January 1947 in the American zone, as compared with

36,710 in the previous December. There were 450 tribunals working on denazification; more than 200,000 cases had been tried, some 370,000 Nazis removed from their jobs, and there were 1,300,000 still to be heard. A former inmate of a Nazi concentration camp, Eugen Kogon, whose book *The SS State* had sold out overnight its entire edition of 40,000 copies, wrote an article on his visit to one of the camps where former SS men were awaiting trial as members of a criminal organization. He found apathy, despair, and resentment among them. At the rate the men were being tried, he calculated it would take five years to hear all their cases. That there were villains among them may not be doubted, but thousands of young men had been drafted into the Waffen SS whether they liked it or not.

Herbert Hoover had reported in 1946 on the nutrition of Europe as a whole and had found that, while there were serious shortages and critical areas, there was no longer general starvation in the countries he visited. Early in 1947 he was sent by President Truman to study the food situation in Germany. It was known that there were seriously affected areas there, and the only justification for the Army's sending in the allotments from its store of grains and other provisions was that they were essential to the prevention of disease and unrest. In the light of the Byrnes speech and the conflicting testimony on the state of the Germans' health, there was a need for unassailable and well-publicized facts and figures that would make possible a comparison of the needs of Germany and those of other countries whose hunger was owing to the German attack and occupation. There were shortages everywhere; Hoover had reported one third of the world hungry. Why should the Germans be fed along with their victims? This was essentially the question Hoover was to answer.

The Hoover report in late February 1947 [1] corroborated the observations of those who had seen the Germans as dangerously undernourished; the situation was far worse than in any

[1] *The New York Times*, Feb. 28, 1947; March 24, 1947.

other European country, and the brunt of the hunger and its secondary effects was borne by the old and the young and those who were too poor to buy what food there was. Germany, Hoover said, had sunk to a level not known in the Western world for a hundred years. The housing situation was the worst in modern civilization. In 1936 Germany had produced 85 per cent of its own food; it now produced 25 per cent. Over half of the children and adolescents he found in a wretched state. Famine edema was appearing among them and among adults too; there were 10,000 cases in Hamburg alone. The population in the Western zones was 9,000,000 more than in 1939, while food production was but 65 per cent of its prewar figure. There had been a sharp reduction in skilled labor as a result of war casualties and the loss of the labor of the prisoners of war who had not returned; more than 3,000,000 of them were in Russia.

The target ration of 1,550 calories was wholly inadequate to sustain a healthy human being, and yet this ration was rarely being attained. Hoover proposed an immediate shipment of ten million tons of potatoes from the United States, where there were so many that American papers had shown them being used for fertilizer. The Secretary of Agriculture later explained that the potatoes were unfit for export; but in England, where two pounds of potatoes were allotted per family per week, and in the rest of Europe, the photographs seemed fantastic. Hoover recommended a feeding program for children, the setting up of soup kitchens, and the issuing of Army rations. He also proposed that seventy Liberty ships lying idle be manned by German crews and used to transport food. German goods could easily pay for the imports if the Germans were allowed to make goods. In Norway, for example, catches of fish were in oversupply; all that was needed to get them to Germany on a paying basis was for Germany to supply the products that everyone in Europe needed.

Other observers corroborated Hoover. Anne O'Hare McCormick of *The New York Times* described women felling trees and, harnessed to carts, hauling away piles of stone. The Ukraine, she said, was more stripped than Germany, but in no other country was the ruin so general and the level of life so low.[2]

Hoover urged economic unity and the rapid retooling of non-war industry in order to end the drain on the United States. The United States and Britain were paying $600,000,000 a year to occupy Germany. The British had never accepted the idea of a pastoral state, but JCS 1067 did in part, and this could have meant the extermination of 25,000,000 people. *Every* industry, Hoover pointed out, was a potential war industry. Light industry needed to be expanded under Allied supervision, but heavy industry was essential too. He proposed that German factories be freed from production quotas subject to Allied controls, that removals and dismantlings be stopped.

The Hoover report was a sober, nonpolitical document—the first official statement to indicate that in JCS 1067 the Morgenthau plan had its descendant. But rations continued at their low levels and emergency supplies were needed to keep them there.[3] Army stocks, however, were made available from American and British supplies for child-feeding programs, which up to now had been largely supplied by gifts of food from private sources abroad.

Accusations were made that the German farmers were not delivering all they could to the city populations but were growing rich instead on the black market. General Clay in April 1947 blamed the Germans for failures in the food program, and he told them other parts of the world were hungrier than they.[4] German officials, and some Americans, denied that the farmers were lax in bringing in food supplies, saying they were meeting 90 to 95 per cent of their quotas. But Clay said he was ready

[2] Ibid., March 1, 1947.
[3] In mid-May it was announced that the United States was rushing grain to Germany to end the immediate crisis; 1,200,000 tons would be sent by the end of July.
[4] *The New York Times*, Feb. 10, April 16, 1947.

to use the Army against hoarders, and the military governor of Hesse warned the citizens that the death penalty would be invoked to curb any disturbances. He too said he was ready to use troops to collect food, and added that martial law might be declared. There were to be no strikes in Hesse, he told the Germans, or any kind of agitation against the military government.[5]

On the day the Hoover report appeared, the Russians announced they would make available to the East zone a supply of 80,000 tons of seeds. The target was now not the Germans but their late allies. They asserted that the Americans were arming the Germans with carbines, and aiding criminals to return to power. While food production in the Russian zone declined —some reports said by as much as half—as a result of the land reform, the continuing lack of fertilizer, and the deterioration of farm machinery that could not be replaced, the Soviet authorities called for unusual measures. Cemeteries and former drill grounds were to be plowed and planted; if a farmer showed signs of being unable to produce what was demanded—many of the new proprietors were inexperienced—he might lose his acreage. Furthermore, he had to run his farm with the help of his family; no hired hands were permitted. Because the quotas were too high and had to be delivered to the government at fixed prices, and the plots were too small for efficiency, many of the farms were abandoned. One member of the East-zone police reported that he had joined the force because he could not live from the land.

In March 1947 Marshal Vasili Sokolovsky announced the end of dismantling[6] in the Russian zone and an increase in German steel production—a 300-per-cent increase, said General McNarney, that had been illegally decided upon without consulting the Western powers. Russian spokesmen continued their efforts to win the German non-Communists. They repeated that

[5] Ibid., May 17, 1947.
[6] This was premature—dismantling continued "spasmodically" until July 1948.

it was essential for German recovery to set up a central administration, and they invited the leaders of the Social Democrats, the SPD, to conferences in the East zone, including even Kurt Schumacher, who had so often been compared to Hitler in the Communist press. The United States was accused of having taken more than $10,000,000,000 in reparations; much of this sum, it was stated, had come from confiscation of German patents in the United States.[7]

At the foreign ministers' conference in Moscow early in 1947 General Marshall, who succeeded Byrnes as Secretary of State, continued the effort to meet the Russian challenge with patience, resolution, and old formulas. Both he and Molotov proposed an increase in German production quotas, but although this was one of the few points on which the foreign ministers agreed, the steel quota was not raised to 11,500,000 tons until the London conference in December. The Russians, in the Moscow conference, continued to press their program for reparations, for uniting Germany, and for four-power control of the Ruhr, which up to now had been solely under the British. The British and Americans were unwilling, however, to repeat in the Ruhr the experiment that had failed everywhere else, and rejected the proposal. They also refused to agree to the Russians taking reparations from current production. Secretary Marshall pointed out that that would mean either the United States paying for reparations or the Germans being kept in their poverty. He warned, however, as had his predecessors, against the threat of a revival of German power and promised immediate aid against a future aggression on the part of Germany. The United States, he repeated, was prepared to stay in Germany for a period of twenty-five or forty years—but this still failed to impress the Russians. Molotov again refused to agree to the French claim to the Saar, a reaction that was profoundly disappointing to Georges Bidault, who could do little, how-

[7] *The New York Times*, Feb. 16, 1947.

ever, by way of reply save to propose a toast "to those of us here who love freedom." [8]

The Moscow conference of 1947, which had no important results, dealt with only one sector of a world-wide scene in which all the foreign ministers present were also taking part. General John R. Hodge reported from Korea that the Russians were arming the North Koreans; the British reported from Greece that they could no longer bear the burden of holding off the Communist attacks without more American help; the French in Indochina were fighting a Communist-led revolt; in China, Mao Tse-tung was arming his troops with Russian help; in the Balkans and Poland the last façades of cooperation between the Communist and non-Communist parties were crumbling.

On March 12, 1947, President Truman asked Congress for $400,000,000 for Greece and Turkey, which he said would otherwise fall before the Communist pressure. The British, who had spent more than $300,000,000 to support the anti-Communist forces in Greece, could not continue to pay the bill; and the Turks, who were spending a large proportion of their budget keeping their military establishment on a war footing, confronted possibly a Russian invasion but certainly bankruptcy unless they got help. The speech was the beginning of the Truman Doctrine, the announced intention of containing Russian power at the points it had now reached, thus far and no farther, and it was to be the basis of American policy from this March day on.

It was, of course, impossible to resist Russia in the rest of the world and not in Germany. So the Byrnes program of September 1946 was extended silently but implicitly in Germany with the announcement of the Truman Doctrine, and the conflict between East and West became in a sense centered there. It would become possible in a few months for Germans to read

[8] Walter Bedell Smith: *My Three Years in Moscow*, p. 219.

replies to Russian attacks on the West in German newspapers; General Clay, who succeeded General McNarney as military governor in March, gave instructions to the bizonal council of German ministers (representing the British and American zones) to take more power and decisions into its own hands. On the second anniversary of VE-Day the Russian-controlled press published accounts of how little the Americans and British had contributed to the Allied victory; it charged the Western powers with having deliberately avoided military targets to concentrate on the destruction of German cities. The United States, moving cautiously to win public opinion in disputed areas that aroused less violent emotions among Americans than did Germany, announced it would henceforth pay the costs of its occupying forces in Austria. And the Germans began to raise their heads. German union leaders said they would back their men who refused to work on dismantling, and they told the British and Americans they could not be responsible much longer for keeping order among the hungry, ill-clad workers who by Allied decree were still receiving the same wages which had been set under the Hitler government but which now bought so little. The plundering of German forests was protested by the ministers president and by Joseph Baumgartner, a candidate for minister of agriculture in Bavaria, who pointed out not only that it contravened the Hague convention but also that the fuel which had been gathered could be equaled by eight days' production of Ruhr coal.[9]

The DP groups reflected the misery and tensions of postwar Europe. In the British zone, where it was said there were 70,-000 employable people among them, those who could work were told they must take jobs or lose their special status. In the American zone General Clay stopped further entry into the camps. There were reports of an organized plan to get the Jews remaining in Poland into Germany and from there to more hospitable countries. At the time Clay's order was given, there

[9] *The New York Times*, May 30, 1947.

were somewhat more than 120,000 Jews in the United States zone, 90 per cent of whom, it was reported, wanted to go to Palestine. These Jews were only one fifth of the DP's who remained in Germany, and they represented a tragic remnant of the Jews of Europe. The victory of the Allies had left them to the mercies of Polish anti-Semitism, which, though sporadic in outbursts and on a smaller scale than the German variety, could be equally violent and lethal.

Polish and German authorities both made efforts to win back people who had fled from their countries. In a camp in Frankfurt in February 14,000 non-Jewish Poles rioted against the liaison officers representing the Warsaw government who were trying to persuade them to return to Poland. For them, too, there was a somber future, whether they chose to go to Poland, to stay in Germany, or to try to migrate farther. The Germans, many of them Jews, who had emigrated during the Hitler period were urged to return by a resolution of the ministers president in June which read: "Our hearts were heavy when we saw them go and we shall welcome their return." These émigrés would be mediators, the resolution declared, between the rest of the world and the Germans in their time of confusion.[1]

An action on the part of military government that created lively debate was the decision to dismiss employees who had not been citizens of the United States for more than ten years. This was immediately attacked as anti-Semitic, since it seemed aimed at the émigrés who had come to the United States from Germany and Austria in the thirties, to return as military-government officers and, with their perfect knowledge of the language and their American uniforms, to work great good and sometimes evil in their assignments. In the new atmosphere of a permissive, nonpunitive occupation and with two years' experience of military government, German-speaking officers were no longer so urgently needed as they had been immediately

[1] Record of the meeting of the ministers president, June 1947, U.S. Army Document Center, Kansas City.

after the war, when only a small fraction of the American-born officers spoke German well enough to get along without an interpreter.[2]

The activities of these former Germans and Austrians gave rise to many stories among the German population, some of which had more than a trace of anti-Semitism. They were often said to disguise their native German with an overlay of imitation foreign accent, and to wear their uniforms on all occasions to authenticate their status not only for the Germans but for the Americans too, since most of them had pronounced accents in English if not in German. There were many men of good will among them who put aside their own humiliations, regarding the enormities of the Nazi period as an aberration in German history, and who did their utmost to help any reconstruction. Some of them had had close German friends in their childhood before they emigrated, and these or the survivors among the families of friends they sought out to help as far as they could. Others, filled with resentment and the power of their status, let both be felt by the Germans with whom they came in touch.

More than 4,000,000 German prisoners of war were still in Allied hands in March 1947. They did all kinds of work, and their treatment varied enormously with the country of their captivity. Many returning from France and Russia looked like walking skeletons; it was rare, despite the Russian propaganda to the contrary, for the relatives of a prisoner in the Soviet Union to hear from him, and a German report said one postcard a year was received from a prisoner of war in France. A photograph showed Germans, clad in an assortment of military and civilian clothes, cleaning the snow off London streets. Thousands of them had been used to help with the harvest in England and

[2] Harold Zink (*The United States in Germany, 1944–1955*) says that 5 per cent knew German fairly well; John Gimbel ("Marburg under Occupation, 1945–52") says that in Marburg, of 63 military-government officers, 41 spoke no German, 17 could use it in conversation, and 5 spoke it after a fashion but not well enough to conduct affairs without an interpreter.

had been publicly complimented on their labors. In the United States, too, they had worked on farms—in Oklahoma and other states. But, well- or ill-treated, their continued status as POW's was contrary to the Geneva convention, which stipulated the prompt return of prisoners to their own country as soon after the end of hostilities as circumstances permitted. The physical condition of many of these men in the hands of the British and Americans was far superior to that of the German civilian population. They received better food—from 1,700 to 2,400 calories was the ration for prisoners held in camps—and this happy state of affairs was also true for the Germans employed on the farms in England and the United States, a number of whom wanted to stay on in these havens as long as they could.[3] In Stalingrad, too, the Germans were working; one photograph showed them cleaning up the rubble with their bare hands. But in this war-smashed area the conviction that the Germans were responsible for the damage was deep and prevalent—and some of the inhabitants of Stalingrad were living in caves.

How many prisoners the Russians were holding was a matter of long and inconclusive controversy. Hoover's figure was more than 3,000,000; the Germans said between 3,000,000 and 4,000,-000; the Russians said 890,542 and that they had returned more than 1,000,000—figures that were unsupported by any evidence. In March 1947 it was reported from Western sources that the British had released 60,000 prisoners and that 170,000 had come from Russia. The Americans, appalled at the state of a portion of the 440,000 men they had turned over to the French, negotiated for their return. France stubbornly maintained that these men were merely doing the work that would have been done by Frenchmen now dead and that their return to Germany would be a crippling blow to the French economy. Many, they said, had been in poor physical shape when the United States delivered them; American officers denied the assertion.

[3] In England 24,000 elected to remain (*The New York Times*, June 14, 1948).

Fifty-six thousand Germans were reported working in mines in France, some 250,000 on French farms. The British had 340,000 German prisoners in England and an additional 90,000 in the Middle East. There were questions asked in Parliament about their status; and the rate of release, which had been 15,000 a month, was stepped up. The last prisoners in the hands of the English were returned in July 1948. All the German prisoners of war in American hands were freed by August 1947.

The French yielded to American pressure and in March 1947 gave their German prisoners an option. In the course of three months they were to decide whether they wanted to return to Germany or to remain in France as free laborers. Those who wished to return to Germany would be sent back at the rate of 20,000 a month, and those who elected to stay would get contracts for one year.[4]

In the midst of these echoes of the war and the feeble signs of any recovery, the speech of the American Secretary of State at Harvard University in June 1947, like that of Mr. Truman in March, was to have long-term results of incalculable proportions. General Marshall extended the policy of emergency aid which had been applied in Greece and Turkey to a long-term program for all Europe. He took note of the failure of Europe to recover in the two postwar years, and he promised help in the form of grants of capital and goods to the countries of Europe with the exception of Germany. Countries behind the Iron Curtain were included in the invitation, as were Germany's former allies, the Italians and the Austrians, and so were the Russians themselves; but the Germans were left out despite the evidence that showed them to be the neediest of all. The omission was in part intended to reassure France, whose suspicions of American pro-Germanism were easily aroused; but mainly, it may be assumed, it was designed to calm the suspicions of the Russians, who would be quick to believe that with the aid of Germany the United States was building up an anti-Soviet

[4] *Germany, 1947–1949*, p. 118.

coalition. The exclusion could scarcely last long; the slow pace of European production, which economists attributed in large part to the failure of Germany to revive, demanded her inclusion in any program of European recovery, as it had already demanded an increase in the level of German industry.

The Russian reaction to the Marshall Plan was delayed. The first reports were that Moscow wanted to study the provisions. After some days had gone by, *Pravda* announced that the crisis in the United States was driving the Americans into an invasion of the economies of other countries. After that the plan was unceasingly attacked by Soviet spokesmen and newspapers as the major effort of American imperialism to conquer Europe. Countries that accepted it were denounced as puppets of the Americans; the Czechoslovakians, who had at first indicated their desire to participate, a short time later withdrew their acceptance. The plan was called a desperate move of the United States to rid itself of its surplus production, and, above all, an attempt to bring the European countries under its political and economic dominance. The Americans, Molotov said, to ward off German competition were bringing to Germany articles that the Germans should produce themselves. The Marshall Plan would do the same thing on a vaster scale for all Europe.

The summer of 1947 was as bad for German production as the winter had been; but a new directive, JCS 1779, which was linked to the Marshall Plan, replaced JCS 1067. "An orderly and prosperous Europe," it declared, "requires the economic contributions of a stable and productive Germany as well as the necessary restraints to insure that Germany is not allowed to revive its destructive militarism." [5] It approved a considerable rise in German industrial production; Germany was to be treated as an economic unit with central administrative agencies. And it repeated the American dedication to the disarmament and demilitarization programs. A higher standard of living was authorized for the Germans, and there were to be no repara-

[5] Ibid., p. 34.

tions beyond those approved at Potsdam. The political objective was to lay the basis of a sound German democracy; the United States wanted a Germany in its own image, made up of federal states and with a central government whose powers and functions were carefully defined and limited. It opposed an "excessively centralized government which through a concentration of power may threaten democracy in Germany and the security of Germany's neighbors and the rest of the world."

The Americans were to help the *Länder* establish and maintain basic civil rights, to encourage the competition of political parties, to foster the independence of the German courts, and to limit military-government controls as far as possible. A basic objective was the establishing of a rule of law, and the directive enjoined General Clay to refrain as far as possible from arbitrary and repressive measures; German legislation was to be disapproved only when it conflicted with military government, and JCS 1779 looked to the earliest possible restoration of German political powers. It continued the ban on cartels and holding companies and stated that Germans were to be taught the virtues of free enterprise, although military government was not to interfere with tendencies toward public ownership. In effect the directive marked the end of collective punishment for Germany. As the head of military government in Bavaria said, henceforth the democratization of Germany would be the primary policy.

The new directive foresaw no limits to the eventual German industrial capacity under Allied supervision. The United States and Britain, over French objections, agreed on a revised level of industry for "Bizonia," as their two economically merged zones were called. Steel and other production was to go up, heavy machinery to 80 per cent of prewar, while 35 per cent instead of 60 per cent was to be taken as reparations; light machinery was to be 119 per cent of prewar, and 23 per cent instead of 33 per cent was to be delivered as reparations. The manufacture of aluminum, vanadium, and other materials that might be used for warlike purposes was still prohibited, and there was to be no change in the levels of production of ball bearings, ammonia, synthetic rubber, gas, and oil.[6]

It was announced in the light of the new policy that American doctors would aid the recovery of German medicine, which had fallen to a low estate under the Nazis. Hospitals and laboratories were in ruins, German medical men had been cut off for years from knowledge of scientific research in the rest of the world, and the help of Allied doctors was essential if there was to be a revival of German medicine. Doctors had to be trained and retrained; about one fourth of them in the American zone had been denied the right to practice in 1946 under the denazification rules.

An American soldier describing himself as "a little man" wrote a letter asking his superiors if he might have permission to help the Germans rebuild bombed-out houses in his spare time. He thought this a good method of showing Germans a practical way to democracy, and the Army approved his request. American troops were told that the rights given the Germans under the *Länder* constitutions were to be respected; there was no conflict between American security and those constitutional rights.[7] German guests were now authorized to enter homes of Americans, although the Americans were not to be allowed to draw special rations if they stayed to dinner. Germans were to be permitted to enter the American Red Cross building. A German-American women's club was started in Munich and was followed by others; they did practical jobs such as collecting linen for children's clinics and orphanages.

None of this could occur without opposition. The voices of protest were many and of various political timbres. Sumner Welles warned against Germany's having an opportunity to rebuild before there was general security in Europe. The Mar-

---

[6] *A Decade of American Foreign Policy*, pp. 563–8.

[7] *Der Mittag* reported that General Clay would welcome German criticism of the American occupation.

shall Plan, he said, would not be worth the paper it was written on unless the democracies of Europe were ensured against German aggression. Our fundamental error, said Welles, was the assumption that because we pay the bill we alone can decide. The German people, he thought, were far more dangerous in 1947 than on VE Day.[8]

William Shirer wrote that the United States was making the same mistakes as after the First World War, and that the Germans were merely awaiting a new Fuehrer.[9] Delbert Clark said the differences among the Allies were deplorable because they confirmed the Germans in the belief that they were right after all. "Neo-Nazism," he wrote, "is rising, denazification is breaking down." [1] William Attwood in the New York *Herald Tribune* detected a new German nationalism. The Marshall Plan was attacked by Senator Pepper, who declared the conditions insupportable, by Henry Wallace, and by the Society to Prevent World War Three, which had found even the Hoover report sinister; its recommendations, the Society said, would make Germany the greatest industrial power in Europe.

The Germans, in the midst of the high politics and the dry summer of 1947, continued to go hungry. Crops withered in the fields; and in the treeless Tiergarten, where rows of vegetables had been planted, water was brought in pails and any kind of battered container to save the plants. Rations rose slightly, but remained under 1,400 calories. Posters were put up telling of the marvelous effects that sunlight had on human metabolism, how it helped prevent tuberculosis; but people were starving in the brilliant summer sun that burned on them day after day.

In Vienna and Berlin people who were conspicuous anti-Communists were kidnapped and taken across the sector boundaries at a rate of sixty to a hundred a month. Some of them

[8] *Washington Post*, Sept. 14, 1947.
[9] New York *Herald Tribune*, Sept. 7, 1947.
[1] *The New York Times*, Sept. 7, 1947.

were abducted by strong-arm methods, forced into a waiting car before friends or police could intervene, and driven off; others simply vanished. More indirect methods were also used against political figures. A former Communist was chosen as mayor by the Berlin City Assembly—the vote was 89 to 17—despite Russian warnings that they would veto his election. He was Ernst Reuter, who had returned to Berlin after having been in Turkey during most of the years when the Nazis were in power. The Russian veto prevented his taking office; this was the beginning of the split that was to result the next year in Berlin's having two governments.[2] For a long time the Russians succeeded in keeping the opponents of communism from taking over offices of authority. Despite the results of the Berlin election, the Communists continued to control the Berlin administration because of their hold on the unions, the city agencies they had established before the Allies joined them in Berlin, and Russian support of their activities in the Kommandatura. For more than two years the Western Allies contented themselves with protests.

Sometimes in fact they did even less. The Russians in Berlin were losing deserters to the West, and in addition were seeking to repatriate by force citizens of the Baltic states who had man-

[2] Reuter had had a brilliant and checkered political career. A spirited member of the Social Democratic party, he opposed the voting of credit to the German Army when World War I started and most European socialists capitulated to the war fervor. He had been captured on the Russian front and after the Bolshevik revolution had wholeheartedly adopted the cause of the young Communist state that would bring peace and socialism to the peoples of Russia and then of Europe. He had been appointed commissar of the Volga Republic of Volk-Germans (people of German descent) and then had returned to Germany, where as a Communist organizer he spent a short period in jail and became one of the leaders of the party. Lenin and Stalin had praised his brilliance, although Lenin thought him too independent. Reuter, like so many others in that period, saw his vision of communism fade in the light of the glaring Moscow dictatorship, and left the party. After Hitler came to power he spent some time in concentration camps, and later fled to England and then Turkey, where he taught economics. In October 1946 he was given permission to return to Germany. Two months later he became an SPD city councillor and director of utilities; in June 1947 he was elected lord mayor.

aged to stay in Berlin. The Soviet authorities therefore asked the Western powers in Berlin to join with them in raids against undesirable characters, including "war criminals" and deserters. While the Americans refused to help the Russians arrest any Baltic nationals, since the United States did not recognize the Soviet claims to the Baltic states, they did agree to join in the raids if they were to be conducted in a humane fashion. This led to another large-scale Allied action in Berlin in which two thousand Germans, Russians, and others were arrested. Six hundred were picked up by the Americans in their sector, some of whom were turned over to the Russians. Among them were doubtless a number of the deserters the Russians were looking for, but it is impossible to tell how many were guilty of nothing more than anticommunism.[3]

In West Germany small beginnings were made in reviving German manufactures. Coal production had risen as a result of incentives given miners in the form of shoes and textiles and liquor, which could be traded for food. In Munich the production of porcelain reached its prewar figures, and it was announced that four hundred pairs of stockings had been made. German production had so deteriorated that even such figures were publicized as a hopeful token of the future. More than a hundred new enterprises were started making glass and musical instruments. Some of these industries had been set up by refugees coming from the Sudetenland, one third of whom arrived with nothing, the rest with the 125 pounds of luggage each was allowed to take with him. They had left behind them, it was estimated, 100,000,000,000 Reichsmarks' worth of property in Czechoslovakia. In Berlin, too, a new industry appeared: the reprocessing of the city's hills of rubble. Forty-odd companies were engaged in this work, and some 2,000,000 bricks had been salvaged. If the Germans had cement, the newspapers said, almost all the bricks could be used; but there was no cement. Production rose with painful slowness. In 1947 it was 40 per cent

[3] *The New York Times*, April 10, 11, 1947.

of 1936, only 6 per cent higher than in 1946. The Germans continued to lose weight. In October their health was reported worse than the year before.

Not until December 1947 was it announced that Germany would be included in the Marshall Plan, but the change in sentiment was already evident in pronouncements by American spokesmen as well as in the trend toward higher quotas in production and consumption. The Ruhr authority was established, giving the Germans an equal voice with the British and Americans on the Control Council and leaving problems of production to the Germans. The steel quota went up, despite opposition from the French, who found themselves caught between two overwhelming political forces that left them with little bargaining power of their own. A French trade delegation was invited to Moscow to work out an exchange of French manufactured goods for Russian wheat. It set out before the French municipal elections took place, but had to return home without an agreement after the Communists failed to increase their representation in the elections. The Russians no longer had any interest in the negotiations after their propaganda purpose had been served. There were French successes, as when the Saar voted to incorporate itself in the French economy; but even this had to be brought about by maneuvers strange for a country that was bringing instruction in the practices of democracy to Germany. The sole way a Saarlander who was opposed to unification could vote "no" was by abstaining or voting Communist; of the four authorized parties three were pledged to favor the French tie, and only the Communists were allowed to be in opposition. As a reward for their voting, the Saarlanders were given a ration of wine, and ice cream appeared in their shops.

The French believed that the American and British desire for an increase in German production in the Ruhr was aimed against them; Bidault declared that the American efforts to help Germany would lead to a Communist government in France.[4]

[4] Ibid., Aug. 22, 1947.

France found herself buffeted by an inflation and a political struggle that could have extreme results. The cost of living had gone up 50 per cent while wages had risen only 25 per cent. This was one cause for the ruthlessness of the French occupation. French families—wives, children, and sometimes grand-parents—joined the troops in Germany, and they fared well. In 1947 a British observer reported that the entire meat ration produced by the French zone was divided between 100,000 Frenchmen and 6,000,000 Germans; one Frenchman got the same amount of meat as did 55 Germans.[5] In France there were strikes and sabotage and other signs of political and economic disorder. De Gaulle's party in the city elections polled 38 per cent of the votes cast, the Communists 25 per cent; in other words, 63 per cent of the electorate opposed the principles of the parties that were governing the country. In Indochina there was a revolt against French rule. One spokesman for American military government said the French wanted a veto in the decisions of Bizonia but accepted no responsibility; their main interest was how much coal France was to get.

While the British and the Americans made plans for putting Germany on her feet, the dismantling continued. German threats to strike against it were met heatedly by General Clay, who said he would tolerate no opposition in the matter. The United States announced that it was releasing $100,000,000 worth of Army surplus—uniforms and shoes to be used by German miners; and American spokesmen also pointed out that as a result of the decisions of the Moscow conference only 682 plants were now on the list for removal, a 60-per-cent reduction from the original 1,800 scheduled.[6] For the first time questions were asked in the American Congress, as they were being asked in the German parliaments,[7] about the reasonableness of taking

[5] Montgomery Belgion: *Victor's Justice*, p. 99.
[6] Robert A. Lovett: Reply to House Resolution 365, Dec. 18, 1947, in *Germany, 1947–1949*, pp. 413–20.
[7] Speech of President Erhard, Jan. 1947, *Drucksachen des Hessischen Landtags*, p. 21.

away the means of livelihood of a people while exhorting them to increase production. American and British authorities in Germany continued to defend the dismantlings, but the anomaly was pointed out by more critics now, British and American as well as German. General Clay, defending the official position as best he could, announced that 104 war plants had been delivered to countries that could use them to manufacture for the benefit of Europe. West Germany, he said, should put her energies into reaching the level permitted under the new directives, and the losses owing to the dismantling would hardly exceed what the United States and Britain were contributing to the German economy in one year.

The British, because they regarded German competition as dangerous to their own economy, which had to increase its exports or wither away, were more determined on dismantling than were the Americans. They blew up the harbor installations at Hamburg, in spite of strong opposition from officials who wanted the equipment at least saved for use in England; they dismantled German watch-making machinery; and one of the difficult decisions for them was whether to let the Volkswagen be manufactured for export. The Volkswagen would be in direct competition with British automobiles, and British officials were well aware of it from the start. In the American zone the rigid denazification rules would have prevented the employment of Heinz Nordhoff, who was responsible for the revival of the Volkswagen plant. Having been an official of a major German automobile company during the Nazi period, Nordhoff would automatically have been classified as eligible only for ordinary labor in the American zone. The British were torn between the economic and political urgency of increasing German production and taking full account of their own needs. Austerity was a key word in Britain in 1947, when London was still blacked out for lack of coal and Britain had to increase its sale of goods to other countries or reduce even further on its impaired diet. On the other hand, it was necessary to get German production moving for the immediate benefit of the British taxpayer as well as for the revival of Europe. In this case at least, British officials made a generous decision that was bound to be costly to their foreign trade.

On the whole, 1947 was a year of promises, not of fulfillment. Secretary Marshall said the Americans had put $19,000,000,000 into Europe since the end of the war and yet Europe was worse off than before.[8] The reason was not far to seek. As the experts kept saying, there could be no general European recovery without German recovery. Marshall proposed $597,000,000 worth of immediate aid to France, Italy, and Austria, and a long-term program of from $16,000,000,000 to $20,000,000,000 in aid to last until 1952, by which time he believed Europe would be back on its feet and no longer in need of outside funds for reconstruction.[9] General Clay said that Germany would require over $2,000,000,000 during a period of four years. President Truman asked Congress for $17,000,000,000 for the long-term Marshall program. The British and the Americans agreed that currency reform must precede any German recovery and would have to be undertaken even though it would reinforce the division between East and West Germany with the additional barrier of two currencies. The mark was valueless outside the country, and no plan for increasing foreign trade could be pursued on a large scale unless the Germans had a currency in place of the cigarettes that were the real international medium of exchange from 1945 until the reform in 1948. The Harriman Committee, appointed by Truman to survey European needs, called Germany the most disorganized area of Western Europe, and the worthless mark its symbol.[1]

The Russians strengthened their lines against the Marshall Plan. The Comintern was re-established in October 1947 to organize the anti-American forces in France and Italy. Russia

[8] *The New York Times*, Nov. 13, 1947.
[9] *A Decade of American Foreign Policy*, p. 1276.
[1] *The New York Times*, Nov. 13, 1947.

again proposed, at the London conference of foreign ministers
in December, the setting up of central German administrative
bodies to facilitate the flow of goods through Germany; she
wanted Bizonia dissolved and a united Germany in its place.
On the economic front in East Germany, the Russians initiated
a system of incentives through piece work, higher rations, and
slogans of equal pay for women doing the same work as men.
They pointed to trade statistics that showed the virtue of the
dismantling they had done. Production, they said, was 58 per
cent of 1939 in the Russian zone and only 38 per cent in the
Western zones. Furthermore, they charged the Western Allies
with trying to keep German industries from competing with
their own, with taking hidden reparations such as forest products
(about which the Germans too had complained), and with
buying up German factories for contemptible amounts. Vyshinsky said in September that the United States was attempting
to dominate the world and was seeking war to that end.

But General Marshall, returning from the London conference, pointed out in a radio speech on December 19, 1947, that
while the United States and Great Britain had been paying
$700,000,000 to sustain their zones the Russians had been
plundering East Germany, extorting huge sums—$500,000,000
in the year, he had announced a few days earlier—from dismantlings and current German production, forming a gigantic
trust of the German plants they expropriated,[2] and acquiring a
monopolistic stranglehold over East Germany. He reported as
part of the evidence of Moscow's intransigence that the three
Western powers had agreed the Saar should be detached from
Germany and integrated into the French economy but that the

[2] In the American zone the battle for decartelization was violent. Ten
officials resigned, charging that the program was being delayed and softened,
and their cause was given a friendly hearing in the American press. General
Clay's decision was on the side of moderation, in part because the British refused to accept the American formula to break up concerns employing 3,000
people. American military government now declared in Cartel Law No. 56
that any concern employing more than 10,000 people was to be investigated
for excessive concentration.

Russians had refused to commit themselves. The United States, however, while unwilling to determine the Polish-German border until the peace conference, wanted Poland to have *more* resources than it had had before the war and at the expense of Germany. He repeated the American desire for elimination of the zonal barriers and for the free movement of persons and ideas across the boundaries, and he also said that currency reform was essential. But there had been no agreements of any importance at the London conference other than that of increasing the steel production allowed Germany to 11,500,000 tons. Molotov had proposed that German industrial production be raised to 75 per cent of that of 1938, to permit reparations schedules to be met; but the Western Allies would not agree that Russia was owed, in addition to the enormous sum the Soviet government had received from dismantlings and other reparations, the $10,000,000,000 Molotov continued to demand. Its payment, the British foreign minister pointed out, would have meant that the German economy would turn over one seventh of its production to the Russians. Any such stranglehold over the West German economy would mean, as Marshall said, the same power of life and death over the future economic life of all Germany that Russia already held over the East zone.[3]

These were the events on the diplomatic front. On the cultural side, the Russians had 27,000,000 books available in their zone for 4,313,000 students, compared with the French supplies of 6,000,000 books for 900,000 students and the American 4,400,000 books for 2,700,000 students. The Russians offered to supply the schools in the American sector of Berlin with textbooks: editions of Mark Twain and Jack London and a collection of Stalin's speeches; but the Jack London and Mark Twain books had introductions on the evils of capitalism, and the offers had to be refused. There were still no history courses in the Berlin schools in 1947 because the four powers could agree on

[3] The Germans calculated that more than $10,000,000,000 was taken in reparations from the 18,000,000 people of the East zone in 1945–53.

neither facts nor interpretations. This was one point, however, where a compromise was to be reached in the months to come. German historians managed the delicate task of revising the histories in a fashion satisfactory to all four powers, and Berlin children were able to study the past.

These were very nearly the only signs of common policy. In Berlin in October a Russian colonel, Tulpanov, told a German audience [4] that the United States was seeking war, thus echoing in the conquered city what Vyshinsky was saying at the United Nations. Tulpanov's speech deeply disturbed General Clay, for it was the first time, he said, that an official of one Allied power in Berlin had appealed to German sentiment against another; and he asked Marshal Sokolovsky whether the statement was official and had his blessing. Sokolovsky said that it applied to certain reactionary monopolists in the United States, whom he was sure General Clay would not wish to defend. General Clay in October authorized replies to be made to these attacks in a program of education and information in the press which would explain to the German people the basic concepts of democracy as opposed to communism. There were to be no criticisms, however, of specific governments or individuals; the controversies were to be kept as remote as possible, limited to the ideologies as such. Nevertheless, the battle was now joined by a second Russian officer, who told another German audience that reactionary forces in England and the United States had plotted the Second World War to bleed Germany and Russia alike. A third Russian spokesman said the statements that the United States would stay in Berlin were pompous and warlike and that Germans who had faith in such promises would be left stranded.

[4] His speech was made before a meeting of the SED.

VIII
THE YEAR OF THE BLOCKADE

1948 WAS the year of change for Germany. It was the year of the blockade, of the reform of the currency, of the start of economic revival. But, above all, it marked the beginning of the return of the Germans to the civilized world, as the West praised the fortitude and stubborn resistance that only three years before had contributed to the destruction of so many German cities. It was the year of West Berlin, the half-devastated center of the struggle between the East and West, where threadbare and hungry people walked the desolate streets and alleys between the mounds of rubble but refused to eat the food offered in the Soviet sector or warm themselves with its coal.[1] Both could be had if the West Berliners would lend themselves to the Communist propaganda, cross the sector boundaries, and register with the borough authorities in East Berlin.

1948 was the year of the opening of the large-scale offensives of the Soviet against the West—an extension of the forays that had been met by Allied intervention in Greece and that would be followed by the notable victories of the Red Chinese armies in the Far East. Berlin itself was assaulted from every quarter and from inside the Western sector as well; it was attacked by the invisible constrictions of the blockade, by kidnappings and

---

[1] Eighty-five thousand West Berliners out of a population of more than 2,000,000 registered to accept the Russian offer. Twenty-five thousand of these would normally have bought their food in the East sector because they worked there or lived near the border shops, and there were also some who registered twice, so only 60,000 West Berliners took the Russian bait. (W. Phillips Davison: *The Berlin Blockade*, pp. 165–7.)

stratagems, by threats and allurements, by every device short of massive armed force.

As we have seen,[2] there were no written documents attesting the Western powers' unrestricted right of access to Berlin. There had been an exchange of letters on June 14 and 18, 1945, between Marshal Stalin and President Truman. Truman said he had agreed to the withdrawal of the advanced American troops who were deep in the Soviet zone, on condition that the American and Russian military commanders work out mutually satisfactory arrangements for supply of the Allied garrisons in Berlin. What then had occurred was a matter of interpretation: the American troops had been withdrawn and routes of access had been agreed on, but these were clearly under Russian border control from the beginning. The American Army officers showed no interest in the matter during the discussions on the zonal boundaries which took place in London. General Clay, who was deputized by General Eisenhower to work out the arrangements for occupying Berlin with the Russians, made no attempt to put the right of free access into written agreement. His personal notes show that the matter was discussed and that apparently the Russian commandant had agreed that the Allies should have the unrestricted right to supply their troops; but there was nothing in writing because, as Clay pointed out, to have specified routes would have implied some limitation in American rights in a city under the shared control of four powers. In any event, the Russians could interpret a document to their purposes as readily as a verbal agreement. But even while these conversations were going on, the Soviet government was evidencing its reluctance to let the Western powers come and go as they pleased. Clay had asked Marshal Zhukov for the right to use three railroads and two highways in withdrawing the American troops from their positions in the Russian zone, and for nine days in which to do it. Zhukov said nine days were too many, four were enough; that the Americans shouldn't need

[2] Cf. above, Chapter 3.

three railroads and two highways; that one highway and one railroad should be sufficient in view of the Russians' need to move their own troops. In London, Ambassador Winant, a devout believer in co-operating with the Russians, reacted strenuously against Churchill's suggestion that the forward positions of the American troops be used for bargaining purposes. But Winant did want a written agreement specifying the right of free entry to Berlin. It was perhaps because his principal concern was with the broader aspects of postwar collaboration that Winant urged a formal and legal arrangement on what were relatively minor points. The Army, on the other hand, was perfectly aware of the problem of supply. But, secure in its sense of power after the historic victory, it was unconcerned with legalisms. The very presence of American troops in Berlin surrounded by a Russian zone was based upon the premise of four-power collaboration.

From the first days of the occupation of Berlin, the Russians had made it plain that they regarded Berlin as primarily under their control. There was no road to it or escape from it except by way of the railroads and highways that went through their zone or the air corridor over it. The Allied troops entering Berlin had had to keep to stipulated routes, the trains that passed through the zone were subject to Russian checks at the border and depended on Russian maintenance of the railroad right-of-way. From time to time there were unexplained delays and blocks as trucks were stopped which hitherto had been allowed to pass the check points, and the Russians held up trains because they said there were undesirable people or goods on them and demanded that these be removed. Thus they had emphasized that rail and motor traffic, and air traffic too, ran by the writ of their approval. Three air lanes were allotted to the Allies by the Allied Control Council late in 1945, but they too had an uneasy use. Planes were buzzed and sometimes they were shot at as the Russians declared they were off course and intruding in the territory of the East zone. This was part of the Russian show of force to impress upon the Germans and the satellites that it was Russian power which counted and that they must look to the Russians for protection; it was part of the same strategy that sent East-zone policemen across the border into Western territory to arrest Germans conspicuous for their "anti-Russian" or "pro-Western" activity.

There had long been rumors that the Western Allies intended to pull out of Berlin.[3] Before there was talk of a blockade Americans in the city had said that Berlin lay in an awkward geographical position: it was too far from the center of bizonal administration in Frankfurt; too exposed if the Russians decided to move in. These rumors were always rejected by American and British authorities, but when they were printed in East- and West-sector newspapers they were the first shots in a psychological offensive against the Berlin population. The Berliners already had experience of a Russian occupation and a good idea of what it would mean to be marked as anti-Communist if the British and Americans should decide to leave. There was now little or nothing in the Soviet press to distinguish between those who were called fascists and those called lackeys of the imperialists. The rumors that the Western troops would withdraw were denied, but no one knew precisely what the denials meant. One American general said that in case of dire emergency the Army could supply its own personnel by air but that the responsibility for feeding the civilian population would rest on the Russians.[4] There were evidences, too, in the summer of 1947 that some kind of Russian move was in the making; Soviet spokesmen referred to the likelihood that the Western powers would leave

[3] Early in 1946 a German newspaper writer, Arno Scholz, in the *Telegraf*, referred to these rumors. In April 1947 a *New York Times* dispatch said it was believed that the Allies would leave the city and the Russians take over. On October 12, 1947, the *Times* reported a denial by military government that the Americans would leave.

[4] General George P. Hayes, *The New York Times*, Jan. 13, 1948.

Berlin. Early in January 1948 the *Tägliche Rundschau* said there was no room in the city for adherents of the partition of Germany.

As the Russian propaganda attack became more violent in reply to the Marshall Plan—one noted commentator said in late 1947 that the provincial Ku-Kluxer and later haberdasher of Jackson, Missouri, vied for laurels with the little corporal from Munich [5]—Communist positions were buttressed everywhere in Europe and Asia. In December 1947 the king of Rumania abdicated, thus clearing the way for complete Communist domination of the country; in Germany the SED called in November for a people's congress for unity and a just peace; the CDU leaders Kaiser and Lemmer were refused permission to head their party in the East zone and were replaced by men who would heed the Soviet call for unity. In the Far East there were riots in the American zone in South Korea and demands that UN officers and Americans be withdrawn; [6] in mid-February 1948 the founding of the People's Republic of Korea was announced, with an army estimated at 200,000 men. At the end of the month came the Communist *coup d'état* in Prague.

In Germany the countermeasures of the English and Americans produced a new agreement in December 1947 to reorganize and strengthen the administrative agencies for Bizonia. Conferences with the ministers president in January 1948, despite French protests, led to a widening of the membership and authority of the German Bizonal Economic Council. The new council, although it would remain no more than an agency of military government, would include an executive and legislative body.

On January 20, 1948, in the Allied Control Council, Marshal Sokolovsky demanded immediate dissolution of the bizonal agreement; in February the East German "democratic organiza-

[5] Boris Shub: *The Choice*, p. 84, quoting Gorbatov in the *Literary Gazette*.
[6] *The New York Times*, Feb. 15, 1948.

tions" were invited to participate in the administration of the Soviet zone. On January 22 British Foreign Minister Bevin called for a West Union with the participation of all Western Europe including Germany; this was followed by the first meeting of the London six-power conference of the Benelux nations —Belgium, the Netherlands, Luxembourg—with France, England, and the United States, and the second took place from April to June. These London conferences ended with statements in favor of the close co-operation of Western Germany with the rest of Europe.

The Communist seizure of power in Czechoslovakia in late February was followed shortly by the suicide of Masaryk, who had pursued a policy of loyal collaboration with Moscow. For the future Czechoslovakia even more than for Poland, many people in the West, and the Czechs too, had cherished high hopes. In Poland, Mikolajczyk and his opposition party had been defeated and he had fled to England, but it had been evident since 1945 that no serious political opposition would be permitted there. The Czechs, though, had joined the Russian camp of their own free will; Masaryk and Beneš had made it plain after Munich that they were relying on Russia, not on the West, for protection; the offer of Marshall Plan aid that had been accepted by the Czech government was abruptly rejected when Stalin opposed it. The coup was proof to almost everyone that collaboration even by devoted friends and admirers of the Russians could lead only to complete Communist control. Many pro-Russians outside Czechoslovakia, however, remained unconvinced. Henry Wallace, for example, blamed the events in Czechoslovakia on the United States. It was American opposition to Russia, he asserted, that had made the move necessary, and more like it would follow.[7] Wallace did not have long to wait to see his prophecy come true; Stalin, a few days after the Communists took over the government in Czechoslovakia, invited the Finns to join Russia in a mutual-defense pact.

[7] Ibid., Feb. 28, 1948.

Under this menace of a rapidly spreading Communist power, President Truman called for a temporary draft and universal military training in the United States; [8] and the Benelux powers, together with France and England, announced on March 17 the Brussels Pact, a defensive alliance to last for fifty years. The United States, Britain, and France began discussions on the fusing of their three zones; the British and Americans hoped the French would accept merging the zones now that the Saar was detached from Germany and a security system was being patched together against both the Russian and the German threats. This was a step which the French were most reluctant to take, as they were reluctant to see Frankfurt made the new economic capital of the American and British zones. The French zone remained outside Bizonia; if they were to join, the French had said, it would widen the breach with Russia. The only kind of West German state they favored would be nothing more than a loose confederation, and this was unsatisfactory to the British and Americans. The Russians continued their cold reception of any French pretensions to act either as a major power or as mediator between East and West. In July, when the three powers sent a note to Moscow asserting their right to remain in Berlin, the Russians addressed their reply to the British and Americans only. It was the departure of Marshal Sokolovsky from the Allied Control Council, General Clay said, which convinced the French that they would have to join their zone to those of the British and Americans—either that or run it alone, and isolation was more alarming to the French than even a union of three German zones.

Marshal Sokolovsky appeared at the March 20 meeting of the Allied Control Council resplendent with forty medals gleaming on his chest, but he read from a nondescript mimeographed paper he held in his hand. He read so rapidly that the interpreters had trouble keeping up with him, and then he and his deputy

[8] Forrestal noted in his diary that Truman for the first time named Russia as the nation blocking all efforts to make a peace treaty (March 17, 1948).

and their assistants left the room. The burden of his remarks was that by meeting in London without Russia the three powers had acted illegally and the quadrupartite government of Berlin was consequently at an end. Berlin was part of the East zone and the four-power government there was dependent on the harmonious four-power administration of Germany as a whole. If the decisions of Potsdam were not carried out, then the Western Allies were no longer entitled to a part in the governing of the city and must leave. What was their legal claim, the Russians asked, to be there in the heart of the Russian zone?

The three powers replied that they were there by right of conquest, that the Russians had recognized their right; and they stated they had no intention of getting out. The British minister for Austria and Germany, Lord Pakenham, said that he liked Berlin too much to think of leaving, and General Clay declared bluntly that the Americans would stay. But what could they do if the Russians imposed a complete blockade? There were 3,500,000 people in the city, more than 2,000,000 in the West sectors, entirely dependent on the hinterland for their food and fuel. In addition, there were 6,500 troops of the Western powers, of whom some 3,000 were Americans with wives and children in Berlin. A writer in *The New York Times*[9] said the Allies could supply their own garrisons but any idea of their being able to feed the Germans should be instantly dismissed. It was a judgment that many others agreed with, including the man who would be responsible for making the decision to try to supply the city—Lucius D. Clay.

General Clay shared the opinion of the Germans which so many of his countrymen held. He had accepted without question the official views of how the enemy should be treated: JCS 1067, the wholesale denazification program, the low production levels. In January 1946 he had said that military government made it plain that within the framework of Potsdam it was up to the Germans to solve their own problems. He had defended

[9] Jan. 18, 1948.

dismantling in the same news conference in which he protested against Colonel Tulpanov's charge of American warmongering. When he came to Berlin he sharply rebuked people who were in any way critical of Russian activities. One of his advisers said he had, up to the end of 1946, a five-year plan of poverty for Germany.[1] He tolerated no opposition; he wanted no dissenting opinions from his subordinates; he was against an early British proposal for increasing steel production in Germany and threatened to leak it to the papers if the British persisted in urging it. Even so, by October 1947 he was ready to say in public that the United States opposed communism in every form and that it was American policy to give the Germans a free choice between East and West. It is one of the paradoxes of recent history that Clay became the allied proconsul who established what was almost a comradeship with the late enemy. It was Clay, above all, who bore the responsibility for waging the battle of Berlin; but it was not the Clay of 1946 for whom the Berliners would name one of their broadest avenues. He came to or was forced to adopt conclusions different from those he had held, and the story of how his mind changed is the story of the change of many American opinions. Clay was a military prototype of the average American; but he had one single advantage over others who thought as he did. He was in Berlin; he dealt directly with the Russians and with the Germans. He was also a man of courage and duty. It is unlikely that a more subtle or more politically schooled commander could have done better than he in the end, though such a one might have changed his views sooner.

Clay spoke no German and showed little evidence in his early reports as military governor of making any distinctions among Germans save as they accepted or rejected what military government wanted them to do. In his official reports there is no trace of criticism of the Russians until suddenly in October 1947, as though the irritations had been accumulating, he tells of the

[1] Personal interview.

difficulties they are making for the Western Allies. In his correspondence with his subordinates he is invariably sensible; he has a keen eye for the details of running the occupation; he is remote, cool, and stern with the Germans. He rebukes them for failing to bring food to the cities, although some of his subordinates say the farmers are doing everything they can to make deliveries despite difficulties of supply and transport. He cannot understand the Russians' behavior; their savage personal attacks on Truman are one of the decisive factors affecting his thinking. Russian spokesmen called Clay himself the chief gangster in 1948; but as late as 1948 [2] he maintained that differences among the four powers in Berlin were exaggerated. The Russian attacks on the United States had gone on for months without Clay's authorizing a reply in the German papers under American control. He was efficient. hard-working, the best kind of engineering officer—and the Army sets a high value on its engineers. He had cleared the harbor at Cherbourg with great dispatch, and, according to Army standards, such a man would do well in administering a country that also needed to have its broken steel and stone and Nazis cleared away. Once he had made up his mind to defend Berlin, he organized the operation of the airlift with skill and purpose.

Truman in February said he was no believer in the Morgenthau plan but neither did he want to see Germany rebuilt. Forrestal quotes him as saying at a meeting in June: "Berlin will be held. Period." But in July, Forrestal reports, Truman said the United States had a fixed determination to stay "until all diplomatic means had been exhausted in order to come to some kind of accommodation to avoid war." Marshall was fearful of strong measures. Washington was filled with brave words and indecision. It was Clay who caused the decisions to be made.

The coils of the blockade tightened slowly. On March 31, 1948, the Russians issued an order forbidding the entrance of

[2] *Neue Zeitung*, March 28, 1948.

military trains into Berlin unless baggage and personnel were first checked by Soviet officials. The next day it was announced that no freight could leave Berlin without Russian approval. At Helmstedt, one of the check points where East and West zones met, eight British truck convoys were stopped; and the main railway line was tied up as American and British trains were held for inspection. On the following day Soviet guards stopped all barge traffic, an important link in the city's supply system. The remedies prescribed by the Russians were as vague and complicated as the reasons they gave for their necessity. A new kind of permit—a proof of identity—would be needed for the trucks; the Russians demanded special passes of the Germans without telling where they could get them; bills of lading had to be approved; baggage of the Allies was to be subject to Russian examination except for personal articles. The Americans replied that they would supply the Russians with certified passenger lists, but they would not allow Soviet soldiers to board their military trains; neither visit nor search would be permitted. The Germans riding the nonmilitary trains were not so fortunate. They had no rights they could enforce, and they were taken off trains, just as they were kidnapped from the Western sectors of Berlin.

The Russians demanded that the occasional German using an American military train be subject to questioning. This too was part of the display of force: to demonstrate that the Russians determined how and where a German in the border zone could live and travel. But the Soviets made use of other measures besides fear. They announced the end of denazification; food and clothing were to be supplied in their zone in larger quantities; and they proclaimed themselves the protectors of a unified Germany as against the split and humiliated areas under the Western Allies.[3] As the West moved to merge the three zones and to reform the currency, the Bank Deutscher Länder was established, which the Russians charged was but another evidence

[3] *The New York Times*, June 3, 1948.

of the desire of the West to perpetuate the division of Germany for its own purposes. The Allied Control Council was described as only a cover for the plan to keep Germany divided and powerless, a vassal of American capitalism. This, indeed, was one of the reasons the Russians gave for the Council's having to be broken up.

The measures of the blockade, then, were countermeasures against the designs and concealed purposes of the West. They were intended to control the goods and people and sinister rumors that were infiltrating the country. The restrictions were actually designed, the *Tägliche Rundschau* said, to increase traffic by routing it through fewer check points, so that it could be handled more expeditiously; there was need for order along the demarcation lines, otherwise the Soviet zone was threatened with unrest. As for food in Berlin, the Russians offered to supply that; in April they said they would bring 40,000 tons into the city.

There was industrial reform in the East zone too. The Russians announced that 8 per cent of the industries, supplying 40 per cent of German production, had been turned over to the German people—that is, nationalized; the rest had been given back to its former owners, whether public or private, or had been incorporated in the mixed Russian-German companies. Occupation costs would be cut, although reparations would be held at the same level; and the German share in the trade of the Eastern states—Poland, Hungary, Bulgaria, etc.—would be bigger.[4]

In May, Stalin proposed that the four powers make a peace treaty with Germany and withdraw their occupation forces. A new party was founded in the East zone: the National Democratic party, especially designed to enroll the former National Socialists, who had been debarred from joining the CDU or Liberal Democrats and who had found the SED too sharp a turn from their allegiances of a few years back. The party, like the German police army that was being formed, had nationalist

[4] *Tägliche Rundschau*, April 18, 19, 1948.

overtones, and both had a theoretical place in the battle for winning German adherence to the Soviet system. The alternatives, the Russians told the Germans, were the marionette regimes of the West, slavery to American capitalism which hid under the benevolent Marshall mask the true face of the imperialist exploiters who sought the utter impoverishment of the German people. It was a marvelously topsy-turvy picture that Soviet propaganda drew. The blockade was aimed at increasing interzonal traffic,[5] the Western plans for aid sought to dry up German production. Communist writers denounced the forced labor of German workers in the West at the same time that thousands of Germans streamed across the zonal borders to escape slave labor in the uranium mines of Silesia or the camps of Soviet Russia, or merely the daily conditions of work in the East. Cartoons showed the East Germans the fat, scheming, predatory capitalists and politicians of the West, and the shades of the Nazis in the service of the United States and Britain. One cartoon showed Goebbels being summoned back to take his place in the propaganda wars. The East-sector papers reported a reign of terror in the West: the immigration from the Western zones was so great that it threatened the food supply of the East zone; men seeking to escape were being hunted with dogs in the American sector; the Ruhr was being annexed; the Americans and British planned to continue the occupation indefinitely.[6] When the currency reform took place in June the Russian press said it fixed the division of Germany; it was a heavy blow against the German workers, and to protect their interests as well as the economic stability of the East zone the rest of Germany would have to be sealed off.

Other Soviet devices too would make communication with Berlin more difficult. General Clay and his colleagues were told by Marshal Sokolovsky that Russian planes were planning to

[5] On April 1 a *Tägliche Rundschau* headline described the Soviet measures as "Widening of Interzonal Traffic."

[6] Ibid., May 26, 1948.

maneuver in the air corridors and that it would be dangerous to continue the regular transport flights. All in all, Berlin and its approaches were to be increasingly uncomfortable for anyone but the Russians and their sympathizers. Schumacher said the only people in Berlin who felt safe were the Communists. At the same time, the anti-German sentiments of Germany's neighbors were played upon. The Warsaw conference of eight powers, including Czechoslovakia, Poland, Hungary, and Yugoslavia, charged the West with creating a Germany with a considerable war potential, and, like the Russians, they demanded four-power control of its rising strength.

There was no precise day or hour when the partial blockade began. Controls had been imposed, tightened, relaxed, and reimposed with new and stricter regulations. As the American trains were delayed and stopped and then started again, the Americans repeated that they were prepared to give the Russians a list of passengers and a copy of their orders but that no Russians would be allowed on the trains. Soviet authorities replied that there could be no unrestricted access to the city, that all sorts of shady characters were arriving in Berlin and committing crimes on East-zone territory. To this an American general replied that he knew of no shady characters who were traveling on this line and expressed his willingness to meet any the Russians might care to produce.

As the Russians announced the new regulations, General Clay ordered that supplies for the American troops be brought by air. On April 5 a Russian and a British plane collided; the Russian fighter plane, apparently attempting to buzz the transport, dove into it, and fifteen people were killed, including the Russian pilot. On the same day the Moscow radio broadcast that the Allied Control Council was through; the dismemberment of Germany was an accomplished fact. The Soviet authorities then declared that air restrictions might be imposed in view of the accident and the danger of collisions. General Clay replied that he would reject any Russian flight restrictions. Clearly, if the

Western Allies were to stay in Berlin at all it was here that they would have to take their stand. The British announced immediately that they would provide their transport planes with fighter protection. Sokolovsky said no interference with British flights was contemplated, and the British commander in Berlin, General Robertson, thereupon withdrew his order for fighter escorts.

The West, still wary of the Germans, was quicker to react to Russian provocations now. Secretary of State Marshall and General Clay continued to defend dismantling despite mounting protests in the United States, but an American officer walked out of a Vienna meeting when the Russian representative said the United States was planning a war. In Berlin, German papers were permitted to publish the documents of the Russo-German pact of 1939. General Clay told the Germans they had touched bottom and henceforth they would have more to eat and wear. The British commandant in Berlin went further. Speaking in German first and then in English, General Robertson equated the Russian regime with that of the Nazis, and the Germans with the forces of democracy. "Make up your mind," he told his German audience, "to stand together against these gentlemen who with democracy on their lips and a truncheon behind their backs would take away your German freedom from you. The prospects are good; go forward and seize them." [7] In Bad Homburg a requisitioned hotel was returned to its German owners; General Marshall, too, compared the iron-curtain regimes with Hitler's; and President Truman ordered that the German art collections which had been brought to the United States for safekeeping be returned. (A Senate committee had declared earlier that they were private property, not war booty.) There was a sense of imminent danger all through the West. The American Army Chief of Staff, General Bradley, said he was not sure that war did not lie in the near future; Trygve Lie, Secretary General of the United Nations, declared that Europe

[7] *The New York Times,* April 8, 1948.

lay under the fear of open hostilities. The Central Intelligence Agency in April was able to extend for only sixty days its March forecast that war was not probable within a two-month period. General Clay reported to Washington that something was brewing—perhaps a new war. He sensed that something was going to happen not from intelligence reports but from the attitude of the Russians.

In the midst of this gathering tension, German voices were heard too. Schumacher believed the Germans should have a democracy of their own, neither a Russian nor an American brand of economic and political theory, and should build a bridge between the East and West, a bridge at long last of reconciliation. Konrad Adenauer said military government and democracy were contradictions in terms; an army was accustomed to giving orders and expected to be obeyed. A member of the Bremen Senate prepared a balance sheet of reparations and declared that the Germans had already paid a total of $70,000,000,000, including the territories lost without compensation, the dismantlings, the confiscations of property. Jakob Kaiser said the methods of the Russians were those of Hitler; but he refused to join the Bizonal economic council, which he thought would prejudice the future unity of Germany.

President Truman accused the Soviet Union and its agents of destroying the independence of a whole series of nations; their ruthlessness, he said, had brought about the crisis in Europe. Czechoslovakia had fallen; Greece continued under military attack; in Italy the Communist party was making a determined and aggressive effort to take power; Finland was under heavy pressure. Seven Finns had gone to Moscow to work out a mutual-security pact and treaty of friendship with the Soviet Union, and it was no doubt the stiffening of the Western attitude which enabled them to refuse the Russians the right to decide when Soviet troops could enter Finland in the interests of mutual defense.

The British and Americans agreed that the Germans could

produce aluminum under strict supervision, and they invited the Germans to submit estimates of their needs under the European Recovery Program. When the German estimates were made, they were promptly declared too high; but they were not scaled down seriously. The Germans were even able for the first time in many years to order fruit from Italy—$3,000,000 worth. And Italy was worth buying from, not only because of the succulence and vitamins of its fruit: De Gasperi won the fiercely contested Italian election with 48 per cent of the votes, which meant that he could govern with a democratic coalition. The Communists remained in formidable numbers; in the Italian electorate, as in the French, one out of every three voted Communist. Nevertheless, observers were agreed that it was a notable victory both for the Italian anti-Communist forces and for the Marshall Plan.

While President Truman and other Allied leaders called attention to the peril of the West, another kind of battle went on inside the American military-government apparatus, as it had since 1945. In 1948 for the first time there were security checks of American occupation personnel. Some of the effects were devastating; one branch was summarily shut down in Berlin because many of its members failed to get FBI clearance.[8] The struggles over the decentralization of German industry continued, and much of this was reported in the American press by correspondents who praised the courage of the little band of trust-busters who were valiantly fighting against the revival of German big business. Here again were two camps: one that wanted German recovery, even if it came about with the help of enterprises employing 10,000 people or more, and the other ideologically committed to decentralization, either because of old-fashioned trust-busting principles or because it was following the Communist line, which had long and faithfully been represented in the Treasury Department. General Clay, under the influence of the reconstructionists and the events in Berlin, continued to side with the moderate members of his administra-

[8] Personal interview.

tion; and decentralization proceeded cautiously, concentrating on sure targets such as I. G. Farben.

Along with the decisions of military government there were other moves toward reviving Germany. The Benelux powers at their April-to-June meeting joined the Americans and British in favoring internationalization of the Ruhr; the Ruhr, they said, was German and should not be separated from the rest of the country. They agreed too on including Germany in the general European Recovery Program, and they stated that these steps were taken in the interest of the revival of the European economy and that under no circumstances would the Germans be allowed to become too strong or to escape the scrutiny of Allied authorities. Nevertheless, the decisions were regarded by French leaders as a heavy blow: General de Gaulle said that they put France in mortal danger, Bidault that he had tried with all his energies to obtain the separation of the Ruhr from Germany but had failed. To blunt such fears an Allied Security Council was established, which had the right to investigate all German factories without warning and to stop any production it deemed dangerous to the Allies. The body continued to operate for a long time after the Korean War and the decision to rearm Germany—in fact, until the end of the occupation. What its task was became a matter of some debate; the Russians charged that it was a means of industrial espionage, and on this point they were echoed by a number of anti-Communist Americans who thought the Security Council kept more watch on German patents and research than on the military potential of the country.[9]

The close blockade began immediately after the currency reform. The Russians declared that the blockade was made imperative by the Western powers' issuance of the new Deutsche mark, but in fact the two events were connected only by propaganda. When on June 20 the new Deutsche marks appeared in the West zone, they were not issued in Berlin. The Western

[9] Personal interview.

sectors continued to use the old Reichsmarks; the Western powers were, indeed, ready to accept the Russian demand that the new East-zone mark be the sole authorized currency in Berlin. They did insist, however, that they have a part in controlling the amounts to be used in the city; and this the Russians rejected. Before the Deutsche marks became legal tender in the West zone all rail traffic out of Berlin had been stopped, as had all passenger traffic to and from the city; the Autobahn was open for Germans and the Allied personnel only if they had documents approved by the Russians. When the four powers failed to agree on the control of the East marks to be issued for Berlin, the East-zone currency was nevertheless introduced in the city by the Russians on June 23; and after June 24, while the Allies introduced the West-zone marks (imprinted with a "B" for Berlin) in their sectors, the East-zone currency was also valid there.

On June 24 the full blockade started. Everything that moved by land or water stopped; in West Berlin the power was effectively cut off, for the source of almost all the city's electricity lay, like so much else, in the Soviet sector. Inside Berlin the SED circulated leaflets telling the Berliners that Germany was an indivisible democracy; in Washington the State Department published a list of thirty-seven violations of agreements by the Soviets since the Potsdam conference. Marshal Sokolovsky, addressing the East-zone CDU, proclaimed the end of denazification, the release of prisoners of war, the end of the sequestration of property and of land reform as well as of any one-party system; and he promised that the Germans would get 14,000,000 pairs of shoes and 45,000,000 meters of textiles.[1] The last meeting of the Kommandatura had been held on June 16; the Russians had stalked out of it, as Sokolovsky had earlier left the Allied Control Council. The city was now almost completely divided. The Magistrat—the executive branch of the Berlin government—and the City Assembly continued to meet in the City Hall in

[1] *The New York Times*, June 3, 1948.

the East sector, but the first staged riots against the non-Communist majority in these bodies began with the announcement of the currency reform.

The Russian attack inside Berlin was adroit and well organized; it lacked now what it had always lacked, what the first elections in Berlin had shown was missing: mass support. Police from the East sector made raids into the Western areas, arresting men who were active in the independent, non-Communist union, or in the non-Communist parties. They kidnapped West-sector policemen—anyone who might serve as a conspicuous example of the fate of anti-Communists. People simply disappeared into the East, sometimes after a public raid, sometimes quietly.

Demonstrations were organized in the Western zones. These took the form of unsuccessful strikes in the Ruhr and elsewhere, protesting against the hidden depredations of the Marshall Plan and the splitting of Germany. Again there simply were not enough strikers to do any serious damage to the burgeoning revival. And outside Germany, where the Comintern and the Russian apparatus were recruiting their forces, shrewdly identifying the aims of the Communist party with the independence movements among native peoples, came the first revolt against Moscow. It was directed against the policy of complete subordination of political and economic life in the satellite countries to the requirements of the Soviet state. The new course that many Communists had believed in 1945–6 was to foster a degree of autonomy in the Communist parties outside Russia never developed, and Yugoslavia broke loose from the Soviet lines. Tito, with the advantage of no common frontier with Russia, was able to resist the authority of Moscow, and was read out of the party.

This was the scene as Berlin faced the summer of 1948. The Americans and the British said they were resolved to stay in the city and to attempt to supply it by air if the Germans could stand up under the privations they might have to endure for a long time. General Clay asked the opinion of Mayor-elect Ernst Reuter, who earnestly assured him that he could rely on the stoical Berliners. They would be neither intimidated nor bought; they would never under any circumstances go over to the Communists. Reuter had another meeting with a number of Clay's deputies at Harnack House in Berlin, the American-occupied guesthouse and club in the relatively undamaged suburb of Dahlem. There had been many of these occasions since the beginning of the occupation, the Germans being given their instructions and then returning to their jungles. Only a year before an American officer had been told by a superior that he should not allow the mayor to sit down unless invited to.[2] But Mayor-elect Reuter by 1948 had the respect and good will of the Americans with whom he dealt. He said he had heard that the Americans planned to fly in supplies not only for their own forces but for the civilian population as well, to attempt what seemed the hopeless task of supplying a great city by air. Reuter said that he was grateful for the motives and sentiments that lay behind the American decision. He was certain that the attempt must fail. Nevertheless, he added, he would not leave the city, nor would his colleagues. They could not defend Berlin or hold it against the invisible nets of the blockade and the divisions of the Red Army that lay in a vast area surrounding it.[3] But they could stay on to resist with all available means as long as possible and to share the fate of the city. Conversations such as these were reported to General Clay and were believed to have made a deep impression on him, as had the Communist attacks on President Truman in 1947. He had made the decision to try to fly in supplies—the first planes carrying food for the civilian population started on June 26—but he too had no confidence that the city could be given anything but emergency aid. When he announced the start of the experiment to the editor of the *Neue Zeitung,* he said as he snapped his fingers: "I wouldn't

[2] Personal interview.
[3] Personal interview.

give you that for our chances." [4] How could he think otherwise? Supplies had been flown in quantity across the hump in Burma, and for short periods food and ammunition had been brought by air for large bodies of troops; but how could a city of millions with only two airfields be supplied with fuel and food? Although one of the airports, Tempelhof, was among the largest in Europe and lay in the center of Berlin, the other, in the British sector at Gatow, was little more than a country airfield. An air operation of this magnitude had never been attempted, and no one, American, German, or Russian, thought it could be carried on for long. It was something to be used as a stopgap, to give time for negotiation.

Once, however, the decision to fly in supplies had been made, retreat would be difficult. If Berlin was defended, the rest of Germany too would be brought into the defense perimeter of the West. The London conferences had laid the basis for a German state; the ministers president were to meet with the military governors; and a Constituent Assembly was to adopt a constitution. Not only did the French feel this decision a mortal blow, but Germans too were unenthusiastic. Both Adenauer and Schumacher pronounced themselves unwilling to take part in this German state; it would widen the break between East and West and would for many confirm the Communist assertion that West Germany was a creature of the Allies, going through predetermined motions to found a state controlled by foreigners. Nevertheless, it would be an entity, a Germany of however amorphous a shape; and in Berlin it would have a frontier that would be defended by the Allies and Germans.

General Clay explained that this decision to create a West German state was no *diktat*; [5] the Germans were to take part in discussions with the Allies and have a voice in the decisions; the West had no intention of forcing this measure of independence down their throats. And they would be protected because Amer-

[4] Personal interview.
[5] *The New York Times*, June 13, 1948.

ican troops were garrisoned in the former capital. To put the United States out of Berlin would mean war, General Clay said in a speech at Heidelberg on June 24. Foreign Minister Bevin and also a Conservative, Harold Macmillan, told the House of Commons on June 30 that the price of staying in Berlin at the risk of war must be accepted.

Americans and British stopped coal shipments from the Ruhr to France because the French were not returning the railway cars in which the coal had been delivered to them. But hopes of a reconciliation with the enigmatic Russians were still cherished. President Truman, despite his firm words and acts, told reporters that he liked old Joe, that he had got along with him personally very well, but that he thought Stalin was not so powerful as he seemed; the Politburo could circumvent his friendly intentions.[6]

This view continued to influence American policy. On July 6 the United States, France, and Britain informed Moscow that they were in Berlin because of the defeat and surrender of Germany, that they had the right of access to the city and would not be induced by threats, pressures, or other actions to abandon this right. Yet they were eager to resolve the controversy in the spirit of fair consideration for all concerned. The Soviet reply, addressed to the United States and Britain, sharply rejected the Western contentions and repeated that the West had lost a legal claim to remain in Berlin. The note seemed to leave open a possibility of further discussion when it said that four-power conversations would be useful only if they were not limited to Berlin but extended to questions that affected all Germany. The three Western ambassadors to Moscow then asked for a meeting with Molotov, but were told that he was on vacation and Vyshinsky, too, was unavailable; they might see the deputy foreign minister, Zorin. They informed Zorin that the matter was of the utmost importance and asked if a meeting with Stalin could not be arranged. On August 2 Stalin saw the three Western

[6] Ibid., June 12, 1948.

envoys; he was his old self, sensible, sympathetic, tractable, a sharp bargainer but easy to deal with. He said that he understood the economic but not the political necessity for a merging of the British and American zones. The purpose of the blockade was not to drive the Western powers from Berlin—"After all, we are still allies," he told them. And suddenly he asked the American ambassador, Bedell Smith, if he would not like to settle the matter that very night. There followed what appeared to be an agreement except for technical details. The East mark would be accepted as the only legal currency in Berlin, and simultaneously all transport restrictions would be lifted. Second, while the Soviet government would no longer ask as a condition the deferment of a West German government, this was to be regarded as its insistent wish.[7]

Seemingly, another crisis had been passed. Ambassador Smith was optimistic; in a report to Washington he pointed out that Marshal Tito and Moscow had broken relations in July and this, together with the early success of the airlift, had made a softening of Soviet policy likely. Then the recurrent trouble arose which had blighted the hopes raised by other conferences; the details first proved difficult to work out and then impossible. Molotov said the creation of a West German state must be delayed as a condition of raising the blockade; Russia was prepared only to restore traffic that had been stopped since June 20, not to cancel the earlier restrictions.

A second meeting with Marshal Stalin was arranged for August 23, to resolve the differences, and he met the Western representatives with a plan he had prepared. Smith and his colleagues also had brought a proposal. A paragraph-by-paragraph comparison of the two disclosed, Smith reports, that they were in many respects in close accord. Stalin said he was ready to lift all restrictions of any consequence; he proposed that the East-zone mark should be the sole currency, and that the zone bank of issue be controlled by a financial commission under

[7] Walter Bedell Smith: *My Three Years in Moscow*, pp. 244–5.

the four Berlin commanders. He added that there should be something in the agreement about the plan to establish a West German government. He suggested that the final communiqué should say that the question had been discussed "in an atmosphere of mutual understanding." Smith thought that such a statement signed by the Allies would be interpreted by the Germans and the rest of Europe as a decision to abandon a West German government for some concessions on the blockade. He and his French and British colleagues would go only so far as to say publicly that they still desired a four-power agreement on a central government for Germany and that the London decisions did not preclude one. Finally on August 27 compromise was reached, not on the wording of a communiqué to be given the press but on a directive to the military governors. Within a week they were to find practical ways of lifting the blockade and introducing the Soviet-zone currency under four-power supervision.

The technical discussions were held in Berlin during the week of August 31 to September 7. Marshal Sokolovsky, like Foreign Minister Molotov, had objections to raise: he demanded control over civil aircraft entering Berlin, control over East-West and foreign trade of the city, and over the currency. After a week of deliberations the military governors were unable to submit a report; Sokolovsky said truly that there was nothing to report.

Notes went back and forth between the governments, and on September 22 the Allies wrote: "It is clear that the difficulties . . . derive not from technical matters but from fundamental points of view . . . as to the rights and obligations of the occupying powers. . . ."[8] Their note proposed continuation of discussions by the foreign ministers, who would soon be meeting in Paris.

The reply of the Soviet government said the position of the Allies complicated reaching an agreement, and reaffirmed the need for Soviet control of the airlanes.

[8] *Germany, 1947–1949*, p. 217.

The Russians were playing for time; if they could not succeed in delaying the creation of a West German state, they
could await the arrival of an old ally, winter. It was one thing to
fly planes into Berlin around the clock in the early fall; it
would be something else in the fog, snow, and darkness of the
months to come.

The negotiations failed, and the city settled down to its siege.
The West mark had the overimprint B on it for use in Berlin,
but it had the same magic as the other West-zone mark. By the
end of August it was worth three of the East-zone marks on the
free exchange. City employees who were paid only a quarter of
their salaries in West marks and the rest in the East-zone currency, as well as pensioners who were paid entirely in East marks,
took no part in the buying sprees that went on all over West
Germany. The Russian press in Berlin, while praising the
solidity of the new East mark, complained that goods were still
scarce and that prices, though lower, were not low enough. A
brush that had cost 2.50 Reichsmarks was now one East mark;
a pair of shoes with the material furnished cost 50 East marks,
without the material 100; ceramics were down 50 per cent, and
so were buttons; hairnets had cost 16.50 East marks and were
now 12. Sellers, the papers reported, were friendly again.[9]

There was some improvement, then, in the East, but there
was jubilee in West Germany. Goods appeared from behind
counters and cupboards and warehouses and out of the black
market, and were swept off the counters by famished buyers.
In West Berlin too there was a dependable currency now, but
everything remained in short supply; everything was missing or
on its way, and, no matter what kind of currency was used,
everything had to be brought to the city.

The imports for West Berlin had been filtering in slowly. All
priorities were given to the necessities: food and coal. Calculations varied on what a city would need to stay alive. One American estimate was as high as 20,000 tons a day, another was for a

[9] *Tägliche Rundschau,* July 8, 1948.

minimum of 2,000 tons of food and 5,000 tons of coal daily.[1]
The Germans calculated that 8,000 tons were essential. General
Clay thought a minimum economy could be maintained with
a daily airlift that averaged 4,000 tons for the Germans and
500 tons for the Allied troops. On July 5 American and British
planes—362 of them—brought in 3,000 tons in twenty-two
hours; and the airlift gained steadily in speed and carrying-
power. The British landed Sunderland flying boats on the
Wannsee in addition to the planes using the airstrips of Gatow.
The Americans flew in four-engined C54's carrying ten tons of
cargo to supplement the two-engined C47's carrying two and a
half tons; they came from Kansas, Panama, Alaska, and the Ha-
waiian Islands. A third field was planned in the French sector,
which would have to be built by hand labor without benefit of
much machinery. These three fields would serve during the fogs
and snow of winter; and, counting the good days with the bad,
it was hoped that with the new planes a round-the-clock airlift
would supply 8,000 tons, which was not disproportionate to
what had been brought to Berlin by the restricted schedules of
the railroads.

Russian air traffic in the corridor increased. There was bombing practice near the West sectors; once Russian Yaks seemed
about to land at Gatow, but only skimmed the field and in-
dulged in victory rolls. Landing signals were mixed by the Russian-controlled Berlin radio. The Russians complained that
British planes flying the corridor were at altitudes of only 100
to 300 meters instead of the prescribed 800 meters. They threatened to shoot down Allied planes that violated the Russian-zone
air space by flying outside the corridor lanes. Sokolovsky announced air maneuvers at night and target practice by day; in
addition, Russian planes would fly on instruments. These, he
said, were routine maneuvers; but General Clay replied that he
had never heard of them before.

The Russians were using every device short of military force

[1] Personal interview.

to drive the Allies from the city. In July more than 25,000 non-Communist police officers were discharged, and the principal police offices in the West sectors were moved to the East.[2] The police president, Paul Markgraf, now a diligent Communist, had been decorated by the Nazis a few years before for his exploits against the Russians. He had since repented, and under his direction the reprisals against non-Communist police were carried out boldly and continuously. As a result he had been suspended by the Magistrat, and the police were now divided into two forces as the Magistrat appointed the former assistant president, Johannes Stumm, president of the police in the Western sectors.

Mass meetings were held in East Berlin; the impossibility of provisioning the city through the airlift was a persistent theme. A cartoon in the *Tägliche Rundschau* showed a little boy asking his grandmother in 1949 to tell him the fairy tale of the supply of Berlin by air. Another showed a parrot left by the departed Americans saying: "We stay here." The Russian papers quoted Allied spokesmen who had acknowledged that the city could not be supplied by air; and as the autumn with its rain and fog advanced, the Russian papers assured their readers that the Allies would leave the city by January or February at the latest. But even in September, public-opinion polls had indicated that two thirds of the Berliners thought the airlift would work, although in July less than half had thought it possible.[3] The anti-imperialist propaganda and the promises of a better life for the Germans in the East zone continued. It was announced that 1,500,000 people would be given a warm meal each day, compared with the previous 500,000. Rations were increased; higher production levels were promised, as was German self-government. The airlift was not only ridiculed, it was explained away. Germans were being used, the Communist press said, to unload the small packages that came from the West to Tempelhof, and

[2] Davison: *The Berlin Blockade*, p. 171.
[3] *The New York Times*, Sept. 14, 1948.

Americans loaded the huge crates filled with Leicas, Meissen china, and even grand pianos that went to the West.[4] The Russians would supply the city, the papers said. Food packages were even sent from Russia, and Berliners were urged to get their supplies in the East sector. The city assembly was invaded for the second time by an organized mob on September 6. On August 26 and 27, tumultuous demonstrators had forced suspension of the sessions. The September session too was broken up, West sector policemen who had been deputized by the Magistrat to protect the meeting were arrested, Allied officials were roughly handled, German newsmen and radio reporters were beaten up—though one continued to broadcast while the gangs set upon him.

Non-Communist police took asylum in the American, French, and British liaison offices. On the request of General Ganeval they were granted a safe-conduct by General Kotikov, but when they came out of their refuges, they too were arrested.

The Social Democratic leaders, Franz Neumann and Ernst Reuter, together with leaders of the other parties and the trade unions, called on Berliners to demonstrate against the outrage. But because the meeting was to be held in the British sector near the border it was deemed dangerous, open to incidents, and its cancellation was ordered by the British commandant. A few Americans who felt the demonstration must be held persuaded the Germans to go ahead; it would be impossible for the British to break up such a meeting. And the American radio, RIAS, for twenty-seven hours broadcast the time and place of the gathering intermittently, interspersed with snatches of the "Marseillaise."

The meeting was called for five p.m. on September 9. People came to it by ones and twos; there was no marching, no mass-organized movement. It was a slow, but eventually huge, converging of the population of Berlin, thousands on thousands that stretched from the Brandenburger Tor and away past the Tier-

[4] *Tägliche Rundschau,* July 10, 1948.

garten, block after block as far as the eye could reach until the people became lost in the gray background of the stones and shattered buildings. West Berlin shops and factories had closed at two p.m., and the city emptied into the streets. There was no mistaking the difference both in numbers and in enthusiasm from the apathetic throngs, including schoolchildren freed for the day, who had turned out for rallies at the call of the East-zone leaders. Here there were old and young: 200,000 to 300,-000 of them, it was estimated, including blind paraplegics of the late German Wehrmacht. Neumann asked for a minute of silence in memory of those who had died in the Nazi concentration camps, which now had exchanged the swastika for the hammer and sickle. Reuter linked the fate of Berlin to that of the free world. The crowd was attentive and orderly until a Russian jeep came on its way to the Russian war memorial lying in the West sector. One Russian jeep was too much; stones were thrown at it. A soldier in the jeep fired, and a man in the crowd was killed. The Red flag was torn down from the top of the Brandenburger Tor, where it had flown since the capture of the city. Five men were arrested by the Russians and tried in the East-sector courts, where within days they were sentenced to twenty-five years at forced labor.

The Russians struck hard where the defenses were weak or doubtful, but were unexpectedly cautious. When the British protested against a barrage balloon near their airfield which made landing difficult, the Russians grounded it and never used again what might have become a dangerous weapon. They maneuvered in the air corridor, but brought down no planes except through one inadvertent collision. General Clay sent in a military train with armed guards to try the strength of the blockade; it was shunted to a siding, whence it had to return ignominiously to the American zone. Clay remained convinced, however, that the Russians would not actually risk war, that strong measures would be respected. He wanted to send to Berlin an armored column with a technical force that could repair any damages to the railroad system, which the Russians said were part of the cause of the blockade; the column would have orders to force its way through the East zone. But Clay's superiors in Washington would not permit the risk to be taken, and there were many considerations in such a decision. If the Russians tried to stop them, the Americans would fire the first shot. There would be little enthusiasm anywhere for a war started with one of the late Allies over the belligerent defense of what had three years before been the center of Hitler's Germany. Not least important was the never relinquished hope of winning the Russians back from their unaccountable rejection of the West. These sentiments, however, were being modified by events remote from Berlin as well as in the city: the leap of a woman employee from a window of the Russian consulate in New York to gain asylum in the United States; the accusations against more alleged American agents of Russia.

By the end of September a plane was landing every three minutes, night and day. The millionth sack of coal was delivered. Coal was always a major problem of the airlift; it had to be carried in sacks and wetted down to mitigate the danger of fire. At first the abundant supply of GI duffel bags was used, and when these were gone paper bags were substituted. The operation of bringing food and fuel to the city was called Operation Vittles, and in the course of the autumn there was added to it Operation Little Vittles. This was candy parachuted down to the Berlin children and paid for by the men of the airlift. They had all been impressed by the children of Berlin; one pilot especially had observed that the children never asked for candy but only stood and looked, and were grateful when he gave them some sweets out of his pockets.[5] There was another airlift for the sick children of Berlin, who were flown out by the Allies to the relatively green pastures of the West zones, where

[5] Lieutenant Gail S. Halvorsen started this operation, Davison reports, as a personal project.

they could be fed and cared for more readily than in the beleaguered city. This was something new for Berlin too.

The adult Berliners were having a hard time. Unemployment rose as factories had to shut down for want of fuel and power and raw materials. In July, 20 per cent were closed, and one out of ten previously employed Berliners was out of work. Unemployment gradually went up from 35,000 to 90,000, at the end of the blockade to 150,000. But the city took on a neater look as the newly unemployed joined a labor force that picked and hacked at the refuse still lying over the city. The Berliners were also earning back their self-respect. They were praised continually, and on all sides, for their Spartan courage; in turn they hurled defiance at the Russians on every occasion—the columns of their newspapers were more outspoken than those in the zones. But by November they were freezing; electric current was turned on only two hours during the day and two at night, so that women got up to do their ironing and cooking at one or two o'clock in the morning. A candle cost eighty pfennigs, or more than an hour's wages; petroleum was four marks a liter; there were no fresh meat, potatoes, or vegetables; the subway shut down at six o'clock. Children, blue with cold, were reported always at hand to carry anyone's suitcase; their fathers were earning seventy-two pfennigs an hour working at the rubble.[6]

The Allies imposed a counterblockade on shipments to the East zone. While this could have little immediate effect on decisions that were being made in Moscow, the Eastern part of Germany was dependent on goods and raw materials from the West, far more than the West zones on the East. The countermeasures affected other countries too—Holland, for example; but it was one of the few available weapons that the West was prepared to use, and did use—with small but undeniable effect.

By the autumn of 1948 General Clay had become convinced

[6] *Neue Zeitung,* Nov. 27, 1948.

that he could supply Berlin with its subsistence ration indefinitely. The performance of the airlift was magnificent; it had developed into a precise, belt-line apparatus, with a training center in the United States that simulated the problems of flying in the corridor. And with the new installations ready in December at the French airfield at Tegel, there was no doubt that the airlift would be able to supply the city's basic needs. The Russian offensives had gone to the brink of military action, but had stopped there. German East-zone "barracks police" were brought into the city, as were Russian tanks, but neither the Berliners nor the Allies were easily overawed. The Magistrat forbade Communist meetings in public buildings in West Berlin; the counterblockade was tightened. East-zone police and officials who were known for their brutalities were named in the press. A society—the Battle Group against Inhumanity—was founded to discover and publish information about illegal activities and excesses committed by the party and administration in the East zone. The tanks stayed in a huge semicircle around the West sectors, but they did not move, nor did the Allies. The "barracks police"—ready, if all went according to plan, to answer the call for help of a "spontaneous" rising in the West sector—stayed in their barracks. It was plain to Moscow that it would take more than the blockade to get the British and French and Americans out of the city. In December a Russian-zone paper pointed out that Berlin and the stir over the blockade were dwarfed by the dazzling successes of the People's Army in China. There were articles on the false alarm over Berlin, over a nonexistent blockade.[7] Peiping was captured by Mao's forces, and Russia announced that her own army would be out of Northern Korea by the end of the year.

Preparations for founding the West German state went ahead. In September Konrad Adenauer, who had become persuaded that a West German government was essential, was elected president of the Constituent Assembly, or Parliamentary Coun-

[7] *Tägliche Rundschau*, Dec. 9, 21, 1948.

cil, as the Germans called it. The East zone too announced plans for a new constitution. While the former leader of the Social Democrats, Grotewohl, addressed an audience on the subject, it was noted that his colleague Wilhelm Pieck read a newspaper. The enraptured, spontaneous demonstrations would come later.

The Russians' efforts to take over the city government succeeded only in dividing it. The City Assembly and Magistrat, minus the Communist party, the SED, were established in the British sector. At the end of November the East Berliners were presented with a new government, headed by Fritz Ebert, son of the first president of the Weimar Republic. In early December the elections to the Berlin Assembly provided for under the city's constitution were held in the West sectors. These had been delayed at the insistence of the Russians, who had of course known that their outcome would overwhelmingly favor the non-Communist parties and the West. The Communists now called for a boycott, but over 85 per cent of those eligible voted, and Reuter was again elected lord mayor; this time he could take office. The new Assembly met in overcoats and by candlelight in unheated rooms, but there were no further attacks by the Communist mobs. There were two police forces now and two city governments, and General Clay said it was possible that a solution of the Berlin crisis could be found in recognizing both governments and the sole validity of Russian-zone currency in the city.

The University of Berlin lay in the East sector. Before the blockade started, there had been a movement among students and faculty to found a new university free of Communist authoritarianism.[8] The blockade hastened decisions, and the Free University opened in Dahlem early in December on funds that had been accumulated by profits of the American-controlled German press and with a faculty assembled from the University of Berlin and other German universities. Its chancellor was Ed-

[8] Personal interview, Edwin Redslob.

win Redslob, Goethe scholar and editor of the West-sector news-paper *Tagesspiegel*, long the target of the Communist press and political leaders.

The Russian-controlled papers displayed a map used in the French zone, showing not "Germany" but a series of separate *Länder*,[9] representing, as everyone knew, the stubborn French hopes for a confederation of German states. But in Berlin the French were under other influences besides those of the Quai d'Orsay, and they produced one of the unexpected events of the blockade. The Soviet radio tower lay in the French sector; like the broadcasting station that had been in the British sector, it was a vestige of the time when the Russians had been the sole occupiers of the city. One day the French threw guards around the tower and blew it up, announcing that it was a danger to the airplanes using the Tegel field. Their action surprised not only the Russians but some of the French as well. It had been taken on the responsibility of the local French commandant, General Ganeval, who was as tired of the Russian blockade as were his British and American colleagues. A few days later, however, it was announced that the village of Stolpe—which lay in the French sector, and over 90 per cent of whose inhabit-ants had voted in the Berlin elections despite Communist de-mands for a boycott—would be surrendered to Russian con-trol. Since the French had originally said they needed Stolpe as part of the space for an airfield, its importance to them had dis-appeared in theory with the construction of Tegel. To Ber-liners, however, it seemed to be a sorry *quid pro quo*.

The Tegel landing field had been built by 20,000 Germans, men and women, mainly by the same sort of hand labor Gen-eral Clay had seen carving out the airfields of China. A few bulldozers, dismantled by an "acetylene expert," had been flown in sections from Frankfurt to Berlin and reassembled.

As Christmas neared, one of the holiday wishes of the popula-tion, the *Neue Zeitung* reported, was for a mild winter. A small

[9] *Tägliche Rundschau*, Dec. 21, 1948.

extra ration of coal was issued, cigarettes were distributed, British and American soldiers gave presents to the Berlin children; but the city had to celebrate on meager resources. Trees in the Grunewald were chopped down for fuel, as was every second tree in the city streets. The Russians took pictures of the half-destroyed Grunewald and "quoted" the Americans as saying that what they had spared from the air they would now destroy on the ground.

The Berliners were cold, gaunt, and hungry; the population was notably lacking in young men. Although the city as a whole had fewer people in it than in 1939, there were more older women and young girls than there had been before the war; there were, however, far fewer women of twenty-five to forty, and less than half the number of men in this age bracket. The city's political leaders, back from exile or the concentration camps, were older than those in other areas of the West, and some were women. One of them, a deputy, was Jeanette Wolff, a "non-Aryan" who had miraculously survived two of Hitler's most notorious death camps. She was severely beaten when the Communists invaded the Assembly, and she spoke convincingly to her colleagues about her contempt for secret police and concentration camps, whether Nazi or Russian. "I have only one life to lose," she said, "and this life belongs to freedom." Turning to the SED members: "And if it should cost my life on your account, gentlemen, and Berlin could remain free, I declare myself ready for death." [1] Another was Louise Schroeder, modest and housewifely but a fanatical and eloquent democrat, who had become acting mayor when Reuter was debarred from taking his office. She lived in a furnished room and during the blockade took the subway to work, although one of the rare Berlin automobiles was at her disposal. It was a city held together by a vast contempt and hatred for totalitarian states; [2]

[1] Davison: *The Berlin Blockade*, p. 114.

[2] Berlin had never voted for the Nazis—only six out of nineteen deputies in the City Assembly were members of the party when Hitler came to power. The Berliners had the abiding wit and cynicism of the people of great cities.

lacking everything, finding substitutes for what people had in cities that were intact; owing its life to the foreign pilots, who a few years before had brought destruction and who now took the place in its affections of the German heroes whose busts had once lined the paths of the Tiergarten. When American planes crashed, there were long lines of mourners, and flowers were left anonymously at the site. The gifts the Berliners showered on the pilots and men of the air bridge were brought from a minuscule store. Some of them the Americans insisted on returning because they thought them far too costly.[3]

The Christmas of 1948 was not only lean; it also overturned old customs. Among the traditional symbols of the season were candles; and Berliners expressed the wish that the next Christmas might be celebrated in warm rooms and without candles; even these had come to have another meaning.

In December the average daily tonnage of the airlift was 4,500; in the next two months it climbed to 5,500. This provided no fuel for industry or for homes; it kept the electric generators going and the population fed. The cargoes continued to increase despite the hazards of the winter weather, and by spring the average tonnage reached 8,000 a day. In April in one day 12,941 tons were landed by 1,398 planes that came in every 61.8 seconds. As the records were broken, Berliners rushed out on the field with flowers and gifts for the airmen. It was plain now that the blockade could be beaten in the sense that the city could be supplied with food; in fact, the ration of the average Berliner rose during the blockade, although he got only twenty-five pounds of coal with which to keep warm and he lived in the latitude of Labrador.

As the blockade turned out to be porous, there were other responses to the actions of the Soviets. On March 20, 1949, the

---

During the worst period of the bombardment someone put up a splendid new sign which stretched for thirty feet across the blasted windows of a burned-out building: "We greet Adolf Hitler, the first worker of the Reich."

[3] *Tagesspiegel*, Aug. 4, 1948.

West mark was declared the only legal currency in the West sectors. The North Atlantic defense alliance was signed in the early part of the year. The United States protested to Russia against the continued detention of 400,000 German prisoners of war. A Russian mission, consisting of four officers and four enlisted men, was ordered out of West Germany by General Clay, who said there had been enough time for them to arrange for voluntary repatriation of Soviet citizens.

The Russians organized their East bloc into an economic trading area and a military alliance paralleling that of the West, and armed the East-zone barracks police with machine guns. But they had lost the battle of Berlin. The magnitude of the successes of the Red Army of Mao Tse-tung in China enabled Stalin to withdraw from his claim to Berlin with some dignity. In February an American correspondent asked him a number of questions about his views on peace and Berlin, and Stalin's answers made no mention of the currency question. The American Department of State noted the omission, since this had been the cause most frequently alleged for the blockade. The American deputy representative on the Security Council, Philip C. Jessup, took occasion on February 15 to ask the Soviet member, Mr. Malik, whether the omission had any significance. A month later Malik replied that Stalin's failure to refer to the currency was "not accidental," that the Soviet regarded the currency question as important but felt it could be discussed in the council of foreign ministers if a meeting of that body could be arranged to review the German problem as a whole. Mr. Jessup asked whether this meant that the Soviet government had in mind a meeting of the foreign ministers while the blockade was in progress or whether the restrictions would be lifted in order to permit the meeting to take place. On March 21 Mr. Malik replied that the restrictions on trade and transportation could be withdrawn reciprocally and the blockade could be ended in advance of the meeting.

After further discussions the three Western powers announced on May 4 to the Secretary General of the UN, where the blockade had long been on the agenda, that they had concluded an agreement with the Soviet government providing for lifting the blockade as of May 12; on May 23 there would be a meeting of the council of foreign ministers in Paris to consider questions relating to Germany and problems arising out of the situation in Berlin, including the question of the currency.

Despite Stalin's former emphasis on postponing the establishment of the West German state, the talks progressed this time without major disagreements. On May 8 the German Assembly approved the new constitution, or Basic Law, and on the following day the Soviet commandant issued orders allowing sixteen trains to enter the city.

The airlift continued through September, although the blockade ended on May 12. The Autobahn was opened to traffic, barges used the canals again, trains came through; but there were stoppages and delays, and the Allied commanders, who had dealt with these matters before, kept the airlift going. General Clay, who left Berlin to return to the United States on May 15, flew out of the city preceded and followed by the planes of the airlift. The State Department was to take over administration of the American zone in Germany, and he could now retire, as he had announced before the blockade started. When he returned to Washington, he made a speech before Congress. In it he paid tribute to the courage of the Berliners, although he added that it was impossible to forget what the Germans had done and difficult to forgive. There had been this change: the Germans had started an aggressive war, and that had been under a dictatorship. He had seen in Berlin the spirit and soul of a people reborn. Berlin had had a second chance to choose freedom.[4]

The blockade had lasted over three hundred days—from June 24, 1948, to May 12, 1949. The estimates varied with the dates ascribed to its beginning; some said it had lasted 315 days, oth-

[4] *The New York Times*, May 18, 1949.

ers 328. It had cost the lives of 45 American and British airmen, had flown in 1,592,287 tons of fuel and food; calculations of its cost varied from $137,498,000 to $350,000,000, if they included the cost of maintaining the Army. As battles go in our time, it was cheaply won.

IX

WEST GERMANY

Berlin was the center of the German moral recovery, but it was in West Germany that the major economic and political changes took place during the time of the blockade. The currency reform that went into effect on June 20, 1948, was a tremendous technical achievement made possible by the fact that Germany was an occupied country. All four of the occupying powers had long agreed that currency reform would have to precede any genuine economic recovery, although some among the German economists believed it would be better to have more goods in production before new money was printed. But as early as May 1946 General Clay's financial adviser, Joseph Dodge, with the assistance of two other American economists, Gerhardt Colm and Raymond M. Goldsmith, consulted with Russian, French, German, and Czechoslovakian experts with experience in revaluing currencies, and then wrote a report recommending the issuing of new marks. The Dodge-Colm-Goldsmith recommendations closely resembled the measures eventually adopted: a ten-to-one reduction in the currency, a reorganization of the public and private debt structure, and equalization of the penalties imposed by the revaluation through what was in effect a capital levy on land and industrial plants. This equalization-of-burdens law, however, was not enacted until 1952.

The Russians seemed favorably disposed to the American report during the first discussions in the Allied Control Council, but soon demanded that two sets of plates be available for printing the currency, one of which would be kept in Leipzig in the East zone. The British and French were ready to let the Russians have the plates, but the Americans, with vivid memories of their last experience of sharing the printing of German marks with the Russians, countered with the suggestion that one set of plates be made and that the currency be printed in Berlin in an enclave under four-power control. This, however, the Russians declined to accept, and the reform languished, along with much else on the agenda of the Control Council.

In 1947, as a result of rumors that the Soviet might at any moment introduce a revalued currency in its zone, the United States Treasury printed new marks in what was called Operation Bird Dog. These, before the end of the year, were secretly shipped to Germany, where they were stored against the emergency of any sudden Russian move on the economic front.

Mr. Dodge returned to the United States, to be succeeded by Jack Bennett, another expert made available to military government by the Treasury Department. In Clay's opinion, it was he who now became mainly responsible for the success of the reform.

The Germans were given the job of administering the issuing of the currency, and German technical advice was often sought and given in the course of the formulation of the plans. But the Germans tended to be skeptical; even the impassioned proponent of the free market, Ludwig Erhard, was reputed to be lukewarm to many of the provisions.

The rigorous decisions were ones that no democratic government responsive to the pressures of large portions of the population could have made. Germany had gone through two inflations, and the currency reform of 1948 again shrank savings that a thrifty people had accumulated, this time by more than 90 per cent. The new currency was to be exchanged at the rate of ten Reichsmarks to one Deutsche mark, but later this was scaled down and the eventual conversion rate became 100 to 6.5. The reform was heavily on the side of the producer and the shopkeeper; for people who had goods or food to sell, there was the pent-up demand of years behind the consumers' storming of the shops. Every German could exchange 40 of his old marks against 40 of the new; 20 more marks, also to be exchanged at a one-to-one ratio, were to be made available in two months. Savings had to be registered; one half of the new marks was made available to their owners almost immediately; of the rest, one fifth was released later and one tenth was put in blocked accounts for investment. The remaining seven tenths were later extinguished when the whole reform seemed in danger.[1]

West Germany took off on an enormous buying spree. Goods were magically on the counters—food, clothing, and drink—and everyone had at least forty marks to spend. It was a Kafka-like fairy tale, with the buyer in the midst of shops, many of which were little more than window displays in front of bombed-out interiors, a market place where shopkeepers and manufacturers were kept deliberately short of working capital so there would be a powerful incentive for a rapid turnover and cash receipts would be spent promptly for new supplies.

The Germans were drunk with their opportunities. Some of them, indeed, found the liquor supply the most desirable of all there was to buy; some stuffed themselves with food they had dreamed of; some bought shoes or a dress; but all of them bought, and the goods were there to buy. They came from new production and from old, hoarded stocks that had been kept against just such a bright day when again the markets would be open to everyone and streams of goods and solid legal tender would refresh the parched longings of buyers and sellers. It was Christmas, it was carnival, and it was very nearly another inflation. The Bank Deutscher Länder almost immediately took steps to limit credits as far as possible, raising its requirements for minimum reserves and urging that the banks restrict credit to essential uses of imports and production. This could not immediately affect the consumer, but the rate of credit expansion

[1] H. C. Wallich: *Mainsprings of the German Revival*, p. 69.

slowed down. The most important anti-inflationary force was the forbearance of labor in not demanding higher wages. The German unions were well disciplined, and both the rank and file and the leadership knew from hard experience what a rising spiral of wages and costs did to the economy. With the productive capacity of German labor less than that of prewar years, rising wages could have been disastrous. Wages stayed where they were despite all the pressures of mounting industrial prices, and their stability was helped by price controls on basic foods and rents. After a few months foreign imports began to come in, which cooled to some extent the fevers of domestic manufacture.

The economy bounded forward. Production doubled in the second half of 1948. Those who benefited most were the ones who had something to sell—there could scarcely fail to be a demand for it, whatever it was. And the technique of the reform had been skillfully designed to keep people producing. Debts were cut down at a ratio of ten to one. There were tax remissions for investments and savings. Office furniture could be written off, profits plowed back into more goods. The income tax, while heavy, was designed with loopholes for the benefit of the entrepreneur. The German producer had to get his capital from current sales, which meant long hours as well as a quick turnover. It meant that a great advantage lay with those who had a start, a supply of goods or the means of making them; and after the first buying surge was over, people with small incomes and those living on savings or pensions watched the country enjoying a recovery in which they had only a small share.

It was a spectacular and brutal boom that was to last for years, to become one of the wonders of the postwar world. It was a triumph for the economists, both Allied and German, who had designed the model for precisely what was accomplished. When the reform started, Germany was economically leveled; except for a handful of people who had kept jewelry and such personal possessions intact, there were no rich, there were no large fortunes, no great enterprises. What automobiles there were ran by dispensation of the Allied authorities and Allied stocks of gasoline, or they were converted to wood-burning vehicles that transported what little there was to carry. The Germans had been brought to economic equality, and in this respect there was little to distinguish between the East and West zones.

There were other brakes on inflation; one was the amount of money the consumer had to spend. With a 20-per-cent price rise, people were unable to buy many of the things they wanted; and by the turn of the year, with imports and increased production, there were signs of a buyer's market in some commodities. Had food prices gone up, it is doubtful that the wage line could have been held, but these remained fixed; and, as the first surge of buying was primarily the food wave (which was to be followed by the clothing wave, and then the repair wave, and finally the travel wave), the German worker, however tempted to increase his share of the bounty, continued at the old rate of pay. There was more to his stoicism than his judgment of what the economy needed. Unemployment figures continued to rise despite the new production, owing largely to the continued influx of refugees who came from the East zone by the thousands,[2] and widespread strikes would have had damaging results for employed workers. Furthermore, no one in Germany wanted to cloud the dawning prosperity. They had all known too many years of dearth; it would have been political suicide to advocate a course that could be viewed as slowing or stopping the recovery.

Savings were drawn on; 600,000,000 of the new marks were spent from savings in the period from June to December. The trend toward spending was stimulated not only by desire but also in part by prudence. The Allies in October of 1948 lowered the rate at which blocked balances would be exchanged,[3] and in this move was the threat of further depreciation of savings.

---

[2] McCloy reported their rate of entry in the last quarter of 1949 at 30,000 a month (*First Quarterly Report*).

[3] *Report* of the Bank Deutscher Länder (1948–9), p. 4.

For those who had small savings or none, or were dependent on pensions or sickness insurance, for the war widows, the orphans, the old, the infirm, there was at best a subsistence living. As it was, at least 15 per cent of the German national product went to the pensions and upkeep of these people; the gamble, and one that no representative government would have dared take, was that an economy based on the profit motive would have the essential dynamism—and only such an economy would have it—to stir production out of the superannuated machines, the lowered vitality of the workers, the apathy toward slogans and exhortations which had followed the bankruptcy of National Socialism.

The decisions of the Allies were cut to this pattern. Although there were many critics of the decentralization and deconcentration programs, the Americans in particular had succeeded in changing the economic landscape to a degree. The guild tradition had resulted in the *Länder*'s continuation of the former practice of licensing new businesses; as a result of American prodding, at the end of 1948 all such laws were rescinded. With the exception of fields requiring skills affecting the public welfare, such as medicine and dentistry, new businesses could start without the approval of a local board on which sat future competitors of the applicant. So it was possible in the early days of the currency reform to set up a business on a tiny amount of capital and cause it to burgeon in marvelous fashion. Here the refugees, with their need to find a new place both in the economy and in their own minds, were important, and they had a spirited effect on a native population that without them might have been tempted to slow down.

By the early part of 1949 the danger of inflation was over. The increase in short-term credits, which had risen from 1,300,000,-ooo D marks in July 1948 to 3,800,000,000 in October, slowed noticeably, as did the increase in prices. While the rate of production went up much less steeply, competitive production was lively, foreign goods appeared, and customers became more selective. Because of the relatively high prices and the need for everything, many wives worked to increase the family income. To keep prices within reach of the buyers, entrepreneurs used their ingenuity to rationalize, to simplify the processes of production wherever they could, and this had an unfavorable effect on the employment figures. Before the currency reform there had been only 450,000 unemployed; at the end of 1948 there were 760,000; by June 1949 they numbered 1,300,000; by the end of January 1950 there were nearly 2,000,000. It was a lopsided economy, not only as compared with East Germany, where there was little unemployment and little production for consumers, but within the boom. Yet even the mass of pensioners and the unemployed could be supported by the doles it made possible, and many of them were eventually absorbed into the economy. Nevertheless, the ostentatious buying of luxuries that began on the part of the newly rich as early as the start of 1949 was in sharp contrast to the shabby state of millions of their countrymen, many of whom had left a lifetime's hard-won savings in the East. These new men and women of affairs who were parading their own escape from poverty were resented, but the resentment was diverted for many by the possibility of joining them.

There was a considerable variation in the unemployment figures within West Germany. In Schleswig-Holstein, with its swollen population of refugees, they were high: 15.4 per cent. In Württemberg-Baden, with its larger urban centers of production, they were 2.5 per cent.[4] Another factor was the housing situation. There were often jobs open in mining and industrial areas, but no place to live for a family wanting to move there. In 1950 a quarter of the German population shared their living-space with friends, relatives, or strangers, or lived in bunkers or cellars. Employment actually went up in that year, but not enough to match the increase in the labor force.

[4] *Germany Reports*, p. 208.

Unemployment was recognized as a major threat. It had been in large part the failure of the Weimar government to deal effectively with this problem that had brought Hitler to power, and both the Germans and the Allies were aware of its dangers. Plans were formulated; building programs, reconstruction projects—"made" work—was to be the answer, reflecting the experience of the United States and the other Western powers in the thirties—where, however, such projects had met with indifferent success until the arms boom had got under way.

The Allied Joint Import-Export Agency gradually permitted the importation of foreign goods in quantity. By the end of 1949 these importations were an important factor in releasing excess pressures on domestic production, and in the late autumn prices turned down and production went up. People began to save money again, something they had been reluctant to do after their experience of the inflations of '23 and '45, the threat of further reductions in the value of their savings, and the hunger for the things on sale. The pattern was set for the long-range economic recovery of the West zones.

Germany was not the only country in 1949 to show signs of deflation and unemployment. Prices in Britain and the United States had turned down too, and in Britain the pound was devalued in September. As a result, the mark had to be devalued; the new rate was .238 instead of .30 to the dollar. The change was accepted calmly by a public that might well have been dubious of any revaluation of a currency so recently established. Confidence in the new currency remained unimpaired. This time it had to be good; there had been enough paper in the form of money and enough money in the form of cigarettes to last the Germans for a long time. Along with the currency reform came heroic doses of Marshall Plan aid. The flow of ECA-financed goods began to reach Germany in December 1948; Clay reported that imports for the year were $417,000,000 financed from German exports, and $101,000,000 from ECA funds. The Marshall Plan money was most important in the critical period when Germany needed to increase her imports without having to export to pay for them.

The political changes in West Germany paralleled the economic ones, although they were far less spectacular. On July 1, 1948, the eleven ministers president of the Western *Länder* had met with the Allied military governors and decided that the Constitutional Convention would meet in September. With the blockade tightening at this time, it was the British and the Americans who were pushing the Germans to make decisions and take responsibility. General Clay complained of the reluctance of German leaders to move ahead and grasp the opportunities for self-government which were being pressed upon them.[5]

German uncertainty came in part from the still raw surfaces of the Nazi past. There would be no serious, wide-scale neo-Nazi movement in the postwar years, although neo-Nazism was often discerned by both Germans and Americans, and from time to time, beginning in 1948, splinter parties would be formed which, however small and absurd, could remind an observer that Hitler and his brown shirts had once been both. With the economic revival and the beginnings of an independent political life, former Nazis and men who had been officials under the Hitler government took part in the new organizations, some of them in far too important positions. The Bank Deutscher Länder made a place, Americans charged,[6] for two such who had been directors of the Reichsbank. In Bavaria 85 per cent of the civil servants who had been removed were reinstated by 1949, and there were reports that it was hard for those who had not been Nazis to get jobs. Former Nazis were reported back at their high industrial posts in the Ruhr. A party known as the Association of Independent Germans, called nationalist and reactionary, was founded in June 1949; and in March 1950 the only neo-Nazi party that would gain more than 5 per cent

[5] New York *Herald Tribune*, July 17, 1948.
[6] *The New York Times*, April 27, 1949.

of the vote in local elections, the Socialist Reich party, was started with a program described as a Mussolini-like corporate state. Some of its support, Chancellor Adenauer charged, came from Communist sources. As the licensing of newspapers was abandoned in the summer of 1949, it was freely predicted that undesirable publications would reappear staffed by those who had been unable to obtain licenses from the Allies.[7]

For years the scandal of an appointment of a former pillar in Hitler's Reich to a position of respectability and authority in the federal or state government would make intermittent headlines in the press. As time went on, men who had been judges and prosecutors under the Nazis were much too often appointed to high judicial posts, a concentration-camp doctor who had been living obscurely but well in West Germany would be discovered, a former SS concentration-camp guard would run for office. The press always set up a hue and cry. Resignations and prosecutions followed, but allegedly repentant Nazis slowly returned to high places in the West as well as the East. The unanimous outburst of the press against them as well as their reappearance in public life made manifest the continuing dilemma of a country that had followed Hitler too long and too faithfully.

But among the neo-Nazi manifestations none of these clouds grew larger than a man's hand. No important Nazi-like publications developed; the established papers, in fact, continued to retain three quarters of the circulation of all the newspapers—the newcomers had to divide the rest. There was never any mass support for either the far Right or the Left. The West Germans had had their throats stuffed with the total state, as the elections would show; the votes for communism or for the neo-Nazi parties would never be more than the 11 per cent the Socialist Reich party polled in Lower Saxony in 1951—a year in which the Communist vote was half that of 1949—and they would diminish. In Berlin, riots accompanied the showing of a British

[7] Ibid., Aug. 25, 30, 1949.

film, *Oliver Twist*, which was criticized for anti-Semitic overtones, and Mayor Reuter joined those who signed protests
against it.

What had happened to the Nazis? This was a question which
the Germans as well as the Allies asked themselves many times.
A hard Nazi core was still there in 1949—some 10 per cent, the
polls indicated. Jewish cemeteries were defaced, a Bundestag
deputy made an anti-Semitic speech, a newspaper printed an
anti-Semitic letter. But the reactions to such events were always
intense. The deputy was assaulted for his speech, crowds paraded in protest against the letter to the newspaper. German
anti-Semitism had not been eradicated, but there was a consciousness of its meaning which had never before existed.

Every German had to take account of the past even if he
denied any responsibility for it. Memorial ceremonies were held
in 1949 at Dachau, and the members of the Bavarian Landtag
were urged to go. A priest, a minister, and a rabbi were to speak.
One of the deputies said Dachau had to be seen to be believed.
"I have the impression," he told the House, "that the men in
the black uniforms with the death's heads on their caps have
pressed deeply on our brows the Cain mark of fratricide." (Cries
of "very true" from all sides of the House.) The speaker said he
wanted the German officials to ask the Allied authorities' permission for the Landtag to visit the camp. Another member rose
and said that a camp at Flossenberg should be visited too, where
ashes three and four meters high were still piled up, and even
two years ago there had been signs of half-burned corpses and
shoes of children who had been murdered there. A member
seconded the speaker and repeated that the House had to see
those places. He himself (apparently a former inmate) had carried bodies in his arms for two years. The presiding officer said
he took it as the unanimous wish of the House that they visit
both Dachau and Flossenberg.[8] Every German in his own way
would have to visit these camps.

[8] *Verhandlungen des Bayrischen Landtags*, Dec. 13, 1949.

The French were more reluctant than the Germans to see the new political developments move so quickly. What General Clay had called the "weak and limited administration" of the German authorities in Bizonia [9] he said the French regarded as "the prelude to a powerful centralized government." In the matter of the currency the London *Economist* wrote on November 6, 1948: "By reinflating and undermining confidence in the new German D Mark the decision [for the disposal of German blocked accounts] has halted progress toward stability. If the results of bringing France into Anglo-American councils are all to be of this nature it would have been better to do without them."

The Americans and British had agreed, in return for the French zone's joining Bizonia, that no major decisions would be taken without the consent of the French representatives. As a result, measures affecting the British and American zones were long delayed. Although General Clay and Foreign Minister Schuman could agree on general measures affecting Germany, Clay was sure that Schuman's subordinates would try to defeat his efforts. He wrote: "There is an increasing conflict between American and French policy which leads to almost daily disagreements in our operations in Germany." [1] What started out to be a courtesy call of the French commandant in Frankfurt on Generals Clay and Robertson, an American correspondent reported,[2] turned into a five-hour session, in which a last effort was made to hold up the currency reform and the creation of a West German state until another attempt had been made to come to an understanding with Russia. Not only did the De Gaullists and the French Communists make common cause, but among more moderate parties too there were similar sentiments. In July 1948 both Léon Blum and Vincent Auriol announced that they favored further talks with Stalin.

The French could not impose their views once a determined opposition to them developed. Even in 1946, when the French

[9] Lucius D. Clay: *Decision in Germany*, p. 179.
[1] Ibid., pp. 416, 427.
[2] Edwin Hartrich, New York *Herald Tribune*, June 17, 1948.

representatives in the Allied Control Council vetoed the establishing of central German administrative agencies, a Russian general expressed his disbelief that the French could be doing this without secret American approval in view of the enormous financial aid the Americans were providing. Now the United States, in contrast to the period after World War I, was dealing directly with the postwar problems and taking a major share of the responsibility. Its representatives in Europe, faced with political and economic realities in place of the sentimental flushes that had colored the Lafayette-we-are-here period, turned cool toward France and its negative policy. One American reporter, writing of the situation when the West German government was being debated, said that great concessions would have to be made by one side or the other in the American-French disputes and that if they were made by the United States there would be wholesale resignations of the American staff.[3]

General Clay and other highly placed Americans thought the dogged French rejection of a quasi-independent German state or of German economic recovery might be affected by further guarantees of French security, and in this matter the French were far more impressed with American promises than were the Russians. The six-power conference in London had announced that none of the countries present would withdraw its forces from Germany "until the peace of Europe is secured . . ." and "it was further recommended that the governments concerned should consult if any of them should consider that there was a danger of resurgence of German military power." [4] On June 7 the United States had stated its position: "It has lately become apparent, even to those most fearful of the consequences of German economic revival, that German reconstruction is essential to the well-being of Europe. . . . In these plans there is no intent that German economic recovery shall have priority over the needs of other participating countries but only the

[3] Ibid., Dec. 21, 1948.
[4] *Germany, 1947–1949*, p. 78.

intent that Germany shall share in the common effort and the common welfare. . . . Ruhr resources may never be used for warlike purposes." [5]

The differences between the British and the Americans were unimportant in principle. Although when the Basic Law was approved the British *Länder* were without constitutions, the British zone had more centralized administrative machinery than the American, and the British favored more centralized German authority in the future German state than either the French or Americans. Even after Marshal Sokolovsky had walked out of the meeting of the Control Council and a German state with a federal structure had been decided on, there was no agreement on details. The French opposed giving the future German government powers over taxation or police; in addition they wanted a veto in the three-power control of West Germany; in the event that one of the powers found itself in a minority it would have the right to appeal its case, which again would have made for long delays. When the Parliamentary Council met, the French professed themselves alarmed at "what they believed," General Clay reports, "to be a trend to dangerous centralization in the work." [6] They urged—against the views of the British and Americans, who wanted the Germans to have a clear definition of their powers—that the future German state should be permitted to legislate on financial and economic matters only after Allied approval. Similarly, they wanted the High Court to have advisory authority and to function without German participation. General Clay reported that powers which the London conference had agreed to give the German government the French later wanted to reserve to the Allies; and Clay came to believe that the French were trying to retard German economic recovery, that they did not want what all four countries in the war of the blockade were saying they wanted: a unified Germany with Berlin as its capital. Together

[5] Ibid., p. 81.
[6] Clay: *Decision in Germany*, p. 413.

with their search for security, he thought, the French were interested in preventing the rise of German industrial competition.

The Americans now opposed the further territorial changes asked for by Holland, Belgium, Luxembourg, and France.[7] They felt it was inconsistent to demand that the Eastern border be undefined until a peace treaty had been signed and yet give their consent to small but significant changes in the Western boundaries, even for the sake of tidier political and economic frontiers. Changes were nevertheless made, although Belgium and Luxembourg refused to accept their acquisitions and agreed on minor border adjustments in direct negotiations with the Germans. In this case the French too, Clay reports, made concessions.

The people who were most enthusiastic about the new German state were the Americans. German leaders had not been eager to participate in any development that might give color to the Communist accusation that what they and the Allies were doing confirmed the splitting of Germany. The law that was drafted, therefore, was not a constitution but a Basic Law, and the body that produced it was a Parliamentary Council, not a "Constituent Assembly," as the Allies had first called it. "Nothing," the ministers president wrote to the military governors, "should be done to give the character of a state to the organization which is to be formed, notwithstanding the granting of the fullest possible autonomy to the population of the territory." [8] The state that was set up was a provisional one against the day of German unity.

The preparations for the Basic Law as well as the withheld powers continued to reflect the Allies' ambivalence toward the Germans and the Russians. The delays, which seemed endless to General Clay and his colleagues, were owing to French internal politics as well as the desire to find, if possible, some way of doing business with Moscow. The Germans too required

[7] Ibid., pp. 402–3.
[8] Edward H. Litchfield: *Governing Postwar Germany*, pp. 39–40.

time for consulting precedent, for adjusting their thinking. The Basic Law was to be a carefully detailed blueprint that took full account of past failures. It was a restoration of a means toward sovereignty; but as it turned out, it functioned well, long after the occupation was over. Its provisions were subject to approval by the Allies before they were adopted, and could be abrogated in important particulars afterward; their force lay in Allied approval of the forms of continued co-operation of the Germans with the West. Nevertheless, it was mainly a German document, hammered out by men who had seen another democratic system collapse.

The Western Allies made clear to the ministers president what kind of German government they wanted. Powers necessary to fulfill the fundamental purposes of the occupation were reserved by the military governors. These included, for the time being, the right to conduct Germany's foreign relations; to exercise a measure of control over German foreign trade, the Ruhr, reparations, the level of industry, decartelization, disarmament, demilitarization, aspects of scientific research;[9] to protect the prestige and ensure the security of the occupation forces and observance of the constitution, which the Allies would approve. In any emergency threatening security, they would resume the exercise of their powers, and any amendment to the constitution would require their approval. In the absence of their disapproval, laws and regulations of the federal government would come into force within twenty-one days. The military governors would assist the federal and state governments with the democratization of political life, social relations, and education.

The military governors asked the ministers president to submit their observations on these principles, which might then be

[9] The scrutiny of scientific research under the Central Council law had been very wide. All research came under its surveillance; it forbade scientific investigations into methods of shipbuilding, and permission had to be obtained for research on ball bearings, synthetic fuels, and rubber. Its tasks included supervision of finances and personnel, of the development of ideas, and, in the French zone, of the development of methods of testing materials.

modified, to the Constituent Assembly as a guide to that body in preparing the constitution. After the military governors had approved the constitution for submission to the states, they would publish simultaneously an Occupation Statute so that the West Germans would understand that they accepted the constitution within the framework of the statute. The constitution would be ratified by a simple majority of the voters in each state and would be in force when approved by two thirds of the states.

By the end of August 1948 representatives of the parliamentary council had been elected by the Landtags—the state legislatures—on the basis of the proportional strength of the parties at the last election. There were 25 delegates from the United States zone, 32 from the British, and 8 from the French. Most of them were government officials; and at the meeting of the council at Bonn they elected Konrad Adenauer president of the council.

On November 22 the military governors sent an *aide-mé-moire* [1] to the council outlining their interpretation of the documents they had given the ministers president. They said that they favored a bicameral legislature in which one of the houses would represent the states, that the executive must have only those powers prescribed by the constitution, and that emergency powers of the executive must be so defined as to require prompt legislative or judicial review. The powers of the federal government must also be limited to those stated in the constitution and in any case would not include education, cultural and religious affairs, local government, and public health (except to secure such co-ordination as might be essential to safeguard the health of the people in the several states); the government's powers in the field of public welfare and police would be limited. The powers of the federal government were to be restricted in the fields of finance and taxation; there was to be an independent judiciary to review federal legislation and the exercise of

[1] *Germany, 1947–1949*, p. 278.

executive power, and to adjudicate conflicts between federal and state authorities. Every citizen was to have the right to public office; a public servant, if elected to the federal legislature, should resign his office with the agency where he was employed before he accepted election.[2]

The latter provision was a product of the belief that the German bureaucrat had had too great importance and insufficient independence in the past when he was a legislator as well as a government servant. The Allies thought that men should be chosen for democratic parliaments without the dual allegiance to a government apparatus and the district they represented. Only in this fashion could they take a proper part in free debate.

These observations reflected the continued concern of the Allies with what they regarded as the evil root of the German past, the undue centralization of power. A state must not be too large, for then it might take over the smaller ones, or too small, lest it be swallowed by a bigger one. To this end the possibility of changes in the boundaries of the *Länder* was to be considered by the ministers president.

The Germans had wanted to include Berlin as a *Land* in the new West Germany, but the Allies opposed this on legal and political grounds; it would have complicated, among other things, their claim to being in Berlin as a result of a four-power agreement. The Christian Democrats, too, may have been reluctant to see a Berlin delegation that would be strongly Social Democrat added to the Bundestag. When the Germans proposed that Berlin have 15 members in the Bundestag, the military governors said the number was too high; they would not approve more than 8. These members would take part in the legislative debates and proceedings, but were not allowed to vote. The Allies kept in touch with the deliberations of the parliamentary council, and since their approval was required before the Basic Law could be submitted to the *Länder*, their views had weight.

[2] Ibid., p. 278.

Disagreements were mainly of a kind that could be compromised: the election of government officials to the parliament, the degree of centralization of federal power. There were no serious disagreements on objectives or the general framework. The tone of the communications from the military governors was far from peremptory. A memorandum of March 2, 1949, said:

> My colleagues and I have asked you to come here today in order that we might comment to you upon several provisions of your proposed Basic Law. A number deviate from the principles of the *aide-mémoire*. . . . However, on viewing the document as a whole we propose to disregard some . . . but feel it necessary to call to your urgent attention others that depart from these principles. Three powers of the Federal government are not defined with sufficient clarity. . . . We suggest that you delete articles 36 and 36c, and substitute a new article 36 based very largely on your own language and which might read substantially as follows . . .[3]

When the draft of the Basic Law was approved by the parliamentary council, the accompanying Allied approval was again friendly but admonishing. The military governors said that they were disturbed over "the very wide powers" [4] given the federal government in the administrative field, and that the high commissioners who would now replace them would have to give careful consideration to the exercise of such powers "in order to insure that they do not lead to excessive concentration of au-

[3] *Parlamentarischer Rat.*
[4] The German delegates, with their eyes on the deficiencies of the Weimar state as well as on the Allies' recommendations, struggled with the problems of fixing responsibility in a parliamentary system without concentrating too much power on the president or chancellor or allowing the chancellor to be unseated by a resolution that might be purely destructive. At the end of the Weimar period the Nazis and Communists had been able to prevent any government from functioning. Now it was decided that a vote of no confidence could be taken only if the Bundestag proposed a new candidate.

thority." [5] The military governors nevertheless agreed that conflicts between *Länder* and constitutions and the federal Basic Law should be resolved in favor of the central government. They complimented the members of the parliamentary council on the job they had done and "on their devotion to the democratic ideals toward the achievement of which we are all striving." These were brave words and they were also precisely the ones that General Clay had used in congratulating the Bavarian Constitutional Assembly in October 1946.

On May 8, the fourth anniversary of the end of hostilities, the parliamentary council approved the Basic Law; on May 12 it was approved by the military governors in a meeting with the ministers president and the representatives of the parliamentary council; at the same time the military governors promulgated the occupation statute. Between the 12th and the 22nd the Basic Law was approved by the Landtags—and also by the City Assembly of Berlin, which adopted it unanimously.

The Basic Law, consisting of 146 articles, provided for its own demise. It became invalid, according to its last article, when a constitution "adopted in a free decision of the German people comes into force." This provision, like the use of "Basic Law" instead of "Constitution," was intended to keep the way open to a united Germany. Meanwhile the almost three quarters of Germany represented in the Western zones took over the responsibility of its self-government under the mild gaze of the high commissioners.

Proclaimed on May 23, the Basic Law summed up many things out of the experience of a democracy that had failed, of a Reich that had horrified the world, and of the ideas of the Western powers. It stated that Germany was "filled with the resolve to preserve its national and political unity and to serve world peace as an equal partner in a United Europe," and that West Germany acted also on behalf of those Germans to whom participation in it was denied; and it called on all Germans

[5] *Germany, 1947–1949*, p. 279.

to achieve by self-determination the unity and freedom of Germany. It proclaimed the dignity of man as inviolable and gave everyone the right to development of his personality in so far as he did not infringe the rights of others or offend the moral code. All men, it said, were equal before the law. Men and women were to have equal rights; no one was to be prejudiced or privileged because of sex, descent, race, language, or political or religious convictions. Freedom of faith and conscience was guaranteed. No one was to be compelled against his conscience to perform war service as a combatant. Art and science, research and teaching were to be free from government control. Germans were guaranteed the right to peaceful and unarmed assembly; but, with an eye to the past, it was added: "For open-air meetings the right may be restricted by legislation or on the basis of a law."

The right to form associations to safeguard and improve working and economic agreements was assured everyone and all professions. Germans were to have the right to choose their occupation, place of work, and place of training. The dwelling was inviolable; all searches must be ordered by a judge or, in the event of imminent danger, by other authorities. Property and the right of inheritance were guaranteed. No one could be deprived of his citizenship; loss of citizenship could occur only on the basis of a law, and against the will of the person involved only if he was not rendered stateless. The politically persecuted had the right of asylum.

The internal organization of all political parties must conform to democratic principles; parties seeking by their aims or the behavior of their members to impair the free and democratic basic order or to jeopardize the existence of the Republic were unconstitutional. Sovereign powers might be transferred to international organizations. Any activities that disturbed peaceful relations between nations, and especially preparing for aggressive war, were unconstitutional.

A Bundestag and a Bundesrat were established. Under the

law, the members of the Bundestag are elected for four years; it elects its own president; it can demand the presence of any member of the federal government at its sessions; it can set up investigating committees, and has a standing committee to safeguard its rights in relation to the federal government.

The *Länder* participate in the legislation and administration of the federation through the Bundesrat. The latter consists of members of the *Land* government, each *Land* having at least three votes, with proportionately more if the population is larger. It elects its own president, and the members of the government have the right to take part in its debates. The *Länder* hold reserve legislative powers; that is, they have, as do the American states, all rights of legislation not specifically given to the federation.

The president of the Bundesrepublik is elected by the members of the federal convention to serve for five years, and he can be re-elected only once for a consecutive term. The federal convention is composed of the members of the Bundestag plus an equal number elected by the representative bodies of the *Länder*. The president represents the federation in all matters concerning international law, concludes treaties, appoints and dismisses judges, and may be impeached by either the Bundestag or Bundesrat. The federal chancellor is elected by the Bundestag on motion of the federal president, and his ministers are appointed and dismissed by the president on the chancellor's recommendation. The chancellor determines and assumes responsibility for general policy. If he fails to get a vote of confidence in the Bundestag, he may dissolve it and call for an election.

A federal constitutional court, elected half by the Bundestag and half by the Bundesrat, interprets the Basic Law. The court decides whether the president and parliament have acted in accord with the constitution, and also is charged with protecting the fundamental rights of the individual. All judges are independent and subject only to the law. The Supreme Federal

Court has jurisdiction where the decision is of fundamental importance for the uniformity of the administration of justice. There is no death penalty.

"Germans" were defined broadly for the conferring of citizenship. They included people who had been accepted in the territory of the Reich as of December 31, 1937, refugees or expellees of German stock or the spouses or children of such persons, and also former German nationals who, between January 30, 1933, and May 8, 1945, had been deprived of their nationality for political, racial, or religious reasons. These former nationals were considered not to have lost citizenship if they took up residence in Germany after May 8, 1945, and wished to remain German. Their descendants were to be regranted citizenship on application.

The federation agreed to bear the expense of the occupation and other burdens arising out of the war. The powers reserved to the Allies were considerable.[6] No German court was to have authority over a member of the Allied occupation, although German courts did have jurisdiction over Allied nationals not connected with the occupation. The Allied courts could take jurisdiction of any case and could set aside the decision of any German court violating the occupation statute.

Elections were held on August 14, 1949. Twenty-four million people voted, but a rather high proportion—20 per cent—abstained. Some observers thought this was because the election confirmed the splitting of the country. Deputies were chosen in part by direct vote, in part by proportional representation. The Christian Democrats polled 7,590,000 votes, 31 per cent of those cast, and won 139 seats in the new Parliament. The CDU had turned away from its earlier socialism and was often called Rightist, both in Germany and in the United States. It stood, after the currency reform of 1948, for a system of capitalism diluted with the virtues of Christian responsibility for the common weal. It was a party of the new Germany, of expanding

[6] A Decade of American Foreign Policy, pp. 586–8.

businesses, of *Sozialwirtschaft*, which means as much free enterprise as possible but with an acknowledgment of duties and obligations to society as a whole. In its early period it counted among its members conspicuous anti-Nazis as well as anti-Communists, who opposed as a matter of conscience and principle any undue power of the state, whether over the individual or the economy. It was a direct descendant of the former Catholic Centrist party; much of its support and leadership was Protestant, and in appealing to the electorate it emphasized broad religious and humanitarian principles rather than any denominational ones.

Its strongest rival and the second-largest party was the traditional German Socialist party—the Social Democratic party, the SPD. It received 6,900,000 votes, 29 per cent of those cast, and won 131 seats. In 1949 it remained the traditional party of the workers—anticlerical, with a Marxist background, but implacably anti-Communist. It had a loyal, unshakable foundation of supporters, many of whom voted SPD as their fathers had and because its mild socialism still seemed to them the hope of a new Germany, a new internationalism, and a better world. At the head of the SPD was the fiery Kurt Schumacher, who had refused to participate in the parliamentary council, who had spent ten years in Dachau, and who had battled for full equality for Germany ever since he walked into a British military headquarters in 1945 just after the German collapse and asked for a license to organize his old party. The world had never been as decent as he thought it deserved to be; he never hesitated to denounce both the West and the East, as well as his own country, for their failures.

Among the smaller parties, the Free Democrats and their associated parties polled 2,800,000 votes and obtained 52 seats. The FDP had changed their name from the Liberal Democratic party, but they continued to be anticlerical and to favor the conservative principles of the free market and a more centralized government. The German party, with 939,000 votes, 4 per cent of those cast, won 17 seats. It represented a conservative, anti-Prussian, Protestant tradition, a party of farmers and businessmen which, like the CDU, favored federalism over centralism. The Communists, burdened with their Russian association, polled a small vote in the first West German election, as in all subsequent ones: 1,316,000, 5 per cent of the total, giving them 15 seats. Although in the pre-Hitler years their party had been a major force in German politics, it had nothing to offer in Western Germany. For practical purposes it disappeared as a political opposition.

On September 7 the Parliament met in Bonn, which by a narrow margin had been chosen over Frankfurt as the capital. Around the delegates were decorations of black, red, and gold, the same colors as those of the Weimar Republic; and an orchestra played Beethoven and Mozart.

Theodor Heuss was elected president. He was sixty-five years old, a Free Democrat, and a journalist. Although he had once voted to give power to Hitler, he had fortunately broken with him at an early stage, and in 1933 two of his books had been burned by the brown shirts. Konrad Adenauer, aged seventy-three, was elected chancellor by a majority of one vote. There were 202 votes for him, 142 against, and 44 abstentions. For election a majority of the 402 members was needed, and while Adenauer's election at this point was as close as possible, he had a clear majority among the absentees, whose votes would have been recorded on later ballots. The abstentions were mainly those of the far Right and Left, the Communists among them. Adenauer appointed 8 CDU ministers to his cabinet, 3 from the FDP and 2 from the German party. This coalition of the Center and the Right, although not the extreme Right, was to stand up over the years in spite of many vicissitudes and reflect a remarkable unity on essential questions of economic policy and foreign affairs. The Bonn government has been able to function without the aid of the splinter parties that had contributed to making the democracy of Weimar impotent. These parties had pursued their private and particularist programs when the crisis of the depression and the rise of extreme Left- and Right-wing groups had demanded firm decisions and a consensus among the democratic parties. The government would be shaken from time to time by secessions from the coalition, but the tendency of West Germany after World War II, despite the degree of proportional representation, was to move more toward the two-party and away from the multiparty state.

Adenauer created three new cabinet posts: for the Marshall Plan, for All-German Affairs, and for a liaison with the Bundesrat. He appointed some of the members of the cabinet with the consent of Heuss but against his advice—the first tug-of-war over the respective powers of the heads of the state. It was won by the chancellor, who maintained that the president merely confirmed cabinet choices without participating in them. Adenauer, however, did submit his cabinet to the Bundestag for a vote of confidence, which, under the Basic Law, he was not required to do.

Military government was replaced by a civil administration operating under an occupation statute, with high commissioners replacing the military governors. The high commissioners were the chief officers of the occupation. While the military commanders retained authority over the troops and military decisions, they could be called on by the high commissioners to assist the civil administration, and policy was in the hands of the civil authority.

The American High Commissioner, John J. McCloy, was a lawyer. He had been Assistant Secretary of War under Henry L. Stimson, and was accused during the Senate hearings on his appointment of being anti-German and of having had a part in the framing of the Morgenthau plan. McCloy denied that he had ever favored the Morgenthau plan for an agrarian Germany, and a statement by Stimson was cited on his behalf attesting that both had opposed it.[7]

[7] Conference records bear out McCloy's defense. He did oppose the Treas-

McCloy was to become one of the most popular figures in Germany, owing perhaps in no small measure to the fact that, unlike General Clay, he was the dispenser of large sums of American aid to a German economy that was beginning to boom. This was a circumstance recognized by Clay, who asked to retire from his post in Germany in part because he was associated with the earlier punitive period of the occupation. McCloy had no such association in the mind of the Germans, and his assignment was different from the one given the military governor. The German views of what should be done would differ considerably from those of the West on many occasions, but these would be tactical debates, however heated; the controls and the repressions were loosening; McCloy would be a guide and counselor of the new half-free state.

It is doubtful whether at this stage the attitude of the High Commissioner was the important factor in relations with the Germans. During the war McCloy, like his superior, Stimson, had made decisions that were highly questionable from the point of view of those who wanted Germany to be cured of its militarism and taught the virtues of a democracy. It was he who, with Stimson and Roosevelt, had permitted the Army in 1942 to move more than 100,000 Japanese, of whom two thirds were American citizens, from the West Coast of the United States to camps in the interior. This unprecedented invasion of rights of American citizenship was, it may be thought, precisely the kind of arbitrary rule by a combination of army officers and government officials which the Germans had long been told had been their undoing. Yet, like many of the choices made in the Bundesrepublik which on their face seemed to mark a return to militaristic and authoritarian ways, the American appointment of McCloy was to be a remarkable success.

---

ury draft for JCS 1067 in 1944. In March 1945, however, apparently for administrative reasons, he supported the Treasury's proposed revision of the directive against the less severe measures advocated by the State Department (Paul Y. Hammond: "The Origins of JCS 1067").

X

PETERSBERG AND THE NEW CRITICISM

O<small>N</small> S<small>EPTEMBER</small> 21, 1949, the newly elected Chancellor of the Bundesrepublik was received by the high commissioners at the Petersberg, the hotel on the hill of the same name near Bonn where Neville Chamberlain had lodged while having his stormy talks with Hitler. Konrad Adenauer came with his newly appointed cabinet and was formally and cordially welcomed. The French High Commissioner, François-Poncet, who had been ambassador to Germany during the Nazi period, expressed in German his own and his colleagues' pleasure on the occasion and on hearing Adenauer's words of gratitude for the Allied help given Germany during the military occupation, without which, Adenauer said, many Germans would have starved.[1] It was a day of mutual congratulations and temperate rejoicing; the Chancellor shook hands with the three high commissioners, to whom he presented the members of his cabinet. The cabinet members, on his instructions, did not shake hands, because Adenauer wished to indicate the separation of his government from the occupation. He wanted to avoid any implication that this was a government of the Allies; there was no question about his representing the West German government to the occupying authorities, but its members, it had to be made clear, were German appointees and as such were represented even in small

[1] *Germany, 1947–1949*, pp. 321–3.

courtesies by their chief. It was with the aid of such subtleties that the new government could attempt to gain dignity and stature.

In late November 1949 another meeting at the Petersberg resulted in a new agreement between the Western Allies and the Bundesrepublik. This was the first negotiated agreement since the war; and it provided for reduction in the number of plants to be dismantled, for a stop to dismantling in Berlin (the Berlin plants that had been affected by dismantling were again to be put in working order), for the right of the Germans to build an unlimited number of ships of not more than 7,200 tons, including fishing vessels of not over 650 tons. West Germany was to send consular representatives to foreign countries, and the protocol reiterated the purpose of the Allies and the Germans to bring Germany into the European international organizations as a peaceful and equal member. In return Chancellor Adenauer promised on behalf of his government to join the Ruhr coal-and-steel authority, to accept a higher export quota for the coal produced, and to continue to consent to the supervision of German research and investigation on anything that touched on military security—which meant, in effect, supervision of the technical developments of German industry.

This Petersberg meeting was another milestone; it was negotiation in the place of directives. It expressed again the compromise between the American wish to see the Germans free, productive, and eager to join the West by their own choice and the French demands for guarantees and assurances that nothing that happened in Germany would damage their own economic and political security.

Signed on November 22, the Petersberg protocol said: "The discussions were animated throughout by the desire and the determination of both parties that their relations should develop progressively upon a basis of mutual confidence. Meanwhile, their primary objective is the incorporation of the Federal Republic as a peaceful member of the European community and to this end German association with the countries of Western Europe in all fields should be diligently pursued." [2]

The German government repeated its determination to maintain the demilitarization of the federal territory and to endeavor by all means in its power to prevent formation of armed forces of any kind.

German-American rapprochement was making rapid strides. But the foreign ministers of the West and Russia had met in Paris from May 23 to June 20, 1949, without coming to an agreement on the future relations of the four countries to Germany. The conference provided a ceremonial way out for Stalin from his unsuccessful blockade; the negotiations that lasted for almost a month were face-saving proof that the Allies were staying in Berlin by common consent. Vyshinsky repeated Russia's proposal that Berlin be placed under the Kommandatura which had governed the city before the blockade, that a government of Germany be established under four-power control, and that the Allies agree to withdraw their troops a year after the signing of a peace treaty. This resembled the formula that had been used in Korea, where after the period of tutelage the Russians and the Americans were to withdraw. The Russians had, in fact, just announced the evacuation of their garrisons from North Korea, and the United States would soon leave the South.

The Western powers, on their part, proposed at Paris that the East zone accept the Basic Law of the Federal Republic, after which a four-power occupation statute would be issued; and they wished to have majority rule, not the unanimity principle, in the Control Council. They also wanted guarantees of individual freedom and of free political activities for the whole of Germany. Vyshinsky repeated the old accusations; he said that the West wanted to prolong the occupation, that it had produced a pseudodemocratic government in Bonn which maintained monopolists and reactionaries in positions of power; and

[2] *A Decade of American Foreign Policy*, p. 1010.

he repeated, too, that the federalization of West Germany split the country. He proposed that Berlin have one Magistrat again, that the so-called mass organizations of loyal Communist groups be permitted to take part in national elections along with the approved political parties; and he demanded that Russia participate in the administration of the Ruhr.

These proposals were unacceptable to the West. Dean Acheson, who had succeeded General Marshall as Secretary of State, said it was impossible to plan a peace treaty with Germany without knowing who would represent the country or what its borders would be, and that it was the unanimous opinion of the Western foreign ministers that the Bonn Basic Law with its guarantees of freedom could readily be extended to the East zone.

Russian policy inside the Soviet area had hardened as a result of the defection of Tito. In the satellite countries there were wholesale arrests, and leaders suspected of Titoism were executed. Gomulka and other long-standing party members in Poland were accused of nationalist deviation and imprisoned; Rajk, the foreign minister of Hungary, was tried and executed as a traitor and agent of the West; in Bulgaria and Rumania the same charges were made against dissidents. The Tito deviation was having its effects, too, in other spheres, as the Greek guerrillas, cut off from their Yugoslav supplies, began to melt away before the onslaughts of the government troops. But in the Far East the Soviet cause was triumphant. Chiang was completely defeated; and in Korea, in Malaya and Indochina, even in Japan, with which no peace treaty had yet been made, there were vast possibilities of further successes.

To counterbalance the West German state, an East German state was proclaimed on October 7, 1949; and there were rumors in the Western press that it would include an air force as well as an army disguised as police. A provisional People's Chamber was elected by delegates chosen from a single list of candidates, including representatives from West Germany. It announced the founding of the German Democratic Republic, with a manifesto attacking the enslavement of the people of the West zone and setting the goal of a unified, independent, democratic Germany. This united Germany would then demand the annulment of the Ruhr statute and the withdrawal of the autonomous regime of the Saar; it would be a Germany, like Mr. Vyshinsky's, with which a treaty of peace would be concluded and from which occupation troops would be withdrawn as rapidly as possible. Sovereignty would be restored, battle would be waged against the betrayers of the German nation and the warmongers —the agents of American imperialism. On October 12, 1949, Wilhelm Pieck was unanimously elected president of the People's Democratic Republic, and Otto Grotewohl minister president of the provisional regime. Leaders of the bourgeois parties —the LDP and CDU—were given minor but decorative posts. Nuschke of the CDU and Kastner of the LDP became ministers for foreign affairs.

The new government recognized the Oder-Neisse boundary and was sent a telegram of good wishes from Marshal Stalin, who said the founding of the peace-loving German Democratic Republic was a turning-point in history. There was no doubt, he declared, that a peace-loving Germany alongside a peace-loving Russia completely excluded the possibility of war and the enslavement of the people of Europe by the Western imperialists. If the peoples of Germany and Russia, who had suffered most from the war, were determined to fight for peace with the same energies they had used on war, then the tranquillity of Europe could be held assured.[3]

In early November, just before the Petersberg meeting, the three Western foreign ministers met again in Paris. They discussed dismantling and the safeguards against German military revival, and repeated their assurances that they looked forward to the increasing participation of the West German state in the organizations of European recovery. The Germans were now

[3] Boris Meissner: *Russland, die Westmächte und Deutschland*, p. 216.

members of the European Payments Union, started in the summer of 1949, and of the OEEC, the Organization for European Economic Co-operation, through which American economic aid was administered to twelve countries; [4] and the foreign ministers desired to see the German government take on increasing responsibilities. From Paris, Acheson went on to Bonn and Berlin. He promised the Germans every assistance, but added that the real effort must come from them.[5]

Thus a new plateau was reached in late 1949, with the East Germans and the Soviets exchanging ambassadors, and the West resolutely set on repair of the German economy and political life under German administration, linked to the West by the occupation and by the long-term interests of both parties. Before the end of the year Chancellor Adenauer said he hoped West German contingents could take their place among the armed forces of the West as part of an anti-Communist striking force. Since, as the American Secretary of State pointed out, the troops of the North Atlantic Treaty countries were overwhelmingly outnumbered by the Soviet forces and those of the satellites— the largest peacetime accumulation of power in history—there can be no doubt that Adenauer's words were welcomed if not inspired by the people in the American and Allied camp who looked with far graver disquiet on the formidable Soviet military machine than on any possible revival of German armed forces.

In this new atmosphere there was opportunity for more outspoken German criticism of Allied practices. The chief complaints had to do with dismantling, occupation costs, and the continued requisitioning of housing. The criticisms were by no means new, but they had been more circumspect when the license of a newspaper could be taken away if it printed anything the Allies considered harmful to the prestige of their armies.

[4] Clay had complained in July 1948 that Germany was given loans instead of the outright grants made to other countries by the Economic Co-operation Administration (ECA).

[5] *The New York Times*, Nov. 14, 1949.

One of the first acts of the new government was to protest against the continued gutting of the factories. While the blockade was going on and the bridge of planes brought sustenance to Berlin, dismantling continued. In Cologne the archbishop and his parishioners prayed against it; strikes were threatened; but the program went on, although with diminished objectives. Its great damage was not so much to the German economy as to German morale. American and other defenders of its purposes had long argued that the plants could not be used by the Germans anyway, that the lack of fuel and raw materials as well as the limitations imposed on production prevented the factories that were left from using their capacity. What the ordinary German saw in his threadbare life was machinery being destroyed or shipped away, leaving shells of buildings (in some cases the buildings were torn down too) and the threat of unemployment then and in the future. German economists calculated that from 158,000 to 200,000 people were unemployed because of the dismantling in the West.[6]

Dismantling in the East zone was finished in 1948. The Germans estimated that the Russians had taken away plants that had produced 45 per cent of the output of the zone. In addition, plants were shipped to the Russians from the West, since under the Potsdam agreement they were entitled to 15 per cent of the reparations from the Western zones. The balance of reparations from the American, French, and British zones, which came to 8 per cent of the productive capacity of West German factories, was allocated among eighteen countries, all of which had been damaged by the German occupation or by German weapons.

The Russians were wholesale and quick dismantlers, ruthless and inefficient.[7] Much of the machinery they took was badly

---

[6] André Piettre: *"L'Economie allemande," Revue économique et sociale,* April 1950, p. 127.

[7] Russians defecting to the West reported that the early days of their occupation had been like a gold rush. Seventy thousand officials were assigned to reparations in the summer of 1945. The Russian dismantling section in 1947 still had 150 officials for the Western zones alone. In addition, "trophy

damaged in the process, and there were many reports of its rusting on the sidings of railways in the East. German accounts tell of the waste and clumsiness of the sledge-hammer methods that destroyed machines and were sometimes followed by accusations of sabotage against both Russians and Germans, as the Soviet bureaucracy had to account for the results.

The chief criticism of the Western dismantlings came from the Russians, the Germans, and some Americans. The Russians said that the American dismantling enabled the United States to send its finished goods to Germany as part of its imperialist plan of dominating the economies of Europe, and that the Western powers thus got rid of unwanted German competition. Germans in all walks of life—economists, workers, politicians—had protested as soon as they could. Statistics showed that by 1947 the Germans had paid huge sums to the Allies. One detailed report [8] said the amount came to over $71,000,000,000, including the worth of the property beyond the Oder-Neisse and the worth of the Saar, and the confiscations; of this, over $3,000,000,000 came from dismantling. Another calculation was that almost half the substance of the Germany of 1938 had been destroyed in the war or lost through cessions of territory, the destruction or surrender of shipping, reparations, and the removal of machinery. Other calculations reduced these figures, but there is no doubt that the dismantling, from the Germans' point of view, seemed of great and punitive proportions, adding little to the restoration of Europe but much to the hopelessness of their lot.

Not only the loss of the plants themselves was damaging; there were also side effects of destroyed capacity on other factories and utilities. Plants manufacturing ball bearings were dismantled, although bearings were urgently needed by the German railroads, which were transporting goods and materials to

---

brigades" had been sent to Germany to collect bicycles, clocks, food, trucks, etc., to send to Russia (Robert Slusser, ed.: *Soviet Economic Policy in Postwar Germany*).

[8] G. W. Harmssen *et al.: Reparationen, Sozialprodukt, Lebensstandard.*

the factories that were permitted to operate. Coal was in short supply throughout Europe, but coal-mining equipment was hauled away, as were rolling-mills, synthetic-oil and -rubber plants, and steel and cement plants. The program was full of cross-purposes. Most of the German industrial capacity lay in the British zone, and there the heaviest dismantlings occurred; long after the Berlin blockade started and ended, the British continued their demolitions; yet it was the British who had wanted to set the steel production figure in 1946 at almost double what was decided on.

The American House of Representatives in December 1947, stirred to action by protests as well as by the paradox of being asked to vote funds to aid German production while factories were being disassembled, called on the Secretaries of State and Defense for information. Under Secretary of State Lovett replied that the plants being removed were capable of production for peaceful uses, and indeed that was the idea: that they be given to countries which would use them for such purposes. He said the Dutch had been given machinery that would increase manufacturing by $400,000 a year, and $100,000 more might be expected from optical equipment; the French, too, had produced crankshafts with German machinery, and British shipyards had been supplied with equipment.[9]

Secretary of State Marshall testified that the British and French opposed modifying the program, that Russia and Poland were getting only the remnants of three plants that had already been largely dismantled. He said the State Department, too, wanted to continue the reparations program, which would not hamper the recovery of Europe.[1]

This was the defense; but by 1949 it rang hollow amid the pronouncements that Germany must rebuild. No one could miss the incongruity of flying bulldozers into Berlin and dismantling the factory that could have produced them. American

[9] *Germany, 1947–1949*, pp. 413–20.
[1] Ibid., pp. 374–5.

pressure to cut down the dismantling came now from many sides; the Marshall Plan administration tried to get the British and French to agree to a delay; the Adenauer government and the Social Democratic opposition were united in petitioning for a halt to the destruction of the Ruhr plants, and workers went on strike. At the Petersberg meeting the list was cut again. Nevertheless, 1949 was the peak year of dismantling. The plants still on the list were energetically attacked. In 1946, when the lists were long—some 1,500 plants had been originally scheduled —the actual removals had not been so large as when the program was declining.

The Germans said dismantling sometimes resulted in a complicated series of unplanned and unforeseen events. From Salzgitter dismantled machinery was sent to Yugoslavia and to Greece; but since the technicians of these countries were unable to put it together again, it was sold as scrap to the United States, which in turn was bringing new and more modern equipment to Germany under the European Recovery Plan.

German papers now reported on these anomalies. McCloy was quoted as wanting the auditorium of one factory taken off the dismantling list because it would be useful for religious and other peaceful purposes.[2] But dismantling, he said, would be stopped only when Germany had given guarantees of security and restitution. At a press conference in March 1950 he declared that the goal was the removal or destruction of all facilities at Salzgitter for steel production for military purposes. On March 11 the *Neue Zeitung* announced that $552,900,000 worth of goods was coming to Germany, the second allocation of American aid; and on March 15 it reported that the last chimney at Salzgitter had been blown up.

The value of dismantled plants has been variously estimated. The 1,500 plants scheduled for destruction were reduced at successive meetings to 859, then to 700; calculations of their worth varied considerably. The Germans said that in many cases the

[2] *Neue Zeitung*, Sept. 7, 1949.

cost of dismantling a plant was far more than its value as reparations. Four Krupp furnaces cost 20,000,000 D marks to disassemble and had a reparation value of 9,500,000; included in the 20,000,000 marks were the costs of carting away 35,000 cubic meters of masonry.[3] The country, German sources said, had paid the Russians alone in dismantlings from 1945 to 1947 over 5,000,000,000 marks.[4] The loss in the West they calculated, at the 1936 value, as 1,032,000,000 D marks, or, at 1949 current prices, 2,500,000,000. Germany was credited by the Allied Reparations Agency with 587,000,000 marks, which was only 40 per cent of the current worth of the machinery. American computations placed the value of the dismantled plants at 2,000,000,000 marks.

Whichever of these figures is correct, the worth in the West was at most a fraction of the Marshall Plan and other aid that was brought to Germany during 1945–54, which in all came to over $4,000,000,000. But the people who saw their livelihood blown up or shipped away could scarcely have been comforted by such figures.

The Western armies and their dependents lived well in Germany during the occupation, especially the French and the Americans. The French lived off the country; what was left the Germans could have. The Americans, on the other hand, took little except housing, services, and by way of the black market; but they walled themselves off from the natives. The visible partitions came down, but the separation remained. In Frankfurt there had been a symbol of the barriers between them in a wire fence nine feet high, which had been erected by German prisoners at a cost of $40,000. Until mid-1948 it enclosed the complex of buildings, houses, and shops providing the standard American foods and packages without which the transplanted Americans—1,030 families and 3,500 bachelors—found their environment too unfamiliar. The fence kept marauders away

[3] Piettre: "L'Economie allemande," pp. 114–15.
[4] Richard Lukas: Zehn Jahre, p. 189.

from the riches of the settlement—and all other Germans too, except those who were provided with passes for special occasions. Germans who had business in the area had to wait patiently for admission into this marvelous oasis in the midst of the city's ruins. They waited in the guardhouse, or greenhouse as it was called, until their passes were checked and the security of the area was assured.

The fence could serve its purpose in a Germany being punished, but not in one exhorted to take its place among the freedom-loving nations. The event that precipitated its dismantling occurred when German officials in May 1948 were invited to a ceremony inside the American compound and, according to the ritual, were kept in the greenhouse until their passes were checked. This took so long that they missed the occasion entirely, and high American authorities were irritated. The fence came down, despite protests on the part of Americans who thought its disappearance a danger, subjecting them to the depredations of an unruly native population, especially at night.

By 1949 there were no longer tall fences separating the Germans from the "golden ghettoes" of the Allies. The differences now were more subtle and, as the Germans discovered when their newspapers printed long accounts, more expensive. They were to be observed in the occupation costs. The Germans had been paying them since 1945; before then they had imposed similar costs on the countries they had occupied. The principle was established in the Hague convention and in the Basic Law. The Hague convention, however, stipulated that costs of occupation be imposed only "for the requirements of the army" and to an extent "commensurate with the resources of the country." The question, then, concerned their amount and what they paid for. There was no doubt of the duty of Germans to pay the immediate costs of the occupation—support of the troops and of the occupation authorities. But the German papers now printed itemized lists showing that there were four Germans serving every American soldier in some form: maids for every

American household; service battalions for the troops; secretaries, technicians, chauffeurs—all paid for by the Germans. So were such items as 30,000 brassières used by DP women, a ton of water bugs that were used as food for the pet fish owned by an American general, a bedspread of white Korean goatskin for a French official, an electronic microscope sent from the United States to London, lawn-mowers, diapers, and false teeth. One general was reported to have given a party where cigarette cases worth 288 marks each were presented to his guests and charged to occupation costs. In 1948 *Die Welt* had published figures showing the occupation costs in the East zone to have been 438 Reichsmarks a year per head in 1946-7, while they were 122 in the American zone and 194 in the French zone. Up to the end of 1947 the *Neue Zeitung*, the paper sponsored by the American Army, was paid for by the Germans at a cost of 5,000,000 D marks a year, as were the radio programs. From 1949 these costs were met from American sources—Government Appropriations for Relief in Occupied Areas (GARIOA) and ECA funds.

In 1948 one German economist calculated that occupation costs would consume 46 per cent of the tax income for the year; in 1950 they were 36 per cent of the budget of the central government, and 22 per cent of the budget of the *Länder* and the Republic combined. In reply, American spokesmen said the Germans were responsible for their own sorry financial state; there were too many officials and pensions were too high, also Germany was paying for construction that would remain in the country. Twenty per cent of the costs, the Americans said, were for permanent improvements—rebuilding of streets, airfields, etc.—and the United States was spending far more than it took in. Occupation charges, they pointed out, were 20 per cent less than they had been the previous year and would not go up the next year despite higher costs. Whereupon a German paper referred to the "gallows humor" of the military-government spokesman, but added that a man in the hairy shirt of penitence was not in a position to bargain about such matters. Someone writing in the *Neue Zeitung* said that as the war was the most expensive in history, so was the occupation.

There were three phases of German reaction to occupation costs. The first was one of apathetic acceptance; these, like the other misfortunes, had to be borne, and with a worthless currency they made little difference. This attitude dominated up to the time of the announcement that Germany was to be included in the Marshall Plan and in the general design for the recovery of Europe. The second phase came between the Berlin blockade and the Korean War, when it became possible for the Germans to be heard, to criticize, and to be taken account of, and after the currency reform had given meaning to the balance sheets. The last phase came as Germany became part of the defense of the West.

There is no doubt that in all three periods many things were charged to occupation costs which would better have been paid for by the troops. The soldiers and their families could vacation at de-luxe hotels that had been requisitioned from the Germans at low rates; since the hotels and services were supplied by the Germans, $1.50 a day paid for first-class accommodations. They traveled in railroad trains at a fraction of the regular fare. Forty thousand domestic employees were provided free. One American directive said households should be limited to two inside housemaids and one outside gardener, fireman, etc., to avoid unnecessary burdens on the German economy.[5] Every American employee of the High Commission office was given living-quarters, free gas, light, heat, and maintenance, and maid service. In addition there were cheap telephone rates, tax-free cigarettes, and liquor supplies from the PX.

At a meeting of American wives in Germany, the wife of the American High Commissioner asked the purpose of the extraordinary coffee ration, which she called an invitation to black-marketing: 24 pounds of tax-free coffee, she and others pointed out, were allowed every American each month. Coffee

[5] Directive of Jan. 1947, Army Document Center, Kansas City.

was scarce on the German market and sold at $3.00 a pound. From time to time arrests were made as Americans were found by military authorities to be selling such commodities to the Germans.

The economists worked out figures that were appalling to a frugal population. Fifty-four per cent of the German automobiles exported in a six-month period in 1949 went to the occupation forces but were paid for by the Germans. Two hundred thousand people in the occupation used almost as much electricity as 8,000,000 Germans.[6] One paper listed 66,000 chauffeurs and other "transport workers" moving the occupiers from one place to another, as well as 12,000,000 marks' worth of rugs and window curtains for Allied homes.

The Bundestag appointed a committee to look into the problem. The committee reported that from October 1948 to September 30, 1949, the bill came to 4,500,000,000 D marks, with a cost to each German of 95.45 D marks. That was a comparatively low figure. In 1945 the cost was 45 marks per person; in 1946, 114; in 1947, 122; in 1948 the costs went down to 98; in 1949 as low as 86; in 1950 to 96; in 1951 they went up to 160; and in 1952 to 176. The Bundestag report pointed out that account had to be taken of the military, political, and social effects of the occupation costs; if the economy was seriously damaged, this would affect the entire society.

The *Stuttgarter Zeitung* said that the whole French Army in 1949 had cost France about 4,500,000,000 D marks, or 10,000 marks a man; these included the costs of garrisons, maintaining troops in the colonies and in Germany, and the war in Indochina, and equaled almost exactly the cost of the occupation troops per man to the Germans. In 1946 occupation costs in the French zone exceeded the value of the entire production of the zone.

Debates raged in the *Länder* parliaments; in Bavaria a speaker said that the United States had done much for Ger-

[6] *Occupation Costs*, pp. 51–2.

many, but that nevertheless the occupation cost Bavaria 186,-000,000 D marks a year. A voice asked what the Russian occupation would have cost, and the speaker denied that that was the same thing. An East Berlin paper said that locusts were less destructive than the occupation costs of the West, that there were 700,000 Germans working for 100,000 American troops.[7]

The Germans also protested against the sums being used to support the DP's. Many of these people, they said, had come voluntarily to Germany, and those from the iron-curtain countries who refused to return were more properly a charge on the whole economy of the West than on the Germans alone. The costs of maintaining the DP's were the largest of the so-called secondary costs of the occupation.

One of the reasons for the figures being in dispute was that the bookkeeping was arbitrary; each of the occupying powers did its own. The French took machines from the Bosch works in Reutlingen in their zone and sent them to the Saar, alleging that there had been insufficient manpower to run them. They called this action decartelization, although no cartel was involved; the company had already been split up. Sixty per cent of their occupation costs the French charged as lump-sum levies, which made it difficult to know exactly what the funds were being used for. The so-called "irregular requisitions" were those undertaken without benefit of the usual form the Allies used when taking goods, and any German injured by them was prevented from making a claim for restitution in the French zone.[8]

Nor was it easy to estimate whether charges were excessive. In the early days of the occupation the French had a staff of 3,000

[7] A careful German estimate in 1950 indicated that two Germans were employed for every member of the occupation. The majority were young people who would otherwise have been engaged in productive enterprise in an economy short of workers in their age brackets (*Berliner Zeitung*, Nov. 2, 1950).

[8] *Einwirkungen der Besatzungsmächte auf die Westdeutsche Wirtschaft*, pp. 51, 177.

running the railroad system in their zone; this was reduced by 1948 to a little over 100. One hundred thousand Germans were working on the administrative staffs of Allied agencies in 1949, paid by the German economy.

The German press was being encouraged to speak up, to break with the habits of the authoritarian past; but the issue of the paper that printed the story of the DP brassières was banned. The Allies countered German attacks with detailed analyses. The *Westfälische Nachrichten* quoted Allied figures showing that their contribution greatly overshadowed the German; that in 1949 and 1950 the Germans had spent 5.7 per cent of their income on the occupation and it was thought that in 1951–2 the proportion would be 4.6 per cent, whereas in the period under Hitler they had spent 19 per cent on the military budget. A spokesman for military government reported in the *Neue Zeitung* that the United States was contributing 80 pfennigs for every 20 the Germans paid. A release from the offices of the High Commission (HICOG) said that for 1951–2 the occupation cost for Germany would be 6.3 per cent of its gross national product, compared with armament costs of 15.7 per cent for the United States, 9.7 per cent for France, 6.3 per cent for Italy, 6.5 per cent for the Netherlands, and 21 per cent for the Soviet Union. American and British troops were paid by their own governments, the Americans explained, and they spent money in the German economy that helped the German dollar balances.

The Germans pointed to their burden of expellees and of others who were in need of substantial help. Allowances for families of the unemployed or individuals who could not otherwise support themselves were only 110 to 120 marks a month, and for those getting partial assistance 33 to 38 marks. One third of the population needed government assistance of some kind; 20 per cent of the state income went for this support, 600 marks from each wage-earner. As a result of the reduced economy and the influx of refugees, the Germans had only a fraction of their income to spend,[9] compared with the French, British, and Americans. As for the Americans leaving money in the country, Germans said they left the currency but obviously took goods and services that would have been used by the natives.

There were occasional brisk skirmishes. During one news conference a German remarked to the American High Commissioner that the number of refugees in Germany was owing to the generosity of Messrs. Churchill and Roosevelt and the Yalta agreements. The costs of such generosity, he said, should be paid by the people who made the gift, not by the people burdened with its consequences. McCloy replied heatedly that it was Hitler who had set these events in motion, and, while it was not considered good form to mention it, he had nevertheless existed and had brought these troubles to Germany.[1]

Public sentiments were checked by polls, and it was found that 38 per cent of the people in the American zone, 61 per cent in Bremen, and only 29 per cent in Berlin thought the Germans were paying all the occupation costs. The higher the income bracket of the person asked and the better educated he was, the higher he thought the German share. Only one in ten gave the occupation costs as a major cause of the imbalance of the *Länder* budgets, which was contrary to what the German officials were telling them.[2] Germans were sure, whatever the reasons given, that occupation costs could be reduced. Some estimates— that of the *Stuttgarter Zeitung*, for example—declared that they could be cut by 60 per cent; others said by half.

With the Korean War the German case became stronger in theory but lost much of its steam. Carlo Schmid, vice-president of the Bundestag, said in November 1950 that the Allies would have to cut out occupation costs that did not directly concern

[9] German disposable income in 1949 was 6 per cent of the German national product compared with 18 per cent for France, 22 per cent for Britain, and 32 per cent for the Americans (*Deutsche Zeitung*, Nov. 11, 1950).

[1] *Neue Zeitung*, June 19, 1950.

[2] *Some German Opinions on Occupation Costs.*

the common defense. Speaking for the Social Democratic party, he said that only when the Allies "bound their fate" to that of Western Germany would the SPD take part in the defense effort.[3] In 1950 the Americans urged West Germany to prepare a defense budget of her own as a substitute for the occupation costs, and then a new argument developed as to how much Germany could afford to pay for her own defense. The Germans held to their view that social costs and occupation costs had to be regarded as a whole; their contribution to defense should be as high as possible but not beyond their strength.

Like so much else, the debate faded away with the growing certainty in every German's mind that if the Allies were not in Germany the Russians would be; and with the Russians there would be no articles in the newspapers about the luxurious living of the occupation, no political investigations into improper expenditures, no economic commissions at work on the data, no debates in the Bundestag.

The Allies found ways to reduce the conspicuous waste; they cut personnel; they assumed some of the charges the Germans had borne. The occupation costs became defense costs, and although German economists could show that these, too, would be onerous—the cost of a jet bought in the United States would be a good deal higher than the Germans could pay, and the expense of starting up any German defense industries would be a heavy charge against the economy, especially in absorbing scarce manpower—the argument now became one about details of what the country could properly afford.

[3] *Neue Zeitung*, Nov. 8, 1950.

XI

THE RECOVERY

Nations, like individuals, have runs of good luck and bad. Before and after Hitler came to power there was nothing Germany could do that ended well. Just as the economy was overcoming the results of the First World War and the inflation that followed, the depression struck. After Hitler took over the government there was a burst of prosperity for some of the population, but it came through rearming, repressive controls over the economy, and domestic and foreign policies that could lead only to war. It became clear to people among the opposition that Hitler must somehow be got out of the way. Leading generals planned to arrest him if he went to war over Czechoslovakia, but the Munich agreement saved him. There were plots to arrest and finally to kill him, but, thanks to his wary intuition and a series of coincidences, he escaped: he failed to keep to a planned schedule, or a bomb mechanism failed to detonate. And since the Allies would neither negotiate with nor make any commitments to the German opposition, World War II had to be fought to the bitter end, which meant death and destruction not only for armies but also for cities and thousands of the civilian population. There was no way out for Germany. Hitler had been able to wring concessions from the Allies after the far more modest proposals of the governments of the Weimar Republic had been rejected, but Hitler had fantastic goals that could be won only by war. Almost everything the Allies had conceded to the Weimar democracy had been badly timed; when reparations were cut down not even the lower figures could be paid.

Now the time had come when whatever the Germans did contributed to their attaining both international respectability and economic recovery. Prices rose rapidly in 1948 in Germany. But a deflation hit the rest of the Western world in early 1949. Imports to Germany during 1949 soon helped to level and then send prices down there too, as shopkeepers were forced to sell their goods to pay bills. With unemployment mounting and the Allies prodding the new German government to take vigorous action to make work, the Germans used up their credit balances buying raw materials in the world market, a procedure that could have had disastrous results. But the Korean War came in the summer of 1950, sending a panic rush of buyers to raw-material sources, increasing demand for every kind of industrial production; and the Germans by March 1951 were for the first time exporting more than they imported. Their exports continued to increase month by month; they had done exactly what they would have if they could have foreseen the events. From having been an extreme debtor to the OEEC, they now became an extreme creditor. German dollar reserves more than doubled before the end of 1951; industrial production was up 20 per cent. The trade deficit that had been $700,000,000 in 1950 was cut to under $30,000,000 in 1951.

On the political side, the Russians provided the help the Germans needed. Despite the French, despite the stereotypes that American officials brought with them to their task, despite the springs of hatred the Nazis had left, the decisions of the Kremlin did not permit the West to proceed with its plans to keep Germany weak, divided, and poor. The Russian attack forced the West to countermeasures, and Germany always lay in the center of the struggle. The West German officials made the decision that the country's future lay in co-operating above all with the United States; and Adenauer, as he thanked the Allies at Petersberg for the help they had given, was being more than polite when he used the word "allies." It was the United States that had supplied the encouragement and the bulk of funds and materials for German reconstruction, as it was doing for all the Marshall Plan countries; if the Germans could win the approval of the Americans, all the rest would fall into place. It would matter little what the French hoped for in the way of German territory or feared from the German recovery if the Americans wanted something different.

Nor in the long run would it matter if the British blew up the shipyards of Hamburg. If the Americans wanted these rebuilt, they would be. Whether conscious or unconscious, this was the German policy under Adenauer. Early in 1950 he said that never in history had a conqueror done so much for the nation she had conquered. McCloy and the other American representatives might scold the Germans for their incorrigible nationalism and political shortcomings and urge them to accept such penalties as dismantling, but behind their rhetoric was the desire to see the Germans get on their feet again.

Both the desire and the means were vastly increased by the attack of the North Koreans on the South Koreans in late June of 1950. As soon as it became evident that the Communist invaders would overrun the country, the United States intervened, first with air force and navy, then with ground troops. Although Mr. Truman called the operation a police action, it was not easy for the public, and especially for the troops, to tell the difference between this and war. American resources were mobilized, economic controls imposed, a state of national emergency declared; the nation sought to strengthen its alliances wherever it could. Billions were voted for the rearmament of the United States and its allies. It seemed that a full-scale war might come at any time—and that Germany could be another Korea. There were German military formations in the East zone; there had been a gathering of East German youth in May 1950 in Berlin. Five hundred thousand boys and girls and 10,000 of the new units of the East zone "barracks police" had paraded and demonstrated. The East-zone leaders had said the Free German Youth would invade West Berlin;[1] but those who came over were peaceable and friendly—400 asked for asylum in the West—and likely to be critical of their government. Nevertheless, it was a powerful demonstration of fanatical propaganda as the blue-uniformed ranks marched and shouted "Friendship," clapping their hands over their heads. Winston Churchill, who in March had called a German contribution to the defense of Europe vital, now warned that time was not on the side of the West and that World War III threatened. Governor Dewey called war with Russia inevitable;[2] an American major general came out in favor of a preventive war;[3] a Russian spokesman said the West must yield or there could be war. In all these ferments and calls to arms there could be no ignoring the need for German co-operation and contingents. The members of the North Atlantic Treaty Organization, with the exception of France, were agreed on the need for German forces and wanted them right away; and even influential French voices were raised in favor of the principle of a German contribution to European defense. The foreign ministers' conference, meeting in New York in September 1950, declared that there would be no German army as such but that German contingents should be included in a European army. The foreign ministers recommended the end of the state of war and announced that any attack on Germany would be the equivalent of an attack on the Western Allies.[4]

The economic rise in West Germany that accompanied the fighting in Korea was prodigious. In the place of the down-spiraling prices of German goods (stores, in order to keep liquid, had sold overcoats for as little as 1.5 marks in early February of 1950)

---

[1] When it became apparent that the West would not permit demonstrations, the slogan "Free German Youth Storms Berlin" was changed to "Free German Youth Greets Berlin."

[2] *The New York Times*, Sept. 9, 1950.

[3] Ibid., Sept. 3, 1950.

[4] *American Foreign Policy*, pp. 1711–13.

there was an upsurge of demand both inside and outside the country. Unencumbered with the manufacture of war goods, the new and rebuilt factories could concentrate on products for the world markets, and the most efficient part of the working force could be used. There was no army to draft young men out of employment.

The Germans took the Korean War seriously, especially in the early days when the American troops were being thrown back by massive drives of North Korean soldiers armed with Russian equipment, including in one battle 80 tanks. For the Germans and the Western Allies the question was whether Korea might not be a preview of what would happen next in Europe; and there was little time to prepare against the overwhelming Russian forces, which were said to number 500,000 in East Germany alone. Against them and what were believed to be some additional 200 divisions, the Western Allies could perhaps muster 20 to 30.[5] Unless the atomic bomb were to be used, the disparity was too overwhelming to prevent the Russians from overrunning Europe rapidly and with little loss to themselves.

While many Germans, including the leaders of the main parties, saw the peril, there was a wide difference of opinion as to what they could or should do about it. Adenauer had immediately asked the Western Allies for a guarantee of German security and—pointing at the East German barracks police, estimated at 50,000—he asked for a West German defense force.[6] Schumacher, too, favored German rearmament, a German role in the defense of Europe; but he was suspicious of Allied strategy, which he thought might call for a retreat from German territory; he wanted all Germany defended with an attacking force, not a delaying action, and full equality with the other powers.[7] There was powerful antiwar sentiment in the country,

---

[5] S. Brant: *Der Aufstand*, pp. 106, 140.
[6] *The New York Times*, Aug. 18, 1950.
[7] Ibid., Aug. 24, 1950.

however, ranging all the way from neutralism to a refusal to bear arms. Polls showed only 43 per cent in favor of German rearmament, although the figure had risen from 26 per cent and less in 1949. German youth leaders declared that, while they opposed the Russians and communism, they also opposed joining an army to fight them. The SPD, which (despite Schumacher's concessions in the emergency) either rejected rearmament or wanted it to come more slowly than did the CDU, gained over the CDU, which suffered severe losses in Hesse, Württemberg-Baden, and Bavaria in the elections in the autumn of 1950.[8]

The dam had now broken, and aid, both moral and economic, flooded over the country. McCloy even earlier in the year had asked his staff, on the urging of Chancellor Adenauer, not to criticize the German administration in public, and the Chancellor could now ask that the Allies help in restoring the honor of the German soldier, and the German sailor too; he suggested that the admirals be released from prison. Persuading the German people to accept the need to make a defense contribution would, he pointed out, be a considerable job.

Sentiments other than antiwar were affecting German public opinion. The Security Commission of the Allies, which was to stand guard against German rearmament, set up its establishment at Koblenz, using fifty villas and two hotels, and sent out an eighty-two-page questionnaire to German plants. The questionnaire required answers in the smallest detail: the number of employees and shifts, the amount of fuel used each day, the number of cranes and their lifting capacity, their age, and so on.[9] The commission forbade many things; one paper headlined its account "The Nyet out of Koblenz," referring to the refusal to permit the rebuilding of the mills at Thyssenhuette, Salzgitter, Dortmunde Haide, and the shipyards of Blohm and Voss. The *Hamburger Echo* said the commission had a piece of

[8] *Jahrbuch der öffentlichen Meinung, 1947–1955*, pp. 360–1.
[9] *Deutsche Zeitung und Wirtschafts Zeitung*, Feb. 10, 1950.

Potsdam, a drop of Morgenthau, and traces of re-education in it. In 1950 the commission permitted 75,000 hunting weapons to be placed on sale for the season—25,000 rifles, 50,000 shotguns, but no revolvers, pistols, or automatic weapons. The Russian papers said the commission was actually a general staff with 3,000 American and British officers designed to function between the Elbe and the Rhine. "It continues the colonization of Germany—an American monopoly through which the annexation of Germany is secured." [1]

There were still levels of German industry and taboos of certain kinds of manufacture which the commission enforced. No searchlights more than 45 centimeters in diameter could be produced, no kites or model airplanes of any dimensions. No machine tools of possible use in war were to be manufactured. Even the ships that were to be built, despite the limitations on their size and speed, were to be investigated by a committee for features that could be converted to war purposes. Under the Petersberg protocol, the need for the destruction of research facilities for synthetic oil and rubber was reaffirmed. [2]

Public-opinion surveys showed the Germans on the whole favorably disposed to the Americans. The *Frankfurter Rundschau* reported on June 10, 1950, that 31 per cent of the Germans in the American zone found the Americans the most sympathetic among the occupying powers, with 7 per cent of the votes for the British and 4 per cent for the French; 16 per cent had no opinion and 42 per cent said they preferred none. In the British zone 30 per cent preferred the United States, 9.8 per cent the British, .6 per cent the French, and .4 per cent the Russians. In the French zone 22.6 per cent preferred the United States, 14.6 per cent the French, 2.6 per cent the British, and .1 per cent the Russians. Two thirds of the Germans interviewed said they knew no Americans, six out of ten said they never or rarely saw American troops, and the same number said the con-

[1] *Tägliche Rundschau,* Jan. 25, 1950.
[2] *A Decade of American Foreign Policy,* pp. 1002–9.

duct of the troops was good. In Berlin the favorable percentages rose; 80 per cent of the population thought well of the behavior of the Americans, and eight out of ten said they had had no unpleasant experiences with American soldiers.

In contrast with these surveys, the German papers printed many articles on cases of rape, drunkenness, and robbery involving Americans. MP's were accused of beating up Germans in Augsburg, and representatives of the German papers met with American resident officers to discuss measures to be taken.[3] The commanding American general had agreed that there could be objections to the conduct of the MP's, and the newspaper reported that in the last ninety days eighteen soldiers had been brought before a committee of officers and eleven had been sent back to the United States. German criticisms of the American troops were that they were too young, too undisciplined, given too much leave, and drank too much.[4]

Requisitioning continued to distress the German communities. Not only were the houses taken, the Germans pointed out, but also they had to be supplied with furniture. One American colonel was sentenced to two years' imprisonment for selling $10,000 worth of furnishings from the house requisitioned for him. Furthermore, the houses often were occupied by what the Germans thought a disproportionately small number of people and sometimes, the Germans said, by none at all. The Army explained that it must be sure of having enough space for its requirements, that the personnel fluctuated, and that returning a house only to have to requisition it again was considered poor policy. When McCloy came to Germany, for example, he was given a house that had been saved for just such an occasion; no one had been living in it.

The *Frankfurter Presse* in October 1950 said that thousands of persons were still kept out of their homes, though the Americans replied that most houses had been returned. In the city

---

[3] *Schwäbische Landeszeitung*, Nov. 22, 1949.
[4] *Deutsche Allgemeine Zeitung*, April 20, 1950.

of Frankfurt 2,200 apartments and one-family houses remained in the hands of the occupation, as against 10,800 in the early postwar days. Between 1948 and 1950, another paper reported, 7,000 requisitioned structures had been returned. These included 4,000 dwelling-places, 216 barracks, 45 schools, 28 hospitals, 191 hotels, 106 warehouses, 50 factories, 190 office buildings, 1 airport, and 1 post office.

The Americans continued to see dangers as well as hopeful signs in the new Germany. McCloy in his first reports said that nationalism and nationalistic groups were now more vocal than they had been during the period of military government; he observed, too, that there used to be in Germany an aggressive spirit, an extensive and efficient industry, and national pride. "If security is to be maintained," he wrote, "these elements must be contained within safe limits." [5] The signs of nationalism that he and others saw were visible in such matters as the German protests against the French taking over the economic resources of the Saar. The German White Book on the Saar, Mr. McCloy said in his second quarterly report, showed the strength of this latent nationalism.

The Americans conceded, however, that the denazification program had been a failure. The program, it was now clear, had attempted too much; it had not taken into account the German reaction to the regime that had led the country to such inconceivable disasters. Even Goering's widow had come to learn of Hitler's intention to have her child killed when he discovered what he considered Goering's perfidy; and one of the useful results of the Nuremberg trials had been the widespread publication of the facts of the concentration and extermination camps. There were few in Germany, whatever they had once believed, who would again entertain the notion of an authoritarian state. But it was also a fact that the Nazis had run the country for thirteen years with a large bureaucratic apparatus and with a fluctuating but always substantial support from the country at

[5] John J. McCloy: *First Quarterly Report*, pp. iv, 10–15, 41.

large; consequently, the job of dealing with those members of the party who were guilty of committing or permitting its excesses was a formidable one.

McCloy wrote in his fifth report in the last quarter of 1950 that the denazification proceedings, now virtually at an end, had been the most extensive legal procedure ever undertaken. They had involved 13,000,000 people; almost 3,700,000 (27 per cent of the adult population) had been found chargeable; 3,500,-000 had been tried. It would have been wiser, McCloy wrote, "to have applied the penal aspects . . . more promptly and effectively to the real activists . . . treating the great mass of lesser Nazis more leniently." [6]

Also he thought the scope of the trials too broad. The big Nazi was sometimes a man of influence, he said, who urged his employees to join the party, but he himself might not have persecuted anyone. The little man, on the other hand, might have been the fanatic. Teachers had been reinstated in Württemberg-Baden who had held high positions under the Nazis, and the United States had urged the ministers president to reconsider their appointments. These teachers had been pardoned by the German authorities, but the American High Commissioner reported that he was continuing to press for their dismissal. Had the prosecutions been more widespread, McCloy said, they would have separated some 30,000,000 people from the community—8,000,000 party members and their families. Now it was German public opinion that forced the resignation of a man from a federal ministry because of his previous party history; the German people themselves, McCloy thought, despite what he had just written about the schoolteachers, were to determine the standing of these people in the country.

McCloy's views of the failure of denazification were widely shared. The official HICOG history said the program failed to meet the objectives set by American policy; lesser offenders were brought to trial quickly and often severely punished; major

[6] McCloy: *Fifth Quarterly Report*, pp. 51, 52.

offenders postponed their hearings and got off easily as the surge
of hatred subsided. By 1948, the history reported, 85 per cent
of the officials removed in Bavaria had been reinstated; by 1950
the denazification tribunals were closed down, and there were
now new outcasts: the personnel of the tribunals. In Ludwigs-
berg 400 of these former denazification employees were trying
to find jobs, while in May 1950, 60 per cent of the government
employees in Württemberg-Baden were former Nazis. The
American *Land* commissioner, General Gross, exchanged bitter
words on this subject with the minister president, Reinhold
Maier, who charged him in turn with interfering with the German administration.[7] McCloy announced himself as fully backing General Gross and said that Maier had made a bad error in
defending an unsuitable person's right to a job—a position with
which the majority of German newspapers agreed.[8]

Many Germans felt, as did the Americans, that former Nazis
were treated too lightly, had divested themselves of their allegiance too readily; but there was neither time nor means to stop
to make another accounting of the past, although a Bundestag
committee set out to investigate the use of former party members in the government and forced some resignations.

But the time had gone by when denazification and disputes
over appointments were to have an important bearing on decisions, and McCloy summed up matters very clearly in his report in the last quarter of 1950: "As the free world was speed-
ing measures for defense . . . the Federal Government moving
toward a position of equality . . . was offered by the Atlantic
Pact Council an honorable share in the arrangements for common security."

[7] *Neue Zeitung*, April 29, 1952.
[8] In defense of its attitude the German administration said that repentant
or re-educated Nazis, if they had not been major offenders, should not be
excluded from the German community and from jobs they were competent
to hold; if they were, another source of frustration and hatred would be
made permanent. Adenauer's declared policy in 1950 was to use former
Nazis, but only in positions where they were flanked by men who had opposed the party.

The Korean War hastened and sharpened the Allied reaction to Russian belligerence. Secretary of State Acheson in February 1950 had spoken of the need for total diplomacy in dealing with the Russians—the need to meet the threat wherever it arose, and to build the defense out of the economic, political, and psychological resources of the democratic countries. A month later he offered Russia the other choice: to join in control of the atom, to make peace treaties with Germany, Japan, and Austria, to agree to the unification of Germany under a free government, to withdraw its troops from the satellite countries, to desist from subversive activities in Europe and Asia, to permit free elections in the satellite countries, and to stop its scurrilous attacks on the United States.

French policy too showed signs of responding to something more than a nostalgia for times past. In February 1950 the government concluded an economic agreement with Saar authorities linking the Saar to the French economy for fifty years, a step which the British said they approved but which Chancellor Adenauer bluntly denounced as a blow to European unity. Adenauer had proposed an international status for the Saar and a plebiscite, but the French wanted neither. Proposals by Bidault and Schuman, however, were of a different character. Bidault made a speech in April, when he was premier, in favor of a new European conception, a high authority that would concert plans for a European economy and defense system; and later in the month the idea was carried forward by Schuman, who as foreign minister proposed that Germany, Austria, and Switzerland be included in such a body, although without participation in its military committee. In May he suggested a Franco-German agreement to pool coal and iron production in an arrangement that would be open to the other European countries.

In late October 1950 the new French premier, René Pleven, drew up a plan for the inclusion of German contingents in a European army; although this was a counterproposal to the demands for a separate German army, it seemed, together with the Schuman plan, to bring nearer than ever before the possibility of a solid French-German collaboration.

In the East zone, as the October elections for the new Parliament drew near, the Liberal Democrats and Christian Democrats were forced to accept the SED proposal for a single list of candidates. Seventy per cent of the candidates were assigned to the SED, the "mass organizations," and the SED's satellite parties—the National Democratic party and the Democratic Farmer party. The two bourgeois parties shared the remainder.

The Russian bloc lined up against the plans for West German armed forces and worked on French fears of German rearmament. The Prague conference of eight powers, including the People's Democratic Republic of East Germany, with Russia, Albania, Czechoslovakia, Poland, Rumania, Hungary, and Bulgaria, met October 20 and 21 and scored the plans for a West German army. It said the Hitler generals would now return; the army would be a tool in the hands of the British-American aggressors to be used against the democratic forces in France and West Germany. The conference favored establishing an all-German council to prepare the way for a provisional regime and a peace treaty to be concluded without delay. Occupation troops, following the usual formula, would be withdrawn a year later.

The Americans were determined not only to integrate West Germany into the political and economic security system they were building but also to reconstruct its administration. They continued to regard many of the habits of thinking of German officials as archaic as well as dangerous. The federal government had not dealt vigorously enough with the problem of unemployment in 1949, when there were 2,000,000 out of work; it failed to channel investment; it permitted the importation of luxury foods and consumer goods on too great a scale.

During the early part of the Korean War, with German unemployment at a high figure, the Americans urged action on the federal government as well as price controls to keep down an incipient inflation. An American correspondent reported the third critical memorandum on the subject within two weeks from the Allied high commissioners.

Still a major cause of distress in Germany was the housing shortage, which was also linked to unemployment. In Western Europe more than 7,000,000 houses had been totally or partially destroyed; more than half of these were in Germany, where 2,250,000 had been destroyed and 2,500,000 damaged. Hundreds of thousands of refugees were living in barracks or in what had been Nazi concentration camps. Rebuilding had been slow. Up to 1948 it had occurred largely in rural areas, where there were means of trading food for materials. Little was done on a large scale until 1949, when over 215,000 dwellings were either repaired or rebuilt, and in 1950 this figure rose to 362,000. In scheduling new housing, the Americans wanted priorities for areas near factories, for the refugee population, for those who had suffered under the Nazis or who had been bombed out. Surveys were made of the needs of these areas and groups, and where the concentrations of refugees were highest, as in Bavaria, the building program was most active. More than 350,000 rooms were newly built or repaired in Bavaria between 1947 and 1950; and in 1950, 60,000 apartments were added to them. The largest program was for Schleswig-Holstein, where the 1939 population of 1,500,000 had risen to 2,650,000 because of the refugees. Schleswig had the highest unemployment rate in Germany; 20,000 new dwellings were planned for it in 1950 at a cost of 85,000,000 D marks, of which ECA was to put up 40,000,000 marks. Thirty-five million marks came from the *Land* government, 10,000,000 from co-operatives and private sources. In the Ruhr, where out of 300,000 dwellings only 74,000 had been left undamaged, 281,699 units had been built for miners by 1950.[9]

[9] Anna E. Brauer and Elizabeth Erdman: *The West German Housing Problem, 1945–1953.*

Surveys were made to determine what new industries could be started. Manufacture of textiles, glass, optical instruments, mechanical and leather goods, iron, and steel was considered promising, and actually a great transformation was made. In Kiel, for example, the capital of Schleswig-Holstein, the Germania docks that had produced U-boats were turned into factories to produce small and medium-size machine tools. Yards where warships had been built now manufactured electrical and mechanical instruments. The Navy yard produced precision instruments, and the former Navy maintenance shops turned out knitting-machines, kitchen stoves, and car bodies. Other plants produced chemicals, pharmaceutical supplies, clothing, furniture, locomotives, and eventually merchant ships. Twenty-two hundred new apartments were built for the 10,000 workers who found jobs in these plants. At Wahstedt a former Navy arsenal was turned into a coffee-processing plant, a furniture factory, a textile-and-knitting plant; hundreds of new jobs were provided, and 350 houses built. In lower Saxony 30,000,000 D marks were allocated for refugees, for whom 10,000 dwellings were built; 15,000,000 marks went for refugee resettlement in the Rhineland and the Palatinate.[1]

The Germans had discovered in 1946 that the rubble could be used instead of crushed stone in manufacturing concrete slabs. Before building supplies had become available, they had painstakingly picked out bricks from the rubble; these they had cleaned and made usable one by one, by hand; the official estimate was that 1,700,000,000 bricks had been processed in this colossally inefficient fashion.

The Americans introduced contests for architects and builders; fixtures were standardized and central purchasing agencies were organized. A Reconstruction Loan Corporation was established with American funds in Frankfurt in December 1948 to give immediate aid, with a capital of 81,500,000 D marks to

[1] Ibid.

be divided among eight *Länder* for making mortgage loans. The European Recovery Program (ERP) did not have to charge interest on the loans it made, and not more than 3 per cent was required from refugees, never more than 5 per cent from any borrower—extremely low rates for Europe.

The cost of a house was usually about 10,000 marks; there were tax concessions for new buildings and many incentives for private builders; above all, there was almost limitless demand. Self-help projects were started, where people pledged themselves to spend so many hours working on the new construction; some of these were sponsored by churches, which gave money and land; factories gave materials to their employees or lent money for housing construction at no interest. In the view of the churches a Christian life was more than ever difficult in crowded barracks and bunkers; the Lutherans and Catholics as well as the Quakers, joined later by American foundations, put money and land at the disposal of these private groups.

The building program in Berlin and West Germany was to continue for many years. In 1951, 410,000 new units were built; in 1952, 443,000; in 1953, 515,000—almost 2,000,000 in the period since 1949. More than 5,500,000 people were provided with new homes, one out of every nine persons in West Germany, and there was still a shortage of some 2,000,000 units.

American concern for the German economy reached into all its corners. Experts were critical of the efficiency of agriculture. The holdings were scattered, owing to the German system of inheritance by division of the farms among the children; and many a farmer spent a third of his time traveling from one of his small plots to another, often at the other end of the village. German agriculture, the Americans thought, was too backward to compete with that of other countries, and because of its inefficiency had to be paid subsidies by the government. American authorities set out to increase incentives for production, providing credit and introducing modern farming practices. There had in the past been notable scientific work by German researchers in agriculture and forestry, but the Nazis and the war years had taken their toll of both the research and the land.[2]

The German farmer had been less affected than any other group in the country by the war and the inflation, and by 1949 in the American view he was back at his old unintelligent ways, with the help of a Farmers' Union that aimed at agricultural protectionism. The Americans regarded the Union as mainly an organization in restraint of trade, whose purpose was to protect German agriculture from competition with that of foreign countries.

In 1950, with credit and machinery available, the use of tractors reached a new high; the Americans were encouraging the Germans to join international agricultural congresses and to learn new methods; women were urged to form Farm Women's Associations, independent of the Farmers' Union. Late in 1950 West Germany became a member of the Food and Agriculture Organization, the first time since the war that the Germans had achieved full status in an international body.

The ancient farming practices improved in a short space of time. Land was reclaimed, refugees were settled on it; some holdings were consolidated, although to have done the job completely would have cost too much—one billion marks, it was estimated. The Americans urged the Germans to plant more green land and fodder crops, to use scientific methods of soil-testing and disease control, especially in the vineyards and among the cattle. The TB rate was high in the German herds. Credits were given dairies, research was aided, and in addition there were wide-scale food programs for a population that had been undernourished for years. In Württemberg-Baden three quarters of the children were given lunches, and in Berlin they received them without charge. Seventy per cent of American dollar aid in 1949 was for food; in 1951, 1,800,000 children were given 350 calories a day through the lunch program, for which

[2] McCloy: *Seventh Quarterly Report*, pp. 77–85.

half of them paid nothing; but the average German was still consuming only 2,780 calories daily as against a prewar figure of 3,000, and, as the Americans pointed out, the increased work load called for increased proteins.

Decartelization laws were now administered by the Germans, and the minister of economics, Ludwig Erhard, held much the same view of the pernicious effects of restraints of trade as did the Americans. He presented to the Parliament a bill to outlaw cartels except in cases of emergency or where the rationalization of industry made them useful. The Allies had forced one soap company to stop setting minimum prices and had imposed a stiff fine on the officers of a company manufacturing abrasives for similar practices. The great combinations in the Ruhr had been broken up into eight companies; I. G. Farben and a number of other large combinations had been divided. The single company that had controlled the German motion-picture industry had been immediately dissolved; in its place came a large number of small producers that turned out some competent pictures but fewer experimental films, because with small capital they could ill afford losses.

From the beginning the Allies had favored the growth of labor unions, and a good deal of practical and strategic guidance was supplied them from labor unions in the United States and from official policy. After a sluggish start the union movement in West Germany soon became a center of the anti-Communist forces, as labor leaders struggled to organize workers in Berlin and in West Germany.[3] At first union activity had been almost entirely concentrated on improving the bare living-conditions of workers—obtaining housing, higher ration cards for union members, and paper, typewriters, and gasoline for the organizers. In the early years of the occupation there was no bargaining for increased wages or the fringe benefits that were characteristic of union aims in other Western countries.

By 1949 the German Trade Union Federation had on its rolls

[3] Interview, Irving Brown.

90 per cent of all the union membership and 40 per cent of all those gainfully employed. Under the German constitution independent unions have a monopoly on organizing labor—there are no company unions. Backed by both major parties as well as most of the smaller parties, the labor unions secured what appeared to be one of the most revolutionary reforms of the economic life of any country. This was co-determination. A measure proposed first in 1920, co-determination had been put forward again by German labor leaders during the period of military government; then as well as later, under the high commissioners, the occupying authorities remained neutral in the matter. The reform was designed to give labor a part in making policy decisions, to keep the powers of industrial capitalism from allying themselves again with reactionary forces, whether political or military. In the coal and steel industries there were equal numbers of workers and management on the board of directors, plus one neutral member. The labor directors, like those of management, got a house and car and the very considerable salary of 25,000 to 50,000 marks a year. Co-determination had little effect on industrial decisions; more than anything else it was a symbol of a new order that on the one hand would outlaw unholy alliances and on the other would lead the workers into the bourgeoisie.

The labor potential rose some 2,000,000 between 1948 and 1953. There were jobs for almost all of these people, and with the standard of living rising rapidly, the old socialist doctrines had little influence on political thinking. The SPD became a party of criticism as the nation, in the midst of its prosperity, moved toward a middle-class, free-enterprise point of view. The West Germans had not only their present exhilarating boom to rejoice in; they could also compare their freedom with their experience of the unrestrained power of the state, and always at their door was the planned economy of the East zone to contemplate.

Between the time of the currency reform in 1948 and September 1953 the West German population, largely owing to the immigration from East Germany, rose by 2,600,000. Production in 1948 was two thirds of 1936; by 1950 it was up to 113 per cent, by 1952 144 per cent. In 1947 imports were $43,000,000 and exports $15,000,000; in 1948 each of these doubled approximately, and by 1951 they totaled $3,500,000,000.[4]

In West Berlin, matters were different. The city was a ward of the West and of the federal government. But it remained something besides a deficit area. In October of 1950 General Clay returned to Berlin for the dedication of the Freedom Bell in the presence of 400,000 people. A replica of the Liberty Bell in Philadelphia, it bears a variation of Lincoln's words: "That this world under God shall have a new birth of freedom." The bell could be heard in East Berlin, and from there thousands came to visit a fair held in the West sectors, where optical products and manufactures made of heavy steel were among the goods on display. None of these could have been manufactured a few months earlier in the West, and although they also were being manufactured in the East the German population got none of them.[5]

Production was up in Berlin, but so was relief. Loans were made from American funds for the repair of houses; $3,900,000 was given to build hotels that would stimulate tourism. Supplies left over from the airlift were sold cheaply, and double shifts worked on the rubble. There were investments of ERP funds in heavy industry; 57,000,000 D marks was given to industry, 35,-000,000 marks to housing. The Americans found the German bank and city officials who were responsible for approving these loans "very conscientious." There were loans for research work, for druggists, for publishers, for the vehicle industry. There was indemnification from the Economic Co-operation Administration for damage suffered during the blockade. But by the middle of 1950 unemployment in West Berlin was up to 309,000, twice

[4] *Deutschland Heute.*
[5] *The New York Times*, Oct. 25, 1950.

as much as at the end of the blockade. One American economist's suggestion of how to meet the crisis favored a drastic paring of the city budget, the encouragement of only such industries as could pay their way; but he left out of account the requirements of a city that was also a monument of the West in enemy territory.[6] The West Germans introduced the *Notopfer*, the emergency contribution for Berlin by way of a stamp affixed at two pfennigs a letter to all letters mailed in the West. In addition, for the benefit of the city there was a tax of one per cent on all salaries and wages. These measures met with opposition in West Germany, despite the widespread admiration professed for the Berliners. The taxes, while not large, were perceptible in strained budgets, and the symbol of Berlin was less important to some than the daily grocer's bill. Nevertheless, the taxes were voted in all the *Länder*.

The housing situation in Berlin remained critical for a long time. Five hundred and fifty thousand apartments had been destroyed, and 70 per cent of the remainder had been damaged. Of the 700,000 dwelling-units remaining in West Berlin, 50,000 were such places as cellars, ruins, garden huts, which could only be called temporary refuges. According to the American surveys, the Western sectors urgently needed 70,000 new apartment units to house the population. There was a shortage, therefore, of 120,000 apartments, if the wretched 50,000 makeshift quarters were to be replaced. In addition, 50,000 dwellings in West Berlin were in need of immediate repair.[7]

Rebuilding was intensive and widespread. By 1951 twenty new sport centers were built, rubble heaps became terraces and parks, hospitals and schools were repaired, old-age homes were built with the aid of funds from the Magistrat. New apartments were planned at a rate of 10,000 in 1952, rising to 20,000 for 1955. Priority for employment in restoring the city was given to men and women supporting families; white-collar workers were

[6] Hubert G. Schmidt: *Economic Assistance to West Berlin*, p. 33.
[7] Brauer and Erdman: *The West German Housing Problem*.

taken on for investigations and surveys. There were thousands of them needing jobs in a city that had once housed the complicated apparatus of government and private business. The pay of the 50,000 Berlin emergency workers was only one quarter of a building worker's. Up to 20,000 of them were used in garden projects, planting the banks of the city's canals to keep down the clouds of dust that rose when the wind blew over the rubble and the flinty soil left by the bombardment. The Tiergarten was replanted with trees; Bremen sent a gift of bushes to the city, and other cities followed suit. On behalf of the United States government McCloy presented Mayor Reuter with a check for 5,000,000 D marks for a library: 90 per cent for the building, the rest for books. Hostels for the homeless were built, as well as maternity homes, swimming pools, and homes for handicapped children; and as many supplies as possible were bought in Berlin.

By the end of 1951 West Berlin began to take shape again; a showcase, as it was called, of what the West could do. New hotels glittered, shops were filled with things to buy, neon lights shone on the Kurfürstendam. The West mark was worth five East marks on the free West Berlin market, although the official East-zone rate was one to one. Production, which during the blockade had fallen to 17 per cent of 1936, was now 51 per cent. Yet, despite everything, almost half of the city's population was supported by public funds; that is, they received pensions or worked on city projects.

The causes are not far to seek. West Berlin was a showcase, but there was no shop behind it. To it had streamed the refugees from the East. Some of them were then flown to West Germany, some stayed on legally, and some of them could not pass the screening process and remained "black," "unrecognized" by the authorities, ineligible for relief, eager to work at anything to stay alive and out of the East zone.

In the golden flood of American aid, there were only minor signs of Allied disapproval of the details of the German renaissance. Early in 1950 the high commissioners turned down the budget of Schleswig-Holstein on the grounds that it showed a paper deficit of 94,000,000 D marks when the actual deficit was 220,000,000 marks. They disapproved Bavarian laws covering damages during the Nazi period and against importing game, a Bremen law for a consumers' co-operative, a Hesse ordinance on DP's, a Hamburg tax-reduction for motion pictures. No federal law was ever disapproved by the Allied High Commission. There were tentative disapprovals of the Federal Civil Service bill and the income-tax revision, but such conflicts were resolved by a compromise or by one party conceding that the other's position was sound. Twenty-six *Länder* laws were acted on adversely at some stage, eight finally. Adverse action was taken in only four cases of federal legislation, but none was final. American observers believed that the very existence of the Allied power of disapproval made German legislators cautious in their lawmaking, but this has scarcely been borne out by the enactments of the German parliament after the restoration of sovereignty.

In April 1950 the German minister of economics said Allied disapproval of the proposed income-tax law was absurd, but this dispute too was one largely of the details of economic doctrine. Neither the Germans nor the Americans questioned the need for the law nor for the high taxes; the differences came in deciding how the burden could best be borne and how the capital could be provided to keep the economy on its upward course. The Allies were constantly on the alert for any signs of undemocratic measures, and a tax that permitted entrepreneurs to put more earnings into capital had suspicious features.

The Americans by the end of 1950 were urgently calling for a German contribution of manpower to the defense of Europe. In October, even before the Chinese had joined the war in Korea, Acheson had recommended a build-up of ten German divisions, although he said there should be no national army or general staff, thus adapting his views to those of the French and British. No one, in fact, in Germany or elsewhere, expressed a desire for a separate German army, and the resistance to the idea of any armed forces was so strong that not only did the opposition speak against it but members of Adenauer's cabinet resigned on the issue. Acheson warned both Bonn and Paris that the Russian danger was real, and the United States readily accepted Adenauer's view that German contingents in whatever number must join the Western forces as equals, and that German public opinion needed to be stimulated to accept rearmament. President Heuss, on New Year's Day of 1951, said the best type of German soldier upheld the ethics of his profession as well as the best type of any other nation. In January the commander in chief of the NATO forces, General Eisenhower, journeyed through the Allied countries, including West Germany, and in the course of his travels made two notable announcements. He spoke of his former enemies as "honorable comrades." "I have come to know," he said, "that there is a real difference between the regular German soldier and officer and Hitler and his criminal group." [8] In another speech he said the West felt no enmity toward the German state, certainly none toward the German people; he wanted equal status for Germany with the other countries of the alliance, and for him bygones were bygones. He assured the country that the German soldier had retained his honor during the war; the only dishonor had involved individuals who had brought it on themselves.[9]

[8] *The New York Times,* Jan. 24, 1951.
[9] Ibid., Jan. 21, 1951.

XII

THE ALLIANCE

The Germans quickly adopted the language of the late alliance against Hitler. The meetings between representatives of the Allied High Commission and the West German government held in January 1951 at the Petersberg on the creation of a German army were called "discussions on the German contributions to the maintenance of the peace." The West Germans were now to become a part of "the alliance of the freedom-loving nations." The East Germans mechanically took their place with the "peace-loving nations," to which their own and the Russian leaders continually referred as the Soviet attacked the NATO alliance, American bases in Europe, the peace with Japan made without Russian participation, and the plans for a West German army.

The West Germans took their place in the anti-Communist alliance with remarkable speed. In his second report early in 1950 McCloy had recorded that the German White Book issued by the federal government on the Saar illustrated "the reviving strength of latent German nationalist feeling, of which there are increasing evidences." By 1952 when his tenth report was written he was able to speak of the Saar as a detached observer. In his letter of transmittal to the Secretary of State he wrote:

> The fact that attempts, though still undeveloped, were again made to remove the Saar question as a constant irritant in Franco-German relations was a hopeful sign, partic-

ularly as many of the proposed solutions involved a so-called European dealing with the issue. . . . The Saar question has long been a serious obstacle to the building of harmonious relations between France and the German Federal Republic. . . . Yet the determination of the Western Foreign Ministers and Chancellor Adenauer to prevent the Saar, located in the heart of Europe, from becoming a stumbling block in the realization of the century-old dream of European unity, and the understanding of the situation demonstrated in the German and French Parliaments, were evidence that this concept of European solidarity has transcended the debating stage.[1]

For the Americans, Chancellor Adenauer had taken on the proportions of an eminent European as well as a German statesman. He spoke the language of European unity; the French foreign minister found it a pleasure to work with him as they negotiated on the Schuman plan; he made difficult concessions for the cause of a French-German rapprochement, and by accepting the need to sacrifice a degree of sovereignty for the sake of new European conceptions, he put his antagonists, whether German or French, at a disadvantage when they claimed more than he was ready to give. A short time before, some American observers had found him "tactless" and a prototype of the authoritarian, father-like figure to which the Germans were hopelessly addicted. Now, although the Americans thought the Federal Republic's political progress admirable in many ways, they wanted it to hurry up with its arming, to subdue the forces of neutralism and pacifism; and Adenauer wanted the same things. The country was in danger, McCloy told the Germans; they could not rely solely on others for defense, and in December he warned them that Marshall Plan aid could not be taken for granted. Prompt action was needed, the United States made clear, both in ratifying the Schuman plan and in creating a German defense force.

[1] John J. McCloy: *Tenth Quarterly Report*, pp. iii-iv.

The British High Commissioner, Sir Ivone Kirkpatrick, urged on the Germans full association with the West without equivocation. Neutralism was out of the question,[2] he said; and British spokesmen told the Germans that if only they would assume the German prewar debt, a status of virtual sovereignty could be granted.[3] And now the Germans, of whom so much new thinking was being demanded, stated the case for a regenerate people. They demanded full equality with the West in the negotiations on the new contractual status that was being discussed, and on the European Defense Force.

In debates in the Bundestag [4] the conduct of the trials of some of the war criminals who were under sentence was attacked. It was charged that they had been convicted through third-degree methods: the German-born American prosecutor (since returned to Germany to practice law) had threatened a German prisoner with trial by the Russians if he did not confess; matches had been driven under the nails of seventeen-year-old boys at the Dachau interrogations, and staged hangings of prisoners had been conducted to organ music. In addition, it was pointed out, many of the prisoners had been under sentence of death for months, which was itself cruel and unusual punishment.

The hearings and trials had been sharply criticized both in Germany and in the United States, and the critics included two American judges who had taken part in them.[5] Petitions for clemency now came from Chancellor Adenauer and President Heuss, from German veterans' associations, newspapers, and the families of the convicted men. The American High Commissioner and General Thomas T. Handy early in 1951 commuted 21 death sentences of the 28 still to be executed, and reduced 36 out of 41 terms of imprisonment, 32 of them to time already served. Alfried Krupp von Bohlen-Halbach was released and

[2] *The New York Times,* Jan. 13, 1951.
[3] Ibid., Jan. 14, 1951.
[4] Proceedings, Report 168, Vol. IX.
[5] *The New York Times,* Feb. 23, March 2, 12, 18, April 14, May 15, 1949.

his property, which had been ordered confiscated, was returned. The sentences of 11 men convicted of participating in the Malmédy massacre of American troops during the Battle of the Bulge were among those commuted.[6]

Doubts were expressed in many quarters about the intention or ability of the West to defend the Federal Republic if war should come. Adenauer demanded and obtained a guarantee that the Allies would defend German territory, but a number of critics thought this could mean defending Germany as an advanced base. Articles in newspapers pointed to the explosive chambers that the Allies had placed in bridges, which might be regarded as a plan to retreat from rather than to defend West Germany. Polls of German public opinion showed that these doubts were widely shared. Thirty-four per cent of the population were skeptical that the Americans would put up a good fight in the event of a Russian attack. Twenty-seven per cent believed the Americans would fight well, and those interviewed had a lower estimate of the French soldier. The Germans placed the Russians next to their own troops in fighting quality, although they liked the American soldiers; two thirds of them thought the GI's behaved as well as German soldiers would under the same circumstances; they just did not have much confidence in them as combat troops.

The Americans, in their urgent desire to see Germany armed quickly, came under heavy fire from British and French quarters. Winston Churchill and other British spokesmen had long seen the necessity for the German troops the United States was calling for, but the governments in London and Paris did not share Washington's sense of emergency. Now it was the United States that called on the free world to perceive its peril; the

---

[6] In 1948 there had been a Senate investigation, in which Senator McCarthy took an active part, into the methods by which convictions had been obtained. Spurious Catholic priests had been used to get confessions; there had been faked hangings and physical torture, according to the American report.

British and French were more fearful of American impetuousness than of an immediate Russian attack.

American surveys in 1951 indicated that 65 per cent of the Germans were in favor of an association with the West, while only 16 per cent wished for neutralism.[7] Other reports were less optimistic. One German paper said that of the university students polled, 88 had repeated the slogan "Without Me," 27 had been in favor of joining the armed forces, and 18 had no opinion.[8] McCloy reported that polls taken at the universities of Munich and Erlangen had shown that none of the students wanted to be soldiers, but seven out of ten thought it inevitable that they would be.

On April 3 the Allied High Commissioners raised the German steel quota to 14,000,000 tons of production, with a permitted capacity of 15,500,000 tons. Limitations on the size and speed of merchant ships were canceled, the manufacture of synthetic oil and rubber was authorized, as was the production of ball bearings, but the controls over electronic valves remained in force.

A new list of nonmilitary items charged to the German account by the Allies appeared in the German press. Publication of one paper, *Der Stern*, was suspended by the Allies in January 1951 because of its article headed "Hoopla, We Live on Occupation Costs," describing the sybaritic life of the Americans. Again long lists appeared: 564,000 D marks for false teeth, 41,000,000 for furniture, 5,000,000 for excelsior for fragile wares being shipped abroad. One paper listed a Turkish carpet at 16,200 D marks, a desk for a general at 80,000 D marks, a silver tea service at 15,323 D marks, 150,000 meters of material for sleeping garments, 264,000 meters of cloth for shirts, 64,000 diapers, 30,000 girdles, 14,000 D marks for rubber pants, 4,000 D marks for bibs. An American soldier, the Germans calculated, cost them 9,650 marks a year; each man of the new West German border-police formations, by contrast, cost 2,034.

[7] *The New York Times*, April 15, 1951.
[8] Ibid., July 31, 1951.

The Americans again made careful replies. They repeated that the United States was spending more on the occupation than Germany, and that many of the personnel they were employing would have a hard time finding work in the German economy. A large proportion were German refugees from the Eastern territories and from the East zone, and expellees were the last hired when German factories took on help. In Bonn and Bad Godesberg the Americans were paying for the construction of apartments for 1,000 Germans and 500 Americans, which would become the property of the West German state; meanwhile the Bundesrepublik was paid rent for them. But the German criticisms again had an effect; it was decided that HICOG employees who wanted German servants could pay for them themselves. When military authorities wished to requisition houses, they would first take the matter up with the resident officer; he would approach the local German authorities, and if they approved, the Army would go ahead; if they did not, the differences would have to be resolved by finding other accommodations or by mutually acceptable compromise. No American families were to displace Germans unless other quarters could be found for the German family. The American high command was sensitive to German criticism. When the commandant at Berchtesgaden wanted to cut down trees to make space for a bowling alley, the burgomaster protested to General Handy, who ordered the project stopped.

By the end of 1951 the Germans wanted an end to occupation costs, and the term replaced by "defense contribution." Allied officials emphasized the equality of the Germans' status in the discussions about the new army, in the negotiations for the contractual relationship, in everything but the discomfiting vestiges of the period of occupation, which were now, however, to be seen in small matters only. Whatever they were called, occupation costs had to be met, and with Germany's rising prosperity and the additional troops the Americans were sending, they could actually be increased. The Allies asked for a contribution of 10,000,000,000 marks; the Germans thought they could afford 8,000,000,000, which was more than they had been paying with the Allied luxuries included.

Relations with Russia remained critical. There was much talk of peace on the Soviet side; the Russians said they would gather 500,000,000 signatures from all the people of the world for a peace petition. But the war went on in Korea, and when the deputy foreign ministers met in Paris in the spring of 1951 the Russian delegate, Andrei Gromyko, referred to Winston Churchill as a "criminal" and to a British representative, Ernest Davies, as a cannibal.[9] The Russian propaganda offensive, designed to stifle or slow the coalitions building up against their further advances in Asia and Europe, now emphasized the world's need for peace and the threat of West German rearmament. In East Germany the head of the CDU, Otto Nuschke, like the SED leaders, made a speech accepting the Oder-Neisse boundary and the permanent loss of the German eastern provinces to Poland and Russia.[1] It was the boundary, he said, the Allies had helped to establish in 1945 by agreeing to the deportations of millions of Germans from the territories beyond that line. Mass demonstrations were planned for West as well as East Germany, with people of all political colors marching against the war plans; in West as in East Germany the Communists made a special effort to win the Right-wing groups of former Nazis and Army officers, in the West zones for neutralism, in the East zone for rearming.

In the summer of 1951 a huge youth rally was staged in East Berlin. One hundred and four countries, the Communist press said, were represented, including the United States—a festival of militant youth which the East-zone papers reported would be attended by two million people. A million and a half came, Western observers estimated—Scots in kilts, Spaniards, Frenchmen, Italians, West Germans, Chinese, and North Koreans—

[9] Ibid., April 26, 1951.
[1] *Tägliche Rundschau*, Aug. 12, 1951.

and they marched in impressive parades shouting "Friendship" and clapping their hands over their heads as had the German young men and women in the previous summer.

The rally was held to oppose the "imperialist aggression" of the United States and its allies; and speakers recounted the iniquities of the Western powers; a Korean woman orator who had journeyed to Berlin called the American troops "dogs." [2] It was part of the global peace offensive the Soviet was waging against the rearming of the West, but it also seemed an impressive display of zealous devotion of young people to the Communist cause. And yet, despite this evidence of the success of the indoctrination and the slogan of "Germans at one table," urging Germans of the East and West to unite and make their own future, 1,000 East German marchers sought asylum in West Berlin. Some 700,000 of the paraders visited the Western sectors, and many of them professed far less admiration for communism than would have been imagined from seeing them march rank on rank shouting *"Freundschaft."* Nevertheless, this rally, like the one of the year before, was a sobering spectacle seen in the light of the Chinese Communist successes against the UN forces in Korea. The visitors to the West sectors were given meals through contributions of the West Berliners, the British, and the Americans; and so many visited that finally the Communist leaders organized demonstrations at the sector border so the West Berlin police would be forced to break them up and thus give a pretext for stopping the border crossings. [3]

Neither the speechmaking nor the marching was new for Berlin. But the dynamism of Communist power seemed evident enough; communism appeared to have made disciplined converts of a large proportion of these young people, and in China it had transformed an army that had been dispersed by Japanese units a fraction of its size into a superior fighting force. And Berlin was continually, month by month, reminded of its vul-

[2] *The New York Times,* Aug. 10, 1951.
[3] McCloy: *Eighth Quarterly Report,* pp. 46–50.

nerability. The Russians demanded that a new tax be paid on motor vehicles traveling on the Autobahn to and from the city, and the lines of trucks waiting at the check points once again extended from four to eight kilometers. A busload of American sightseers was fired on while making an authorized tour of East Berlin. The electric current coming to the West from the East sectors was shut off, and West Berlin retaliated by stopping shipments to the East.

On April 18, 1951, the treaty for the Schuman plan was signed in Paris. It provided for the merging of the French and German coal and steel industries—a step designed, as Schuman had written to Adenauer, to make war between France and Germany not only unthinkable but impossible. Four additional powers were part of this union: Italy and the Benelux countries. The plan looked to the eventual removal of tariffs and quotas in a single market area. A High Authority made decisions that were binding on the participants, and with the founding of the union the international authority of the Ruhr was dissolved and all restrictions on its steel production were lifted. Agreement on the size and character of the German army also seemed to have been reached. Everyone was agreed that there must not be a separate German army but that from ten to twelve divisions would be welcomed into the European Defense Force by the NATO powers. Schuman's effort to have the Germans' service limited to labor battalions had no success against the American insistence on troops capable of front-line duty. In Bonn the Chancellor said that Germany had restored the balance between East and West.

England and France in July ended the formal state of war with Germany, and President Truman asked Congress to pass similar legislation. On October 19 he signed such a bill. By the close of 1951 employment in West Germany was up to 14,582,-000; and while unemployment was still high—1,650,000—it compared with 1,690,000 for the year before, when employment had been 14,163,000.

Many articles in the German newspapers told of friendly relations between the Germans and the Americans. One woman gave a party for GI's because in 1945, she said, an American soldier had knocked on her door and presented her and her three children with candy and food for that grim Christmas season. There were pictures in the papers of American and German officials dining together; Germans, it was announced, could live in the American housing developments.

Despite all the pleasantries of the new relationship, the idea of rearmament still failed to appeal to a majority of Germans. The CDU continued to lose ground in the 1951 elections; the SPD continued to campaign against a German army; and in Lower Saxony the Socialist Reich party was the first of the neo-Nazi parties to win an important following. Neutralist and anti-American, in the May elections it won 367,000 votes and elected 16 candidates in the 158-man state legislature. In Hanover it got 6 per cent of the vote, and in Bremen it ran fifth, with over 25,000 votes to the CDU's 31,000 and the SPD's 130,000. The success of the party in Lower Saxony was attributed by some observers to the large concentrations of refugees in the area and the high rate of unemployment, but further analysis showed that its main support came where the Nazis had once been strongest. Similar parties had appeared in widely separated areas as early as 1948, but none had succeeded in winning 5 per cent of the votes cast. They had appeared only on regional lists; their leaders had fought savagely with one another; and they had disappeared after a short time for lack of support. The Socialist Reich party was more ominous, and the federal government took steps to bar both it and the Communist party by bringing charges of antidemocratic activity against them before the Constitutional Court. The government charged that the Socialist Reich party was a successor to the National Socialists, and that it and the Communists sought to impair the liberal democratic system of the Republic. In actions taken by German states, two of the Socialist Reich leaders were sentenced to jail for three months for defamatory statements. One was Major General Remer, who had helped put down the July 20, 1944, revolt. The court found him guilty of slander, but it also found that he could not be charged with dereliction of duty for having acted against the plotters in 1944.

These were the outward and visible signs of the new Germany. There were no werewolves. There was a large antimilitarist sentiment along with a quasi-Nazi movement of some strength, and there was a determination to deal firmly with it and its totalitarian relatives of the Left. That a party of the character of the Socialist Reich group had succeeded in getting even their relatively small proportion of the vote was disquieting.

How strong was the new movement? Charges of covert or open pro-Nazism had been made for years. American papers as responsible as *The New York Times* had reported evidence of it in headlines and articles, with which the denials could never quite catch up. The few anti-Semitic incidents, the slow pace of restitution, the intense German reaction to the DP's (a small but conspicuous part of whom had been Jews) were indications that the German population still had traces of the disease along with the antibodies. Of the prewar Jewish population only 22,-000 remained in 1951, and these included some 7,000 Jews from outside Germany. Not many of the prewar Jewish emigrants had returned, although they were urged to come back by German officials. For the most part neither the Jews nor the non-Jews who had emigrated returned; they stayed away because they either felt they would be uncomfortable in the land of their birth or had taken roots in their new environments. There were exceptions among the labor leaders and politicians especially; the mayor of Hamburg, Max Brauer, who had become an American citizen, returned to Germany almost immediately, as did Ernst Reuter to Berlin and former Chancellor Bruening. There were also Jews among those returning, but very few.

Investigations into the German attitudes toward Nazism and the Jews continued to be conducted by statisticians and inquirers of all kinds, German and Allied, and a picture began to emerge. It emerged slowly because many investigators, overly eager to find Nazism and anti-Semitism, contributed distorted reports. Like crime, any slight evidences of anti-Semitism made news, and where it did not exist it could be invented. Thus, the early American polls on the subject were widely criticized for the complexity of the questions, the small samples, and the exaggerated interpretation of the replies. One in 1947 showed 60 per cent of the Germans "deeply imbued with racial feeling." [4] A more widely based sampling of German sentiments on the Jews was made by the Americans in 1951. It disclosed that a majority of the Germans—more than two thirds—favored restitution for the Jews; but there was a tendency to put them last on the list, after the victims of the war, the widows and orphans of German soldiers, the survivors of the July 20 plot. Even a majority of former Nazi party members, however, supported compensation for the Jews.[5]

There were a Brotherhood Week, a society of Christian-Jewish reconciliation, and a searching of souls. Delegates of the Christian faiths had met immediately after the war and asserted the responsibility of the Christian church and its membership for the events of the Nazi years. This was the well-known Stuttgart Confession, which stated: "We proclaim that by our inaction and silence we are guilty before the God of Mercy for the crimes committed against the Jews by men of our nation." The Catholic Church had its day of Social Conscience and of Love; there were no attempts on the part of the religious groups to whitewash the past. Jews, it was asserted, were sorely missed in the intellectual life of the country; as audiences as well as creators they had played a large part in the German theater and literaature, both of which continued at a low ebb after the war. The theater subsisted largely on revivals and translations; German

[4] March 3, 1947, in *German Opinions on Jewish Restitution and Some Related Issues.*

[5] Dec. 5, 1951, ibid.

writing, it was generally acknowledged, was mediocre; the energies of the country were going into rebuilding the outer, not the inner, world.

When the facts about the concentration and extermination camps became known, it was impossible for anyone to defend what had been done.[6] Jews could and did testify to many acts of courage and kindness on the part of individual Germans during the Nazi years, and to the revulsion shown by some communities to the Nazi brutalities when they saw the SS transporting Jews or watched the forced-labor battalions go off. There was also the awareness that either by participation or by default the German people had permitted these things; but Jews who went to Germany often reported on the friendly attitude of the population.

A majority of Germans interviewed by the Americans in the autumn of 1951 disclaimed any general guilt for the atrocities in the Third Reich or obligation to right the wrongs. Sixty-three per cent of those polled said they felt neither guilt nor obligation, and only 25 per cent said they should accept both. Ninety-six per cent thought that the widows and orphans of German soldiers should get help, with only 1 per cent opposed; 93 per cent favored help for those who had been bombed out, with only 3 per cent opposed; 90 per cent thought refugees should be helped, with 6 per cent opposed. Seventy-three per cent wanted restitution for the relatives of the men killed as a result of the 20th of July revolt, and 13 per cent were opposed. Sixty-eight per cent favored restitution for the Jews, and this was opposed by 21 per cent. The reasons given by those who believed in low priority for the Jews were various and often stock. "They

---

[6] Evidence that the Germans in general had not known of the extermination camps comes from many sources, including anti-Nazis and Jews. For example, Jews who were sent to Theresienstadt from Berlin reported even late in the war that they had heard rumors of extermination camps but did not believe them. The general population had known, of course, about the concentration camps; Germans of all faiths had been their chief occupants up to 1940. But the extent of their brutalities could only be guessed at.

have made fortunes; they are businessmen; they can solve these problems more easily than others; they get international support; they have been helped by the Allies, by the Germans, by the United States, or by others." Some one per cent said words to this effect: "I am an old Nazi and against the Jews" or "Other groups are worse off." Those who placed the Jews last to get help said much the same things as those who opposed their getting any payments: "They have enough; they get help; they have exploited us; they are foreigners." To the statement "What happened during the Third Reich was partly the fault of the Jews or not their fault," 53 per cent said it was not the fault of the Jews, 21 per cent said the Jews were responsible, 26 per cent had no opinion. Twenty-seven per cent wanted the few Jews remaining in Germany to emigrate, but of those, 50 per cent thought they should be compensated for their losses. Of the Germans who wanted the Jews to stay in Germany 83 per cent favored restitution. Thirty-eight per cent of those polled favored a law against anti-Semitism, and 33 per cent opposed one. Of those opposed, the objections were that "It goes too far to punish someone for not liking someone." Those favoring such a law said: "Jews are human just like everybody else. It's the best way to counteract prejudice. The Third Reich should not be repeated." Even among those who reported that they saw more good than evil in the Nazis, 52 per cent wanted to pay the Jews damages.[7]

In the beginning of 1947 there had been 166,000 Jews in Germany, most of them DP's. By 1951 there were 22,000, of whom 15,000 were of German origin. The 15,000 were survivors who had somehow lived through the Hitler period, who had been hidden or married to Gentiles, partners of the so-called privileged marriages; and their average age was fifty-five. By 1953 there were only 2,000 Jewish businessmen in Germany, some 300 lawyers, a few physicians, 20 to 30 publishers, 140 Jewish judges, and officials in the federal and state governments.

[7] Dec. 5, 1951, in *German Opinions on Jewish Restitution.*

There were three Jewish deputies, all belonging to the SPD, and a Jewish weekly, the *Allgemeine Wochenzeitung*.

Germany had lost its great Jewish community: the writers, scientists, musicians, poets, clerks, lawyers, businessmen, and housewives—above all, the children, without whom the community would never return. There were weary echoes of the old struggle: in 1955 there was still a street in Cologne that had only one-story houses on it because the Germans in possession of them were unwilling to rebuild higher and make the buildings profitable. If they did, they said, a New York Jewish organization would be ready to claim the property when the opportunity presented itself. The German owners were waiting for sovereignty to be restored to the Republic, when such cases would be tried in German courts.[8] The Allied courts held that any Jew who had sold his property during the Hitler period had been under duress and should be awarded full damages, a practice that has since continued. Germans claimed that in many instances they had paid the government the full value of the property purchased from Jews; and that was likely to be true, since the Nazi state had set the selling prices. The Jewish owner, however, seldom if ever received from the Nazis the full sum paid. The state kept all or most of it, and as far as the former owner was concerned the house was confiscated.

Restitution actually was voted by Parliament in 1952 after negotiations with the State of Israel and organizations representing Jewish interests. By the time the autumn elections of 1953 were held, the Socialist Reich party was finished as a national party; it polled only 220,000 votes—less than the 5 per cent needed to keep it on the ballot. Nazism, whether new or old, was a corpse. A residue of anti-Semitism remained, but in the German awareness of the past, in the general will to compensate to this degree for the evil, there was a trace of the ashes of the four million who were killed.

[8] The cases were reviewed, however, by an international tribunal sitting in Nuremberg. It included two American and two German judges.

The American effort to reform German education had an effect on the constitutions of the German states. Every state now provided for the education of the children within its borders without regard to the race, creed, or class of their parents. Some provided free tuition, all of them granted scholarships. In the universities American aid provided funds for dormitories and student centers; hitherto the German student outside the fraternity system had had a lonely life. Student aid was felt to be inadequate by American standards, but in the Free University in Berlin the federal government contributed 8,000,000 marks for scholarships in 1950; and scholarships were also available in other universities.

The ratio of teachers to pupils in 1951 remained abnormally low; there were often sixty pupils in a class, and two million children went to school half time. One half of the funds the United States gave for special projects was spent on education. The special projects included aid to returned prisoners of war and war wounded, homes for the aged, kindergartens, youth and community centers, X-ray machines, an iron lung, and the establishment of a silicosis hospital in north Germany, where half the miners who had worked for ten years had the disease.

In 1951, when the Germans had been free for two years to establish their own book-publishing houses and newspapers, those which had been licensed by the Allies nevertheless continued to dominate the field. This was true even though most of the printing plants taken over in the early days of the occupation had been returned to their owners, who would often have preferred to see a new enterprise started in the place of the one that had been licensed. As controls were lifted, new papers were started, but with remarkably little success. The *Wiesbaden Tageblatt*, for example, a Socialist paper, gave away as many as 90,000 copies of an issue, but could not persuade the hoped-for 20,000 of the public to buy it. The new publications that succeeded were largely based on American models such as *Time* and *Newsweek* and the picture magazines. The celebrated pre-

Hitler German papers had had superior reviewing staffs and excellent criticisms of the theater, music, and the arts; and these were maintained in the new press. What was added was the general paper, representing no party, reporting with far more objectivity than had the newspapers of the past. In 1951 the Americans provided 15,000,000 D marks for German newspaper subsidies or for the overt press—that is, the direct organs of the occupation; these subventions were strongly objected to by Germans such as Pastor Niemöller, who felt they meant foreign control of German information. The total circulation of the German press in 1951 was 13,000,000, and the formerly licensed press had three times the readership of the new papers.

In the field of radio the Americans had been stern advocates of decentralization; one report said that only at the time of the Berlin blockade was the principle relaxed. German radio-users paid a fee of two marks a month for listening to broadcasts and so were deprived of the commercials to which their American preceptors were accustomed. The programs up to 1951 gave a half-hour a day to the Voice of America; after that the time was cut to fifteen minutes.

The direct effect of the Americans upon the cultural life of Germany was not great. The America Houses, which started early in the occupation, supplied the Germans with American books, periodicals, and lectures. They were widely used both by people who wanted to get warm and by those who wanted to learn what had happened in the outside world while they had been cut off from it under the Nazis and in the first years of the occupation. The America Houses showed moving pictures, provided concerts, lectures, classes in English, and exhibitions of work and enterprise in the United States. In Berlin the America House was especially important to the men and women who came over from the East zone to read publications they could not otherwise see. For their own security they were not required to register; and small, easily folded copies of newspapers were given them to carry back to East Berlin. The America Houses also arranged for the translation of American books, which it was hoped might clarify German views of the United States and of world events. A student-exchange program was started in 1948 and run by the Houses to enable German students to travel to the United States for a year of study. German leaders and experts in various fields were also sent to the United States: public-health officials, physicians, nurses, research workers, labor leaders.

American assistance to religious bodies came largely in the form of direct aid from private sources. The widely prophesied religious revival did not take place in Germany after the war. It had been predicted in the belief that after the repressions of the Nazi era, the blight of hatred and suffering and the dissolution of so many values for which the solidarity of the Nazi organizations had in part compensated, the church, purified and aware of its supranational mission, would be a haven. This was not the case. In 1945 only 47,000 Catholics took up membership in the Church again, a tenth of those who left it during the Nazi years. Before the war Germany had been one-third Catholic and two-thirds Protestant; after the war, with the loss of the dominantly Protestant east and north, the country was about evenly divided.[9] But communities that were formerly entirely Catholic now had large Protestant populations as expellees, who were mostly Protestant, moved into such areas as Bavaria.

In the Soviet zone, which had 14,500,000 Protestants and 2,000,000 Catholics in 1952, the churches were under the same attack as churches elsewhere in the Communist-dominated countries. The East-zone government sought to bring up the new generation of young people and to prevent their elders from interfering by way of religious training with their indoctrination.

It is nevertheless in the East that the churches have shown remarkable strength. In Leipzig in 1954, 650,000 people came to the final ceremonies of a convocation. A meeting in Berlin

[9] *Deutschland Heute*, pp. 363–77.

brought 100,000 from the East zone. The Federal Republic with its freedom of worship has had far less dramatic convocations, and the influence of the churches, both Protestant and Catholic, while still considerable, is less than in the pre-Hitler days. In Schleswig-Holstein, for example, 22 per cent of the members of the legislature reported that they had no religious affiliation, a very large figure in Germany, where even in the Hitler period only 6 per cent of the country had reported not belonging to a church.

Both Protestants and Catholics organized vocational groups and meetings to consider social and economic problems. The Protestant Evangelical academies and the Catholic Castle Rothfels were centers for discussion of the difficulties and problems of contemporary German life. The churches' position, like so much else in Germany, has been uncertain. Although there were Nazis among them, the record of both the Catholic priests and the Protestant ministers in resisting Hitler was far better than that of the professors in the universities or other leaders of secular organizations, with the possible exception of the members of the Communist party. The concentration camps had their pastors and priests who spoke out against the Hitler state and the persecution of the Jews; and later when the victorious Allies came, many did not hesitate to speak against the excesses of the occupation.

Along with grants to the institutions of public information, the Americans sent resident officers into the field whose duty it was to help plant and tend a grass-roots democracy. The resident officers arranged community meetings and the showing of educational and cultural films; they set up parents' advisory committees, discussion groups, women's groups, civic activities. One of them saved the life of a child suffering from coeliac disease, for which bananas were a cure, by collecting money from Americans to buy bananas at the PX. Another resident officer conducted a meeting in Swabia, which was attended by 210 people; he reported that after he had led a two-hour discussion three hands were raised in favor of his proposal to found a citizens' committee. His principal mission, however, although he did not say so, had clearly succeeded: the Germans were making up their own minds.

XIII

THE CONTRACTS

In May 1952 West Germany moved close to complete sovereignty, in the view of government spokesmen and the Allies. The High Commission was abolished, the commissioners became ambassadors, the German consuls in the United States, Britain, and France became chargés d'affaires, and the occupation was officially declared ended. The Western troops became defense forces, and the occupation statute was replaced by a contractual agreement. In principle German sovereignty was established; the Allies retained only such special rights as the protracted crisis demanded: to station troops, to decide when an emergency existed and how to deal with it, to act on behalf of the federal government in negotiations with Soviet Russia, and to continue to govern Berlin. They agreed to pursue their efforts to unify Germany and to defend it as a "forward, exposed, strategic area." [1] The Germans were free to conduct their domestic political and economic affairs without Allied interference; they could repeal or amend Allied statutes; no German could be tried in Allied military courts. On its part the West German government assumed the prewar external debts of the Hitler government, which were somewhat scaled down by the willingness of the United States to forgo the repayment of part of the postwar loans it had made. The federal government also agreed to take no action prejudicial to the rights of the Allies, to conduct its policies in accordance with the principles of the United Nations and the Council of Europe, and to participate in the European defense force.

[1] *The New York Times*, May 27, 1952.

The contractual status was in fact only quasi sovereignty, since the Allies alone would decide how and when their emergency powers had to be used. The SPD and the Free Democratic party objected to the rights reserved by the Allies, saying that the decisive controls were still in the hands of the Western powers. West Germany could join the deliberations, but the ultimate decisions lay elsewhere. The government conceded that the agreements granted less than it had wanted, but said they were nevertheless a step forward and the best that could be had at this time. On May 27, the day after the contractual agreements were signed in Bonn, the foreign ministers and Chancellor Adenauer met in Paris to sign the European Defense Community (EDC) agreements. Later ratified by the parliaments of West Germany, Belgium, Luxembourg, and the Netherlands, these nevertheless never came into force, because after long delays the French National Assembly rejected them. The objections of the French took many forms. While accepting the need for German soldiers, they refused to sign the EDC agreements until they had obtained Anglo-American promises to keep troops on the Continent and to see to it that no German contingents would leave the European defense force and go off to form a national army. When these demands were met, new objections were raised.

Five years were to go by before there would be Germans in uniform. The idea of a European defense force was French; it originated with the Pleven government, which fell, however, soon after the plan was proposed. The governments that followed always found obstacles to making the idea an actuality. Instead, in the early part of 1952 it was announced that the French High Commissioner to the Saar would henceforth be an ambassador and the French delegations to foreign capitals would include a representative of the Saar. This seemed a heavy blow to the Germans. They said that a shadow had fallen over Europe, that Germany had deserved better of France than to suffer this unilateral decision with its implications of the final loss of the

Saar at the very time when, by signing the treaty for the Schuman plan and agreeing to the use of German troops in a European army, the Bonn government had demonstrated its good faith and readiness to make sacrifices for European solidarity. The German protests were not confined to one party; the opposition groups were as outspoken as was the government; and with the Americans and British this time far less impressed by the French arguments than in the past, and with the Russians in stony opposition, the French had to move cautiously. In the course of the year there were conversations between Adenauer and the French foreign minister, Robert Schuman; the Bundestag voted to instruct the federal government to bear in mind that the Saar was German and under no circumstances was the German title to it to be ceded, and it was evident that some sort of compromise was inevitable.

The Russians presented two faces in their foreign policy. One spoke of coexistence, the unification and neutralization of Germany, the need for the two systems of the East and the West getting along with each other;[2] this was part of the peace offensive. Over 50,000,000 signatures were collected for a peace petition, on behalf of which meetings were held by workers' groups, women's organizations, and churches throughout the Communist and non-Communist world. The other approach was made under the banners of "Hate America";[3] it was the call to action against the United States. This, too, was a peace offensive, but the enemy was named, as were his methods: waging germ warfare in Korea, arming accomplices in Japan and Germany, and constructing bases that threatened the peace-loving peoples of the world. The enormous Communist postwar gains of territory were now at a stop, with NATO and the EDC in the West, the military balance in Korea, the American plans to rearm Japan and to form an anti-Communist coalition in the East. Now was the time for an attempt to break up the anti-

[2] Boris Meissner: *Russland, die Westmächte und Deutschland*, pp. 290–3.
[3] *The New York Times*, April 3, June 22, 1952.

Communist alliances, to recruit support in the West, to prepare for the opportunities of the period when the innate self-destructive tendencies of capitalism and its battle for markets would make possible the next wide-scale advance. The Russian offers were, as always, baited with glistening appeals for war-weary populations. Vyshinsky proposed late in 1951 an armistice in Korea, the troops to be withdrawn to both sides of the 38th parallel, after which the foreign contingents would be evacuated. A disarmament conference would outlaw the atom bomb and permit inspection of the facilities for manufacturing atomic weapons. In addition the Soviet government asked the Western powers to acknowledge that membership in NATO was incompatible with the purposes of the United Nations, and to accept Communist China as a party to the treaties that would be negotiated.

There were words of many timbres. The tone of the East German leaders became harsher. At the SED party congress in Berlin in July 1952 they bitterly denounced the Americans and the "traitorous" Adenauer government, and warned the West Germans that in joining the European Defense Community they could be held guilty of the crime of war.[4] They called for the overthrow of Adenauer and said they would welcome talks with the members of the bourgeois parties and the SPD who opposed his and the West's enslavement policies.[5] A delegation of five members of the East-zone parliament was sent to Bonn to urge unification on the basis of the Russian proposal made earlier in the year for a treaty of peace with all Germany. The Russian blueprint was alluring, but it would be difficult to build to its specifications. In Germany, as in Korea, the occupying troops were to withdraw from their zones within a year; German elections would be held, the country would enjoy full freedom of speech, religion, press, and politics, and former Nazis and officers would be rehabilitated if they were not under sentence.[6]

[4] *Tägliche Rundschau*, July 11, 19, 1952.
[5] Richard Lukas: *Zehn Jahre*, p. 96.
[6] Meissner: *Russland, die Westmächte und Deutschland*, pp. 290–2.

There were to be no limits to German industrial production, and German factories could produce arms for the new German army. This united Germany would join the UN, and no organizations unfriendly to democracy and peace would be permitted on its soil; it must be neutral and have no part in any alliance or coalition. It must also, the Russians said, be bounded by the Oder-Neisse on the east. Some observers, however, believed that, despite repeated statements by Soviet, Polish, and East German spokesmen that the boundary was inviolable, there lay in the future something quite different: the possibility of a new partition of Poland for the benefit of Russia and of a Germany that with such rewards could be detached from the West.

The Russian proposal could be nothing more than a propaganda offer. No free election in Germany would return a pro-Communist government, and the Allies in their answer to the Russians insisted on free elections as a condition of any German settlement. Refugees were still streaming from the East across the zonal borders; from mid-1951 to mid-1952 there were 218,-730; from July 1952 to July 1953 338,896.[7] The increasingly harsh measures of socialization and repression were driving down the standard of living, purging the SED—over 150,000 were expelled from the party in 1951—narrowing the small areas of freedom remaining. More than 300,000 people, it was reported, had been sent into exile from the East zone.[8]

But the Soviet proposals in themselves were not without appeal for large groups in Germany and Western Europe. The Germans were told that it was an essential attribute of sovereignty for every country to have its own armed forces and that the West's plan to incorporate the Germans in a European army was aimed at making the country a protectorate. The East German government officials spoke eloquently on the need for German soldiers in the People's Republic for defense against the Western powers, and promised that a similarly independent

[7] Lukas: *Zehn Jahre*, p. 99.
[8] Ibid., p. 92.

army would be recruited from all Germany once it was unified.[9]

For the benefit of sections of British and French opinion, the Russians accused the United States of arming West Germany as part of its plan of world domination. Stalin pointed out that in 1952, with the Soviet Union and its allies dominating such vast territories, it was now more than ever necessary for the capitalist powers to fight for markets; it was from this circumstance that World War III would come, he said, rather than from the rivalry of East and West.[1] At the same time Russian spokesmen attacked the encirclement: the alliances and the bases ringing Soviet territory, and the warmongers who planned to make use of them as soon as the time was ripe.[2] The time might seem nearer with General Eisenhower as President, who spoke of the roll-back of communism in place of containment. Moscow used every weapon; it vetoed the entrance of Italy into the United Nations because of Italy's acceptance of membership in NATO.

The Federal Republic bobbed along in the wake of these world-wide events, but Adenauer clung to the alliance with the West and made no attempt to come to terms with Russia, as many thought he would one day be bound to do. He spoke out steadily for the Western orientation of the new Germany; although he placed the need for unity first on the list of goals of West German policy, it was not to be brought about through the neutralization of the country. For Adenauer, both German unification and the peace of Europe could be secured only through a Western community; the new state of affairs demanded new politics centering in an increasing co-operation of the West European nations. These views accorded with American policy and were also held by most of the German population, only 6 per cent of whom, polls indicated, opposed the unification of Europe. Adenauer, whatever his motives—and some

[9] *Tägliche Rundschau,* April 19, 1952; May 3, 1952.
[1] *The New York Times,* Oct. 3, 1952.
[2] Ibid., Oct. 6, 1952.

critics thought him lukewarm about the Eastern provinces because they were largely Protestant—was painstakingly building up German moral credit, a credit that had been as bankrupt as any in history. He was patient and stubborn on big issues, flexible and ready to compromise on small ones. When even members of his own party declared themselves disappointed with the Bonn treaties, he replied that they were the best that could be had under the circumstances; when the French reached for the Saar he denounced them, but this did not prevent him from pursuing imperturbably his basic policy of Franco-German collaboration and of the unification of Western Europe. He refused to accept the accomplished fact of a separate Saar, but was ready to negotiate on the issues. When the Saar plebiscite was held in 1952 and the French, under the party-licensing law that prevented any pro-German party from participating, seemed to have won a victory, Adenauer declared the election to have been neither free nor democratic and said that Germany would not consider herself bound by the results. It was this combination in Adenauer of resoluteness with a willingness to discuss and to make concessions, as well as the insecurity of the French position, lacking now both American and British support, that led to a meeting of Adenauer and Schuman soon after the plebiscite to talk about changes in the status of the Saar. The French could not force a policy on their allies; they were in need of help in too many sectors—in Europe, Indochina, North Africa, and France itself.

Adenauer had first declared he would not sign the defense treaties of the EDC until there was an agreement on the Saar.[3] The forces inside and outside Germany opposing German rearmament were so powerful that the Americans promptly lent their aid to the chief spokesmen of those who were urging the German legislature and people to take action. They too urged a meeting between Adenauer and Schuman, but expressed the hope that neither the Saar question nor French fears need

[3] Ibid., Feb. 5, 1952.

delay German rearmament. The British, while they would not pool their army with that of the European Defense Community, had agreed in advance to sign mutual-security pacts with the signatory powers in order to obtain French approval of having German forces in a European army.

When the Bonn conventions were signed, the East reacted immediately. In Berlin, telephone communications with the West were cut; trucks and cars were held up at the zone border;[4] a prominent member of the investigating committee of free German jurists, which exposed Communist political persecutions in East Germany, was kidnapped from West Berlin and disappeared into the East, where the Russians for a long time denied any knowledge of his whereabouts.[5] The East German government announced the establishment of a prohibited area some three miles wide along the zonal border; there would be no access to it without a pass, and the people living there would be resettled elsewhere. Within a control strip ten meters wide, trees were cut down and the land was cleared so the border could be watched day and night. Anyone crossing this area could be shot on sight by the border police. The East-zone police invaded small enclaves of the West Berlin sectors that lay within East Berlin and ordered the inhabitants to leave.[6]

Personal relations between the West Germans and the Americans continued to be fostered in a systematic fashion. The Army attacked the problem on a broad front. Germans still pointed out defects in the defense role of the American soldiers: 250 swimming pools used by the troops and their families were off bounds to Germans, and many of the pools were not much used, they said; American cars were driven too fast for the narrow German roads, a complaint that would seem more dubious in later years when the German accident rate was among the highest in the world. But American soldiers helped

4 Ibid., May 31, 1952.
5 Ibid., June 1, 1952.
6 Ibid., Aug. 7, 1952.

rebuild youth centers, parachuted candies from helicopters, built swimming pools and playgrounds the Germans could use, painted cribs and buildings, and went about the task of recon- struction with even more enthusiasm than they had brought to the bombings. The Army held open house, and 60,000 Allied soldiers spent the Christmas of 1952 in German homes. An Operation *Kinderlift* flew children, some of them from Berlin, to visit American families; thousands of dollars were collected for orphanages; one American field hospital took over the re- sponsibility for the care of 50 children; at Wiesbaden some $30,000 was collected for an orphanage from the profits of a roulette game organized for the purpose. "The world's largest Christmas party" was held for more than 14,000 German or- phans at the air depot outside Munich; 72,000 Christmas pres- ents were given away, including 3,500 pounds of chocolate; children were provided with food and clothing. Among adults, too, there was camaraderie: General Handy thanked Chancellor Adenauer for the interview he had given *Stars and Stripes* on the friendship between American soldiers and the German popula- tion.[7] Adenauer had praised the frank, upright, and humane conduct of the GI in the face of many problems. American sol- diers sang for 300 German war wounded at Berchtesgaden; Germans were invited to visit American airfields and military installations that had been out of bounds to them for many years. McCloy told the Germans that since the Americans were defense troops whose mission in Germany was the same as in the United States, the Germans should behave toward them in the same way the Americans were accustomed to act in their own country.

Americans joined in the criticisms of exorbitant defense ex- penditures. An article in *The New York Times* showed some of the comparative costs of American life and recreation in Ger- many and in the United States. An Army captain and his wife living in an eight-room villa in Stuttgart that would have cost

[7] *Neue Zeitung,* June 9, 1952.

some $30,000 in the United States were given the house rent free; in addition they could sell extra cigarettes, coffee, and PX commodities to pay all their expenses, leaving the captain's salary for other things.[8] An American correspondent reported that a medical officer who needed a piece of equipment costing $600 in the United States was told to get it in Germany, where it would cost 6,000 D marks but would be charged to occupation costs.

The State Department clearly wished to end the luxuries of Allied troops, which were estimated to be costing the German taxpayer $45,000,000 a year—a low figure, as later calculations were to show. HICOG was reported by the New York *Herald Tribune* in April as saying that this free ride for the Army must stop.

American senators and congressmen joined in the protests; one said that if the Army did not end its extravagances, Congress would. Some American Army wives were reported by the *Christian Science Monitor* as saying that having a servant for the first time in their lives freed their energies for the good works they were doing among the Germans.

But the criticisms again had their effect. Henceforth, it was announced early in 1952, Army as well as HICOG personnel would have to pay their own servants, saving the German taxpayer nearly $50,000,000 a year. Eleven million D marks, it was decided in October 1952, would be paid the owners of requisitioned property for damage done their crops or property, and the Amerian Army of the Rhine announced cuts in its budget; HICOG, too, planned to reduce its German personnel by 20 per cent. Three hundred ninety-two houses and 178 apartments were "derequisitioned" in the American zone, 736 houses and 2,582 apartments in the French zone, and 7,745 houses and 136 apartments in the British zone. The Americans announced that a 100-ton motor yacht they had kept since 1945 for outings on the Rhine was being returned to the city of Cologne. A little

[8] *The New York Times*, April 18, 1952.

later they added that the special trains and compartments reserved for the use of the Allies at a cost of $13,000,000 a year were returned to the Germans, with the exception of the military trains running through the East zone to Berlin.[9]

The Security Commission was still under fire. Under the heading parodying *"Die Wacht am Rhein," "Fest Steht und Treu das Sicherheitsamt am Rhein,"* the *Südeutsche Zeitung*[1] said the bureau had had 300 soldiers and experts at its disposal and now had 150; it called the office "the reverse Pentagon on the Rhine" and wondered if some positive function might not be found for it.

There were protests in the Bundestag and newspapers concerning other matters too. It was asserted that Germans had been trained by American intelligence officers to serve as saboteurs in the event of a Russian invasion. Their assignments were rumored to have included the liquidation of German liberals such as Mayor Brauer of Hamburg, and Ollenhauer, the head of the SPD, in the event of war. The crisis cooled quickly when officials announced that the program, of whatever proportions, had been dropped, and Adenauer said there would be no similar one.[2]

1952 was the year when the first unforeseen results of the occupation appeared in the schools in the small persons of 3,000 *Mischlinge*[3]—half-Negro, half-white children born of colored American fathers and German mothers. These were some of the 94,000 "occupation children" being reared by German mothers after the departure of their soldier fathers, or, in a few cases, being adopted by American or German families. The German experts methodically canvassed the situation. An explanatory bulletin told the teachers they must exercise great tact: these colored children had been brought up in neighborhoods where they were known and accepted; now they would come for the

[9] *Neue Zeitung*, Oct. 2, 1952.
[1] April 19, 1952.
[2] *The New York Times*, Oct. 9, 10, 14, 24, 1952.
[3] *Neue Zeitung*, March 13, 1952.

first time into schools where some of the children had never seen a colored child before. The pamphlet urged the teacher to make sure he or she was without prejudice.[4] The possibility of separate classes had been debated but abandoned. These were German children, the bulletin emphasized; there were special problems connected with them, but they were to be treated no differently from their white classmates. One colored American published an article reminding his readers that in the past a quarter of a million Negroes had lived in Europe, among them such celebrated men as Pushkin.

The German press as a whole was critical of the Negro soldier. A sampling of newspapers from June to November 1952 showed that of 284 articles in which Negroes were mentioned, only 3.2 per cent were favorable and 79.2 per cent were unfavorable. Although many Germans paid tribute to the generosity and good will of the colored soldiers in the early days of the occupation when the Germans were still outcasts, a large proportion of the crimes of violence committed by the American troops were attributed to Negroes in the German press.[5] Analysis of German newspaper reports on American soldiers in general in 1952 showed 26 per cent to be favorable, 43 per cent unfavorable, and 31 per cent neutral. By December 1953 this was to change to 60 per cent favorable and 22 per cent unfavorable, with 18 per cent neutral.[6] The crime rate of American soldiers, including acts of violence and robbery, seemed high to the Germans; but the Americans said it was approximately that of any large American city, and when curfews were imposed on the troops in areas with a high rate of incidents, the rate went down 25 per cent.

The life of the German refugees who were still in barracks remained bleak; they had no part in the spreading prosperity. American investigators reported that they were beaten, that they

---

[4] *Maxi, Unser Neger Büblein.*
[5] *Report* of the Public Information Division, U.S. Army, June–Nov. 1952.
[6] *Report* of the Public Relations Branch, U.S. Army, 1952–3.

showed little disposition to help themselves and were passively waiting for the federal government or the Allies to do something for them. Their state was described as one of "apathetic disgruntlement"; they feared getting a job and leaving the wretched security of the camps; they said, for example, that they were afraid they would not be able to get a house. They did not expect that they would be able to return to their old homes, and almost half of them reported that the local industries preferred to employ native Germans rather than refugees. Although two thirds of them said they would take any job offered to them, only 53 per cent thought it would be better to leave the camps than to stay in them.[7]

There were some 10,000,000 German refugees—those expelled from the Eastern and other territories and those who escaped from East Germany—and their numbers were increasing. Over 2,000,000 had come from the East zone up to 1954. Observers thought that those outside the camps were, for the most part, getting along pretty well. Eight out of ten of them said they were better off in the West than they would have been in the East. The refugees constituted some 20 per cent of the German population, but they were never widely distributed throughout the country, largely because of reluctance of the states to assume heavier burdens; and up to 1952, despite the many official plans for resettling them in districts where there was most need for their labor, only 320,000 were resettled. By 1954 the figure had increased to 653,000. American and German funds were spent generously to help the expellees start life in West Germany; in many areas small shops were set up with the aid of loans, as were industries such as the Gablonz glass manufactures that had once flourished in Czechoslovakia. By 1953, 6,000 businesses had been started and 55,000 artisan enterprises. The federal government reduced railroad fares for refugees; clothing was provided for 2,000,000 children; 29,000 farmers got land; and in 1952 the law for equalization of burdens

[7] *Hard Core Refugees Evaluate Their Situation.*

was passed, assessing up to 50 per cent of the value of property in West Germany for the benefit of refugees and native Germans whose homes had been bombed out.[8] There was, once the recovery started, a shortage of skilled labor in Germany, and a continuous demand for it in such areas as the North Rhine and Westphalia. But the refugees came with no possessions; everything had to be supplied them: public services, schools, roads, and housing. They absorbed more than 40 per cent of the amounts spent on social security. From the beginning they were recognized legally and officially as Germans, but they constituted 37.9 per cent of the unemployed in West Germany in 1949 and one third in 1952. In Schleswig-Holstein half the unemployed were refugees.

McCloy reported that 300,000 were still in camps in 1952 and two thirds of the remainder were in quarters worse than the camps. American proposals to aid them were for more investment, resettlement, and new housing. An expellee bank was established with ERP counterpart funds; there was a concentrated program to create employment and refugee enterprises. More housing developments for refugees were started with a priority over those for the native population, and in the course of the next years, with the virtual disappearance of unemployment, the problem largely found its solution. But the influx from the East zone continued; the number of arrivals increased in the second half of 1952—in part composed of those forced to move from the three-mile border zone between East and West Germany—and was to go higher as the East German state in 1953 progressed to the next phase of socialism: more farmers were to be forced into the collective farms, and publicly owned enterprises expanded at the expense of the 20 per cent of the economy still in private hands.

[8] *Deutschland Heute*, pp. 164–71.

XIV
THE UPRISING OF JUNE 17, 1953

With every change in Russian foreign policy, internal policies in East Germany veered sharply. 1945 had been the time of Communist collaboration with the bourgeois parties; the East zone was to be the center of antifascist, antimilitarist unity; the large landowners were to be dispossessed, but not the large farmers; private enterprise was to be encouraged. East Germany was to make its own way to socialism; and meanwhile the non-Communist parties of those who had opposed Hitler would join in the rebuilding of a peaceful German state. This was the program that even German Communists believed possible of fulfillment, but the reality was different. The bourgeois parties were under constant pressure to conform to the main lines of Communist purposes. Jakob Kaiser and Ernst Lemmer were forced to resign their CDU posts because they spoke in favor of the Marshall Plan. Their successors and the leaders of the LDP in the East zone dutifully backed the peace petitions and joined in the anti-Western oratory. In 1952, 79 per cent of the East-zone enterprises were run by the mixed Russian-German companies, directly by the People's Democratic Republic, or indirectly as people's co-operatives. By the end of the year the percentage was expected to rise to 81 per cent; the remainder under private ownership was to be liquidated. The true socialist state, with the dictatorship of the proletariat, farm collectives, and state enterprises, could now be foreseen. Stern measures were taken against what remained of the old order. A relentless class war was declared in July 1952 against private enterprise

326

on the land, in trade, or in industry, and against the "bourgeois ideologists" of the CDU and the LDP.

The production quotas in the first quarter of 1953 had not been met. Agriculture was down, the economy as a whole was producing only 96 per cent of 1936, although the five-year plan called for doubling the production of 1936 by 1955. People would have to work harder. There was a shortage of three million tons of potatoes and a half-million tons of grain. With the main economic effort concentrated on heavy industry, consumer prices rose in the government HO (*Handels Organisation*) stores and wages did not. On the contrary, the norms— the amount of production expected of each worker—were constantly increased as the People's Republic lurched toward the new phase of socialization. Farmers with more than twenty hectares of land were to be outlawed in effect, penalized by a series of unequal, forced deliveries of produce and payments based on acreage for the use of farm machinery. The large farmer had to deliver to the government more food per acre than the small one, and paid three to four times as much for the use of tractors and machinery for plowing and harvesting. The big farmer was required to deliver 504 liters (about 132 gallons) of milk per hectare (approximately two and a half acres), the medium 494, the small farmer 414. There were similar differentials for eggs: the big farmer had to deliver 143 per hectare, the medium 138, the small 110. Grains had still more of a differential, from 5.2 hundredweight for the small farmer to 18.7 for the large. The rates for potatoes were 104.7 hundredweight for the large farmer, 79.3 for the medium, and 38.4 for the small holders; for meat they were 130.6 kilograms for the large, 119.1 for the medium, 84.9 for the small farmer.[1] The state had taken over 47,800 farms, and as a result 440,000 hectares were lying idle. Not only were prices at the HO stores high in comparison with earnings, but often there was not much to be bought; weeks went by with no margarine or meat for sale. Fish and potatoes were the staples.

[1] Richard Lukas: *Zehn Jahre*, p. 179.

A quart of milk cost 2 marks, the equivalent of $.50; a pound of butter 10 marks or $2.50; a pound of steak 14 marks or $3.50.[2]

Non-Communist organizations were under heavy pressure. Leaders of the CDU and LDP were arrested; the churches and their youth organizations were violently attacked; boys and girls who belonged to them were denounced in the schools and universities.

"Voluntary" contributions were demanded of the workers. From time to time they were ordered to pass resolutions declaring their desire to overfill the quotas, which by May 1, 1953, had already been raised 35 per cent over those of the previous year. Machinery was often in poor shape and broke down, but there could be no excuses; poor machinery or not, production had to go up. The standard of living went down steadily, but the workers were promised rewards in the socialist state of the future; when they produced more they would earn more. Meanwhile, their meetings touched on political as well as economic matters. One resolution read: "I pledge myself to work with all my strength for the conclusion of a peace treaty and the withdrawal of all occupation troops." [3] The factories, the workers were told, were their own, not the dens of exploiters who fed on labor as in the West. The words, however, could not conceal the raw economic facts. East Germany, separated from the Ruhr and the factories of West Germany, had to build up its own heavy industry to contribute to the East bloc's economic and military requirements. The standard of living had to be kept low if the main effort was to be put into heavy industry; it was the same problem confronted by all the Communist countries, including Russia itself. A German worker said in early June: "You want us as cows for milk and meat both. There is no such animal."

There were occasional strikes—eleven of them from April to

[2] "Der Aufstand . . . ," Der Monat, Sept. 1953, pp. 595–624; Oct. 1953, pp. 45–6.
[3] Theodore Lit: "The Proletariat against the Dictatorship," Problems of Communism, II (1953).

June in 1953, sporadic and short-lived. With all the power on one side, they could always be broken; the mere threat of taking away an employment card, without which a man could not live, was usually enough to send him back to his bench. There were also incentives. If a man found a way to raise the production rate with an improvement, he was permitted to work at the old norms for four months. In 1948, in imitation of the Russians, a worker named Adolf Hennecke had been chosen to produce a record-making output of coal. He was drilled and trained for the day of his performance with the annointings and rigors of an Olympic athlete, and he topped the norms by some 380 per cent. Hennecke became a "hero of labor"; he was given a prize of 100,000 marks and feted like a champion. He also became the source of many bleak jokes: "Hennecke is dead," one went. "How did he die?" "He drowned in his own sweat."

A man in the East had to work two to three times as long as a worker in the West to attain the same standard of living. Shoes were three times as expensive in the East, butter more than three times, sugar about two and one-half times; only potatoes cost the same.[4] The wage differences were much greater than in the West. Highly skilled technicians earned as much as 4,000 marks a month; a few specialists might be paid as much as 15,000 marks (and there were low rates in the government stores for the privileged). On the other hand, a hod-carrier got 1.40 marks an hour, a transport worker 1.10 marks.[5] The rank and file of employees were being worked to the limit of their endurance and beyond; some of them had no Sundays off for weeks as the government tried to raise production to meet the plan. Thousands fled over the zonal borders; almost 340,000 between July 1952 and July 1953: 58,000 in March, 36,000 in April, 35,000 in May. Thirty-seven thousand went to the West from farms. On May 28 the Council of Ministers ordered all norms to be raised 10 per cent, "complying with the request

[4] *Europa-Archiv* (Aug. 5, 1953), p. 5831.
[5] S. Brant: *Der Aufstand* . . . , p. 30.

for a general revision of work expressed by a wide circle of the working people." [6]

On June 9 the party line swung around to the opposite pole; it was announced that HO prices would go down, farmers who had been dispossessed would get back their farms and be given credits to develop them, and forced deliveries would be reduced. Serious errors were admitted by the Politbüro of the SED in the methods that had been used: in the increased taxes, the injuries done individual farmers and businessmen and intellectuals. Henceforth the standard of living would go up for these people, too many of whom the Politbüro admitted had been driven from the country; production of consumer goods would rise; private enterprise would be permitted again, as would the non-Communist youth organizations. "Economic criminals" serving one to three years in prison were to be freed. In mid-June it was announced that some 4,000 people would be released within a few days.[7] Credits were to be made available for privately owned businesses. The New Course was proclaimed, a marvelous transformation of almost all the economic measures that had driven hundreds of thousands of people from their homes to start over again in West Germany and to accept the risks of an uncertain future. The 10-per-cent rise in the norms remained, however; it was to take effect at the end of June.

The strike that was to become a revolt began among the elite corps of workers which was building Stalin Allee in Berlin. "Brigades" had been dispatched there from all over the East zone to build the monument of housing that not only honored the great Stalin during his lifetime but also offered evidence of "socialist realism" in architecture and the comforts the proletarian state provided for its workers. The construction men were well paid; they earned from 150 to 160 marks a week with overtime, and the rise in norms would mean a drop of some 30 per cent in their income. They were not only well paid, they were

[6] Sherman, p. 2, quoting *Der Monat*.
[7] Lukas: *Zehn Jahre*, p. 104.

"activists," workers of unusual efficiency who were what the party hopefully called politically conscious; but the police state, far from turning them into cowed party members, had merely made them sure of one another and of their deeply felt opinions of the East German leadership.

On Friday, June 12, the workers on Building Site C South were told by union leaders that some of the men had volunteered to raise their production quotas, and there were shouts from their sophisticated ranks: "Where are they? Show them to us!" The next day there was a boat trip on the Müggelsee near Berlin, and the workers of Building Site C South, with some of the colleagues they had asked to come along from Block 40, drank beer and talked about little but the rise in norms. On Monday the 15th the men of Block 40 decided to stop work and to send a delegation to Ulbricht and Pieck to thank them for the New Course the government was adopting and to ask at the same time that the proposed increase in norms be canceled. On the morning of the next day, June 16, they read in the *Tribune*, the Communist trade-union newspaper, that the new norms must go into effect; and instead of sending the delegation, they called for a vote. Those in favor of going on strike and presenting their demands as a group would step to the right and any opposed to the left. Every man moved to the right; and they marched off in their working clothes, some wearing wooden clogs, some walking barefoot to save their shoes. They carried a sign: "We demand lowering of the norms"; it was painted on the back of a sign that read: "In honor of May Day, Block 40 has volunteered to raise its norms 10 per cent."

As they passed the other buildings of Stalin Allee, masons and carpenters and hod-carriers poured from them. One group was held back for a time by party workers and became the target of a chorus of catcalls and yells; they broke through and joined the marchers. The men from Block 40 were joined by hundreds as they marched down the length of Stalin Allee, and in an hour there were 2,000 of them. A party functionary tried to appeal to them and was roughed up; a policeman came to his assistance and the men shoved him from one to the other until he retreated. As their ranks grew, the idea of what they wanted changed. They had started with the simple demand for the return of the norms to the old level, but before long they had begun to shout for free elections, for lower prices, and against the Communist leadership. "HO *macht uns KO*" ("HO knocks us out"), they chanted, referring to the Handels Organisation—the government stores. "We want to live like free men." "Of Pieck, Ulbricht, Grotewohl, we have our snouts full." The ranks of the marchers continued to grow; what police there were did not interfere. A photographer who took a picture was made to destroy the film. The policeman at the Alexander Platz turned off the traffic lights and detoured all motor cars, under the impression that this was a government demonstration, the only kind he had ever seen. Another policeman tried to stop the marchers and was swept out of the way.

By the time the crowd passed the Alexander Platz there were more than 5,000 shouting: "We don't want a People's Army; we want butter." As they moved down Unter den Linden they were joined at the old Lustgarten, now Marx and Engels Square, by the workers rebuilding the opera house; and they called for the students of Humboldt University to join them. When they reached the government buildings on the Leipzigerstrasse, they yelled for Grotewohl and Ulbricht. Two members of the government appeared at a window and then came downstairs. One of them, Selbmann, minister for foundry construction, climbed onto a table that he and two others had dragged out of the building and began: "Fellow workers . . ." There were shouts from the crowd: "You're no worker." Selbmann held up his hands to show his proletarian calluses, but he could no longer make himself heard. A professor from Humboldt University followed him to lecture the crowd on the economic situation, and he was shouted down. A man stepped from the crowd and climbed onto the table. "We represent not only Stalin Allee but the people of Berlin. This is a people's rising." Another speaker took his place; he said he had spent five years in a concentration camp under Hitler and would gladly spend ten years more if it would bring freedom. "If you don't see me here tomorrow," he added to the men around him, "you'll know what happened to me."

Selbmann could not quiet the crowd even when he said the norms would be lowered, nor did the news, brought by loudspeakers, that the Politbüro of the SED would reconsider the increase in the norms. A girl in the uniform of the Free German Youth got up to talk; the crowd started to shout her down, but she took off her party jacket and called on the young people to join the strikers. There were voices now shouting for a general strike, for a free vote, for the downfall of the regime. Small groups of party workers tried to tell the demonstrators their demands would be met, but these attempts had no success; either the speakers were knocked around and fled or they joined the ranks. Loudspeaker trucks sent by the party to announce the plans for reappraising the norms were taken over by the crowd. A delegation of three [8]—two workers and a salaried employee—crossed the sector boundary to RIAS in West Berlin and told the story of what had happened. They asked to be put on the air to present their demands and to call a general strike for the next day.

They raised a difficult problem for the directors of RIAS. It was certainly a moment for which the Americans and West Germans had long been waiting: the first rising of the workers against the total state, the workers' state. It was unpremeditated, unplanned, orderly, and for the most part good-humored, but growing conscious of its strength and certain of the justice of what it wanted. But the directors of RIAS moved cautiously; they put the account of the demonstrations on the air and broadcast the demands of the workers: no increase in norms, immediate reduction of prices, free and secret ballots, no reprisals

[8] Rainer Hildebrand, in *The Explosion*, says there were five.

333

against the strikers.[9] None of the delegation of three, however, who had risked prison to come over to the West and tell the story was allowed to broadcast. Nor did the broadcasts repeat the call for a general strike which was being shouted in the East-sector streets. That could be the signal for a general rising, and responsibility for such a move must come from higher sources than the management of the radio station. The broadcasts were accurate, professional, and sympathetic; and they were also sensible. One speaker, after describing what had gone on, told his hearers to demand the possible; he reminded them that the ultimate decisions would lie with the Russian occupiers and asked his audience in the fastnesses of the East zone to decide each for himself what could be demanded. More, he said, had been achieved than had been thought possible,[1] but the final word had not been said by the power that would really determine how far the demands of the workers would be met. "Be brave, be cautious," he told them. Jakob Kaiser, Minister for All-German Affairs, spoke, and said that everyone in West Germany and in the free world was with the strikers, but he too asked them to be prudent.

The first day of the strike had seen little interference by the regular police force or by the brown-uniformed barracks police. At the Alexander Platz two of the crowd of marching workers had been cut off from the rest and taken to the police station; but the crowd, hearing of this on the loudspeakers, shouted for the release of the men, and the police hastily let them go. There had been little violence; the police obviously had been given orders to quiet the demonstration as peaceably as possible. Now, as the general strike was called, there was a counterdemonstration before the Friedrichstadt Palast. This had been planned some days earlier as part of the propaganda for the New Course; at eight p.m. Grotewohl and Ulbricht spoke to 3,000 of the

[9] Interview, Gordon Ewing.
[1] In the evening the announcement was made over the East Berlin radio that the government, following a recommendation of the Politbüro of the SED, would lower the norms to their old figure.

faithful, admitting errors in an outburst of self-criticism, but saying nothing of the day's events.

RIAS, while it did not announce the general strike, did report that a meeting had been called for the next morning at seven o'clock at the Strausberger Platz on the Stalin Allee. The night of the 16th passed without serious disturbances, although the streets of East Berlin were filled with crowds. There was a demonstration in front of the women's prison; propaganda posters were torn down. It began to rain. There was no leadership, no central committee, no direction; there were the announcements and the speeches from RIAS, and the speakers who mounted the table in front of the government buildings, but that was all.

Daylight lasts for a long time in Berlin in mid-June, and people were in no hurry to get to bed. Little groups clustered until late, and at six a.m. a voice from RIAS told them to go to the Strausberger Platz for the meeting. By seven the square was filled, and the workers moved off in uneven ranks, seven or eight abreast, toward Alexander Platz and then down Unter den Linden. Now violence broke out. As the crowd converged on the government buildings at the Leipzigerstrasse, the police formed a line to bar their further advance. The people in the rear could not see them and pushed forward. The men and women in the front lines, marching with their arms linked, collided with the line of police, who began to use their clubs. Some of the policemen made only gestures, raising their arms but not striking; others hit out, and blood began to flow. The crowd drew back and found its own ready-made weapons in the stones of the rubble, a limitless supply of which lay all over Berlin. They also managed to take some of the clubs away from the police and returned to the battle with their makeshift weapons, among them umbrellas they were carrying against the rain.

The workers of East Berlin occupied the city. Marchers moved on the Charlottenburger Tor, where the red flag waved after having been torn down in the demonstrations of 1948; now it came down again. Two young men climbed the huge gate and then the flagpole. They had a hard time tearing the flag from the mast, but at last it fluttered to the ground and was burned in the sight of Russian soldiers, who, like the East German police, made no move. As the young men climbed the flagpole for the second time to fasten the Bear flag of Berlin to the mast, shots rang out from the East-sector police massed at the border, and the boys hastily fastened the flag halfway up the mast. But the crowd cheered wildly, and when the boys came down, Americans tossed them cigarettes.

The government was also on the move now. The night before, the barracks police had been alerted to a state of emergency; they were to sleep in their uniforms. Each man was issued a carbine and thirty cartridges. They came into the East sector from the countryside around Berlin; and on the way, too, were Russian armored cars and tanks.

The demonstrations were getting far out of hand. There were risings in the provinces as news of the events in Berlin reached the cities and villages of the East zone. Members of the secret police were beaten up whenever they were spotted. One of them in the city of Thale in Sachsen-Anhalt was pointed out by an eight-year-old boy as the man who had sent his father to jail; as he hit the child to silence him he was set upon by the crowd and beaten so badly that, although he escaped to the protection of the police, he did not survive. Mobs in Halle and Jena and other towns attacked the jails and freed the political prisoners, carefully examining the dossiers, when they could, to tell which were the criminals and which the men and women under political arrest.

In some places the police were remarkably docile. They readily surrendered their arms and even joined the marchers. "Colleagues," the marchers called one another; the word took the place of the old and now shabby term of the revolution, "Comrades." The Russians had remained more aloof than the German police. When they saw attacks on the prisons they refrained from interfering, and some of the Soviet officers and men showed signs of sympathy for the marching, shouting people they had conquered, patting them on the back and putting arms around their shoulders.

Stalin had died in March and the question in the minds of many of the Russians, as later defectors to the West reported, was whether there might not be a New Course for Russia too. The words the Germans were shouting against the police state were foreign, but they undoubtedly touched on hopes the Russians cherished. One Russian officer who later came to the West reported that the Soviet soldiers felt themselves to be in the same oppressive role as the troops of the tsar they had been taught to detest.[2]

As the violence increased and the revolt spread, the atmosphere changed. Russian tanks lumbered down the streets of Berlin and the provincial cities. They zigzagged to clear the crowds, but they did not shoot. Sometimes when they appeared, strikers shouted that they were not against the Russians, only against the German leaders of the People's Democratic Republic. "Don't shoot the German proletarians," voices called out in Russian over the loudspeakers. It was a sensible appeal. Everyone knew the Russians would decide what reforms would be conceded, what errors admitted and what ignored, and who would replace the unseated if the Soviet decided to take action against the German officials who had let matters get out of hand. But the tanks were there not only to restore order but also to put down a revolt. The Russian commander of Berlin, Major General Dibrova, announced a state of emergency, making it illegal for more than three people to gather together in the streets on pain of the wartime penalties for disobedience of the occupying power. A curfew was imposed from nine p.m. to five p.m.

The mobs refused to disperse. For the first time they turned

[2] "*Der Aufstand* . . . ," *Der Monat* (Oct. 1953), p. 46.

their anger against the Russians. "Ivan, go home," they shouted; "Ivan, go home." The tanks fired now, but they aimed over the heads of the rioters. The workers retaliated as best they could. The briefcases that every German, East and West, carries were stuffed into the exhausts of the tanks; the crowds threw rocks, used crowbars on the treads, and yelled defiance. But these were small weapons against the heavy T-34's. One man was killed, crushed by a tank, and others were injured as some of the armored vehicles were driven into the crowd at speeds of twenty to twenty-five miles an hour.

The Russian soldiers had orders not to turn their guns on the crowd unless fired upon, but real shooting began. Workers jumped onto the tanks, they pushed sticks of wood into the firing-slots, they tore down the antennae. The demonstrations became a riot. Policemen turned firehoses on the crowds, the crowds captured the hoses and turned them on the policemen; HO selling-booths were set ablaze, along with Communist posters and slogans and the barriers set up by the police. The crowd set fire to party buildings, Columbus House, Café Vaterland, and police cars.

As the Russian tanks and armored cars cleared the streets, the crowd taunted them, shouting the words the Russian soldiers had so often used when they had plundered and raped the city in 1945: *"Uhri, Uhri; Frau komm."* It is unlikely that many of the soldiers who had been part of the invading army eight years before were still in the city, and the meaning of the words was doubtless lost on the troops that were now there. They were permitted no direct relations with the people; they strode through the cities with the distance of the occupation between them and the Germans.

The East-zone CDU leader, Nuschke, was discovered in his automobile near the Western sector; a mob broke the windows of his car, and he took refuge across the boundary in the West. Interviewers from RIAS brought him a portable microphone, and he told his listeners that the riots were caused by provoca teurs from the West who had been sent into East Berlin. Nuschke was asked whether he approved the use of the Russians to restore order, and he answered: "Of course." Nuschke had long ago made his peace with the Russians and the East German government; his stay in the West was temporary.

Party workers pleaded with the crowds through loudspeakers. The Politbüro had rescinded the rise in the norms. "Don't destroy what you've created with your eight years of work . . . with your proletarian power." In "Red" Wedding, a district where in the far past the Communists had been strong, where the Hitler brown shirts had been mauled as they paraded through the streets, a sign reading "We greet the Freedom Fighters" was painted. And as 12,000 strikers marched by from the outlying districts of Hennigsdorf on their way from the suburbs to join forces with the rising they had heard about over the radio, they were given flowers and cigarettes and chocolates.

But the workers marching by the thousands on Berlin from plants as far as fifteen and twenty miles away were now opposed not only by the formations of people's police, 3,500 of whom had been ordered from the suburbs to the city, but also by the whole power of the Russian occupation army. In the towns and villages where there were strikes and risings as the news was brought by radio and by travelers who had been in Berlin; in Jena, where in 1918 the red flag had been raised against the Kaiser's government, and the Zeiss workers were now out; in Görlitz, where the jail was stormed and prisoners freed—among them a woman of sixty serving a term of six years for buying ten pounds of coffee in the West; in Leipzig, where thirty were reported killed and a hundred wounded; in Brandenburg, where more prisoners were released, including a man serving three years for stealing some nails that were unobtainable in the stores —wherever the workers had had a few hours of freedom the formidable enemy closed in with tanks and guns. For a day the men and women of the East zone were victorious, unexpectedly and miraculously gathered together singing *"Deutschland,*

Deutschland, über Alles," and the old socialist song they had once long ago shared with Communists: "Up to the sun and to freedom; brothers, up to the light." The party apparatus and the secret police had disappeared, and for a little while the people could imagine that the Soviet military commanders might hear them out and somehow agree that the wrongs and injustices against which they were shouting should be righted. But the Russian commandant had a simple job to do: restore order; prevent the West from making any use of the uprising.

The Vopos, the people's police, were recruited largely from eighteen-, nineteen-, and twenty-year-olds, who had been children when the war ended. They were told that the rising was the result of the machinations of the Western imperialist powers, who had sent provocateurs among them, but they were given only a few cartridges to defeat it. Although the People's Police were provided by the Russians with tanks and were paid well—400 marks a month—the Soviet authorities were careful about giving too much fire power to these young Germans, who were not fully indoctrinated with the mission of the People's Democracy. The Kremlin had little confidence in the satellites, their parties, or their armed forces; even Russian troops were carefully watched for their allegiance. The Vopos did as they were told, for the most part, although some of them, like some of the regular police, joined the marchers, and there were occasional signs of mutiny when they were ordered into action against the demonstrators. By Friday it was reported that 120 Vopos had been arrested for failure to obey orders, and 467 had crossed to the West. German reports said that eventually 1,756 Vopos and Security Police were arrested and 52 were shot.[3]

The mayor of West Berlin was in Vienna when the news of the events of June 16 reached him by telephone. His first question was how serious the situation appeared to be—was it a real rising or a local strike? [4] There had been no preparation or warn-

---

[3] *Europa-Archiv* (Aug. 5, 1953), pp. 5834–5.
[4] Interview, Willy Brandt.

ing; nothing was known of the dimensions or dynamics of the demonstrations, or how far they might go. Ernst Reuter asked the American Army for a plane to fly him to Berlin, but, to his despair, he was told this would not be possible. He returned to Berlin by commercial airline, arriving on the 18th. A broadcast he recorded in Vienna had been put on by RIAS; now he addressed the Berliners directly. He spoke mainly to East Berlin, but to the East zone, to West Germany, and to the entire Western world as well:

"A people," he said, "cannot be held in submission in the long run, with martial law and bayonets and tanks; and it would be terrible if the graves, which are already deep enough, should be made deeper. What we in Berlin and in the East zone have experienced is an exhortation, a beacon for the entire free world. . . . It can finally be understood now as it emerges from its irresolution, its apathy, its disparateness, into political activity. What I saw today at the Potsdamer Platz of these wastes, this dead, empty city, reminded me of my first impression at the end of 1946 . . . in that terrible winter when I first returned to Berlin and saw the Tiergarten. A man's heart could have stopped and it could stop today as we see this city murdered by the forces of history in which we have all been torn.

"We renew our appeal to the entire world; the world must finally understand and I hope must admit that the Germans are a people who know the worth of freedom and are a people who pledge themselves to freedom. The workers of Berlin have not asked for higher wages but for a change of the entire system. Can the world be silent to this call? I think it cannot be silent, will not be silent. We here in West Berlin will go to work to provide all possible help; that goes without saying. But we will do everything to make what we do contribute to the goal that we have set ourselves of the unification of Germany." [5]

Now there were direct appeals to the West for help; on one side of the Brandenburger Tor were the lights, the security, and

[5] Translated from Brant: *Der Aufstand.*

the power of the Western Allies; on the other the dead and wounded, and the spirit of rebellion that the West had wanted to kindle. For many of the people on the spot, both Germans and Allies, it was terrible to stand and watch. But what was the West going to do? What could it do? The Russian tanks at the sector boundaries could be matched only by other tanks. The official Communist story was that the rising came from the West; few people in the East zone would ever believe that. The mobs that stormed the prisons found people in them who had been sentenced for trivial political crimes; they found cells, some of them knee-deep in water and with ceilings only a little over four feet high so the prisoner could neither sit nor stand upright. They found political prisoners crowded eight to a cell; some were rescued and got to the West, many more were caught as the police returned. Some were spirited away by the Security Police before the crowds with their battering-rams of telephone poles and bulldozers could get to them. But the East Germans could do no more without outside help, and outside help on a scale large enough to do any good would mean another Korea at the least.

The rising spread even to the schools, where children threw the Russian textbooks they were forced to study out of the windows and then burned them. Tractor-drivers at the machine stations and the collective farms tore up their party books, as did thousands of workers—the party books which they had been told were the most important documents in their lives. In some 300 towns and villages, it was estimated, the East Germans demonstrated against the government of the People's Democratic Republic, and in 129 of them the Russians marched in. There was scarcely a factory where the workers did not lay down their tools, even in those run by the Russians.

The countermeasures were wholly successful. In some factories workers were told that unless they went back to their benches, their leaders would be shot. Fourteen East Germans were hanged; 31 were shot during the curfew hours and 141 dur-

ing the period of martial law; 569 were killed in the demonstrations, 1,744 were wounded, thousands were put in jail.[6] An unemployed West Berlin worker, Willi Goettling, who went to
East Berlin to get his unemployment compensation of forty-four
marks a month for himself, his wife, and two children, was
picked up by the Russians, charged with being a provocateur,
and executed the next day; a fifteen-year-old boy was shot by
the People's Police at the sector border.

The rising ebbed slowly. The tanks cleared the streets in routine fashion, pushing the crowds before them, shooting when
resisted. There were wild rumors in the East zone that the Americans were coming: their tanks had been seen, their planes were
dropping weapons. The wholehearted support of the people
west of the iron curtain was assured the East-zone Germans over
RIAS and on the editorial pages of Western newspapers; and
indeed they had it, as the Hungarians and the Poles would have
it in a later year. The newspapers throughout the West—in
Holland, France, Switzerland, England, and the United States
—analyzed the meaning of the rising and praised the spirit behind it. But the West did not move; this was not the unmis-
takable *casus belli* for sending Allied tanks and planes against
the Russian armor. Washington was understandably cautious.
When the Russians ordered their troops to put down the rising,
only the armed forces of the West could have balanced the scale
for the Berliners and the others in the towns and villages and
countryside who were fighting without weapons. Once the state
of emergency was declared, there was one question for the people in Washington to decide: is this the place where we accept
the challenge and roll the enemy back? For East Germany was
beyond the line of demarcation, north of a 38th parallel where
two world forces met and stopped, each on its own side. The
Russians had 25,000 troops in Berlin, the Americans estimated,
some 250,000 in the surrounding area, and more within a few
days' marching distance, as men marched now, by means of

[6] *Europa-Archiv* (Aug. 5, 1953), pp. 5833, 5835.

troop-carriers, trucks, and planes.[7] The rising had set an army in motion; 3 elite divisions had been mobilized; 275 tanks had been used in Leipzig alone—more than twice as many as Rommel had at El Alamein, Germans pointed out.[8]

The West did not move. It excoriated the enemies of the workers; its newspapers and spokesmen pointed out that this was the first rising of the proletariat against the dictatorship of the proletariat; RIAS advised the farmers of the East zone to leave the co-operatives, which they were now permitted to do. As the Soviets took their countermeasures and the flags of the nations of the Council of Europe were put at half-mast for the dead, the trade unions of the free world passed resolutions of encouragement, and aid poured in for the victims: CARE packages and money. The widow of Willi Goettling was given an allowance by the federal government; the other workers of the co-operative to which he had belonged pledged themselves to build her a house; a society of artists made itself responsible for the care and education of the two children. There were criticisms of the behavior of the West. Free elections should have been demanded, it was said; West Berliners should have been allowed to demonstrate at the border; if better propaganda use of the rising had been made, the smoldering revolt might have burst out in many unexpected places.

The stir of the revolt was felt thousands of miles away in labor camps in Siberia, in Czechoslovakia, in Poland, in Russia, and by the German and Russian armed forces in the East zone. After Stalin's death in March there had been signs of change in Russia: fifteen doctors who had been arrested by his order were freed. Beria, one of the new triumvirate with Malenkov and Molotov, was arrested. These were new days with incalculable possibilities. It was reported that among those executed for the uprising were Russian officers who had failed in their duty, and

[7] *The New York Times,* June 21, 1953.
[8] *Der Monat,* Sept. 1953, pp. 595–624; Oct. 1953, pp. 45–6.

there was German testimony to the forbearance and good will shown by individual Russians: an officer who had mud thrown in his face had imperturbably wiped it off, making no effort to retaliate; a colonel repeated, smiling, to the rioters: "Go home, children"; squads of Russian soldiers had watched the prisons broken into and prisoners released without interfering. At Halle the square filled with demonstrators had been surrounded by tanks, but the Russians had watched quietly, the tanks motionless.[9] There had been irresolution in the top Soviet command and among lower officers. Some of the latter, it was said, had refused to fire on the demonstrators, and it was these, perhaps, who paid with their lives. The Soviet soldiers on the whole, however, had obeyed orders; there were no defections, there was no large-scale fraternization.

The new government of the Kremlin showed signs of uncertainty; the question of how to treat the satellites had not been fully determined. Even the Red Army paper in Berlin, the *Tägliche Rundschau,* suggested that the mistakes which had been made were not entirely owing to the East German government; the Soviet Control Commission was in part responsible. *Pravda* between June 22 and July 4 devoted a large proportion of its space to the events in Germany.

The riots stopped; here and there, sit-down strikes occurred, one as late as June 21. On the night of June 18, when Russian troops bivouacked on the Potsdamer Platz, the streets of Berlin were empty. The situation could be kept in hand now by local authorities or readily by the soldiers. The men went back to work slowly; in some places, such as Hennigsdorf, only 20 per cent were at work by the 21st. But they went back: the construction workers, the transport workers, the men from the Agfa factory that was now Russian-owned, the men from Zeiss, from the factories that made artificial rubber and fuel, the coal men,

[9] James P. O'Donnell: "I Led a Riot against the Reds," *Saturday Evening Post,* Aug. 22, 1953.

the steel men, the river men, the tractor-drivers—they went back to work or to prison or to the West. Martial law remained in force until July 12, twenty-four days after the start of the riots.

The East German government tacked, veered, and ran before the wind. The leaders admitted error; they accused the West of responsibility for the uprising; men were arrested; others were freed from prison. The wage cuts were canceled; wages in the low-income brackets were raised. The bonus system was to be expanded, businesses were to be returned to their owners, and credits were to be supplied. Seventy-eight hundred "economic criminals" were let out of prison; 600,000,000 marks was to be supplied for housing.[1] More electricity was to be released for private use; current had up to now been diverted to the needs of industry and had been shut off for household use except for two hours a day. More money was to be spent on workers' rest homes; people who had been ready to work during the strike would recover 90 per cent of their wages; 100 per cent would be paid those who would make up the time lost.[2] Consumer goods were taken out of warehouses and put on sale: 100,000 bicycles, 800,000 pairs of shoes. Farm quotas were lowered, the return of farms was promised, and 3,000 farmers who had fled to the West came back between November 1953 and February 1954. Party leaders purified themselves with confessions of failure and pledges to do better. But there was ambivalence here too. The Minister of Justice, Max Fechner, who had said it was not a punishable crime to go on strike, was dismissed and then arrested. Ulbricht, the long-term party man, held firmly to the line that the rising had been caused by fascist provocateurs and should be sternly dealt with; Grotewohl, who had once belonged to the SPD and had spent years in a Hitler concentration camp, wanted mild treatment for the strikers. Before long the explanations and policies were clarified. An editorial in *Neues Deutschland* as early as June 18 said that Ameri-

[1] *Europa-Archiv*, p. 5832.
[2] *The New York Times*, June 28, 1953; July 26, 1953.

can officers had come into the East zone on subversive missions; that the West, knowing the workers' standard of living was soon to be improved, had tried to cause a revolt. The central committee of the SED, meeting on June 21, declared that the imperialists, defeated in the Italian elections and in their efforts to start a world war in Korea, had sent their agents into the People's Democratic Republic; they had parachuted supplies and, with the help of provocateurs from West Berlin, had succeeded in inciting some politically unschooled workers to strike. The strike had been put down by the vigilance of the overwhelmingly loyal population, its People's Police, and Soviet troops; and there would be harsh measures against those responsible, but no punishment for those who had been used merely as tools. The People's Police rode along the border with loudspeakers, urging those who had fled to return. The renowned East-zone playwright Bertold Brecht sent a telegram of approval to Ulbricht, as did Communists from many countries. In their view, it had been a close call. Some of the people of the East zone were interrogated by Soviet investigators, who asked why had they struck, what were their grievances. The party and the Russians needed to know these things, although it was not possible to predict what changes the knowledge would bring. The party admitted that it had been too authoritarian; it must stop giving orders and gain the workers by persuasion. The workers, it was explained, had not realized that steps were being taken to meet their just demands. Then the tone hardened again. *Neues Deutschland* stated on July 12 that the self-criticism should stop; the zone had made great progress; the Junkers had been dispossessed, people's enterprises now dominated the economy.

In West Berlin the name of the street leading to the Brandenburger Tor was changed to "The Avenue of the 17th of June." On the anniversaries of the rising, signal fires were lighted along the frontier of the zones; they could be seen for miles in the unlighted, silent East, but there were no answering beacons.

XV

A MOST FAVORED NATION

ALTHOUGH A truce was made in Korea on July 27, 1953, the sense of emergency in the United States did not greatly diminish. Additional aid was announced for the French in Indochina, where their troops continued a hopeless fight and the Americans their substantial but ineffectual assistance. One third of the costs of this war, Mr. Acheson said in June 1952, were being borne by the United States, but American opinion was almost as opposed to French colonial policy as to the Communist forces. During World War II President Roosevelt had repeatedly spoken in unflattering terms of the French rule in Indochina.[1] In later years American policy was one of generous help up to a point. The French were supplied with arms and equipment, and American cargo planes with civilian pilots flew to Hanoi, so Secretary of State John Foster Dulles announced in May 1953. The United States was unwilling to intervene further. When the French held tenaciously to their view that the future of the Saar must be settled before they would approve the arming of German contingents, Dulles expressed doubt that the two questions needed to be tied together.[2] The Russians told the French that the United States was ignoring them as a great power, and successive French governments continued to delay asking the National Assembly for approval of the European Defense Community, although influential voices in France as well

[1] *Foreign Relations . . . Malta and Yalta*, p. 770. *The New York Times*, March 2, 1954.
[2] *The New York Times*, March 29, 1953.

as in the United States and England warned that this was a dangerous course and could lead to the Germans being armed without French consent.[3] Toward the end of 1953 Dulles spoke of the possibility of "an agonizing reappraisal" of American policy,[4] and it was reported that Washington now was as critical of the French as the French were of the Germans. The possibility loomed which the French had always most feared: finding themselves without allies against the Germans. Still the government did not demand a vote—in part, no doubt, because of the likelihood that ratification of EDC would be defeated, but largely because with few exceptions no one in France wanted to see German troops.

Before the West German elections, which took place in September, Secretary Dulles strengthened the cause of Chancellor Adenauer with a statement that his defeat would be disastrous and that the Bonn government would be given a part in the decisions on clemency for German war criminals still in Allied prisons. Adenauer for the first time won a bare but clear majority in the Bundestag—244 out of 487 seats. The CDU polled 45.2 per cent of the votes, the SPD 28.8 per cent, the FDP 9.5 per cent. The German Reich party, which as the successor to the Socialist Reich party had disturbed so many Germans and Americans with its Nazi reverberations, failed to get the required 5 per cent of the vote and so lost its right to appear on the ballot as a national party. The Refugee party, the BHE, which many thought might develop extreme Right-wing tendencies, got 6 per cent of the vote—well below what was predicted. Adenauer again evidenced the European point of view that made him so attractive to the Americans; in the midst of the eulogies of his political stature and of West Germany for its political

[3] Schuman said the French should get rid of their sense of inferiority, and René Mayer, who had been High Commissioner for German Affairs, said a purely negative French policy would be criminal (*The New York Times*, Nov. 20, 1953). General de Gaulle announced in January 1953 that he favored a national German army—something the Germans themselves rejected.

[4] *The New York Times*, Dec. 15, 1953.

and economic virtues, he said that Germany must not be praised at the expense of France.[5]

The new American high commissioner or ambassador[6] to West Germany was the distinguished scientist and former president of Harvard, James B. Conant. He succeeded Walter J. Donnelly, who held the office for a short time after the resignation of McCloy. Conant, like so many other scholars of his generation, had deeply admired pre-Hitler Germany. He had been a student there, and had a good knowledge of the language. But he, too, wanted severe curbs on the country in 1945. He had been one of the men responsible for organizing the research that produced the atomic bomb, and, fearful of a revived Nazism and knowing the potentialities of German industry and science, he had wanted to keep even power plants outside German borders. When he appeared before the Senate committee for the approval of his appointment, his earlier views on the treatment of Germany were challenged, but he could say candidly with many others that he was of a different opinion in 1953; and he in fact became one of the strongest proponents of German moral and intellectual recovery and rearming.

The Soviet government announced in August that, as of the end of the year, it would renounce further reparations from East Germany; that occupation costs would not exceed 5 per cent of the East German state income; and that, with the exception of the uranium works, the mixed Russian-German companies would be returned to the People's Democratic Republic. Since Russia would continue to import a large share of the goods produced by these as well as other East-zone factories at prices fixed well below the world market, reparations and occupation costs merely assumed another form.

Building rates continued to rise in West Germany; there were

[5] Ibid., Dec. 23, 1953.

[6] In late June, at the request of Chancellor Adenauer, the high commissioners were given the status of ambassadors, as were the German heads of diplomatic missions in London, Paris, and Washington.

500,000 new structures in 1953. In Berlin over 2,250,000 rooms had been either built or repaired since the reconstruction began, and the average occupancy was lower than in West Germany. The East sector was building too; and while there were fewer new structures than in the West—in 1952 5,700 dwelling-units were built in East Berlin, as compared with 8,200 in the West sectors—the per-capita rate was actually higher and the rents charged were lower. One of the devices used to finance building in East Berlin was the lottery; a man could earn a ticket by working 300 hours at rubble clearance or by contributing 3 per cent of his salary. This was part of the system of volunteer labor.

The competition between East and West Berlin and their guardian powers also continued to be brisk. Nearly $50,000,000, it was announced in 1953, would be made available to West Berlin from President Eisenhower's special funds to create jobs and help balance the budget.[7] After the June 17 rising the United States offered $15,000,000 worth of food for the population of the East zone, but this and a credit of $57,000,000 were declined by Moscow and the East-zone government, as the Marshall Plan had been rejected in 1948. Food packages, including milk and oranges, were offered free in West Berlin to people from the East zone. In the beginning each was worth some five marks, but the value went higher as the program developed and the packages grew larger. Ten pounds of food which would cost $30 to buy was given to everyone from the East who asked for it: the packages included lard, flour, and condensed milk, and people came to West Berlin from a hundred miles beyond the border for them. A million parcels were given away in six days. Then the East-zone police began to confiscate the packages, and the East-zone press printed the names of those who were stopped at the border. Squads said to number 5,000 men were sent from the East to disrupt the distribution. The sale of railroad tickets from the provinces to Berlin was stopped. Border

[7] *The New York Times,* Jan. 20, 1953.

patrols were increased, arrests were made at the sector boundaries; 50,000 food packages were taken from weary East Germans as they returned to the People's Democratic Republic.

East-zone officials went further: they announced that they too would give away food, to the more than 200,000 unemployed of West Berlin (the unemployment figures fluctuated depending on the season and went as high as 268,000); and for this purpose they used the packages they had confiscated, and printed counterfeit coupons.

The West met these tactics by holding up the food distribution for a few days and then starting it again. There were photographs in the Western papers of the East-zoners as they trudged off with their packages, many of them old people who waited patiently in line after having traveled long kilometers to this incredible world where there was food to be given away. By August it was reported that 120,000 had come from the East zone to West Berlin, and 5,000,000 packages had been distributed in eleven weeks.[8]

West Germany produced more food in 1953 than it ever had before. This was in part owing to the American campaign for more use of machinery, the farm loans, and the educational campaigns. Two hundred and fifty-two thousand tractors were in use, 27 per cent more than the previous year; German agriculture now produced more per acre than that of France or Italy, and more per agricultural worker. The Americans continued their good works; they established community houses for women, with sewing-rooms as well as baths and showers; they sent teams of experts around the country to suggest improvements in farming methods; there were free distributions of farm journals, a model farm exhibit in Hamburg, agricultural films, importations and tests of tractors, and courses in home economics.[9]

[8] Ibid., July 18, 24, 25, 26, 27, 1953; Aug. 2, 3, 4, 7, 28, 31, 1953.
[9] *Deutschland Heute*, pp. 202, 203. *Report*, Oct. 1, 1953, from the Office of the High Commissioner.

In industry too the rise continued, although the output per worker remained lower than that of the French and British; the national product rose—at the end of 1953, production was 178 per cent of 1936; unemployment went down; and Germany accumulated nearly $2,000,000,000 in foreign exchange. The population was eating better—not quite so well as before the war, but consumption of meat and milk was up over the previous year. So were the hours of work: 49.7 a week, 3.3 more than the French were working, 1.8 more than the British, but one hour below the Dutch. For every dollar of the American gifts and loans, the official German history reports that ten to twenty dollars' worth of goods and services was produced.

Israel ordered a floating dock and freighter to be built as a result of the restitution agreement, which was ratified by the Bundestag on March 18, 1953; and this could now be done, for the Security Commission had sanctioned the rebuilding of the shipyards of the Blohm and Voss works in Hamburg, although still refusing permission, despite American prodding, for increases in the production of gasoline, oil, and roller bearings.

But while the commission remained stingy, German papers carried more stories of the endless generosity of the GI. At one railroad station two American soldiers had taken the guitar of a legless German veteran who had been playing at the entrance and for five hours had played and sung hillbilly songs for the crowds; they had then returned the guitar, given the man the money they had collected, and disappeared.[1] There were many of these anonymous figures, who appealed greatly to the Germans, brought up as they all were on a fairy-tale tradition of the magical, beneficent, and unpredictable event. A child in worn clothing was taken by an unidentified soldier to a PX and clothed from head to foot in the best the store had to offer: shoes, hat, suit, overcoat. The soldier then simply paid the bill and went off; the child did not know his name. He told the

---

[1] *Frankfurter Rundschau*, Dec. 5, 1953.

story in school and the papers printed it: "a Christmas fairy tale come true," they said.[2]

There were many articles on the GI in German periodicals, some of them indignant, some philosophical. In one house in 1948, a paper said, the Americans had left nothing when they departed: no furniture, no lamps, not even door handles; an expensive piano had been discovered in a horse stall, where the Americans had unaccountably left it. The damages in this case had come to 100,000 marks. An article in *Christ und Welt* explained that 250,000 foreign soldiers could scarcely be expected to know Germany well. The Seventh Army had made a careful study of German criticisms of American behavior; as a result there were now meetings of Germans with American officers, and the Germans in their turn should know more of what the United States did for youth and hospitals and as social work. The writer added, however, that the Americans brought the American way of life to Germany and stayed in it; the Germans knew nothing of it. An American sergeant was paid more than a French colonel. During the last Olympics the Americans had appeared happily in London in their big cars in the midst of the seedy Europeans. Another writer commented that, despite the amity at high levels, the middle and lower groups among the Americans were not always sure they were not dealing with a horde of Nazis and war criminals. He reported that only 8 per cent of the American civilian employees spoke German fluently, 20 per cent could speak it if necessary, and 72 per cent knew not a word of the language; of the nearly three thousand books in a PX library only two were German.

Discussing the serious crimes committed by the troops, a paper observed that the Americans as well as the Germans needed some reorientation in their thinking—the Americans with their high rate of crimes of violence, the Germans with their nagging sense of guilt after the malignant Nazi period. The writer recommended more discipline for the GI's, who, it was often re-

[2] *Frankfurter Allgemeine Zeitung*, Dec. 19, 1953.

peated, had too much time and money. And the Germans protested that there was still a double legal standard for them and for the Allies. A frequent complaint had to do with the differences between awards for damages and court sentences given to Germans and to Americans. A German truck-driver had sped past an Army column; he was pursued by an Army officer, and the two had a violent argument. The officer hit the driver with a rifle butt, giving him a double skull fracture and a severe brain concussion. The German recovered consciousness, chased the officer in his turn, and knocked him down with an iron bar. Both men were hospitalized. The American judge fined the German 600 marks because, he said, "no one has the right to take the law into his own hands." The *Hanover Anzeiger* reported that local emotions were aroused because the German had been badly injured, and when he attacked the American he was no longer responsible for his actions. But the paper also pointed out that the officer was to be court-martialed.

Under the headline "What Is a Backbone Worth?" the *Westdeutscher Tageblatt* said an American backbone was worth 90,-000 D marks, a German 5,000. An American had been hit by a German driving a rented car and an American court had awarded him 90,000 D marks in damages. A German who had suffered similar injuries at the hands of an American had been awarded only 5,000 D marks—and furthermore the American driver had been transferred to the United States, so that the injured German had been unable to collect. All he got was 100 D marks plus friendly visits from Americans who called him "Comrade." These were evident signs of 1945 in 1954, the paper concluded.

There were other episodes, minor but irritating from the point of view of the German proprieties. A German girl slapped an American child because, she said, the snowballs he had thrown at the car she was driving had scratched its paint. She was arrested and questioned for eight hours by military police and then fined 200 marks by an American court. Furthermore, the German papers objected to the court's acceptance of the testimony of the thirteen-year-old child against that of responsible adults.

Such events were overbalanced by the running accounts of camaraderie: the many Army-sponsored concerts and dances, the programs of cultural exchange, the gifts—14,000 children in 106 Bavarian orphanages were given presents at Christmas and 4,800 pairs of shoes bought with the money Americans contributed. A German-American soccer team made a trip to Denmark, a German mayor was made honorary colonel of an American regiment, a former German fighter squadron was entertained at an American air base.

The Army was self-critical too. An Army report said that at one meeting in Frankfurt when the Carl Schurz Society celebrated an anniversary, there had not been enough high American officers among the representatives: only one general was present. Some of the post commanders, the report declared, were still fighting the war, and their staffs took their cues from them.[3] In addition the Army attacked anti-German propaganda. As a result of one of the American polls of German opinion, American newspapers ranging from *Stars and Stripes* to *The New York Times* printed articles on the increase in Nazi sentiment. "HICOG Poll Shows Neo Nazism Gaining" was the headline in *Stars and Stripes*. Drew Middleton wrote that the survey showed that a large majority of Germans could not be counted on. The Public Information section of the Army then set out to analyze the questions and the newspapers' conclusions drawn from the answers, and showed how misleading they were. The questions were often ambiguously phrased, the newspapers' interpretation of the statistics overdrawn. *Stars and Stripes* had stated: "HICOG revealed today that neo Nazism had made sweeping across-the-board inroads on West German popular sentiment within the last 18 months." The Army analysts com-

[3] *Report*, Public Information Division, U.S. Army, Jan. 30, 1953.

mented: "A study of the HICOG report failed to reveal these sweeping across-the-board inroads."

The occupation authorities also warned against organizations that a few years before had been welcomed to Germany. The Office of Research and Intelligence of the United States Information Agency pointed out how the World Federation of Trade Unions was attempting to gain converts by disguising its Communist connections. This was the same organization that had been permitted to send a delegation to the American zone in the early days of the occupation to report on German trade unions.

The East German press played on the theme of unemployment in the West, charging that only the agents of the Americans were well off there. One paper concluded that, just as an American official in Berlin in 1945 had stopped the free distribution of food to children, so today there were jobless among the little people in West Berlin and their children were hungry.[4] Radio Sofia announced that Germans had to work eighteen hours a day on American military installations in order to live, that these men were charged high prices for their food and so the Americans keep most of their scanty pay. In addition the Americans maintained twenty-two traveling bordellos.

The West German government charged that there were 200,-000 Germans in the uranium mines in the East zone being used as slave labor, in addition to 50,000 Germans in other forced-labor camps, and that there were still 84,000 to 103,000 prisoners of war who had not been returned from Russia. The Russians replied that they held only 8,500 and, except for those who had committed serious crimes, all would be released. In Lower Saxony alone 750,000 civilians were sent to Russian camps in the last months of the war, the West German government declared; in addition 1,300,000 soldiers had been reported missing, of whom the German authorities believed 10 per cent were still

[4] *Neues Deutschland*, Sept. 8, 1953.

357

alive. In the autumn of 1953, 9,500 German prisoners, military and civilian, were returned by the Russians; in 1954 an additional 1,100; and in 1955, after the resumption of diplomatic relations between the Federal Republic and Russia, 9,600 more were released—the last of the large repatriations.[5] For the unknown number still in Russia there are annual days of remembrance in the Federal Republic: candles burning in the windows of the houses. But these serve only to recall to the West Germans that millions of their countrymen died uselessly in Russia, and to hold out the hope that from among the relatively few still there a lost one may yet return. Stalin and other Soviet leaders categorically denied that any but a few thousand "war criminals" were being held, although Stalin said it was easy to understand why people wished to think men recorded as missing were still alive. German officials cited testimony of returned prisoners as well as letters coming from Russia to support their argument that large numbers remained in captivity. Sixteen thousand prisoners, they said in 1957, had written to their families. The Western Allies repeated the German charges, the Russians their denials, but there seems little doubt, given the unreliability of Soviet statistics, that the Russians have more prisoners than they admit and little likelihood that many more will return. Russia remains a vast graveyard even for thousands who survived the war.

[5] There are believed to be 180,000 civilian Germans still in the Soviet Union who were deported from German territory between 1944 and 1949. Twelve hundred were repatriated in 1957 and 4,681 in 1958 under a "family reunion" program worked out between the German Red Cross and the Soviet government (*The New York Times*, Feb. 22, 1959).

XVI
THE WAY TO SOVEREIGNTY

In March 1954, more than a year before West Germany, the People's Democratic Republic became sovereign, in solemn meaningless words. It was a device of propaganda. The new state had all the outward signs of an independent democracy, including a constitution and opposition parties and press. It exchanged ambassadors with other countries in the Soviet orbit. But it was free only to do what the Kremlin ordered.

The widely publicized thaw in the East zone drew a sizable migration there from the Federal Republic in 1954; for every three who came to the West, two went to the East.[1] They were about equally divided between those who returned to the East and those who migrated for the first time from West Germany. Life for the refugees who came to the West was hard in its early stages, and for some the future seemed more hopeless than it did in the East. They were put in dreary camps, where they were paid eight cents a day; they were "processed" to determine their true sentiments; and although the prosperous economy in the West made it possible for the able-bodied to get jobs in industry, this was not always what a migrating farmer, for example, wanted. To be "recognized," the refugee had to prove that his life was in danger or his job was threatened; otherwise the Western authorities preferred to have the East-zoners remain home in their discontent until the time would come for unification. The West German government and the opposition too believed that the Federal Republic must be an asylum for the politically

[1] *The New York Times*, Jan. 1, 1955.

359

persecuted, but there is a limit to a nation's capacity to absorb a larger population.

The East zone, too, because it was primarily a producing area for the Soviet Union, could hold out large inducements to scientists and technicians, who often got far higher wages there than in the West. The East German government declared, furthermore, that the bad old days were gone; it made promises of reform that many chose to believe and others hoped might be true. The zone built up its military formations by means of a complicated pattern of armed forces designed to avoid concentrating too much fire power in any one of them. The Society for Sport and Technics trained some 200,000; in the "battle groups" of the party a similar number were recruited as a form of territorial militia attached to the factories where they worked. The police were divided into border police, transport police (the equivalent of motorized infantry), and barracks police, equipped with tanks, artillery, some planes, and small naval units. About 30 per cent of the officers of the barracks police had been officers in the Wehrmacht.[2]

The United States continued to be caught on the fork of its policies in the Far East. Secretary Dulles repeatedly in 1953 and 1954 accused the Chinese Communists of supplying arms to the insurgent Vietminh forces, and the United States poured in financial aid and military supplies as well as advisers to aid the French; but it did not send American soldiers or planes to stop the Communist attack. As the situation deteriorated it became clear that more help was needed, but America would intervene directly only if Britain joined forces, and no one in London any more than in Washington wanted to run the risk of a world war for the sake of keeping the French in Indochina. What the United States offered was all aid short of war; what it wanted

[2] A lightly armed barracks-police force of 30,000 men had been authorized for the West zone by the foreign ministers' conference of September 1950. In October 1950 a force of 10,000 was approved by the federal government and the *Länder*. In March 1951 the government authorized 10,000 additional border police (*Deutschland Heute*, pp. 125–6).

was that the French should grant independence to the states of Indochina, Vietnam, Cambodia, and Laos—without delivering them to the Communists. The Kremlin sought to use the war-weariness of the French and the West's general lack of enthusiasm for the war as a makeweight against EDC as well as a means toward considerable gains of prestige and territory: the recognition of Red China by the governments of the West, the skillful identification of communism with native independence movements and with the mounting tide of nationalism among the colonial peoples.[3]

While the East and West, including a 200-man delegation from Communist China as well as representatives from North and South Korea, Vietnam, and the Communist Vietminh, met in Geneva in May 1954 to discuss a possible basis for peace, Vietminh troops captured Dien Bien Phu. The cease-fire arranged in July was based on a grant of complete independence to Vietnam, Cambodia, and Laos. The division of the country at the 17th parallel added 60,000 square miles and 12,000,000 people to the Communist orbit. The agreement was signed by eight powers, not including the United States, which had attempted to play down the serious nature of the conference by sending a representative of less than ministerial rank, Under Secretary of State Walter Bedell Smith, to Geneva. After the French protested, Mr. Dulles appeared toward the close of the discussions, and the United States associated itself with the agreements by saying it would regard any further aggression "with grave concern."[4] It was a scarcely disguised defeat for the West; despite Vietnam's agreement to remain within the French union and France's retention of minor rights in Laos, it meant the virtual liquidation of French influence after years of fighting and confident statements by Western spokesmen.

With the war in Indochina and disturbances in North Africa, the French had demanded that flexible arrangements be made

[3] *American Foreign Policy*, pp. 87–8, 2387, 2391–5.
[4] Ibid., pp. 750–88.

for their troops in NATO and EDC. They wanted the right to withdraw their forces from the European Army at any time, as well as international controls over the future use of German troops—controls that would be guaranteed by the United States and Britain. The delay of German rearming seemed interminable to the Americans; the NATO decision of 1950 to include German troops in the common defense was still unfulfilled in 1954. In March, Ambassador Conant promised on behalf of his government full sovereignty for West Germany with or without participation in the European Defense Community; in July, British and American staffs began work on a treaty with a sovereign Federal Republic, and the United States Senate voted unanimously to permit President Eisenhower to act during the recess of Congress.

Mendès-France, harried by the United States and the furies of domestic politics, promised that he would bring EDC to a vote by the end of the summer; when he did on August 30 it was defeated. Almost everything the French had demanded had been granted: the British were willing to join in bilateral arrangements to buttress the security system, the United States had promised to keep its forces in Europe, there was to be no German general staff or separate German army. The Adenauer government was ready to come to an agreement on the Saar. Nevertheless, the measure was voted down.

A wave of dismay and indignation arose throughout the West. Anthony Eden made a hurried trip to the capitals of Western Europe; he obtained the agreement of the Benelux powers and of Italy to rearm Germany by way of NATO and by widening the Brussels Pact of 1948 to include Italy and Germany; he consulted with Adenauer, who accepted the plan; and as he went to Paris for talks with Mendès-France, Secretary Dulles announced that he would fly to Bonn and London but not to Paris.[5] It was a calculated detour—"a brutal affront,"[6]

[5] *The New York Times,* Sept. 16, 1954.
[6] Ibid., Sept. 19, 1954.

one writer called it—and it made clear to everyone that the years of indecision had taken their toll of the store of good will for France, that the "agonizing reappraisal" had begun. In London, Eden and Dulles announced in a joint statement that Germany would be rearmed on a basis of full equality. There was no mention of France. The communiqué said: "They agreed upon the need for speedy action and favored the early convening of a preparatory conference to consider how best to associate the German Federal Republic with the Western nations on a basis of full equality." [7] Adenauer refused to attend the Strasbourg meeting of the Council of Europe, where Mendès-France explained why France had defeated EDC, which had gone too fast and too far in the plans for a supranational authority and, above all, had been defective in not including the British. He now proposed that Germany be admitted to NATO, but that an extended Brussels agreement and a dispersed armament be the chief instruments of control over the German troops.[8]

The French, despite their key position for the defense of Europe, were again left without many choices. Quarters hitherto hostile to German rearming now favored it; the British Labour party voted for it, although by a small margin of 250,000 votes out of 6,000,000 cast. The joint Anglo-American communiqué isolated France, and she could not turn East for support. Molotov had made a new proposal in Berlin before the Geneva meeting. He suggested that Germany be unified by combining the West- and East-zone parliaments, that the United Germany have merely police formations in the place of an army, and again that the Allies withdraw their troops except for token forces until a peace treaty was made. A plebiscite would be held in which the Germans would vote for EDC or for neutrality and, assuming a decision for neutrality, a zone of neutral states would be formed of which Germany would be a part. Molotov also proposed that NATO be replaced by a gen-

[7] Ibid., Sept. 18, 1954.
[8] Ibid., Sept. 21, 1954.

eral security treaty open only to European nations. France could scarcely find her cherished security in measures that unified Germany, neutral or not, and outlawed American troops from the Continent. Mendès-France, however, could gain more than a compromise from the West. On the main points—restrictions on the German army and a Saar agreement—he was completely successful. Adenauer shocked many of his own coalition, especially those in the Free Democratic party, by agreeing that the Saar should be autonomous. There was to be a plebiscite, and before it was held the parties within the Saar, including those in opposition, would be free to campaign. Adenauer promised to support autonomy, and to this pledge he remained loyal. When the time came for the plebiscite in October 1955 he urged the Saarlanders to vote for the agreement, as did the French; but autonomy was nevertheless voted down—367,000 votes going to the pro-German parties, 162,300 to the pro-European parties—by a population able to express its views in freedom for the first time since the end of the war. Adenauer's concession had seemed to many Germans in late 1954 a foolish betrayal of German rights for the sake of an unpopular rearmament and another German sacrifice for a Pan-Europe that, so far as it existed, was being made out of German, not French, concessions.[9]

The British gave the specific guarantees the French demanded. They promised to keep at least four divisions and an air force on the Continent; Dulles gave constitutional reasons why he could not make the same guarantees, but said he had no doubt that the President and Congress would continue their policy of maintaining troops on the Continent, including Germany, and he would ask President Eisenhower to reiterate American assurances on the matter. Chancellor Adenauer renounced on behalf of Germany any right to the manufacture of atomic, chemical, or biological implements of war or long-range or guided missiles. The Brussels powers would appoint an agency

[9] Interview, Prince Hubertus Löwenstein.

to determine the size of the German army and to supervise its armament. Thus the way was prepared for Germany and Italy to become members of the Brussels Pact and of NATO.

This time the approval of the French National Assembly was obtained in October, although by a small majority. The vote to restore German sovereignty was 287 in favor and 256 against; for rearming Germany, 287 in favor and 260 against. The British and the Americans declared themselves disappointed by the margin of victory, but after four years twelve German divisions were now authorized, as well as a tactical air force of 1,300 front-line planes. On the other side of the world there were to be Japanese soldiers, and the SEATO alliance of Australia, France, Britain, the United States, New Zealand, Thailand, Pakistan, and the Philippines to guard the uneasy peace. The Japanese, too, were reluctant to rearm; they required much the same persuasion that was being used on the Germans, and the United States voiced similar complaints against their slowness to realize their danger and to put men back in uniform.

A large number of Germans continued to oppose a German army. One American observer said 70 per cent of the Germans were against rearming.[1] A German poll in December 1954 showed that some 45 per cent of the population favored it, 35 per cent were opposed, 20 per cent were undecided; resistance remained especially strong in the generation that would be expected to serve.[2] Two former German chancellors came out against rearming: Heinrich Bruening, who had returned to Germany after spending the war and postwar years in the United States, and Hans Luther. Both favored neutralism. There were large antimilitarist demonstrations in German cities, and the vote for Adenauer's party in the September elections dropped in Schleswig-Holstein, where foreign policy was one of the main issues in the campaign, from 636,510 to 384,870; in North-Rhein–Westphalia it fell from 3,915,000 to 2,856,000.

[1] *The New York Times,* Dec. 9, 13, 1954.
[2] *Jahrbuch,* Institut für Demoskopie.

The years of peace had not been many; the comforting new goods, the houses, radios, television sets, motor bicycles, and automobiles were becoming plentiful in West Germany; and it was hard to think of leaving a well-paid job for the very symbol of what the young men had been told had brought disaster to their country. Besides, there was serious doubt that in the age of the hydrogen bomb, jet planes, and missiles, German contingents could make much difference one way or the other. NATO had 46 divisions, including the Greeks and the Turks. Against them were ranged some 230 Russian and satellite divisions; [3] this was a matter for the superpowers, not the small nations of Europe.

The Americans could explain that the explosive chambers put in the bridges were for certain tactical contingencies only, but many Germans remained unconvinced that the strategy of the Allies would call for an all-out effort east of the Elbe. The opposition was not a matter of party allegiance; the Free Democratic party, which had been part of the Adenauer coalition, joined forces with the SPD in opposing the Saar agreement; many conservatives favored discussions with the Russians. And the Russians, reviving their slogans of 1943, when they had organized Paulus and the other captured officers in the Free Germany Committee, welcomed these Right-wing expressions of patriotic German sentiment. Like the French, the West Germans had little choice; rearmament had to be accepted, in view of the European situation, but they adopted it with not much more enthusiasm than the French felt for German divisions.

The German liking for the Americans became more evident in the news and in the polls, which bore out the stories of the strengthening relationship between the troops and the German people. In 1953, 36 per cent of the Germans interviewed thought their relations with the Americans had improved, and in 1954 this figure rose to 57 per cent. German confidence in the fighting qualities of the American soldier went up. Although many Ger-

[3] *The New York Times*, Jan. 2, 1955.

mans continued to believe that the Russian soldier was the best in the world next to the German, the number choosing the American increased from 12 per cent in 1952 to 24 per cent in 1954. In 1952 only 27 per cent thought the United States would do well in a war with Russia; this figure rose to 38 per cent in 1953 and 41 per cent in 1954.[4]

As in previous years, the attitude of the press toward the Americans was ambivalent.[5] When an American officer refrained from digging in the tailpiece of his antiaircraft gun in order to avoid damage to crops, the fact was reported in the newspapers, which also printed a photograph of American tanks going through a cornfield to get around a stalled truck.

In one of the largest American repair depots in Europe— B. M. W. Allach near Munich, employing 4,600 men—forty German workers were dismissed without explanation; the Army announced only that they had not satisfied security requirements. The German press, Right and Left, exploded with headlines as the Americans had tried to teach them to do: "McCarthy's Shadow over Bavaria," "The Cold War at B. M. W. Allach," "McCarthy Rules in Munich," "Blind Fury of the U.S. Army," "Acts of Fascist Despotism." One of the men had worked at the plant for thirty years; some had been in concentration camps; whatever the merits of the charges or of the men's work, they were given no hearing and no advance notice. Army officials merely said they would do their best to find them other jobs. The forty men could be discharged in this summary fashion only under the occupation statutes, not under German law, a German official pointed out. Some of them were offered a settlement of 9,000 D marks by the Army, but this the Germans felt was not enough; a matter of principle was involved. The chairman of the Metal Industrial Trade Union, to which the men belonged, flew to the United States to mobilize help; and the German papers told how the owners of the plant had re-

[4] *Trends in West German Appraisal of the U.S. Forces in Germany.*
[5] *Report,* Community Relations Branch, U.S. Army, 1954.

ceived neither rent nor compensation from the United States
for damages when part of the factory was dismantled. The losses
were estimated at 170,000,000 D marks. Before the men were
dismissed, a mystifying notice had been posted on the bulletin
board. It said: "It has come to the knowledge of the United
States management of the factory that German personnel have
acted according to directives and regulations which were rescinded. Anyone who continues to work according to these ob-
solete regulations will be released immediately without notice."
Of the forty, eleven declared that they were members of the
SPD and three were former Communists. But the chairman of
the union brought with him to the United States critical reports
of some of the leading American personnel in the factory. One
such said that a secretary who was an "agent" of the East-zone
radio station at Leipzig had been given a responsible job in the
plant. The Army explained that the dismissals implied no
defamation of character, and the German papers disagreed.
One pointed out how unlikely it was that a similar event could
happen in France or Italy, and said the Americans in Germany
were still acting like colonial masters among natives. Another
paper cited the swimming pool and bowling alleys in the plant,
which were open only to the Americans; it recalled that the
German owners had won their case in The Hague when they
had sued for the return of the factory, but that the Americans
had nevertheless remained in possession of it. Finally the Army
announced that it would in any event soon be giving up the
factory and the workers would meanwhile be released and
compensated in accordance with Bavarian labor regulations.

German newspapermen visited jet air bases, where they were
shown the latest equipment; in the Russian zone, they pointed
out, any mention in a newspaper of a Russian plane might mean
a prison sentence. German reporters were impressed by the in-
formal and friendly relationship between American officers and
enlisted men, far more human and personal, they thought, than

had been characteristic of the German Army. The German Navy League was host at a beer party for the crews of American destroyers that had docked at Bremen; the destroyers were open to visitors, and 120 orphaned children were given $200 worth of toys by the seamen. An American patrol boat on the Rhine took children for an excursion; the Frankfurt junior Girl Scouts, the Brownies, were hostesses for their opposite numbers, the Eichkätzchen, or Squirrels; an American Army sergeant invited a handicapped Afrika Korps veteran and his family to be his guests during a reunion of the corps at Heidelberg. As further evidence of amity, railroad tracks were laid by American engineers which would be turned over to the German railroad system.

Longer articles appeared in the German press on such subjects as the danger of the American complex. A writer pointed out that the Germans loved Coca-Cola, nylons, chewing gum, but were nevertheless critical of the United States for having them. The imports of *Unkultur*—comics and jitterbugging— were both resented and adopted; along with jazz and Negro spirituals, of which the writer approved, there were Wild West and gangster movies, an old target of German criticism. Let the German compare his own literature, the writer added, full of empty phrases and provincialism, with the vitality and sensitivity of the American writers. The United States was large and many-sided, and criticism, while it is good, must be based on something substantial. The Germans should not be both attracted and irritated by the mills of mass production.[6] Another writer, referring to the "Ami [Americans] go home" propaganda of the Communists, asked: "Who would defend us if the Americans did go home?" "The adversaries of the United States believe," he wrote, "that it wants to use Europe as a bridgehead, but even England's role has shrunk to that of a connecting link

[6] Karl Korn: *"Über die Gefahr der Amerika Komplexe," Europa und Amerika,* Jan. 5, 1954.

between Europe and the United States. The French too are wrong who would like to escape from the bonds that unite them to West Germany." [7]

A number of neo-Nazi publications appeared in Germany in 1954; some of them had been started earlier, and one, *Der Weg*, was published in Buenos Aires. One or two of these magazines, like the splinter parties, were believed to be financed from Eastern sources to kindle the flame of anti-Americanism; but some were anti-Communist. One, *Nation Europa*, published in its July 1954 number an article by Sir Oswald Mosley on the question of a disarmament treaty with Russia; Mosley thought an agreement for partial disarmament might be worked out. The *Adler Führer* carried an account of the last hours of the battle-ship *Scharnhorst* and printed a reminder not to forget the prisoners of war. The *Wiking Ruf*, a paper of former SS men, ran pictures on its cover of the Waffen SS in battle; it asked for contributions to aid one or another of the black-shirted warriors who were seeking clemency or defending themselves before Allied courts, but it was critical in a gingerly fashion of the late Third Reich. It printed a page for men trying to get in touch with missing friends or relatives, and a slogan, "We Buy from Our Comrades." On the whole, these magazines were far from alarming. They were unimpassioned and uninspired as a group, the kind of publication that a fraternal order might publish, of small circulation and tepid interest. Some of them were merely mimeographed.

By the end of 1954, 47,000 dwellings were still requisitioned by the Americans, although 31,000 had been built for the occupation troops and their families since 1950. [8] A new regulation was the cause of a mixed reception in the German press. Officers down to detachment commanders were authorized to permit the "former owners of appropriated gardens to harvest the fruit that had once belonged to them." "We realize," said the

[7] *Deutsche Zeitung*, Jan. 30, 1954.
[8] *General Anzeiger*, Dec. 30, 1954.

Frankfurter Neue Presse, "that people who planted the trees will feel somewhat bitter about being guests in their own gardens. Yet we ask them to remember that this is a good deal better than being excluded from them, and it won't be long now before this situation is changed for the better." [9]

German-American advisory councils were established to keep relations between the German population and the Army as convivial as possible. The councils were likely to include the burgomaster and his second in command, the local fire chief, and on the American side the commanding officer and the public-information officer. In addition, subcommittees dealt with questions of cultural relations, arrangements for Germans wanting to visit Army installations, or calling for the help of American troops when an engineering unit was needed for leveling ground or otherwise using their bulldozers and earth-shaking equipment.

Some of the German complaints about American behavior were merely political. A candidate for office might know that what he was demanding of the Americans on behalf of his constituents made little sense, but there was no harm in criticizing the occupiers for their disregard of German rights. The Army and the local officials had a constant running battle on the question of firing-sites, which the Army had to have and which the officials knew it needed. But the selection of the time and place for these maneuvers was an open one, and every local inhabitant was likely to be proud of the burgomaster who stood up for the rights of the population against military authority.

The Germans turned eagerly to the United States for industrial examples. Paraphrasing Goethe's "America, you have it better," a correspondent wrote: "America, you have it faster," and showed how Germany still was undeveloped in its consumption of nonalcoholic drinks, television, freezers, and children's clothing, and in self-service; it said firms were considering start-

[9] *Frankfurter Neue Presse,* Aug. 13, 1954.

ing branches in the United States to study American production methods. The writer believed that the Old Continent defended itself too belligerently against American commercialism; it could still hope to keep its separate European stamp, he thought, and at the same time promote the well-being of the masses.[1]

Meanwhile the cold war was highlighted in 1954 by the case of Otto John. Head of the Office for the Defense of the Constitution, a counterespionage arm of the government, John disappeared into the East sector of Berlin in July. Conjectures that he had been abducted were shaken when John held a press conference in East Berlin and said he had quit because of the reappearance of Nazis in the West German government and the threat to peace that they and German rearmament signified. John's brother had been killed by the Nazis in the July 20 attempt on Hitler's life; John himself had escaped to Spain and then to England, returning to Germany after the war. It had been English insistence and influence that had placed John in his job, the German papers reported, and many Germans said they had been doubtful of the appointment from the beginning, on grounds not of loyalty but of his psychological fitness. John, who had apparently gone to the East zone on an impulse, with no well-defined plan, returned to West Germany in December 1955 to stand trial for his defection and was sentenced to two years' imprisonment. The case was of no great moment except to point up the ramshackle nature of part of the new German administrative structure. Thirty-five per cent of the West German Foreign Office, it was charged, was composed of former Nazis, and there was reason enough for a man who had risked his life fighting the party to object that they were reappearing in undue numbers and in too important positions in German life. But John was most useful not to the democratic sections of German public life but to the Communists. In his news conferences he told of the alliance of the Nazis and the American imperialists, and how the Americans were planning a preventive

[1] Jurgen Ekt, in *Frankfurter Allgemeine Zeitung*.

war, something he said he had been told about by a highly placed American official. Thus the John case was another weapon the Russians used skillfully against German rearmament.

The number of refugees from the East temporarily diminished, as did the letters people had been writing from the East zone to radio station RIAS attacking the government and measures of the Communists. The letters came now at the rate of 2,000 a month, far fewer than in former years. For the devoted party worker, life in the East zone might be better than it had been under Hitler. The apartments in the Stalin Allee were for the orthodox middle ranks, and for them the rents were low and wages adequate; a couple with a child might earn 1,000 marks a month and pay only 80 marks a month rent, and their child be cared for in a co-operative kindergarten. In Berlin, where the HO stores were in direct competition with the free-enterprise shops across the border, goods were plentiful by comparison with the East zone and prices only a little higher than in the West, despite the fact that one West mark was now worth six East marks. A good meal cost 7 marks in an HO restaurant in East Berlin, a briefcase cost 77 D marks, an overcoat 107 D marks, a suit 140 D marks, a knockwurst 70 pfennigs. A taxi-driver, however, or an ordinary worker still barely kept alive on his earnings. And the apartments of the Stalin Allee were a thin wedge up and down the avenue; behind them were the battered dwelling-places of the ordinary East Berliners.

While the index of West German production reached 170 per cent of 1936 in the last quarter of 1954, in West Berlin it was only 50 per cent. White-collar employment was especially hard to find, and labor could be had at 15 per cent under the going rate of the West zone because, in part, of the pressure of those living "black." Owing to the various make-work measures, unemployment was down to 176,000 from the 1953 figure of more than 200,000. A problem peculiar to Berlin arose from refugees who came from the east part of the city to the West.

They, too, were Berliners and it was not easy to ship them to Schleswig-Holstein or other parts of Western Germany if they wanted to stay in the West sectors.

The textbooks used in the schools of the sovereign People's Democratic Republic were the same as those in the other iron-curtain countries; the United States was depicted even for small children as the imperialist warmonger. The Asians fought for their independence against its machinations; the Korean and Vietminh people had driven the American "mercenaries" and "colonial oppressors" from their countries; Korea was freed in 1945 by the Russian Army; and the treaty which was made then was broken by the United States in 1950 in its effort to reach the Chinese border. The lot of the South Korean people had worsened under American domination: 40 per cent of the land lay unused, and unemployment was greater than it had been under the Japanese. The destruction of Berlin was the work of the British and Americans. The West divided Berlin in 1948 and the democratic sector became the center of the battle for peace, democracy, and socialism. The United States from the beginning of the occupation had always prepared for war, and the four-power agreement to govern Berlin as a unit was honored only by the Soviet government. The Americans had wanted to rebuild the German war factories; they sent in troops and set up a capitalist regime for the purpose of supplying mercenaries for the American cause. In the Russian zone, with the help of the Soviet Union and German workers, there had been peaceful rebuilding, and miners flocked to Aue, the center of the uranium works, from all parts of the People's Republic. The Marshall Plan countries were undergoing crises; the United States was forcing them to buy weapons and through NATO preparing the plunder of the Soviet and Chinese people and the other people's democracies. The watchfulness of the workers had prevented American spies and agents from making colonies out of middle and southeastern Europe; the Russian-German pact of

1939 had been an attempt on the part of Stalin to preserve the peace, and Hitler had broken it.

The ABC's and elementary grammar were used to indoctrinate the very young children; nouns and punctuation had political uses. When the feminine form of a noun which ends in *in* was taught, an example was given: *"Traktorin,"* the female driver of a tractor, and the pupil was asked: "What does your Mommy work at?" The use of the colon was learned with the example: "Our activist leader says: 'We'll certainly do it!' " [2] Teachers were expected to follow current affairs, to know the party line, and to explain events by its exegesis. Russia in the East German storybooks had discovered Antarctica, and yet the United States, Britain, and Argentina did not permit her to share in its development.[3] No detail escaped the work of these historians. Kant, for example, was born and spent all his life in Königsberg, but nowhere in the account of his life and work in the schoolbooks was there any mention of the city, since it had been renamed Kaliningrad and was part of the Soviet Union. A reader included one poem from Schiller and five from the politically more agreeable Johannes Becher, nineteen lines from Martin Luther and two and a half pages in praise of the "theologian of the Revolution," Thomas Münzer. Goethe was given thirteen pages, Pushkin sixty-three.[4]

Grimm's fairy tales were rewritten.[5] In one story the children of a hard-working collective farmer were kidnapped by the wife of a West German capitalist, given to her husband, and sent to work at forced labor in his factory. They managed to escape and there was a thrilling chase to the East-zone border, where they were rescued in the nick of time by the People's Police.

The blue-shirted FDJ, Free German Youth, like the Hitler

[2] *Unsere Muttersprache. Arbeitstoffe für den Deutschen Unterricht, 3 Schuljahr.*
[3] *Amerika und die Polargebiete. Lehrheft der Erdkunde, 7 Schuljahr.*
[4] *Neue Zeitung,* Aug. 10, 1954.
[5] *The New York Times,* Jan. 16, 1955.

Youth and all the organizations for extracurricular instruction of young people in the Communist countries, was a widespread and powerful group to which the boys and girls of East Germany between the ages of fourteen and twenty-six belonged. Membership in it was essential for admission to a university or technical school. Constant efforts were made to stir and foster the Communist ardor of the membership. There were meetings of self-criticism and mutual criticism, meetings for discussion and for planning spectacular events such as the youth rallies. The FDJ was the propaganda seedbed of the future Communist; from it the boy or girl, if zealous and well indoctrinated, would graduate into the ranks of the party. Meanwhile the FDJ took over direction of the free hours of its members and the activities that in other societies centered around the school, the home, the church, or the gang. It went further, for it was organized not only to provide young people with orthodox political leadership in their thinking and discussions but also to give them an opportunity to learn from one another the meaning of historical and contemporary events as well as their duties and responsibilities, through mutual criticism and through their own desire to master the Communist mysteries. They were taught to want to be activists, to want to improve their marks and attendance in school, to help the boy or girl who needed outside assistance with studies, to bring the new religion of Soviet man to their homes. Like the children of all totalitarian states, they were expected to be constantly vigilant against the enemy, and if this meant informing on their parents or others from whom in Western societies they might have been expected to learn, then it was their duty to inform.[6]

Interviews with the boys and girls who visited West Berlin at the time of the rallies, as well as evidence from refugees, indicated that the FDJ was far from successful with most of the young people in the East zone. The uprising of June 17 showed

[6] Jay H. Cerf: "Blue Shirts and Red Banners," dissertation, Yale University, 1957.

376

the readiness with which members of the organization took off their uniforms and made common cause with the revolt. They had learned to get along with the regime. They went through the motions, but they did not believe. Sometimes in exaggerated deference university students bowed before the statue of Stalin or cheered the mention of his name so loudly and long that a speaker was unable to continue. In one case defectors to the West included almost the whole graduating class of a medical school; the young men for years had outwardly conformed to the organizational discipline, but when they were told they would be sent to some desolate place for their interning they simply moved to the West.

The Free German Youth movement, like many other Communist activities, should in theory be far more successful than it actually is. It attempts to change young people not from above but from within; they are expected not only to learn what is right for them to do but also to want to do it, to devise ways of their own to improve their socialist conduct. Ranged against this, as in all the satellite and occupied countries, are the forces of tradition and, above all, the knowledge that the Free German Youth is the tool of a foreign power. The families, the old mores, and the influence of the churches pull strongly in the other direction. The young people cannot stay out of the movement or they will get no advanced schooling or good job, so they have learned to go along with it as one of the burdens an adult world has imposed upon them, and they turn it to their purposes as far as they can. There are, of course, convinced Communists among them; not all the Free German Youth joined the demonstrators on the 17th of June; some of them graduate to the People's Police and the ranks of the party. But the majority are no more devoted to its purposes than are their elders to those of communism itself.

The East Berliner had only to take a walk to discover that things in the West were different from what he was told. The United States gave $762,000,000 to West Berlin between the beginning of the blockade and 1956, 200,000 new jobs were created, more than a billion marks of long-term credit was granted. In the new library, built at a cost of over a million dollars as a gift from the United States, there were 110,000 volumes. This total compared unfavorably, to be sure, with the more than a million in the East Berlin Staatsbibliotek, but the books in the Staatsbibliotek were mainly those from former collections, not gifts of the Russians. The first building of the Free University was dedicated in June 1954; a third of the students studying there came from the East zone and were completely dependent on scholarships or were otherwise earning their way. East-zone education was almost wholly free because of the state scholarships; its class distinctions were rigidly in favor of the proletarian and of those who qualified for admission to the higher learning from a political point of view. In the West zone, where some 900,000 children graduated from schools or left them, scarcely one fifth continued their education after the age of fourteen. Despite efforts of the government and private industry, it was difficult for boys and girls to find jobs: in 1954 one quarter of the unemployed in West Germany were under twenty-five, and in Schleswig-Holstein there were eight or ten boys for every apprenticeship that was open. The role of the East was important in keeping before the consciousness of government and industry the need for wide-scale efforts to find a place for these young people in the society. On the other side the real and imaginary competition of the West incited the party to ever greater demands for sacrifice and accomplishment in the field of science, in the work brigades, in the willingness to forgo the luxuries of consumer goods for the heavy weapons and industry required for the defense of the revolution. Whatever the East needed to believe about the West could be readily invented; no acts of grace or charity or humanity could exist in the party concepts; every move of the West was shown to be the convulsion and threat of a dying system.

The war had left deep scars in the West German demographic

structure. One million two hundred and fifty thousand children were fatherless and 250,000 more were without both parents; children formed more than half the population of the refugee camps. The illegitimacy rate had risen sharply, as had the divorce rate; between the ages of thirty and forty there were 133 women to 100 men; 10 per cent of the population was over sixty-five, as opposed to 5 per cent before World War I. In East Germany, as will be seen, the changes were even more important.

That the sovereignty, rearming, and rehabilitation of West Germany came about as rapidly as they did was a result of the challenge of the East. Germans in 1954, urging clemency for war criminals still in prison, asked the United States authorities to take account of the charges made by the Chinese Communists that Americans had bombed open villages and waged germ warfare. It was not that the Germans believed these charges of germ warfare allegedly confessed by American prisoners or equated them with the atrocities of the Nazis, but they served as a reminder that it is difficult to believe that justice is administered in the courts of the enemy.

West Germany was among the countries that the Americans believed could be counted on as against the 900,000,000 people and one third of the earth's surface controlled by the Communists. Italy and France were riddled with Communist sympathizers; in each country the Communists formed the largest political party and counted an imposing list of intellectuals and leaders in the economic, political, and even military establishments. West Germany was solidly anti-Communist; neutralist sentiment was a revulsion from the past as well as a dream and a hope. Very little of it came from pro-Communist sources. On the Continent it was mainly to Germany that the Americans felt they could turn for the carrying out of the policy of containment or of roll-back if there should be one. Thus, when a spokesman for the French Foreign Ministry declared at a peace conference in early March 1955 that the British and Americans would no longer back the French claim to the Saar, this was promptly denied by Chancellor Adenauer and there was the silence of consent in London and Washington.[7]

Again there was a hitch when the time came for the official deposit of documents that ratified the granting of sovereignty to West Germany. The French cabinet showed signs of hesitation, and Mr. Conant and Chancellor Adenauer unexpectedly exchanged their documents on April 21, 1955, without the presence of the British and French ambassadors. The sudden Russian readiness to negotiate a treaty of peace with Austria may have hastened the American decision to act, but in any event the Americans were no longer in a mood to accept French procrastination gracefully. France at the last had suggested merely ending the occupation statutes and entering into a new contractual agreement, but the British and Americans would have none of this, nor would the Germans.

Provisions in the documents took account of the practical situation; one had to do with Berlin and the special rights of the Allies in the city which could not be a part of the West German republic. Another reserved to the Allies the right to negotiate with Russia on behalf of German unity and to maintain troops in Germany. Aside from these points and the renunciation of certain weapons, including warships of more than 3,000 tons, submarines of more than 300 tons, and long-range bombers, the West Germans were again free to pursue their own destinies, as free as any other European country.

On the morning of May 5, 1955, the high commissioners formally gave up their duties; at noon, in a small room where Chancellor Adenauer had to elbow his way past the newspapermen to get to the conference table, the Federal Republic became an independent and sovereign power. At three o'clock in the garden of the chancellery the West German flag was raised, during a drizzle. The only ambassador missing was Conant,

[7] *The New York Times*, March 6, 1955.

whose appointment in his new capacity had not yet been confirmed by the Senate.

There were no celebrations—only part of the country was free. People went about their business as on other days; the change made not the slightest difference in the life of the ordinary German, so imperceptibly had the occupation faded away. West Germany was formally welcomed into NATO as the fifteenth power on May 9. Speeches were made by the dignitaries praising the statesmanship and good Europeanism of Chancellor Adenauer. The foreign ministers of the NATO powers wore blue ties with white compasses; the Chancellor of Germany put his on before the German flag was raised to join the others and the band played *"Deutschland, Deutschland, über Alles"* and the *"Marseillaise."*

XVII

A BEGINNING

WEST GERMANY built in many styles on its ruins. In the first stage a roof was put over a ground floor, a theater or a "hotel" was made of an air-raid shelter. Many of the later structures look like American apartment houses and office buildings; others are solid mixtures of concrete and glass or cinderblock, functional, durable, and unimaginative. The cities are hybrid. The Hoch-häuser—the semi-skyscrapers—are likely to stand in no sensible relationship to the architecture around them. Where there were so many wide fields of blasted stone, new buildings sprouted one at a time, or rose in apartment blocks that imposed a sensible order on a small area. These structures often conflicted sharply with the architecture of the old city. In almost all the cities the rubble has left its marks—in West Berlin, for example, where much of it has been moved and planted to form artificial parks and hills.

It was a prosperous Germany that became sovereign. The United States had poured into it more than $4,000,000,000 in aid, in the form of gifts or loans, and the effects had been prodigious, equaled in no other European country, although Germany got a relatively small proportion of Marshall Plan aid. Europe received in all $20,000,000,000 from the United States; in 1954 the figures per capita had amounted to $29 for Germany as against $72 for France, $77 for England, $33 for Italy, and $104 for Austria. But in Germany the help came at precisely the right time, when the accumulated pressures for both physical and psychological reconstruction had reached a bursting-point. The recovery had been intensified too by the continued immigration of the East Germans, who came to the West with the drive and urgency of the uprooted to find a new habitation, who had to make good or be nothing again, for whom work was a boon in which they could lose themselves, shutting out the past and keeping warm and nourished with the present.

The prosperity continued, the rate of improvement leveled off, but year after year there were more goods to consume, there was money with which to buy them. One test of the new German democracy would come if the boom collapsed or even receded sharply. The number of able-bodied workers had not risen a third as much as had those dependent on their efforts. The surge of enterprise which brought Germany its remarkable improvement in the standard of living made the way of a liberal, democratic economy an easy one for the working population to accept and cherish. West Germany lost through strikes from 1949 to 1954 an average of only 103 man hours per thousand employed; this compared with an average between 1952 and 1954 of 151 for the United Kingdom, 1,244 for France, and 1,515 for the United States. The German worker clung to his job: it was the one thing that was sure to make sense.

Such was the bounty of the recovery that from 1954 on some two million Germans a year could travel to Italy, and there were countless excursions of factory workers and other groups traveling through Germany and neighboring countries on trips that had once been possible only for the well-to-do. The Nazis started this movement in their "Strength through Joy" campaigns, but it has continued in the republic on a greater scale.

The philosophy of the free market was developed further by the CDU coalition than by the dominant political parties of any other country. Americans had long preached the crusade against monopoly and extolled the virtues of free enterprise, but the German economic leadership gave these economics a metaphysical form. The minister of economics, Ludwig Erhard, in

1954 attacked cartels, declaring that after fifty years Europe's production, involved as it had been with vertical and horizontal combinations of industries, was still only one third that of the United States and there had been no development of small- and medium-size industry comparable to that in the United States with its antitrust laws. And he added that the new capitalist could not be merely an entrepreneur in search of profits; in a modern society, with the demands made upon it for widespread forms of social security, he had a grave responsibility to the community. Capitalists had been devoted worshippers of free enterprise in the easy bounty of a sellers' market. They had also called loudly for government aid, however, in the form of subsidies and tariffs; when economic developments turned against them they had fixed prices and demanded privileges that were incompatible with their fair-weather creeds. The policy of the federal government was to interfere as little as possible in the mechanisms of the market, but to see to it that the crises of unemployment, the overconcentration of economic power, the interferences devised by business itself with operations of the market were controlled.[1] It was this philosophy of the need for more than practical goals and acts which lay behind the German agreement with men such as Schuman, who were attempting to widen the areas of European collaboration.

The efforts to reduce European tariffs, the Economic Payments Union, the development of the idea of the common market in the European Economic Community, the European Monetary Agreement, the French-German agreements to pool their resources in the development of European and African industry—these were the product of powerful forces in Germany and France and throughout Western Europe. People now recognized that new ways would have to be found not only to deal with the Communist threat outside their borders but also with the anarchy and disintegration within Europe itself. These efforts were not confined to economic measures. Although the

[1] Ludwig Erhard, *Frankfurter Allgemeine*, July 24, 1954.

French had feared Germany's industrial competition almost as much as its rearmament, Schuman and others who wanted German forces as part of a European army thought it best that German industry should be revived in a European context. The settlement of the Saar dispute was an example of this kind of thinking. It came about as a result of profound political changes; yet it was also a decision of reasonable men determined to resolve controversies that were being blown up far beyond their worth to either country alone. The Saar has gone back to Germany, but both France and Germany share in the production of its industries; it has become a place where the two countries meet and collaborate, instead of a cause of endless friction.

More than ever before, the French and the Germans attempted to develop means and methods of mutual comprehension. From the beginning of the occupation the French, despite the arrogant airs of conquerors who had been placed in power by the arms of others, had developed the idea of meetings between small groups from the two countries. Every Frenchman believed that Germany had much to learn from France, and some thought both countries had a good deal to learn from each other. In the first three years of the occupation there were gatherings of German and French youth, and, while it was not until 1948 that the French permitted Germans to travel to France, there were many later meetings of people with special interests in common—of teachers and religious groups. French families, like the Americans, took German children into their homes for holidays and sent their children to Germany, and French theatrical companies appeared before enthusiastic German audiences. In 1957 it was even possible to place French troops under the command of a German general.

A new concept of Europe could grow out of this French-German collaboration; every country has been made aware of what Western Europe, despite its profound historic differences, holds in common. Somewhat awkwardly expressed, a sign in German at the Strasbourg bridge connecting France and Germany read in the mid-1950's: "You are leaving Europe; you remain in Europe." The economic order was changing, blurring old linguistic and ethnic borders; goods and people could move across them with greater freedom. As the curtain closed in the East there was all the more need for common markets, and the intricate measures of mutual defense. It became possible to foresee an end to the mutual destruction, the causes of which were part of the political structure and thinking of other centuries. The murder of an archduke, a Hohenzollern on a foreign throne, one flag or another flying over a splinter of border territory would not be the grave threats to national security in the mid-twentieth century. A common danger made Europe aware of its common heritage; the industries of war and peace made their alliances over the ancient borders. General de Gaulle and Chancellor Adenauer met in the summer of 1958 only to reaffirm the policies of collaboration; there is no place under the long shadow of Russia, in the glare of mid-century science and technology, for any other long-range policy.

With one third of the population under twenty and 10 per cent over sixty-five, the German army threatened to be a serious drain on the already limited supply of able-bodied and productive workers. But the Germans were more concerned with the kind of army they were going to have than with its economic effects. The idea of an army of civilians like the Swiss or American was attractive to a population that would have preferred to be without armed forces of any kind; plans for placing the army under the control of parliament and a civilian minister were approved unanimously in the press, although there were some who thought the amenities were going beyond the nonmilitarist aims when it was rumored that the young soldiers were to serve a nine-hour day and need not salute their officers or wear uniforms when off duty. The look of the old army would be missing: the military haircut was abolished; the uniform was slate gray, noninflammable, proof against infrared rays, and resistant to radiation; helmets resembled those of the Americans; jackboots were replaced by rubber-soled shoes such as the GI wore. Only the East zone kept the helmet and cut of the uniform of the Reich. In the West the recruits were to be served their meals by waitresses without having to wait in line for their food as they did in the democratic army of their American tutors.

Above all, the iron discipline and the military priesthood that placed the deeds and spirit of the army beyond the government or understanding of the civilian were to be done away with. About the old Army there was a good deal of myth which the government was intent on demolishing. The Army had served the Weimar Republic with a lukewarm loyalty; although the General Staff and officer corps had declared that politics was not their business, they had failed to serve the state of President Ebert with the devotion and ardor they had given the Emperor who had preceded him. The Army had had to make political decisions: whether to oppose the Kapp *Putsch*, the SA formations, and Hitler himself, both in 1923 when troops fired on his beer-hall rising and later when they were serving under him. Hitler had always been suspicious of the generals, and with good reason. Most of them disliked and mistrusted him. As early as 1938 the Chief of Staff, General Beck, who had opposed the march into Austria, and his successor, General Halder, with other officers, had planned to arrest Hitler if he attacked Czechoslovakia, for they were convinced that there was no possibility of fighting successfully against the coalition of France, Russia, Czechoslovakia, and Britain. The Munich agreement had saved Hitler. But, despite widespread repugnance, the Army had sworn an oath of allegiance to Hitler; and while many of the officers were ready to break it, many of perhaps equal character, such as Guderian, had refused. In the thirties the Army had seen two generals murdered, and its commander in chief, Werner von Fritsch, falsely accused of homosexuality by the Gestapo; it had permitted the swastika to be made part of the uniform in 1934; it had stood by while Jewish war veterans were humiliated and Jewish officers forced to resign. Hitler had taken over the Army and its officer corps, which had no interest, as it thought, in nonmilitary decisions. Its nonpolitical generals found themselves in the midst of party broils. They were replaced by men who were more pliant politically; Keitel and Jodl were devout Nazis, as was Admiral Doenitz, or they would scarcely have held jobs that kept them in such close contact with the Führer.

Thus, the Bonn government had not inherited from the recent tradition armed forces free of control by the political arm or aloof from its purposes. Hitler, the Secret Police, and the measures of National Socialism had ruled them despite organized resistance in counterintelligence—the Abwehr—headed by Admiral Canaris. The Waffen SS had been an elite corps with its own uniform, and in the regular Army no general or marshal or soldier of any rank was safe from a decision that in the light of his political convictions he was unfit to serve.

Kommiss, the harsh discipline administered by the noncommissioned officers with their high-pitched commands, was a drillsergeant technique practiced for its own sake, different only in intensity and thoroughness from what is practiced on recruits in all armies. It was designed to re-educate them, to turn them into the precision instruments of evenly spaced marching lines, to make them respond unquestioningly to orders, to break them away from civilian habits and remold them as dependable moving parts of the military machine that began with them and ended with the General Staff. *Kommiss* had not been unsuccessful. The German Army had been a model of discipline and fighting qualities. But the Bonn government was ready to trade some of that efficiency for an army of civilians.

There were many evidences of the past in the Law for the German Army which was introduced in the Bundestag in the summer of 1955, and in its later administration. The Minister of Defense, Theodor Blank, was an anti-Nazi trade-union official, a former carpenter who during the war had been a lieutenant in an armored unit and had been captured by the Russians. Officers, the law stated, were to be chosen without regard to birth, religion, or social standing. An order was to be disobeyed if it would lead to the commission of a crime, but if the soldier obeyed without knowing his act was unlawful he was to be adjudged innocent. The army was to uphold the "free democratic order as laid down in the Basic Law." It was to be an army that would have the confidence of the entire people, recognizing the value of personal freedom, and unreservedly devoted to the democratic system. No one was to be accepted for service who was antidemocratic. Former officers who had been forced to resign by the Nazis were to be reinstated in the grade they would have held. A civilian committee of anti-Nazis, including lawyers and members of other professions, would examine all officer candidates for the rank of colonel and up. No one who had been a colonel or general in the Waffen SS was eligible to serve, and anyone who had been an SS officer under the rank of colonel could be commissioned only after investigation had proved that he was now anti-Nazi. Former members of the Security Service of the Reich had to have special approval, as did any former member of the Committee for a Free Germany. The professional soldier was to respect the political and religious convictions of others and therefore—according to a directive of October 14, 1955, of the Personnel Committee—"the decisions of conscience of the men of July 20, 1944." The soldier, Herr Blank said, must not be regarded as a necessary evil . . . isolated from the community. . . . The German soldier "had done his duty bravely, loyally, and obediently. He believed himself to be doing it for his Fatherland. He was misused by a criminal State leadership. There lies his tragedy." [2]

A committee from the Bundestag that included former General Hasso von Manteuffel, now a Free Democratic deputy, journeyed to England and the United States in late 1955. They reported their admiration for the British system of parliamentary control of the Army, the trust between the British Army and its

[2] *Keesing's Contemporary Archives*, X (1955–6), 14567.

civilian superiors; and Manteuffel urged too that the generals be subject to call for questioning before parliamentary committees as they were in the United States.

The Bundeswehr, unlike the Army of the Weimar Republic, would be created by parliament and placed under the control of a cabinet committee. There could be no question of which power was dominant or which one would wield authority over the other. There was opposition to a military academy where officers would be separately trained. Critics objected that this kept the officers out of touch with the common soldier. And German authorities insisted that without mutual trust the army was as separated from the country as when it had been exalted —when the officers, as one CDU deputy said, had been decorated like Christmas trees. An army apart incurred the same danger as in South American countries where the colonels and the generals plotted to make a government more congenial to themselves.

One hundred seventy-two thousand men volunteered for the army by September 1955, 140,000 of whom had served in the war as commissioned or noncommissioned officers. In November the first selections were made, including 2 generals and 100 other officers; [3] in January 1956 the first of the 6,000 volunteers entered the barracks to be trained as instructors for the later draft army. They had the status of civil servants.

Parliament voted conscription in July 1956, but for a service of only one year. As a result the army had to slice away all military trimmings from its training. The troops no longer are taught the traditional close-order drill or the manual of arms. Only one specially trained company knows how to present arms and go through the smart paces that have delighted the hearts of so many generations of shining brass and appalled so many recruits. This company of grenadiers has added the drill to its training procedures; the others have no time for it, although half

[3] Norbert Tönnies: *Der Weg zu den Waffen*, p. 182. *Keesing's Contemporary Archives*, X, 14569.

the army of seven to nine divisions is made up of volunteers. The soldiers are trained to work in small units, as self-sufficient groups of technicians scattered in a countryside where nuclear weapons are at work. Forming part of an international army, they are given instruction in the tact and deportment demanded by relations with the troops and civilians of other nations. The uniform has become somewhat altered in the course of the years; an unlaced combat boot was again adopted in 1957 after many experiments with other footgear; and permission to wear the medals of the Empire and the Third Reich was given, but no swastikas may be attached. In 1956 the air force decided to use the same iron cross on the wings and fuselage which had marked German planes in two wars.

No soldier may serve more than twelve years, a rule designed to give him an opportunity while he is still young to learn a civilian occupation. This, it is always emphasized, is an army of civilians with the rights and privileges of the civilian—a soldier may complain to his superiors—even to the Minister of Defense, who must hear his case—against anything he regards as mistreatment. Commissioned and noncommissioned officers come up through the ranks, where as officer candidates they take the same training as the other soldiers. The officers and men of every unit elect representatives whose job it is to foster comradely relations.

These are significant changes originating in a changed society and related to radically new weapons and strategies. In the time of the hydrogen bomb any army is more than ever part, as a German historian has pointed out,[4] of a complex of industry and scientific research. It is no longer the sole center of a country's defense; it remains an important component in it, but when the laboratories have succeeded in producing one bomb that carries the power of all the explosives used in World War II, the army or air force in a great war becomes little more than the main vehicle of attack or defense. The German army is not likely to be a threat to the democratic state. The soldiers

[4] Walter Görlitz, *Der Monat*, Aug. 1955.

are taught to work in partnership with the civil population out of which they come and to which they return. They are taught this because the societies that produced the officer corps of the old Army as well as the Nazi savages are gone.

The democracy of West Germany is young, but it is successful—enormously successful from the economic point of view, less so from the political. It has produced the satisfactions of a going economy; what is lacking are the sentiments and fervors of the heroic and communal symbols that were so powerful and so debased in Hitler's Germany. Also lacking is a clear way of dealing with the recent past, to get the smell of the gas ovens out of the air.

With the abandonment of Allied vetoes over German appointments there was an increase in the seepage of the old bureaucracy and former party members back to positions of prominence and authority in the republic. Men who had served in the courts of the Reich as judges and state's attorneys even in the Sondergerichte—the special courts where political prisoners were summarily dealt with—turned up in high judicial posts appointed by the governments of the *Länder* or by the Federal Republic. Thus, while there was no neo-Nazism of any consequence in the Bundesrepublik, nevertheless a large proportion of the bureaucracy, the foreign office, and the legal system had served the Hitler state as they were now serving the democracy. In addition, seemingly respectable burghers were sometimes uncovered as former Nazi executioners. In 1958 there were front-page stories in the German newspapers on the trials in Ulm of ten former SS men who had killed some five thousand Jews in the extermination camps and had been discovered and brought to trial only because one of their number had applied for a pension. Another case that made headlines was that of a former prison doctor who, according to witnesses, had experimented on prisoners and killed hundreds of them. He had been quietly living and practicing medicine in Bavaria after having been sentenced to death and then to life imprisonment by an American court. American authorities had later reduced the sentence to seven years, the doctor had been released, and a German court had denazified him on the ground that he had shown signs of a spiritual change and had served a prison term that had satisfied the Allies. Subsequently he was granted 3,000 D marks restitution as "a late homecomer"—one of those in need of financial aid after having come from internment or prison. The new evidence, which was denied by the doctor and his witnesses, led to his flight to Egypt, from which the federal government asked his extradition. In addition to such sporadic cases there were bizarre decisions by German authorities—for example, one that granted the widow of the former chief of the Security Service the full pension of the relict of a man who had been killed in action. In addition she was awarded some $3,000 in back payments for the years when she had received no pension.

One of the judges of the high court of a *Land* had also served as a member of one of the special tribunals under Hitler. Another recent appointee had been a Nazi prosecutor who had opposed the mercy plea of a forced laborer, an illiterate Ukrainian sentenced to death because he had got into an argument with his Bavarian master: the farmer and the Ukrainian had exchanged blows, and the Ukrainian, when the seventeen-year-old daughter of the family wanted to join the fight, had threatened her with a pitchfork. The insult to German womanhood, the prosecutor had thought, deserved the most severe punishment, although the man had done the girl no violence. The Ukrainian had been executed, and now one of his persecutors sat among those administering justice in the republic.

None of these events occurred without a storm of protest in the press. The newspapers denounced the judges, dug into their past, printed heated and documented articles on each case as it was disclosed. The paradox remained, however, and the state and federal governments had no ready solution for it. In October 1958 the eleven *Länder* (in the Federal Republic they, not the central government, administer the criminal law) established a nation-wide agency to investigate and prosecute crimes committed during the Nazi period if the perpetrator had escaped punishment. But the former Nazi officials for the most part remained in their offices. The fact was that the country had belonged once to the party; the denazification process, with its hopeless attempt to judge the cases of millions, had let too many of the big ones off while penalizing the small fry. Like the Nuremberg trials, this process, instead of mobilizing public opinion, had discredited all such attempts to bring the guilty to justice. Letters, anonymous and signed, to the men who wrote the newspaper articles divided sharply into praise and blame for the attacks on the former Nazis.

One of the reasons for the appointment of former Nazis to the judiciary was that the large majority of the judges and state's attorneys in the Third Reich had been party members. The alternative for most of them had been giving up their jobs and their pensions, and, as in the case of the university professors, there had been few heroes among them. They had preferred to stay in their well-paid posts; some of them had salved their consciences by attempting to continue to do their legal duty as fairly as they could; others had merely adopted the views of the party. Like many Germans, they had served the time and the authority, and they asked for nothing more than to be given their old jobs, or better ones if possible, when the penalizing restrictions of the early occupation were removed. The governments could proceed much more easily against those who had committed crimes than against those who had allowed them to be committed while doing their legal duty.

The Hitler state thus remains more than an evil memory; but far more important is the other totalitarian regime to the East. The Germans both East and West have fewer illusions about the Communist state than any other people in Western Europe. Still, observers have thought the time might come when it would be politically expedient and possible to attempt to make an agreement with the Russians, to negotiate on the return of the East zone and perhaps of the states beyond the Oder-Neisse. The Russians have high cards; they alone can restore German unity and the lost provinces without war. Any such negotiations, however, would take place in a far wider context than that of Russian and German relations. Neutralism, a zone disinfected of atomic weapons, for Germany as well as those other border states, Poland and Czechoslovakia, would be possible only as an expression of a balance of forces between East and West. This is the century of continental power, not of the wars of fragmented European states.

A German threat to peace could conceivably come from an uprising like that of June 17 with the East Germans calling to the West for aid as they did then. But in a world that has seen planes of the Russians and the Americans shot down with no more than protests, that has seen contained wars in Korea and Indochina, it is difficult to forecast a major conflict arising out of an incident unless Washington or Moscow wants it.

There are many people in Germany who would like to negotiate with the Russians, however doubtful they may be of the outcome. Conservatives are among them; there are Catholics and Social Democrats, businessmen and members of Adenauer's cabinet. The incentives are strong: aversion to war; the knowledge that the Russians could, if they wished, give and take concessions from which both countries might profit; the desire to be free of any foreign tutelage; internal political currents that might well carry the SPD into office if it was the only party favoring negotiation. There are powerful forces behind the desire to sit down at a table and discuss, and the Russians are aware of them. Sometime they will want to turn them to account.

But the Germans cannot act without the approval of the West. It is their alliance with the West which gives them a bargaining position. The strategic situation is in no way that of the time when Hitler and Stalin made their pact. The Russian demand that West Berlin be made a free city can only be resisted by the West; the Bundesrepublik is bound as few nations have been, by its own sentiments as well as the limitations of its strength, to the decisions of its NATO partners. In the autumn of 1958 the rising military power of the Bundesrepublik was no doubt a factor in the increasing intransigence of the Russians in demanding recognition of the sovereignty of East Germany and attempting to force the Allies to withdraw their troops from Berlin. But German leaders could only participate in the discussions on their former capital, they could not lead them.

Furthermore, the men of West Germany have had a disastrous experience with the *Realpolitik* of Hitler, which left Germany desolate and a pariah among nations. It was not the minor wars of elections which gave Schumacher and Adenauer their detestation of the jackboots trampling down Europe, of the bestialities inflicted upon the individual and public life under Hitler and the Soviets. The new German leaders are not men who operate under the pure forms of *Staatsräson*. It may be argued that their successors will be of a different kind, but there is no official in the Bundesrepublik or among the responsible leaders of the intellectual life of the new Germany who has not had to concern himself with the terrible events of the recent past and the reasons for them. What happened to Germany in the twenty-three years between Hitler's coming to power and the restoration of the sovereignty of the Federal Republic may have provided the ingredient that so many observers had declared missing in German history: the knowledge, won by individual risk and suffering, of the meaning of freedom and the constant vigilance that is demanded for its preservation. It may be that those twenty-three years during which Germans filled the concentration camps as well as the ranks of the National Socialists—years that witnessed the empty sacrifices of millions of men in the snows of Russia and Norway, in Italy and France and the Balkans and on the deserts of North Africa, the useless heroism of the men of the Navy and the Air Force, the stoicism of the civilian population in its bombed-out cities, the long

starvation of the mind and body, the need for self-inquiry
—did for German thinking something like what the barricades
once did for the French. The bearing of the people of Berlin
and the rising in the East zone are indications that this is no
longer the Germany of "poets and thinkers," or of the mobs
shouting "*Sieg Heil.*"

Germany learned much between 1945 and 1955, and so did
the American occupiers. The thinking of Germans and Americans, as well as their uniforms, came to resemble one another.
The ebb of anti-Germanism among the American occupiers began slowly in high and low places, but eventually it went with
a rush of waters. There was nothing the United States could
refuse her new ally. Beginning with the small acts of individuals even before the end of the war, help came spontaneously
and freely until after a few years it transformed all of Germany
it could reach. The early days of the occupation were not unlike
the Nazi period; the civilized world was "off limits." Germans
were beaten, plundered, imprisoned arbitrarily. Had it not been
for the Russians and the lost love affair, the change in American
policy would certainly have taken longer, but it would have
come, because the Americans ultimately demanded nothing of
Germany but to join the good life of the West and to recite the
same political beatitudes. Yet in a tortured time no country,
as the Germans kept telling one another, could have given more
than the United States gave to Germany.

From the East the procession of refugees picked up again
after sovereignty: 252,000 came to the West in 1955, 279,000 in
1956, 261,000 in 1957, and from January to December 1958 over
200,000. The scars of Communist rule were deep; the population of the zone declined in precisely the most economically
productive age groups. The statistical annual of the People's
Democratic Republic reported that 115,000 of those fleeing the
zone in 1956 were in the age group from 25 to 45. Although
stiff penalties for aiding the escape of refugees were imposed,
the attrition continued in 1957, when at least 100,000 more

between these ages left East Germany. From August 1950 through 1957 this section of the population in the People's Democratic Republic dropped 900,000; among the refugees were more than 20,000 of the People's Police.

As a result of the migrations it was difficult, despite coercion and rewards, to fill the ranks of the armed forces in East Germany.[5] The army of the People's Democratic Republic, established in 1956 and headed by former Wehrmacht generals, was integrated with the forces of the Warsaw Pact. A German general sits in Moscow with the combined staffs, and Russian advisers are assigned to the East German army. It numbers some 110,000 men; in addition there are roughly 75,000 People's Police, 100,000 members of the workers' fighting groups, and 65,000 security troops. The Russian advisers give not orders but advice: the suggestions of friends, they say; in the satellite countries it is customary to follow these suggestions. With those of the East European countries the East German contingents make up 120 divisions. But the usefulness of the Hungarian, Polish, Rumanian, and East German forces is extremely problematical.

In 1956 the Hungarian army turned its guns against the Russians. And the continuing flood of East Germans moving to the West indicates that nothing has changed in the potential of German resistance since the rising of 1953. In the Marxist lexicon everyone is subject to call to defend the workers' state, which alone fights the just war; any war against it is illegal. Thus, the North Koreans fought a just war and the defense of South Korea was unjust, as was the defense of Finland against Russia in 1939. Such Marxist fantasies no longer are convincing to anyone but a fanatical core of true believers which is thinning away to cynical placemen who would change their allegiance

[5] In part because of this deficit in young man power, East Germany, unlike the rest of the satellite states and Russia itself, has no conscription. Instead there is a system of quotas, which are filled by "forced volunteers" —boys recruited from schools and factories by threats of being dismissed or being sent to worse jobs, and actual volunteers from the ranks of the Free German Youth who wish to further the cause of the workers' state.

as readily as their hats. The Communist revolution has failed in Germany as it has in the satellites. University professors are paid more in the East than in the Bundesrepublik; doctors working for the state may receive pensions higher than their wages; but highly placed academicians flee the country, and the proportion of doctors to the population is less than half that of West Germany.[6]

These are the privileged groups; among the rest of the population, to make ends meet everyone has to work. More than 2,600,-000 women were employed in 1956 in the East zone. The ratio of women to men working in East Germany in 1956 was 72 to 100, in the West zone 49 to 100. In East Germany in 1956 there were 146 women to 100 men between the ages of 25 and 45; in the West the proportion was 103 to 100; men constituted only 44.7 per cent of the population. Despite the slogans of equal pay for equal work, women receive lower wages than men. In the people's industries that account for 85 per cent of industrial production, more than 80 per cent of the women are in the lowest wage brackets.

The great majority of those who flee to the West leave because they think they will get a better job with more pay or for other personal reasons. In a West German government survey made in 1957, 72 per cent of those migrating said they came for nonpolitical reasons. Sixty-one per cent said they sympathized with Marxism or were convinced of the truth of its *Weltanschauung*.[7] The head of a university may decide, as one did in the summer of 1958, that he can no longer continue to work under the never-ending ideological bombardment, and, despite his privileged economic and social position, he may flee the

[6] A doctor earning 1,000 East marks a month may receive, after deducting taxes and social security costs, some 747 D marks a month. As a pensioner he may get from 700 to 900 D marks. These proportions of course do not hold for the general population, but only for certain privileged groups: technicians, teachers, artists, musicians, members of the People's Police, and the intelligentsia who have done especially constructive work requiring high qualifications.

[7] *The New York Times*, March 24, 1957.

zone. But the party and the doctrine have made their imprint on most of those who reach the West. They want the freedom and opportunities the free world can offer, but they do not believe in its substance.

The East zone has improved its living standards. In the spring of 1958 food-rationing was stopped and food prices were comparable to those in the West. In industrial production, the East zone ranked as the fifth most important producer in Europe; 90 per cent of its industry was now socialized, and the consumer got a relatively small share of what was manufactured. He still paid almost three times as much for a shirt or for a pair of shoes as he would in the West; a suit cost 210 marks, as compared with 115 D marks in the Bundesrepublik. But rents were lower than in the West, and hours of work went down from 48 to 45 per week; bread was 60 pfennigs, as against 85 pfennigs in the West; potatoes were half the Western price. Milk, however, was twice as much, butter 9.80 a kilo as against 7.16, margarine 3.50 as against 2.05, pork 8.80 compared with 5.50.[8] And the political purges continued to throw the party leaders into prison or the seats of the mighty.

West Germany will build her future policy on the alliance with the West, primarily with the United States and England. It is they who have created the German state; it is they who have set the pattern of a democracy that can provide guns as well as butter, and have helped kindle a different sense of political responsibility throughout the country. But the Germans—the Schumachers, the Adenauers, the Reuters, the Jeanette Wolffs, the Reinhold Maiers, as well as thousands of simple workers, teachers, men and women from all the ruined country—met them with at least as much conviction as the great democracies brought to their task. They worked humbly, often without enough to eat or to keep warm with, but knowing their responsibility as Germans for the monstrous past, whatever their individual roles of resistance may have been. It was this sense

[8] *Spiegel*, May 28, 1958; June 11, 1958.

of the past and of the future which united them in the course of time with the men who had begun the occupation hating all Germans.

The People's Democratic Republic has no attraction for the West Germans. It is a part of Germany in a theoretical sense for most of the inhabitants of the Bundesrepublik. But it is the lost and promised land for those who have emigrated from it and for the federal government, which speaks of unification not only on behalf of Germany but for the Allies too. The slogan of German unity must be used on both sides of the iron curtain. The East zone remains the silent claim of the Soviets on West Germany and by extension on Western Europe; its people are drab and dispirited by comparison with the prosperous Westerners. But as in 1953, while discontented with what they have, they profess no love for the economic or political policies of the Bundesrepublik. While two million people—more than 10 per cent of the East-zone population—have fled there in eight years, and the West is regarded as a refuge, a place of opportunity, it is no more than that. Marxism is a *Weltanschauung,* a pervasive philosophy, for some a religion. Its imprint is not obliterated immediately; it fades slowly even for those who have been glad to depart from its homelands.

There has not been much outstanding creative work in the new Germany, no flowering of the novel, the play, or the fine arts such as followed World War I. The government and private enterprise are both spending large sums on scientific research, and German science is again productive. There are splendid concerts but not much new music, and one of its chief creators, Paul Hindemith, prefers to live in exile, as do many of Germany's writers. The arts are without great vitality. Book-publishing still subsists in its production of creative literature mainly in translations and in reissues of German classics. Postwar poetry has been more original, written with more excitement and assurance, than the novel or the play, but nowhere has the German renaissance in cultural matters paralleled the economic one. The nation of thinkers and poets has taken to the roads in its Volkswagens and Mercedes and motorcycles, and its wild humors can be seen in the highest accident rates of any European country. Here again the Germans have imitated the American soldiers' love of speed, about which there were so many articles in the German papers. Now the Germans complain of their own driving; they compare the politeness of the Americans and especially of the British, the dizzying flair of the French and Italians, with the headlong lack of consideration of German drivers.

There are no towering visions, few glimpses of immortality. It is enough for the Germans that they are alive; and the press of bright new toys around them has turned their brooding from the *Lorelei* and *Götterdämmerung* to the Autobahn and the slot machines, the picture magazines, the American cult of success.

German boys walk in blue jeans with the swagger they have seen in the heroes of the American westerns advancing stiff-legged toward the badmen. German girls have adopted the slacks and pony tails of the American bobby-soxers. The federal government has adopted the pace and goals of the American republic. But this is the surface, the unconscious tribute to the victor and the provider of good things. Underneath is an old culture, the bafflements of a provincial people who have suffered as they caused others to suffer, only to see their chief enemy raised to the status of a superpower and in turn become the chief enemy of the West. As in 1918, the Germans did not free themselves from their bondage; again they had democracy and a constitution thrust upon them after a defeat. The difference between 1918 and 1945 was that now they had to live, not with the myth of an untarnished panache of the Army and unmerited defeat, nor with the hypocrisies of a peace of good will and self-determination for all but Germans, but with the recollection of horrors that had invaded their celebrated virtues: loyalty, obedience, selflessness, courage.

The Germans of course are not alone in their confusion; they prosper in it and try to think of things other than the past, which is still heavy on their consciences although some continually deny that it should be. There is less anti-Semitism in Germany than in many other countries; more knowledge of its consequences, of how easily hate can destroy both the hated and the hater. It is, in fact, the voice of a young Jewish girl who died in a concentration camp which is heard in Germany, on stage and off. The lovely voice of a child recalling to the good and evil among men, as only the child, the artist, and in other centuries the prophet could recall to them, the obligation of their common humanity. Anne Frank had her counterparts in the German resistance; there were thousands who in their fashion spoke or felt as she did and who, like her, died for being what they were. In the survivors and in the millions who became aware of what the Nazis had done the voice of the child re-echoes. Not everyone hears it directly and some remain deaf to what they hear. But it is there for all of them, for the people of good and ill will, for the confident entrepreneurs of business and government, for the workers and housewives, the Bavarians, the Rhinelanders, the Prussians in exile. It can never be silent.

BIBLIOGRAPHY

CHAPTER I

Butcher, Harry C.: *My Three Years with Eisenhower*. New York: Simon and Schuster, 1946.

Byrnes, James F.: *Speaking Frankly*. New York: Harper and Brothers, 1947.

Churchill, Winston S.: *The Second World War*, Vol. III, *The Grand Alliance* (1950). Vol. V, *Closing the Ring* (1951). Boston: Houghton Mifflin Company.

Einsiedel, H. von: *I Joined the Russians*. New Haven: Yale University Press, 1953.

Foreign Relations of the United States. The Conferences at Malta and Yalta. Washington, D.C., 1955.

"Fuehrer Conferences on Matters Dealing with the German Navy." Mimeographed. Office of Naval Intelligence, U.S. Navy Department.

Germany, 1947–1949. The Story in Documents. Washington, D.C., 1950.

Gollwitzer, Helmut, Kaethe Kuhn, and Reinhold Schneider: *Du hast mich heimgesucht bei Nacht. Abschiedsbriefe und Aufzeichnungen des Widerstandes, 1933–45*. Munich: Kaiser Verlag, 1954.

Hammond, Paul Y.: "The Origins of JCS 1067." Typescript, 1958.

Hull, Cordell: *The Memoirs of Cordell Hull*. New York: The Macmillan Company, 1948.

Kleist, Peter: *Zwischen Hitler und Stalin, 1939–1943*. Bonn: Athenäum-Verlag, 1950.

Kuby, Erich, ed.: *Das Ende des Schreckens. Dokumente des Untergangs*. Munich: Süddeutsche Zeitung, 1955.

Leber, Annedore: *Das Gewissen steht auf*. Berlin: Mosaik Verlag, 1954.

Leonhard, Wolfgang: *Die Revolution entlässt ihre Kinder*. Cologne and Berlin: Kiepenheuer and Witsch, 1955.

Meissner, Boris: *Russland, die Westmächte und Deutschland*. Hamburg: H. H. Nölke Verlag, 1954.

Millis, Walter, ed., with E. S. Duffield: *The Forrestal Diaries*. New York: The Viking Press, 1951.

Morgenthau Diaries: U.S. Senate, Judiciary Committee, Hearing before Subcommittee to Investigate Administration of Internal Security Act, 84th Congress, 1st Session, 1955.

Müller, Johannes: *Stürz in den Abgrund*. Bollwerk Verlag, 1947.

The New York Times, Aug. 3, 18, Sept. 23, 1944; Oct. 5, 7, 1945.

BIBLIOGRAPHY

Picker, Henry: *Hitlers Tischgespräche im Führerhauptquartier, 1941–42.* Arr. and ed. Gerhard Ritter. Bonn: Athenäum-Verlag, 1951.

Prescott, Orville, in *The New York Times*, Oct. 5, 1945.

Sherwood, Robert E.: *Roosevelt and Hopkins.* 2 vols. New York: Harper and Brothers, 1948.

Roosevelt, Eleanor: *This I Remember.* New York: Harper and Brothers, 1949.

Sayres, Michael, and Albert E. Kahn: *The Plot against the Peace.* New York: Dial Press, 1945.

Standley, William H., and Arthur A. Ageton: *Admiral Ambassador to Russia.* Chicago: Henry Regnery Co., 1955.

Stars and Stripes, July 11, 1945.

Stimson, Henry L., and McGeorge Bundy: *On Active Service in Peace and War.* New York: Harper and Brothers, 1947.

Wagner, Wolfgang: *Die Entstehung der Oder-Neisse-Linie.* Stuttgart: Brentano-Verlag, 1953.

Welles, Sumner: *An Intelligent American's Guide to the Peace.* New York: Dryden Press, 1945.

——: *The Time for Decision.* New York: Harper and Brothers, 1944.

Zink, Harold: *The United States in Germany, 1944–1955.* Princeton: D. Van Nostrand Company, 1957.

CHAPTER II

Bullitt, William C.: "How We Won the War and Lost the Peace." *Life*, Aug. 30–Sept. 6, 1948.

Butcher, Harry C.: *My Three Years with Eisenhower.* New York: Simon and Schuster, 1946.

Byrnes, James F.: *Speaking Frankly.* New York: Harper and Brothers, 1947.

Churchill, Winston S.: *The Second World War*, Vol. III, *The Grand Alliance* (1950). Vol. IV, *The Hinge of Fate* (1950). Vol. V, *Closing the Ring* (1951). Vol. VI, *Triumph and Tragedy* (1953). Boston: Houghton Mifflin Company.

Dallin, David: *Soviet Espionage.* New Haven: Yale University Press, 1955.

Davies, Joseph E.: *Mission to Moscow.* New York: Simon and Schuster, 1941.

Deane, John R.: *The Strange Alliance.* New York: The Viking Press, 1947.

Eastland Committee, Senate Hearings on Scope of Soviet Activity in the United States, Jan. 3, 1955. Report, Dec. 31, 1957.

Foreign Relations of the United States. The Conferences at Malta and Yalta. Washington, D.C., 1955.

"Fuehrer Conferences on Matters Dealing with the German Navy." Mimeographed. Office of Naval Intelligence, U.S. Navy Department.

Hull, Cordell: *The Memoirs of Cordell Hull.* New York: The Macmillan Company, 1948.

Jenner Committee, Hearings, 1953–1954. Committee on the Judiciary, U.S. Senate, 83rd Congress, 1st Session.

Leahy, William D.: *I Was There*. New York: Whittlesey House, 1956.

Meissner, Boris: *"Der Kreml und das Ruhrgebiet."* Ost Europa, Vol. I, No. 2 (December 1951).

——: *"Stalin und die Oder Neisse Linie."* Ost Europa, Vol. I, No. 1 (October 1951).

Mikolajczyk, Stanislaw: *The Rape of Poland*. New York: Whittlesey House, 1948.

Millis, Walter, ed., with E. S. Duffield: *The Forrestal Diaries*. New York: The Viking Press, 1951.

Morgenthau, Henry, Jr.: *Germany Is Our Problem*. New York: Harper and Brothers, 1945.

The New York Times, May 1, 1942; Nov. 18, 1943; Aug. 24, 1944; Feb. 14, 1945; Mar. 18, Oct. 20, 1955.

Perkins, Frances: *The Roosevelt I Knew*. New York: The Viking Press, 1946.

Roosevelt, Eleanor: *This I Remember*. New York: Harper and Brothers, 1949.

Sherwood, Robert E.: *Roosevelt and Hopkins*. 2 vols. New York: Harper and Brothers, 1948.

Standley, William H., and Arthur A. Ageton: *Admiral Ambassador to Russia*. Chicago: Henry Regnery Co., 1955.

Stettinius, Edward R., Jr.: *Lend Lease, Weapon for Victory*. New York: The Macmillan Company, 1944.

——: *Roosevelt and the Russians. The Yalta Conference*. Ed. Walter Johnson. Garden City, N.Y.: Doubleday and Company, 1949.

Stimson, Henry L., and McGeorge Bundy: *On Active Service in Peace and War*. New York: Harper and Brothers, 1947.

Wagner, Wolfgang: *Die Entstehung der Oder-Neisse-Linie*. Stuttgart: Brentano-Verlag, 1953.

Welles, Sumner: *The Time for Decision*. New York: Harper and Brothers, 1944.

CHAPTER III

Butcher, Harry C.: *My Three Years with Eisenhower*. New York: Simon and Schuster, 1946.

Churchill, Winston S.: *The Second World War*, Vol. VI, *Triumph and Tragedy*. Boston: Houghton Mifflin Company, 1953.

Clay, Lucius D.: *Germany and the Fight for Freedom*. Cambridge: Harvard University Press, 1950.

Deane, John R.: *The Strange Alliance*. New York: The Viking Press, 1947.

A Decade of American Foreign Policy. Basic Documents, 1941–49. Washington, D.C., 1950.

Eastland Committee, Senate Hearings on Scope of Soviet Activity in the United States, May 16, 1956; June 11, 1957.

Eisenhower, Dwight D.: *Crusade in Europe*. Garden City, N.Y.: Doubleday and Company, 1948.

Fischer, George: *Soviet Opposition to Stalin*. Cambridge: Harvard University Press, 1952.

BIBLIOGRAPHY

Foreign Relations of the United States. The Conferences at Malta and Yalta. Washington, D.C., 1955.

Frederiksen, Oliver J.: *The American Military Occupation of Germany, 1945–1953.* U.S. Army, 1953.

Handbook for Military Government in Germany Prior to Defeat or Surrender. U.S. Army, for the Military Government of Germany, December 1944.

"Historical Report on the Operations of the Office of Military Government," Berlin District, July 1, 1945–June 30, 1946. Typescript. Karlsruhe, 1947.

Hurwitz, Harold J.: "Press Reorientation." Historical Division, U.S. Army.

Keesing's Contemporary Archives, Vol. V. London, 1943–6.

Kertesz, Stephen D., ed.: *The Fate of East Central Europe.* South Bend: University of Notre Dame Press, 1956.

Knapper, Marshall: *And Call It Peace.* Chicago: University of Chicago Press, 1947.

Leahy, William D.: *I Was There.* New York: Whittlesey House, 1956.

Millis, Walter, ed., with E. S. Duffield: *The Forrestal Diaries.* New York: The Viking Press, 1951.

Mosely, Philip E.: "Dismemberment of Germany. The Allied Negotiations from Yalta to Potsdam." *Foreign Affairs,* Vol. XXVIII (1949–50).

The New York Times, Oct. 14, 1946.

Sherwood, Robert E.: *Roosevelt and Hopkins.* 2 vols. New York: Harper and Brothers, 1948.

Starr, Joseph R.: *United States Military Government in Germany.* Historical Division, U.S. Army, 1950.

Stars and Stripes, May 19, 20, June 18, July 4, 1945.

Stettinius, Edward R., Jr.: *Roosevelt and the Russians. The Yalta Conference.* Ed. Walter Johnson. Garden City, N.Y.: Doubleday and Company, 1949.

Strölin, Karl: *Stuttgart im Endstadium des Krieges.* Stuttgart: Friedrich Vorwerk, 1950.

The Times Literary Supplement, July 26, 1951.

Truman, Harry S.: *Memoirs.* 2 vols. Garden City, N.Y.: Doubleday and Company, 1955.

USFET (U.S. Forces European Theater): Report of Operations, May 8–Sept. 30, 1945.

Wilmot, Chester: *The Struggle for Europe.* New York: Harper and Brothers, 1952.

Zink, Harold: *American Military Government in Germany.* New York: The Macmillan Company, 1947.

CHAPTER IV

Bazel, Rainer: *Die Deutschen Parteien.* Berlin: Schaffrath-Gelder, n.d.

Bergsträsser, Ludwig: *Geschichte der Politischen Parteien in Deutschland.* Isar Verlag, 1952.

Clay, Lucius D.: *Decision in Germany*. Garden City, N.Y.: Doubleday and Company, 1950.

Dokumente der Neuen Zeit. Pamphlet. Dresden, 1945.

Eisenhower, Dwight D.: *Crusade in Europe*. Garden City, N.Y.: Doubleday and Company, 1948.

"Elections and Political Parties of Germany." Typescript. Historical Division, Office of the U.S. High Commissioner for Germany, June 1, 1952.

Gillen, J. F. J.: *State and Local Government in West Germany, 1945–1953*. Office of the U.S. High Commissioner for Germany, 1953.

Grosser, Alfred: *The Colossus Again*. Trans. Richard Rees. New York: Frederick A. Praeger, 1955.

"Historical Report on the Operations of the Office of Military Government," Berlin District, July 1, 1945–June 30, 1946. Typescript. Office of the Military Governor, Karlsruhe, 1947.

Hurwitz, Harold J.: *"Chronik."* MS. Berlin: Forschungsgruppe für Berliner Nachkriegsgeschichte, n.d.

Leahy, William D.: *I Was There*. New York: Whittlesey House, 1956.

Leonhard, Wolfgang: *Die Revolution entlässt ihre Kinder*. Cologne and Berlin: Kiepenheuer and Witsch, 1955.

Lukas, Richard: *Zehn Jahre Sowjetische Besatzungszone*. Deutscher Fachschriften Verlag, 1955.

Der Neue Weg. Einheitsfront der antifaschistischen Demokratischen Parteien. Pamphlet. Berlin, 1945.

Neue Zeitung, Oct. 18, 25, 28, Nov. 4, 8, 1945.

The New York Times, July 9, Oct. 13, 1945.

Oppen, Beate Ruhm von, ed.: *Germany under Occupation*. London: Oxford University Press, 1955.

Post Hostility Pamphlet, by Men Who Know Germany Today. U.S. Army.

A Program for the Occupation of Germany. U.S. Army, Sept. 15, 1945.

SBZ von 1945 bis 1954. Bonn, 1956.

Stars and Stripes, July 9, 1945.

Tägliche Rundschau, Aug. 2, 3, 8, 14, 16, 18, 21, 23, Sept. 8, 9, 14, Oct. 5, 14, 1945.

Treue, Wolfgang: *Deutsche Partei Programme*. Göttingen: Musterschmidt, 1954.

Truman, Harry S.: *Memoirs*. 2 vols. Garden City, N.Y.: Doubleday and Company, 1955.

"U.S. Group Control Council for Germany." MS. U.S. Army Document Center, Kansas City, Mo.

Zentner, Kurt, ed.: *Aufstieg aus dem Nichts*. 2 vols. Cologne and Berlin: Kiepenheuer and Witsch, 1954.

CHAPTER V

Adler, H. G.: *Theresienstadt, 1941–1945: Das Antlitz eine Zwangsgemeinschaft*. Tübingen: J. C. B. Mohr, 1955.

BIBLIOGRAPHY

Assmann, Kurt: *Der Deutsche U-Bootskrieg und die Nürnberger Rechts-sprechung.* Marine Rundschau, January 1953.

Bardèche, Maurice: *Die Politik der Zerstörung.* Im Plesse Verlag, 1950.

Benton, Wilbourn E., and George Grimm, eds.: *Nuremberg: German Views of the War Trial.* Dallas: Southern Methodist University Press, 1955.

Belgion, Montgomery: *Victor's Justice.* Chicago: Henry Regnery Co., 1949.

Bernstein, Victor H.: *Final Judgment: The Story of Nuremberg.* New York: Boni and Gaer, 1947.

Du Bois, Josiah Ellis: *The Devil's Chemists.* Boston: Beacon Press, 1952.

Boutitie, Roger: *"L'Impossible Justice."* Revue politique et parlementaire, March 1953.

Byrnes, James F.: *Speaking Frankly.* New York: Harper and Brothers, 1947.

Calvocoressi, Peter: *Nuremberg: The Facts, the Law, and the Consequences.* London: Chatto and Windus, 1947.

Dallin, David J.: *Soviet Russia and the Far East.* New Haven: Yale University Press, 1948.

Daniel, J.: *Le Problème du châtiment des crimes de guerre d'après les enseignements de la deuxième guerre mondiale.* Cairo: R. Schindler, 1946.

A Decade of American Foreign Policy. Basic Documents, 1941–49. Washington, D.C., 1950.

Dodd, T. J.: *"The Nuremberg Trials."* Journal of Criminal Law and Criminology, Vol. XXXVII, January 1947.

Donnedieu de Vabres, Henri: *Le Procès de Nuremberg.* Paris: Editions Domat-Montchrestien, 1947.

Ehard, Hans: *"The Nuremberg Trial against the Major War Criminals and International Law."* American Journal of International Law, Vol. XLIII, April 1949.

Fitzgibbon, Constantine: *20 July.* New York: W. W. Norton and Company, 1956.

Foreign Relations of the United States. The Conferences at Malta and Yalta. Washington, D.C., 1955.

Gilbert, G. M.: *Nuremberg Diary.* New York: Farrar, Straus and Young, 1947.

Glueck, Sheldon: *The Nuremberg Trial and Aggressive War.* New York: Alfred A. Knopf, 1946.

——: *War Criminals: Their Prosecution and Punishment.* New York: Alfred A. Knopf, 1944.

Görlitz, Walter: *Der Deutsche Generalstab.* Frankfurt am Main: Verlag der Frankfurter Hefte, 1950.

Grewe, Wilhelm, and O. Kuester: *Nürnberg als Rechtsfrage: Eine Discussion.* Stuttgart: Klett, 1947.

Hankey, M. P. A.: *Politics, Trials, and Errors.* Chicago: Henry Regnery Co., 1950.

Harris, Whitney R.: *Tyranny on Trial: The Evidence at Nuremberg.* Dallas: Southern Methodist University Press, 1954.

BIBLIOGRAPHY

Heinze, Kurt, and Karl Schilling, eds.: *Die Rechtsprechung der Nürnberg Militärtribunale*. Bonn: Girardet, 1952.

History of the United Nations War Crimes Commission, compiled by the United Nations War Crimes Commission. London: H.M. Stationery Office, 1948.

Jackson, Robert H.: *The Nuremberg Case*. New York: Alfred A. Knopf, 1947.

——: "Nürnberg in Retrospect." *Canadian Bar Review*, Vol. XXVII, August–September 1949.

——: *Report*. Department of State Publication 2420. Washington, D.C., 1945. Ibid.: Publication 3080, 1949.

Jaspers, Karl: "The Significance of the Nuremberg Trials for Germany and the World." *Notre Dame Lawyer*, Vol. XXII, January 1947.

Keenen, J. B., and B. F. Brown: *Crimes against International Law*. Washington, D.C.: Public Affairs Press, 1950.

Kelsen, Hans: *Law and Peace in International Relations*. Cambridge: Harvard University Press, 1942.

——: *Peace through Law*. Chapel Hill: University of North Carolina Press, 1944.

Kertesz, Stephen: *The Fate of East Central Europe*. South Bend: Notre Dame University Press, 1957.

Lawrence, Lord Justice (Lord Oaksey): "The Nuremberg Trial." *International Affairs*, Vol. XXIII, April 1947.

Leonhard, Wolfgang: *Die Revolution entlässt ihre Kinder*. Cologne and Berlin: Kiepenheuer and Witsch, 1955.

Lippe, Viktor von der: *Nürnberger Tagebuchnotizen November 1945 bis Oktober 1946*. Frankfurt: Fritz Knapp, 1951.

Maugham, Viscount: *UNO and War Crimes*. London: John Murray, 1951.

Maurach, Reinhart: *Die Kriegsverbrecherprozesse gegen die Gefangene in der Sowjetunion*. Hamburg, 1950.

Nazi Conspiracy and Aggression. 8 vols. Washington, D.C.: Office of the United States Chief of Counsel for Prosecution of Axis Criminality, 1946.

Nelte, Otto: *Das Nuremberger Urteil und die Schuld der Generale*. Pamphlet. Hanover: Verlag Das Andere Deutschland, 1947.

The New York Times, Aug. 9, 1932; Nov. 11, 1945; Mar. 10, July 12, 27, Sept. 28, Oct. 21, 22, Nov. 15, 1946.

Pal, R. P.: *International Military Tribunal for the Far East, Dissenting Judgment*. Calcutta: Sanyal, 1953.

Parker, John J.: "The Nuremberg Trial." *Journal of the American Judicature Society*, Vol. XXX, December 1946.

Picker, Henry: *Hitlers Tischgespräche im Führerhauptquartier, 1941–42*. Arr. and ed. Gerhard Ritter. Bonn: Athenäum-Verlag, 1951.

Pompe, C. A.: *Aggressive War an International Crime*. The Hague: Martinius Nijhoff, 1953.

Punishment for War Crimes. The Interallied Documents Signed at St. James' Palace, London, 13 January 1942, and Relative Documents. London: H.M. Stationery Office, July 1942.

Raeder, Erich: *Mein Leben*. Tübingen: Fritz Schlichtenmayer; 1957.

BIBLIOGRAPHY

Rauschenbach: Gerhard: *Der Nürnberger Prozess gegen die Organisationen.* Bonn: Ludwig Röhrscheid, 1954.
Reitlinger, Gerald: *The Final Solution.* New York: Beechhurst Press, 1953.
Springer, Hildegarde: *Das Schwert auf der Waage, Hans Fritzsche über Nürnberg.* Heidelberg: Vowinckel Verlag, 1953.
Stimson, Henry L.: "The Nuremberg Trial, Landmark in Law." *Foreign Affairs,* Vol. XXV, January 1947.
Taylor, Telford: *Final Report to the Secretary of the Army on the Nuremberg War Crimes Trials under Control Council Law No. 10.* Washington, D.C., 1949.
Trainin, A. N.: *Hitlerite Responsibility under Criminal Law.* Ed. A. Y. Vishinsky, trans. Andrew Rothstein. London: Hutchinson and Co., 1945.
Trial of the Major War Criminals before the International Military Tribunal, Nuremberg, 14 November 1945–10 October, 1946 (official text in the English language). 42 vols. Nuremberg, 1947–9.
Trials of War Criminals before the Nürnberg Military Tribunals under Control Council Law No. 10, October 1946–April 1949. 15 vols. Washington, D.C., 1946–9.
West, Rebecca: *A Train of Powder.* New York: The Viking Press, 1955.
Willkie, Wendell: *One World.* New York: Simon and Schuster, 1943.

CHAPTER VI

Byrnes, James: "Restatement of U.S. Policy in Germany," speech of Sept. 6, 1946, in *Germany, 1947–1949* (see below).
Clark, Delbert, in *The New York Times,* Dec. 16, 1946.
Deutschland Heute. Bonn, 1954.
"D.P.'s, 1946–1947." Karlsruhe: Training Packet No. 54.
Drucksachen des Hessischen Landtags, Dec. 1, 1947—Nov. 30, 1950.
Fischer, George: *Soviet Opposition to Stalin.* Cambridge: Harvard University Press, 1952.
Friedman, W.: *The Allied Military Government of Germany.* London: Stevens and Sons, 1947.
Germany, 1947–1949. The Story in Documents. Washington, D.C., 1950.
Hentig, W. O. von, and Giselher Wirsing: "Beobachtungen in der Amerikanischen Zone. Typescript, November 1945.
Hill, Gladwin, in *The New York Times,* Jan. 3, 1946.
"Historical Report on the Operations of the Office of Military Government, Berlin District, July 1, 1945–June 30, 1946." Typescript. Office of the Military Governor of the U.S. Zone, 1947.
Keesing's Contemporary Archives, Vol. VI. London, 1946–8.
Kormann, John G.: *U.S. Denazification Policy in Germany, 1944–1950.* Office of the U.S. High Commissioner for Germany, 1952.
Leonhard, Wolfgang: *Die Revolution entlässt ihre Kinder.* Cologne and Berlin: Kiepenheuer and Witsch, 1955.
Lukas, Richard, in *Europa-Archiv,* Vol. I (1946).
——: *Zehn Jahre Sowjetische Besatzungszone.* Deutscher Fachschriften Verlag, 1955.

BIBLIOGRAPHY

Lusser, Robert S., ed.: *Soviet Economic Policy in Postwar Germany.* New York: Research Program on the U.S.S.R., 1953.

McCormack, Anne O'Hare, in *The New York Times* Oct. 26, 1946.

Nettl, J. P.: *The Eastern Zone and Soviet Policy in Germany, 1945–1950.* London: Oxford University Press, 1951.

Neues Deutschland, May 21, June 27, Sept. 12, 13, 1946.

The New York Times, Jan. 3, Feb. 4, 21, June 10, 11, 16, July 1, 11, 12, 29, Aug. 19, 29, 31, Sept. 3, Oct. 1, 26, 31, Dec. 1, 16, 17, 19, 20, 27, 1946.

Pilgert, Henry P.: "Development of Information Services." Office of the U.S. High Commissioner for Germany, 1951.

——: "The Exchange of Persons Program." Office of the U.S. High Commissioner for Germany, 1951.

——: "Press, Radio, and Film in West Germany." Office of the U.S. High Commissioner for Germany, 1953.

——: "The West German Educational System." Office of the U.S. High Commissioner for Germany, 1953.

Pollock, J. K., J. II. Meisel, and H. L. Bretton: *Germany under Occupation.* Ann Arbor: George Wahr, 1949.

Report of Oberbürgomeister Dr. Klett, in *Verhandlungen der Vorläufigen Volksvertretung für Württemberg-Baden,* Jan. 30, 1946.

Roosevelt, Elliott: *As He Saw It.* New York: Duell, Sloan, and Pearce, 1946.

Salomon, Ernst von: *Der Fragebogen.* Hamburg: Rowohlt Verlag, 1952.

Schmidt, D. A., in *The New York Times,* Dec. 16, 1946.

Starr, Joseph R.: *United States Military Government in Germany.* Historical Division, U.S. Army, 1950.

Tägliche Rundschau, Feb. 26, Mar. 9, May 4, 13, 17, 22, 26, June 6, Aug. 20, 31, Sept. 18, 1946.

Verhandlungen der Bremischen Bürgerschaft, December 1946.

Verhandlungen des Bayrischen Landtags, Dec. 13, 1949.

Weekly Information Bulletin. Office of the U.S. High Commissioner for Germany, Office of Military Government, U.S. Zone, USFET, 1945.

"Wirtschaftliche Entwicklungen in der Sowjetischen Zone seit Potsdam." *Europa-Archiv,* Vol. I (1946), pp. 292–7.

Zink, Harold: *The United States in Germany, 1944–1955.* Princeton: D. Van Nostrand Company, 1957.

CHAPTER VII

Belgion, Montgomery: *Victor's Justice.* Chicago: Henry Regnery Co., 1949.

Clay, Lucius D.: *Decision in Germany.* Garden City, N.Y.: Doubleday and Company, 1950.

A Decade of American Foreign Policy. Basic Documents, 1941–49. Washington, D.C., 1950.

Drucksachen des Hessischen Landtags, Dec. 1, 1947—Nov. 30, 1950.

Germany, 1947–1949. The Story in Documents. Washington, D.C., 1950.

Gillen, J. F. J.: *State and Local Government in West Germany, 1945–1953.* Office of the U.S. High Commissioner for Germany, 1953.

413

Gimbel, John: "Marburg under Occupation, 1945–52." Typescript.

Hoover, Herbert, in *The New York Times*, Feb. 26, 1947.

Leonhard, Wolfgang: *Die Revolution entlässt ihre Kinder*. Cologne and Berlin: Kiepenheuer and Witsch, 1955.

Lukas, Richard: *Zehn Jahre Sowjetische Besatzungszone*. Deutscher Fachschriften Verlag, 1955.

Meissner, Boris: "*Der Kreml und das Ruhrgebiet*." Ost Europa, Vol. I, No. 2 (December 1951).

——: *Russland, die Westmächte und Deutschland*. Hamburg: H. H. Nölke Verlag, 1954.

——: "*Stalin und die Oder Neisse Linie*." Ost Europa, Vol. I, No. 1 (October 1951).

Der Mittag, Nov. 10, 1947.

Nettl, J. P.: *The Eastern Zone and Soviet Policy in Germany, 1945–1950*. London: Oxford University Press, 1951.

Neue Zeitung, Oct. 3, 1947.

New York *Herald Tribune*, July 7, 1947.

The New York Times, July 8, 1946; Jan. 3, 21, 22, 26, 30, Feb. 20, 21, 25, 26, 28, March 1, 2, 6, 14, 24, 25, April 9, 10, 11, 16, May 6, 9, 17, 28, 30, June 5, 7, 22, July 8, 18, 27, Aug. 22, Sept. 11, 19, Oct. 11, 12, 17, 20, 21, 28, Nov. 2, 13, Dec. 14, 1947; June 14, 1948.

Raymond, Jack, in *The New York Times*, March 6, 1947.

Reports of the Military Governor. Office of the Military Governor of the U.S. Zone, January, February 1945.

Schmidt, H. G.: *Economic Assistance to West Berlin, 1949–1951*. Office of the U.S. High Commissioner for Germany, 1952.

Shub, Boris: *The Choice*. New York: Duell, Sloan, and Pearce, 1950.

Smith, Walter Bedell: *My Three Years in Moscow*. Philadelphia: J. B. Lippincott Company, 1950.

Telegraf, May 6, 1947.

Vernant, J.: *The Refugee in the Postwar World*. New Haven: Yale University Press, 1953.

Washington Post, Sept. 14, 1947.

Zentner, Kurt, ed.: *Aufstieg aus dem Nichts*. 2 vols. Cologne and Berlin: Kiepenheuer and Witsch, 1954.

Zink, Harold: *The United States in Germany, 1944–1955*. Princeton: D. Van Nostrand Company, 1957.

CHAPTER VIII

Balfour, Michael: "The Quadripartite Occupation of Germany, May 1945—December 1946." Mimeographed. Royal Institute of International Affairs, 1954.

Brant, S.: *Der Aufstand . . .* Stuttgart: Steingruben Verlag, 1954.

Clark, Delbert, in *The New York Times*, Jan. 18, 1948.

Clay, Lucius D.: *Decision in Germany*. Garden City, N.Y.: Doubleday and Company, 1950.

——: *Germany and the Fight for Freedom*. Cambridge: Harvard University Press, 1950.

BIBLIOGRAPHY

Davison, W. Phillips: *The Berlin Blockade*. Princeton: Princeton University Press, 1958.

Deutschland Heute. Bonn, 1954.

Gailey, Charles K., in *The New York Times*, April 5, 1948.

Germany 1947–1949. The Story in Documents. Washington, D.C., 1950.

Gorbatov, in *Literary Gazette*, cited by Boris Shub in *The Choice* (see below).

Harmssen, G. W., et al.: *Reparationen, Sozialprodukt, Lebensstandard*. Bremen: Friedrich Trüjen Verlag, 1947, 1948.

Hays, General George P., in *The New York Times*, Jan. 13, 1948.

Lukas, Richard: *Zehn Jahre Sowjetische Besatzungszone*. Deutscher Fachschriften Verlag, 1955.

Meissner, Boris: "*Der Kreml und das Ruhrgebiet*." *Ost Europa*, Vol. I, No. 2 (December 1951).

——: *Russland, die Westmächte und Deutschland*. Hamburg: H. H. Nölke Verlag, 1954.

——: "*Stalin und die Oder Neisse Linie*." *Ost Europa*, Vol. I, No. 1 (October 1951).

Millis, Walter, ed., with E. S. Duffield: *The Forrestal Diaries*. New York: The Viking Press, 1951.

Mosely, Philip E.: "Dismemberment of Germany. The Allied Negotiations from Yalta to Potsdam." *Foreign Affairs*, Vol. XXVIII (1949–50).

——: "The Occupation of Germany," *Foreign Affairs*, Vol. XXVIII (1950).

Neue Zeitung, March 28, April 1, Nov. 27, Dec. 11, 16, 1948.

The New York Times, April 22, Oct. 12, Nov. 2, 1947; Jan. 12, 13, 14, 18, Feb. 3, 8, 12, 15, 28, March 8, 15, 21, April 1, 2, 3, 4, 5, 9, 19, 25, May 24, 30, June 3, 12, 13, 20, Aug. 3, 4, 5, 14, 18, 21, Sept. 8, 10, 12, 14, 16, Oct. 1, 23, Dec. 12, 16, 21, 1948; Jan. 2, 10, Feb. 14, May 18, 1949; Oct. 5, 1952.

Shub, Boris: *The Choice*. New York: Duell, Sloan, and Pearce, 1950.

Silvermaster, N. G., in *The New York Times*, Aug. 5, 1948.

Smith, Fred: "The Rise and Fall of the Morgenthau Plan." *United Nations World*, Vol. II, March 1947.

Smith, Walter Bedell: *My Three Years in Moscow*. Philadelphia: J. B. Lippincott Company, 1950.

Der Spiegel, Oct. 18, 1947; March 27, 1948.

Tägliche Rundschau, March 21, 24, April 1, 18, 19, May 26, June 17, 24, 30, July 8, 10, Nov. 13, Dec. 9, 21, 1948.

Tagesspiegel, Jan. 6, 13, March 21, Aug. 4, 1948.

CHAPTER IX

Bank Deutscher Länder: Reports, 1948–9.

Bennett, Jack: "The German Currency Reform." *Annals of the American Academy of Political and Social Science*, 1950.

Clay, Lucius D.: *Decision in Germany*. Garden City, N.Y.: Doubleday and Company, 1950.

415

BIBLIOGRAPHY

A *Decade of American Foreign Policy. Basic Documents, 1941–1949.*
    Washington, D.C., 1950.
Friedrich, Carl J., in Edward H. Litchfield: *Governing Postwar Germany*
    (see below).
Germany, 1947–1949. The Story in Documents. Washington, D.C., 1950.
Germany Reports. Bonn, 1953.
Gillen, J. F. J.: *Deconcentration and Decartelization.* Office of the U.S.
    High Commissioner for Germany, 1953.
———: *State and Local Government in West Germany, 1945–1953.* Office
    of the U.S. High Commissioner for Germany, 1953.
Golay, John Ford: *The Founding of the Federal Republic of Germany.*
    Chicago: University of Chicago Press, 1958.
Grosser, Alfred: *The Colossus Again.* Trans. Richard Rees. New York:
    Frederick A. Praeger, 1955.
Hammond, Paul Y.: "The Origins of JCS 1067." Typescript, 1958.
Hartrich, Edwin, in New York *Herald Tribune*, June 17, Dec. 21, 1948.
Lee, Guy A.: *Field Organization.* Office of the U.S. High Commissioner
    for Germany, 1952.
Litchfield, Edward H.: *Governing Postwar Germany.* Ithaca: Cornell
    University Press, 1953.
McCloy, John J.: *Quarterly Reports: First, Sept. 21–Dec. 31, 1949;
    Sixth, Jan. 1–March 31, 1951.* Office of the U.S. High Commissioner
    for Germany.
New York *Herald Tribune*, June 17, 1948; Dec. 21, 1948.
The New York Times, June 22, Dec. 21, 1948; Feb. 21, April 27, May 20,
    June 24, Aug. 25, 30, Sept. 11, 13, 16, Oct. 17, 30, Dec. 9, 1949;
    Feb. 16, March 23, May 14, 1950.
Parlamenterischer Rat: Proceedings. Bonn, 1948–9.
Piettre, André: *L'Economie allemande contemporaine, 1945–1952.* Paris:
    Génin, n.d.
Plischke, Elmer: *The Allied High Commissioner for Germany, 1953.*
    Office of the U.S. High Commissioner for Germany, 1953.
Reston, James, in *The New York Times*, May 20, 1949.
Tagesspiegel, July 2, 1948; Feb. 20, 1949.
Verhandlungen des Bayrischen Landtags, Dec. 13, 1949.
Verhandlungen des Deutschen Bundestages, Erste Wahlperiode 1949.
    Bonn, 1950.
Wallich, H. C.: *Mainsprings of the German Revival.* New Haven: Yale
    University Press, 1955.

CHAPTER X

Berliner Zeitung, Nov. 2, 1950.
Cooke, Don, in New York *Herald Tribune*, Dec. 18, 1950.
A *Decade of American Foreign Policy. Basic Documents, 1941–49.* Wash-
    ington, D.C., 1950.
Deutsche Zeitung, Nov. 11, 1950.
Echo der Woche, Dec. 27, 1950.
Einwirkungen der Besatzungsmächte auf die Westdeutsche Wirtschaft.
    Tübingen, May 1949.

BIBLIOGRAPHY

Freie Deutsche Presse, Jan. 27, 1951.
Germany, 1947–1949. The Story in Documents. Washington, D.C., 1950.
Grosser, Alfred: *The Colossus Again.* Trans. Richard Rees. New York: Frederick A. Praeger, 1955.
Harmssen, G. W., *et al.*: *Reparationen, Sozialprodukt, Lebensstandard.* Bremen: Friedrich Trüjen Verlag, 1947, 1948.
Hornstein, Erika von: *Andere Müssen Bleiben.* Cologne and Berlin: Kiepenheuer and Witsch, 1954.
Lukas, Richard: *Zehn Jahre Sowjetische Besatzungszone.* Deutscher Fachschriften Verlag, 1955.
Meissner, Boris: *Russland, die Westmächte und Deutschland.* Hamburg: H. H. Nölke Verlag, 1954.
Nettl, J. P.: *The Eastern Zone and Soviet Policy in Germany, 1945–1950.* London: Oxford University Press, 1951.
Neue Zeitung, Sept. 7, 1949; June 19, Nov. 8, 1950.
The New York Times, Oct. 21, 1948; Nov. 14, Dec. 10, 1949; July 17, Nov. 10, 1950.
Occupation Costs: Are They a Defense Contribution? Tübingen: J.C.B. Mohr, 1951.
Piettre, André: *"L'Economie allemande."* *Revue économique et sociale,* April 1950.
Pilgert, Henry P.: *Press, Radio, and Film in West Germany.* Office of the U.S. High Commissioner for Germany, 1953.
Sechs Jahre Besatzungslasten, 1945–1950. Tübingen: J. C. B. Mohr, 1951.
Slusser, Robert, ed.: *Soviet Economic Policy in Postwar Germany.* New York: Research Program on the U.S.S.R., 1953.
Some German Opinions on Occupation Costs. Office of the Military Governor of the U.S. Zone, Feb. 24, 1949.
Der Spiegel, June 5, 1948.
Stuttgarte Nachrichten, Jan. 19, 1950.
Tägliche Rundschau, Jan. 5, 1951.
Truman, Harry S.: *Memoirs.* 2 vols. Garden City, N.Y.: Doubleday and Company, 1955.
Verhandlungen des Bayrischen Landtags, Feb. 9, 1950.
Die Welt, Oct. 19, 1948.
Westfälische Nachrichten, Oct. 27, Dec. 27, 1950.

CHAPTER XI

American Foreign Policy. Basic Documents, 1950–55. 2 vols. Washington, D.C., 1957.
Brant, S.: *Der Aufstand* . . . Stuttgart: Steingruben Verlag, 1954.
Brauer, Anna E., and Elizabeth Erdman: *The West German Housing Problem, 1945–1953.* Office of the U.S. High Commissioner for Germany, 1953.
A Decade of American Foreign Policy. Basic Documents, 1941–49. Washington, D.C., 1950.
Deutsche Allgemeine Zeitung, April 20, 1950.

BIBLIOGRAPHY

Deutsche Zeitung und Wirtschafts Zeitung, Feb. 10, 1950.

Deutschland Heute. Bonn, 1954.

Ford, Franklin L.: "The Twentieth of July in the History of the German Resistance." *American Historical Review*, July 1946.

"Der Französische Plan zur Verteidigung des Westens." Europa-Archiv, July–December 1950, pp. 3518–20.

Gillen, J. F. J.: *Deconcentration and Decartelization.* Office of the U.S. High Commissioner for Germany, 1953.

——: *Labor Problems in West Germany.* Office of the U.S. High Commissioner for Germany, 1952.

Görlitz, Walter: *Der Deutsche Generalstab, Geschichte und Gestalt,* 1657–1954. Frankfurt: Verlag der Frankfurter Hefte, n.d.

Graml, Hermann: *Die Deutsche Militaer Opposition gegen Hitler,* 1941– 43. Bonn: Beilage zum Parlament aus Politik und Zeitgeschichte.

Jahrbuch der öffentlichen Meinung, 1947–1955, ed. Elisabeth Nölle and Erich Peter Neumann. Allensbach am Bodensee: Verlag für Demoskopie, 1956.

McClaskey, Beryl R.: *The Free German Youth and the Deutschland Treffen.* Office of the U.S. High Commissioner for Germany, 1951.

McCloy, John J.: *Quarterly Reports: First, Sept. 21–Dec. 31, 1949; Fifth, Oct. 1–Dec. 31, 1950; Seventh, April 1–June 30, 1951.* Office of the U.S. High Commissioner for Germany.

Meissner, Boris: *Russland, die Westmächte und Deutschland.* Hamburg: H. H. Nölke Verlag, 1954.

Neue Zeitung, Sept. 5, 1950; April 29, 1952.

The New York Times, Feb. 28, March 5, July 16, Aug. 18, 24, Sept. 2, 3, 9, Oct. 25, Dec. 25, 1950; Jan. 1, 21, 24, 1951.

Pechel, Rudolf: *Deutscher Widerstand.* Zurich: Eugen Rentsch Verlag, 1947.

Plischke, Elmer: *Allied High Commission Relations with the West German Government.* Office of the U.S. Commissioner for Germany, 1952.

Reitlinger, Gerald: *The SS: Alibi of a Nation.* London: William Heinemann, 1956.

Ritter, Gerhard: *Carl Goerdeler und die deutsche Widerstandsbewegung.* Stuttgart: Deutsche Verlags-Anstalt, 1954.

Rothfels, Hans: *The German Opposition to Hitler.* Chicago: Henry Regnery Co., 1948.

Schmidt, Hubert G.: *Economic Assistance to West Berlin.* Office of the U.S. High Commissioner for Germany, 1952.

Schwäbische Landeszeitung, Nov. 22, 1949.

Tägliche Rundschau, Jan. 25, 1950.

Truman, Harry S.: *Memoirs.* 2 vols. Garden City, N.Y.: Doubleday and Company, 1955.

Verhandlungen des Bayrischen Landtags, Nov. 17, 1951.

CHAPTER XII

Boehm, Eric, ed.: *We Survived.* New Haven: Yale University Press, 1949.

Bundestag: Proceedings, 168th Session, Vol. IX.

BIBLIOGRAPHY

Deutschland Heute. Bonn, 1954.

Freie Deutsche Presse, Jan. 27, 1951.

German Opinions on Jewish Restitution and Some Related Issues. Office of the Military Governor of the U.S. Zone, 1951.

Germany Reports. Bonn, 1953.

Litchfield, Edward H.: *Governing Postwar Germany.* Ithaca: Cornell University Press, 1953.

McCloy, John J.: *Quarterly Reports: Sixth, Jan. 1–March 31, 1951; Seventh, April 1–June 30, 1951; Eighth, July 1–Sept. 30, 1951; Tenth, Jan. 1–March 31, 1952.* Office of the U.S. High Commissioner for Germany.

The New York Times, Feb. 23, 25, 1948; March 2, 12, 18, April 14, 21, May 15, 1949; Jan. 10, 13, 14, Feb. 1, April 15, 26, May 9, July 3, Aug. 5, 10, 12, Oct. 28, 1951.

Tägliche Rundschau, Aug. 8, 12, 1951.

CHAPTER XIII

Barendsen, Robert D.: "The Communist Germ Warfare Propaganda Campaign, 1952–1953." Dissertation. Yale University, 1957.

Brauer, Anna E., and Elizabeth Erdman: *The West German Housing Problem, 1945–1953.* Office of the U.S. High Commissioner for Germany, 1953.

Bundesfinanz Ministerium: *Einsparungs Möglichkeiten in Besatzungs Haushalt.* Bonn, 1952.

Christian Science Monitor, May 4, 10, 1952.

Deutschland Heute. Bonn, 1954.

Hard Core Refugees Evaluate Their Situation. Report 136, Office of the U.S. High Commissioner for Germany, 1952.

Keesing's Contemporary Archives, Vol. VIII. London, 1950–1.

Lukas, Richard: *Zehn Jahre Sowjetische Besatzungszone.* Deutscher Fachschriften Verlag, 1955.

Maxi, Unser Neger Büblein. Pamphlet. Munich: Münchencr Studien Rat, 1952.

McCloy, John J.: *Quarterly Reports: Eighth, July 1–Sept. 30, 1951; Tenth, Jan. 1–March 31, 1952.* Office of the U.S. High Commissioner for Germany.

Meissner, Boris: *Russland, die Westmächte und Deutschland.* Hamburg: H. H. Nölke Verlag, 1954.

Neue Zeitung, March 13, June 9, Oct. 2, 1952.

The New York Times, Jan. 27, Feb. 5, April 3, 18, May 4, 27, 31, June 1, 22, Aug. 7, Oct. 3, 6, 9, 10, 14, 24, 1952.

Reports (mimeographed) of the Public Information Division (June–November 1952) and the Public Relations Branch (1952–3) of the U.S. Army.

Süddeutsche Zeitung, April 19, 1952.

Tägliche Rundschau, April 19, May 3, July 11, 19, 1952.

Truman, Harry S.: *Memoirs.* 2 vols. Garden City, N.Y.: Doubleday and Company, 1955.

BIBLIOGRAPHY

CHAPTER XIV

"Der *Aufstand in Juni. Ein dokumentarischer Bericht.*" *Der Monat*, September–October 1953.

Baring, Arnulf: *Der 17 Juni, 1953*. Bonn, 1957.

Brand, H.: "The Uprising of June 17." *Dissent*, Winter 1954.

Brandt, Willy, and Richard Löwenthal: *Ernst Reuter*. Munich: Kindler, 1957.

Brant, S.: *Der Aufstand . . .* Stuttgart: Steingruben Verlag, 1954.

Cornides, Wilhelm, and Helmut Löschhorn, in *Europa-Archiv*, July–December 1953.

Eastland Committee, Senate Hearings on Scope of Soviet Activity in the United States, Jan. 3, 1955. Report, Dec. 31, 1957.

Gohlke, Herbert, and James P. O'Donnell: "I Led a Riot against the Reds." *Saturday Evening Post*, Aug. 22, 1953.

Hildebrandt, Rainer: *The Explosion. The Uprising behind the Iron Curtain.* Trans. G. B. Ashton. New York: Duell, Sloan, and Pearce, 1955.

Keesing's Contemporary Archives, Vol. IX. London, 1952–4.

Lit, Theodore: "The Proletariat against the Dictatorship." *Problems of Communism*, Vol. II (1953).

Lukas, Richard: *Zehn Jahre Sowjetische Besatzungszone.* Deutscher Fachschriften Verlag, 1955.

The New York Times, June 21, 28, July 1, 26, Aug. 9, 1953.

"RIAS Coverage of the East Berlin Crisis." Special report, unpublished. Office of the U.S. High Commissioner for Germany, 1953.

Sherman, George: "St. Anthony's Papers on Soviet Affairs: East Germany. The June Days, 1953." Microfilm. St. Anthony's College, Oxford, June 1955.

Der Volksaufstand vom 17. Juni 1953 in der Sowjetischen Besatzungszone und in Ost-Berlin. Eine Kartographische Darstellung. Bonn: Deutscher Bundes-Verlag, 1954.

Wechsberg, Joseph: "A Reporter in Germany—The 17th of June." *The New Yorker*, Aug. 29, 1953.

CHAPTER XV

Brauer, Anna E., and Elizabeth Erdman: *The West German Housing Problem, 1945–1953.* Office of the U.S. High Commissioner for Germany, 1953.

Deutschland Heute. Bonn, 1954.

Foreign Relations of the United States. The Conferences at Malta and Yalta. Washington, D.C., 1956.

Frankfurter Allgemeine Zeitung, Dec. 19, 1953.

Frankfurter Neue Presse, Sept. 25, 1953.

Frankfurter Rundschau, Nov. 19, Dec. 5, 1953.

Germany Reports. Bonn, 1953.

Hanoverische Allgemeine Zeitung, May 13, 1953.

BIBLIOGRAPHY

Der Mittag, April 9, 1953.
Neue Mainzer Zeitung, March 31, 1953.
Neues Deutschland, Sept. 8, 1953.
The New York Times, Jan. 20, March 28, July 18, 24, 25, 26, 27, Aug. 2, 3, 4, 7, 28, 31, Nov. 20, Dec. 15, 1953; March 2, 1954.
Report, dated Oct. 1, 1953, from the Office of the U.S. High Commissioner for Germany.
Reports (mimeographed) of the Public Information Division (Jan. 30, 1953) of the U.S. Army.
Süddeutsche Zeitung, April 25, 1953.
Wallich, H. C.: *Mainsprings of the German Revival*. New Haven: Yale University Press, 1955.

CHAPTER XVI

American Foreign Policy. Basic Documents, 1950–55. 2 vols. Washington, D.C., 1957.
Cerf, Jay H.: "Blue Shirts and Red Banners." Dissertation. Yale University, 1957.
Deutsche Zeitung, Jan. 30, 1954.
Deutschland Heute. Bonn, 1954.
Ekt, Jurgen: "Die Axt im Haus." *Frankfurter Allgemeine Zeitung*, 1954.
Frankfurter Neue Presse, Aug. 13, 1954.
General Anzeiger, Dec. 30, 1954.
Helm, Juergen von: *Die Sowietische Besatzungszone Deutschlands, 1945–54*. Mimeographed.
Jahrbuch der öffentlichen Meinung, 1947–1955, ed. Elisabeth Nolle and Erich Peter Neumann. Allensbach am Bodensee: Verlag für Demoskopie, 1956.
Keesing's Contemporary Archives, Vol. IX. London, 1952–4.
Korn, Karl: "Über die Gefahr der Amerika Komplexe." *Europa und Amerika*, Jan. 5, 1954.
Neue Zeitung, Aug. 10, 1954.
The New York Times, Jan. 19, 21, 26, 31, Feb. 2, 4, 7, 11, 21, March 25, Sept. 16, 18, 19, 21, 30, Dec. 9, 13, 1954; Jan. 1, 2, 16, March 6, May 6, 1955.
Reports (mimeographed) of the Community Relations Branch, U.S. Army, 1954.
Der Stern, Sept. 19, 1954.
Trends in West German Appraisal of the U.S. Forces in Germany. Office of the U.S. High Commissioner for Germany, 1954.

CHAPTER XVII

Bohn, Helmut, *et al.*: *Die Aufrüstung in der Sowjetischen Besatzungszone Deutschlands*. Bonn, 1958.
Bosch, Werner: *Die Sozial Struktur in West und Mittel Deutschland*. Bonn, 1958.
Deutschland Heute. Bonn, 1954.

BIBLIOGRAPHY

Erhard, Ludwig: *Wohlstand für Alle*. Düsseldorf: Econ Verlag, 1957.

Ford, Franklin L.: "The Twentieth of July in the History of the German Resistance." *American Historical Review*, July 1946.

Frankfurter Allgemeine Zeitung, Sept. 24, 1954.

Görlitz, Walter, in *Der Monat*, August 1955.

——: *Der Deutsche Generalstab, Geschichte und Gestalt, 1657–1954.* Frankfurt: Verlag der Frankfurter Hefte, n.d.

Jahn, Hans Edgar, and Kurt Neher: *Taschenbuch für Wehrfragen, 1957–1958.* Bonn: Festland Verlag, 1957.

Keesing's Contemporary Archives, Vol. X. London, 1955–6.

Marcks, Otto: *Die Bundeswehr im Aufbau.* Bonn: Athenäum-Verlag, 1957.

Ritter, Gerhard, *et al.*: "Die Deutschen Soldaten." *Der Monat*, September 1955.

Rothfels, Hans: *The German Opposition to Hitler.* Chicago: Henry Regnery Co., 1948.

SBZ von 1945 bis 1954. Bonn, 1956.

The Soviet Zone of Germany. Pamphlet. Bonn: Federal Ministry for All German Affairs, n.d.

Tönnies, Norbert: *Der Weg zu den Waffen.* Cologne: Markus Verlag, 1957.

Triffin, Robert: *Europe and the Money Muddle.* New Haven: Yale University Press, 1957.

Weymar, Paul: *Konrad Adenauer.* Munich: Kindler Verlag, 1955.

INDEX

Acheson, Dean: on diplomacy with
Russia, 279; and German support in
Korea, 290–91; on Korean war, 348; and
National Council of American-Soviet
Friendship, 98; and Russian press, 126;
on Russian threat, 291; as successor to
Marshall, 252; travels to Germany, 254;
travels to Paris, 254; on unification of
Germany, 279

Adenauer, Konrad: and agreement
with McCloy, 273; and Allied
guarantee to defend Germany,
295; and Allied support, 317; on
American policy and support, 197,
270; and cabinet members, 291, 395;
as chancellor of West Germany, 246;
and denouncement by SED, 315;
and Dulles, 349; on establishment
of West Germany, 203; and France,
279; and Free Democratic party,
366; and German army, 254, 272; and
Handy, 320; on high commissioner
given status of ambassador, 350n;
imprisonment of, 72; and liaison
with Bundesrat, 247; as lord mayor of
Cologne, 51, 51n5; and Marshall Plan,
247; and meeting with De Gaulle,
386; on Mendés-France, 363; Nazis in
administration of, 278n8; at Petersberg
conference, 249, 269; and petition for
clemency of Nuremberg convictions,
294; praise of, 381; as president of
Constituent Assembly, 214, 238; and
promise to join Ruhr, 250; refusal to
attend Council of Europe meeting,
363; and Ruhr coal and steel authority,
250; and Ruhr plants, 258; and Saar,
279, 293, 318, 362, 364, 380; and
Schuman, 300, 314; and sense of past,

400; and signing of EDC agreements,
313; on Socialist Reich, 231; support of,
365

Adler Führer, 370

Advisory Council on Postwar Policy, 19,
20n

Agriculture, 132–33, 160–61, 172, 283–84,
327–28, 352. *See also* Food

Airlift. *See* Blockade of Berlin

Albania, 44, 280

Allgemeine Wochenzeitung, 306

Allied Control Council: and aid for
repairs in Berlin, 155; and air lanes to
Berlin, 184; and bizonal agreement,
186–87; Byrnes on actions of, 147;
criticism of, 193; debate between
majority rule and unanimity principle,
251; and equal voice of America,
Britain and Germany, 175; and
France, 155, 233–34; and permission
for Furtwängler to conduct Berlin
Philharmonic, 129; on proposed
merger of zones, 144; purpose of,
62; Russian comments on, 195; and
Russian obstruction of currency
reform, 222, 223; and Sokolovsky exit
from, 188, 200, 235

Allied High Commission, 290, 292

Allied Joint Import-Export Agency, 229

Allied Security Commission, 199, 273,
322

Allies. *See* America; Britain; France;
Russia

America: and aid to West Germany,
96, 352–53; and alliance with West
Germany, 397, 400; attitude toward
Germans after World War II, 11, 54;
attitude toward Russia, 29–30, 78;
Berlin's American zone, 82, 220; on
communism, 95–96; Communist

423

INDEX

Government Appropriations for Relief
in Occupied Areas (GARIOA), 261
Government of National Unity (Poland),
43, 46, 63, 97
Greece: American support to, 163; British
support to, 163; Communist threats
in, 99, 142, 163, 197; and Danubian
confederation, 23; and division of
influence, 35–36; homeless in, 85–86;
machinery sent to, 258; and Marshall
Plan, 168; as NATO member, 366; and
Yugoslavia, 252
Grew, Joseph, 58n2
Gromyko, Andrei, 298
Gross, Gen. Charles P., 278
Grotewohl, Otto: criticism of, 332; as
minister president of East Germany,
253; and New Course, 334–35; and
Peck, 215, 253; and Social Democratic
party, 93, 215; and Socialist Unity party,
94
Guderian, Gen. Heinz, 387
Gusev, F. T., 60

Hague convention, 260
Halder, Gen. Franz, 387
Halle, 336, 345
Halvorsen, Lt. Gail S., 212n
Hamburg: agriculture in, 357; Blohm and
Voss works in, 353; British attack on
shipyards, 270; in British zone, 135;
dismantling of plants in, 177; displaced
persons in, 290; homeless in, 157; and
Mayor Brauer, 302; starvation in, 159
Handels Organisation (HO), 327, 330,
332, 338, 373
Handy, Gen. Thomas T., 294, 297, 320
Harriman, Averell, 46, 97
Harriman Committee, 178
Heidelberg, 86n, 204, 369
Helmstedt checkpoint, 192
Hennecke, Adolf, 329
Hennigsdorf, 339, 345
Hermes, Andreas, 88
Hess, Rudolf, 108n, 115n, 124
Hesse, 133, 138, 153, 154, 161, 273, 290
Hesse crown jewels, 152n9
Heuss, Theodor, 86n, 93, 246, 247, 291,
294
Himmler, Heinrich, 52, 103, 110, 112
Hindemith, Paul, 401
Hindenburg, Paul von, 100n
Hiss, Alger, 37, 39
Hitler, Adolf: alliance against, 292;
alliances with, as act of war, 128n;

American view of, 54, 101n6; army
of, 123–24n5, 387–88; assassination
plans and attempts against, 4,
105n5, 268, 287, 372; and brown shirt
unit, 120, 230, 339, 387; Byrnes on,
145; Communist threat before, 92;
compared with Russian aggression,
197; and Czechoslovakia, 268; defeat
of, 24; devotees of, 127; and Dutch
strikers, 115; and emigration of Jews,
165; and "Fuehrer Conferences on
Matters Dealing with German Navy,"
17; German acceptance of regime
of, 90; and German economy, 265,
266; and Germany's fate, 148, 268;
Germany's pre-Hitler war plans, 116;
and Goering, 121, 276; and Grotewohl,
346; and Heuss, 246; intentions and
plans of, 66, 100; and killing of citizens,
4; and killing of Russian POWs, 112,
112n3; legacy of, 103, 231, 294; and
Mein Kampf, 12; Morgenthau on,
125; and "Nero plan," 51; newspapers
under, 308; ongoing influences of,
156, 212, 218n, 392; opposition to, 94,
268, 396; pre-Hitler textbooks for
schools, 56; prison sentence for, 50;
and *Realpolitik*, 396; regime compared
with iron curtain, 196; and resistance
to Allied troops, 3, 22, 48n, 49; and rise
to power, 73, 119, 217n, 229; Roosevelt
on, 7; and Russia, 23, 25, 29, 125, 395;
and Schacht, 123; and Schumacher,
94, 162; and Stalin, 16, 17, 22, 26n, 29,
375; suicide of, 57; survivors from
reign, 333; tactics of, 119; temporary
prosperity under, 268; and torture of
Russian troops, 110n, 112, 112n3; and
treatment of Germans unaffiliated
with Reich, 122; tribunals under, 393;
Truman on, 66; and United Front of
the Anti-Hitlerites, 71; word of, as
decalogue, 114
Hodge, Gen. John R., 163
Holland: deportations of Dutch, 113;
employment wages in, 353; on German
boundaries, 236; industrial equipment
minimized, 154; infant mortality in,
85; and occupation costs, 265; and
strike by railway workers, 115; and
Wilhelm II, 100
Hoover, Herbert: on condition of
German people, 135, 158–59; and
criticism by Society to Prevent World

INDEX

Nacht und Nebel, 115
Napoleon, 100
National Committee for Free Germany.
    See Free Germany Committee
National Council of American-Soviet
    Friendship, 98
National Democratic party, 193, 280
National Socialist party. See Nazism
Nation Europa, 370
Navy Department, U.S., 20*n*
Nazism: Adenauer on, 278*n*8; American
    army on, 81; and Anne Frank, 403;
    and anti-Semitism, 56, 111, 166, 303,
    305–6; army of, 29; in churches, 303
    310, 390; Clay's response to, 191;
    Communist attempts to influence,
    298; Communist attitudes toward,
    71; and Communists' flight to
    Russia, 20; compared with nonparty
    member Germans, 11, 15, 19, 103;
    and concentration camps, 53, 281,
    403; and confiscation of property,
    306; continued presence of, 11, 21;
    and Dachau, 122; and destruction of
    Germany, 129; employment of Nazis
    in postwar Germany, 49, 77–78, 134,
    230; heritage of, 81–82; and Hitler
    tribunals, 393; impact on German
    agriculture, 284; introduction of, 7, 127;
    investigations of, 394; and jailing of
    members, 130; and London Poles, 45;
    and medicine practiced, 171; mocking
    of, 194; and National Democratic
    party, 193; Nazis as prisoners of war,
    138; Nazis barred from postwar army,
    13; and neo-Nazi movement, 151,
    302, 370; and Nuremberg trials, 158,
    394; occupation compared with Nazi
    period, 397; opposition to, 70, 73, 87,
    95, 128, 156; and Poncet, 249; and quasi
    movements, 230, 302; resistance to,
    4, 50, 51, 51*n*6, 304*n*; Reuter and, 173;
    Russian communism compared with,
    196; and Schumacher, 94; Stalin on, 18;
    and "Strength through Joy" campaign,
    383; and Stuttgart confession, 303;
    trials and legal proceedings against,
    52, 100, 120, 125, 277; tyranny of, 6, 8,
    16, 166; and weapon development,
    350; and Weimar Republic, 10, 240*n*.
    See also Denazification; Hitler, Adolf;
    Nuremberg trials
Negroes, 55, 322–23
Netherlands. See Holland

Neumann, Franz, 210, 211
New Course, 330, 331, 334, 337
New Deal, 28, 29, 36
Newspapers, 307–8, 357, 366–70. See also
    specific newspapers
New York conference (1950), 271
New York Times, 45, 77, 135, 136, 138*n*8,
    145, 156*n*5, 159, 185*n*, 189, 302, 320, 350
Niemöller, Pastor Martin, 308
Nikitchenko, 105*n*5
Nimitz, Adm. Chester W., 124*n*
NKVD, 110*n*
Nordhoff, Heinz, 177
North Africa, 135*n*, 318, 396
North Atlantic Treaty Organization
    (NATO): and Adenauer, 254; East
    Germany on, 374; France in, 362;
    and German army, 271, 300, 362, 363;
    Italy in, 317, 365; military strength of,
    254, 366; and Russia, 292, 314; West
    Germany as member of, 363, 365, 381,
    396
North Korea, 186, 214, 251, 270, 361, 398.
    See also Korea
Norway, 396
Nuremberg trials: Allied evidence
    barred from, 118–22; America on,
    105–6; Britain on, 105*n*5; compared
    with other trials, 115; crimes against
    Jews, 110–11; crimes of inhumanity,
    109–14; crimes using medical
    experimentation, 113–14; defense
    counsel at, 122*n*; and definition of war
    crimes, 102, 115–19; Goering's rebuttal,
    120; historical background of, 100–101;
    and indictments, 100, 103; and Krupp
    case, 104; legal basis of charges, 116–17;
    and plan for new world order, 101–2;
    precedents of, 100; proceedings of,
    106–9; results of, 124–26; Russian
    actions during, 121–22, 126; Russian
    demands at, 97–99; Stalin on, 104–5;
    treatment of prisoners during, 122;
    verdicts of, 123–24. See also Jackson,
    Robert H.
Nuschke, Otto, 141, 253, 298, 338, 339

Occupation costs, 259, 262–67, 296–98,
    321, 350
Oder-Neisse boundary, 33, 64, 253, 256,
    298, 316, 395
Oder River, 43
Office for the Defense of the
    Constitution, 372

ABOUT THE AUTHOR

Eugene Davidson is the author of numerous books on the Nazi regime, including *The Making of Adolf Hitler*, *The Unmaking of Adolf Hitler*, *The Trial of the Germans*, and *The Nuremberg Fallacy*, all available from the University of Missouri Press. Davidson, who lives in Santa Barbara, California, is President Emeritus of the Conference on European Problems and former President of the Foundation for Foreign Affairs.